ACKNOWLEDGMENTS

Ira had completed his contribution to this fourth edition in the months before his death. All that remained was to organize and edit the material. In addition to the new walks and the new listing in extant walks, the reader will notice other changes in this fourth edition: the order of the walks was changed to follow the grid of the City in a more logical fashion; the maps have been remade and improved; and there are many new photographs.

I also have acknowledgments to make. I am most grateful to Ira, for his trust and love and advice, and for allowing me the honor of working with him on these last four books. My continued thanks go to my mentor and friend, Morton Weisman, who stepped forward in a time of loss and helps ease the grief and solve the problems. I would also like to thank the following people for supplying information and often photographs on the many new listings in this book.

Jean Bellas
Natalie Blake
Larry Booth
William Braker
Bill Brubaker
Jerome Butler
Clementine Calleja
Tom A. Cokins
John Cordwell
Edward Cox
Jerry Eisel
Mrs. O. M. Forkert
Joseph Fujikawa
Brenda Gaines
Michael Gelick
Gaylord Gieseke
Bertrand Goldberg
Jonathan Golkin
Ezra Gordon
Mary Jo Graf
Erik Gregersen

Ingrid Gregersen
Liz Hague
Carol Haley
Wilbert Hasbrouck
Harold Hellman
Bette Hill
Glenn Hjort, AIA
John Holabird
Helmut Jahn
Gene Kohn
Father George Lane
Dan Levin
Mary Ludgen
Jim Lyden
Tim McCarthy
Rob Mier
Steve Mitchell
Bill Moody
Jim Nagle
Harold A. Nelson
Susan Nicolini

Keith Palmer   Rich Tomlinson
Ralph Raby   Harvey Walker
Martin Reinheimer   Bill Ware
Claire Rose   Mayor Harold Washington
Kevin Sarring   Harry Weese
John Schlossman   Mary Beth Weigel
Rima Schultz   Bernard Weisbourd
Joyce Shaw   Malcolm Weiskopf
Stefanie Siegal   Bob Whislow
Jim Stoller   Richard Willich
Stanley Tigerman   Mary Woolever
Michael Tobin   Ralph Youngren

Susan Wolfson
Chicago, May 1986

FOREWORD

I love Chicago. I love the people. I love the neighbors and the neighborhoods. I love the sense of community I feel, each neighborhood with its own special spirit and feeling and style.

Chicago is a livable city. People from all walks of life have found homes here and brought with them a sense of their past. And Chicago is a viewable city—the birthplace of the modern skyscraper, of the Prairie school home, of the Chicago window. Chicago was and is the home base of architects revered the world over. I enjoy walking in the Loop and the neighborhoods. Often on my show, listeners call in to ask for suggestions of where to take their out-of-town visitors for an overall feel of this city. I send them to Michigan Avenue—the Magnificent Mile—or on the boat rides in Lake Michigan to see the city's magnificent skyline from that perspective, but seeing our magnificent city can be enhanced.

Ira J. Bach knew Chicago intimately and he loved the city with a special passion. From his position as Director of the Chicago Land Clearance Commission in the 1940s, to Commissioner of City Planning in the 1950s and 1960s, to Chairman of the Landmarks Commission from the 1970s to the time of his death, and as Director of City Development in the Byrne and Washington administrations, he served the people of Chicago through five mayors' administrations and he had a hand in every major decision for the growth and expansion and rebuilding of our city. No one is a better guide to the great and small beauties of the architecture of Chicago.

Ira rode the CTA bus to work and every afternoon *walked* the five miles from the Loop to his Uptown home, for over 30 years. He used that time, observing and appreciating the city. Ira walked, five days a week, through dark of winter and light of summer, in every phase of Chicago's weather—through the 130 degrees of temperature variance, through hard and soft precipitation. His daughter once remarked that she could tell when it was below zero—when she kissed Ira hello as he arrived home, her lips would stick! Ira knew *Chicago On Foot* and this book reflects his view—as planner, as architect, and as private citizen—of the city he knew and loved.

This updated and expanded fourth edition of *Chicago On Foot* chronicles the city's architectural heritage. And as you read this book, you'll feel as if Ira himself strides beside you, here quickening or there slowing your pace, pointing out features, directing your eye, furnishing tidbits of history, teaching, and sharing your joy on your walks through the city he loved—through the city we love.

Wally Phillips
May 12, 1986

INTRODUCTION

A continued public response to the third edition of this collection of architectural walking tours, combined with major additions to the Downtown area of Chicago, has prompted its updating and revision. What has been a continued source of gratification is its use by the many young foreign and American visitors to the city as well as by Chicagoans themselves.

Leading many group WALKS has been a pleasant dividend for me. People who would enjoy attending group tours can contact the Chicago Architecture Foundation, whose dedicated staff of young docents conduct many WALKS throughout the year for the benefit of the Glessner House, and the Landmarks Preservation Council.

The Northwestern University Evanston Campus, Riverside, and New South Side Housing and Institutional Developments WALKS were eliminated in the fourth edition while two highly significant architectural WALKS were added—the East Lake Shore Drive Historic District and Burnham Park: The South Loop. For this edition, WALK 7, Underground Walkways, has been completely revised to reflect the significant growth of the system in the last several years. WALK 9, Gateway Area: South Branch of Chicago River, WALK 15, The Gold Coast, and WALK 23, Frank Lloyd Wright In Oak Park and River Forest, have been revised for this edition. And most of the Downtown WALKS reflect the new building growth of recent years.

The WALKS proposed here have been selected to present Chicago as a great cosmopolitan city as well as a collection of local community areas, tied together by an intricate web of transportation that makes them accessible to the pedestrian for a closer view.

Since Chicago is a vast outdoor museum of great architecture created in about one hundred years, the major focus of the WALKS is architectural. From 1883 to 1893 the "Chicago School of Architecture" came into being. During that decade a whole galaxy of buildings appeared, reaching the unprecedented heights of 12, 14, 16, and 23 stories. The architects of the Chicago school employed a new type of construction: *the iron skeleton* at that time called quite simply *Chicago Construction*. They invented a new kind of foundation to cope with the problems of the muddy ground of Chicago: *the floating foundation*. They introduced the horizontally elongated window: *the Chicago window*. They created the modern business and administration building. And around the turn of the century, the so-called *Prairie House* came into being here.

Of equal significance is the current work of Chicago architects, often characterized as a continuation of the "Chicago school." The pure forms, horizontally elongated windows, and rugged strength are still to be seen in many of today's buildings. Architects of the present, however, have not hesitated to experiment with their own designs and materials. Though Mies van der Rohe's "Glass Houses" on North Lake Shore Drive and Helmut Jahn's State of Illinois Building may be considered the ultimate development of certain trends of the Chicago school, the cylindrical towers of Marina City bear little resemblance. Their concrete slab construction, circular balconies, and pie-shaped rooms hardly follow the tradition of the "Chicago school" of architects. Nor does the facade of the Henry Hinds Laboratory for the Geophysical Sciences Building at the University of Chicago—though the older school of architects would approve the function origin of the new features.

Complete coverage of buildings worth noting in Chicago cannot possibly be attempted, especially in view of the size of the city. While following the routes proposed here, the pedestrian will many times come across other interesting or beautiful buildings. The frequency with which this may happen is only another tribute to the endless vitality of this tremendous city.

This symbol ◉ appears from time to time throughout the text to indicate buildings and historic sites that have been officially designated as architectural or historic landmarks. The Commission on Chicago Historic and Architectural Landmarks was created on January 17, 1968 by ordinance of the City Council of the City of Chicago. A predecessor commission, known as the Commission on Chicago Architectural Landmarks, was created in 1957 by Mayor Richard J. Daley. Because broader powers were considered desirable, the legislature and City Council acted to replace the first commission by creating the present one. The new commission now includes the preservation of historical as well as architectural landmarks.

The City of Chicago has been particularly unfortunate in having lost Adler and Sullivan's Garrick Theater in 1961 and the old Stock Exchange Building in 1972. Efforts to save these buildings failed because of inadequate landmarks preservation legislation. Indeed, ineffective landmarks preservation is widespread in the United States.

A new ordinance is to be proposed at this writing which will give the Chicago Landmarks Commission greater authority. With proper planning and zoning controls, the owners of a landmark structure would be compensated for preserving their building and the city and general public would benefit by safeguarding another landmark. Other cities in the U.S.A. are likewise considering similar legislation. All agree that some type of financial assistance should be available to owners of landmark buildings.

Chicago is famous too for one of the first comprehensive city plans produced on this continent. The pedestrian will become aware of the planning, especially on the lakefront. In 1909 Daniel H. Burnham and Edward H. Bennett enunciated policies that have been instrumental in shaping the city of today. They established, among other things, the city's shoreline for public use only, by recommending the extension of lakefront parks, and set the pattern for the city's system of forest preserves, linked by highways.

Chicago's street system is the conventional grid, laid out with major streets at mile and one-half mile spacing. There are also a number of diagonal streets, some of them tracing old Indian trails, which bisect the junctions of major streets of the grid pattern, forming six-spoked intersections—creating some of the city's most difficult traffic problems.

More recently, a number of expressways have been built in Chicago. These carry traffic to and from the central business district and also serve large columns of north-south and east-west crosstown traffic. The new roads have considerably shortened travel time within the city and have tied the various parts of the metropolitan area more tightly together. They have also helped to improve public transportation by the installation of rapid transit lines in the median strip of the Eisenhower, Stevenson, Dan Ryan and Kennedy expressways. There is a new extension of the CTA line, which now goes to O'Hare Airport.

The street numbering system in Chicago follows the compass, the east-west division marked by State Street, and the north-south directions divided by Madison Street. The city is about 25 miles north and south, and about 15 miles east and west.

Since all of the city's topography is flat, walking— which is said to be one of the best forms of exercise—will not be strenuous. The routes outlined here for most WALKS are designed for daytime enjoyment.

Instructions for each walk on "How to get there" assume that downtown Chicago—the Loop—the corner of State and Madison streets—is your starting point, and directions to the start of each walk are from that point. Since bus-routes and bus numbers change from time to time, the safest way will be to phone the CTA at 836-7000 (or toll-free at 1-800-972-7000) for precise instructions before starting out—or at least ask the bus driver whether the number you are here told to take will still carry you to your destination.

This book makes no attempt to advise on places to stay or eat. The city abounds with good hotels and restaurants, lists of which can be obtained from the Chicago Convention and Tourism Bureau (at McCormick Place-On-the-Lake, 225-5000).

In the preparation of the fourth edition, I want to thank the many persons who have taken the time to communicate to me additional information or corrections that might be useful now. I particularly want to acknowledge and thank Elizabeth Hollander, Commissioner of the Department of Development and Planning; Carl W. Condit, Hugh Duncan, and J. Carson Webster for their critical statements in *Chicago's Famous Buildings* (University of Chicago Press, 1969), Fredrick Koeper in *Illinois Architecture* (University of Chicago, 1968), which have set a pattern of excellence in reviewing the Chicago School of Architecture; Jonathan Kleinbard, for advice on the University of Chicago campus; Michael Shymanski and Norbert Pointer of the Beman Committee and Charles E. Gregersen for their able assistance on Pullman; William McLenahan, Director, and staff member, Tim Samuelson, of the Commission on Chicago Historical & Architectural Landmarks for their aid; Dennis Mae for providing new maps of the WALKS; David Williams, Alex Sims, and Suzanne Chevrier for additional research; and Olga Stefanos for her excellent new photography; and once again my dear friend Marshall Holleb, without whose companionship and wit I might have given up walking long ago.

Ira J. Bach
Chicago, February 1985

TABLE OF CONTENTS

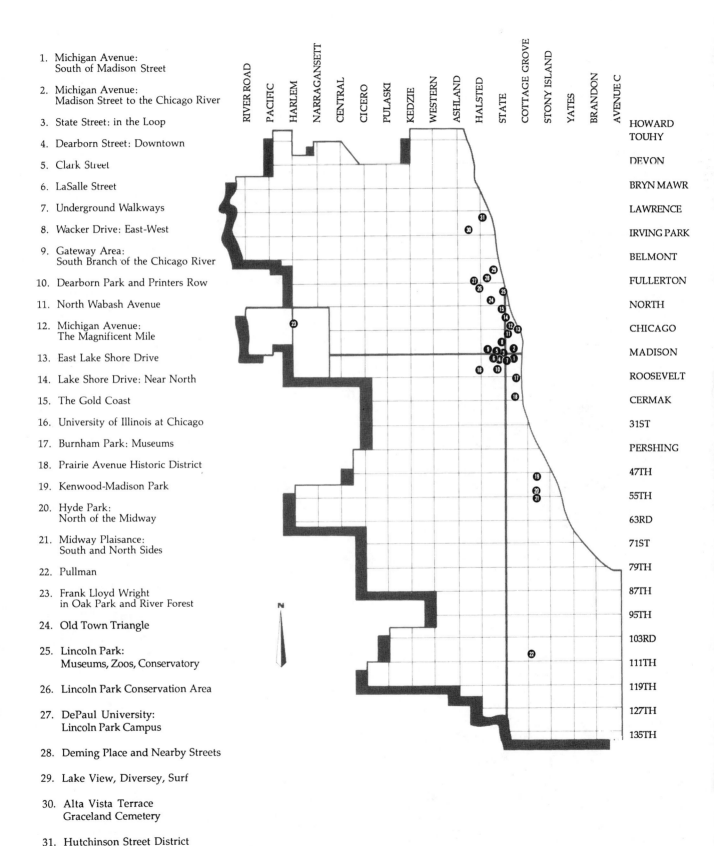

1

1. Grant Park

2. Buckingham Memorial Fountain

3. Chicago Hilton and Towers
   720 S. Michigan Ave.

4. The Blackstone Hotel
   636 S. Michigan Ave.

5. Americana-Congress Hotel
   520 S. Michigan Ave.

6. Auditorium Building
   430 S. Michigan Ave.

7. Fine Arts Building
   410 S. Michigan Ave.

8. The Chicago Club
   81 E. Van Buren St.

9. 318 S. Michigan Ave.

10. Continental National
    American Center
    310 S. Michigan Ave. (Bldg. 1)
    55 E. Jackson St. (Bldg. 2)
    325 S. Wabash Ave. (Bldg. 3)

11. McClurg Building
    218 S. Wabash Ave.

12. Santa Fe Center
    224 S. Michigan Ave.

13. Orchestra Hall Building
    220 S. Michigan Ave.

14. Borg-Warner Building
    200 S. Michigan Ave.

15. Art Institute of Chicago
    Michigan Ave. at Adams St.

16. Peoples Gas Company Building
    122 S. Michigan Ave.

17. Lake View Building
    116 S. Michigan Ave.

18. Charlie Club
    112 S. Michigan Ave.

19. Monroe Building
    104 S. Michigan Ave.

20. Mid-Continental Plaza Building
    55 E. Monroe St.

21. University Club
    76 E. Monroe St.

22. Gage Building
    18 S. Michigan Ave.

23. Chicago Athletic Association
    12 S. Michigan Ave.

24. Willoughby Tower
    8 S. Michigan Ave.

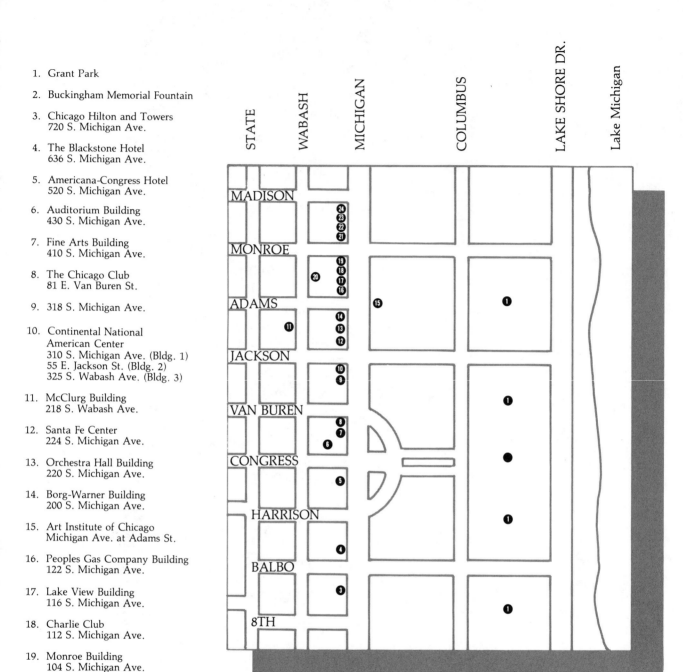

WALK • 1

MICHIGAN AVENUE: SOUTH OF MADISON STREET

WALKING TIME: About 2 hours. HOW TO GET THERE: Take a southbound CTA bus, No. 146 [Marine-Michigan] on State Street. Get off at Balbo Drive [700 S] and Michigan Avenue. Cross Michigan Avenue, and you are in Grant Park.

Chicago's skyline is one of the most exhilarating sights in the world. Day or night the view is magnificent—from an airplane approaching the city, from a boat on Lake Michigan, from a car on the Outer Drive, or from the footpaths in Grant Park. It is always impressive.

GRANT PARK
BETWEEN LAKE MICHIGAN AND MICHIGAN AVENUE (100 E);
BETWEEN RANDOLPH STREET (150 N) AND ROOSEVELT ROAD (1200 S)

Grant Park was no accident. Daniel Burnham designed it as part of the Chicago Plan of 1909. First, the lake was filled from Michigan Avenue east to what is now the Outer Drive, to provide the necessary land space. The park was planned as an immense green expanse following loosely the pattern of Versailles. In the spring, when the park's hundreds of small trees and shrubs are in bloom, this is a place of incomparable beauty. Burnham's original plan for the park was completed when the Monroe Street parking lot, between Monroe and Randolph streets, was decked over and landscaped.

In its midst is the magnificent seated Lincoln, last work of Augustus St. Gaudens. Chicago is the fortunate possessor of this monument because of a $100,000 bequest for a Lincoln statue from John Crerar, the man who also willed the city the John Crerar Library.

Flanking Congress Plaza—near Michigan Avenue in Grant Park—are two American Indian equestrians with drawn bows, created by the Yugoslavian sculptor Ivan Mestrovic. Of heroic scale, they make a sweeping entrance to the enormous Buckingham Fountain, just to the east.

Overleaf: Buckingham Memorial Fountain (Philip A. Turner)

5

BUCKINGHAM MEMORIAL FOUNTAIN
DESIGNERS: BENNETT, PARSONS AND FROST OF CHICAGO
AND JACQUES LAMBERT OF PARIS (1926)

This fountain, modeled from one of the Versailles fountains, is said to be the largest in the world—about twice as large as its model. It has a great central stream with 133 jets of water, some of which reach about 200 feet in the air. Each night from 9 to 9:30 during its active season (May through September) the fountain is illuminated, with shifting colors played on it—longer displays on evenings of concerts in the park. The fountain has become a popular rendezvous for visitors to Chicago. The Buckingham Fountain was donated to the city of Chicago in 1927 by Miss Kate Buckingham in memory of her brother Clarence.

The section of Michigan Avenue covered in this WALK goes from Balbo Drive to Madison Street on the north. From the Chicago Hilton and Towers, on the south, to the Chicago River, on the north—the distance covered by WALK 1 and by WALK 2—Michigan Avenue is rich with sculpture, gardens, and fountains as well as structures of strikingly varied architectural styles.

Start your WALK up Michigan Avenue at the Chicago Hilton and Towers, on the southwest corner of Balbo Drive and Michigan Avenue.

CHICAGO HILTON AND TOWERS
720 S. MICHIGAN AVENUE
ARCHITECTS: HOLABIRD AND ROCHE (1927);
FOR THE RESTORATION: SOLOMON, CORDWELL AND BUENZ (1984-86)

The hotel (once known as the Stevens and more recently as the Conrad Hilton) is 25 stories high with a 4-story tower and two to five basements, supported on rock foundations. The remodeling and renovation by Solomon, Cordwell and Buenz, reduced the number of rooms from 3,000 to 1,620 (larger and more luxurious, many with 2 baths and multiple closets). The hotel's top 3 floors are the Towers, a separate and even more luxurious section with its own added services and separate elevators. The 242,396 square feet of public spaces have been reconfigured, remodeled, or restored. Grand rooms are restored to their original elegance, and new restaurants, lounges, and entertainment areas are designed to harmonize with the older rooms.

An addition contains a porte-cochere entrance, 510-car self-parking garage, exhibition space, and health club. The building is a state of the art, long-span structure with precast concrete facades

6

detailed to blend with the rusticated cut stone of the existing hotel. The porte-cochere becomes the hotel's main covered auto and taxi entrance. There are granite fountains, light fixtures, and paving bricks to carry the design theme of the existing hotel.

On the upper level of the addition is a health club containing an indoor pool, exercise rooms, cushioned running track, saunas, and an outdoor recreation deck. The lower level adds 30,000 square feet of high-ceilinged exhibition space. With the addition and remodeling, the Chicago Hilton boasts the largest single level of exhibition space in any hotel in the world.

Hotel tours may be arranged by advance reservation with the service manager. Phone the bell captain at 922-4000 for information.

Just north of the Hilton, on the northwest corner of Michigan and Balbo avenues, is the Blackstone Hotel.

◉ THE BLACKSTONE HOTEL
636 S. MICHIGAN AVENUE
ARCHITECTS: MARSHALL AND FOX (1910)

This hotel, many times the headquarters for a national presidential nominating convention, offers a rather pleasing exterior of French Renaissance architecture. At the time it was built, in fact, it won a gold medal for excellence of design.

Continuing northward, on Michigan Avenue between Harrison Street and Congress Parkway, is another historic hotel building.

AMERICANA-CONGRESS HOTEL
520 S. MICHIGAN AVENUE
ARCHITECTS: CLINTON J. WARREN (1893);
HOLABIRD AND ROCHE (1902 AND 1907);
HOLABIRD AND ROOT (1956)

In contrast with the Blackstone's exterior, the Americana-Congress has a facade of rugged gray limestone suggesting the influence of Henry Richardson. Its "Peacock Alley" off the main lobby was once one of the city's gathering places for outstanding social events. In the most recent renovation a section of the ground floor, on the north side, was opened up and arcaded, to allow the widening of Congress Street into Congress Parkway. (The south side of the Auditorium Building, across the street to the north, underwent the same kind of change.)

On the northwest corner of Michigan Avenue and Congress Parkway is the Auditorium Building.

Auditorium Building
(Philip A. Turner)

◉ AUDITORIUM BUILDING
430 S. Michigan Avenue
Architects: Adler and Sullivan (1889);
for the restoration of the Auditorium Theatre:
Harry Weese (1967)

The Auditorium Building, now owned by Roosevelt University, is one of Chicago's most famous cultural and architectural landmarks. Its construction was a triumph of the partnership of Louis

8

Sullivan, with his inspired architectural imagination, and Dankmar Adler, with his extraordinary engineering genius.

The Auditorium Theatre, originally surrounded by hotel and office space, has long been justifiably renowned for its large, well-equipped stage and its perfect acoustics. The Chicago Landmarks Commission citation of 1959 reads:

In recognition of the community spirit which here joined commercial and artistic ends, uniting hotel, office building, and theatre in one structure; the inventiveness of the engineer displayed from foundations to the perfect acoustics; and the genius of the architect which gave form and, with the aid of the original ornament, expressed the spirit of festivity in rooms of great splendor.

Disaster threatened the building in 1929, however, when the Chicago Opera Company, which had used the Auditorium Theatre for many years, moved to the newly completed Civic Opera Building; and it became a certainty with the economic depression of the 1930s. By 1940 the Auditorium Building was bankrupt and the theater was closed. From 1942 to 1945 the building was used as Chicago headquarters for the United Service Organization. In 1946 it was purchased by Roosevelt University (then Roosevelt College), and hotel rooms and offices were converted as needed for its new purpose.

The Auditorium Theatre was fortunately left untouched at this time, though all movable contents were sold at auction soon after bankruptcy was declared. Unable to raise the enormous amount of money needed to restore the theater, Roosevelt University nevertheless appreciated its value. In 1958 the University established a nonprofit organization, the Auditorium Theatre Council, which in nine years succeeded in raising the $2,250,000 required for restoration. After twenty-six years of darkness, the Auditorium Theatre opened once again on October 31, 1967, with the New York City Ballet performing to an audience of 4,200.

The University's administration is to be congratulated on having proceeded on a vast and costly restoration and remodeling program of the entire Auditorium Building. The great lobby facing Michigan Avenue has been restored, including a portion of the marble mosaic flooring, onyx wainscoting, and chandeliers. The grand staircase is once again the delightful Sullivan brainchild.

The lobby was one of the showpieces of the Auditorium Hotel when it opened in 1889 and still exhibits many of the great architectural elements designed by Louis Sullivan and Dankmar

Adler. The original floor was made of marble tesserae laid in multicolored design motifs. The central columns in the lobby are faced with an imitation marble called scagliola and contain utility plumbing and electrical connections for the upper stories. There is a 6-foot dado of Mexican onyx around the lobby. Originally the lighting was in rosette clusters of filament bulbs and there were stenciled patterns on the ceiling bays and on the undersurfaces of each of the beams. The restoration, including new light fixtures, was close to the original lobby design and color scheme. Plaster ornament was restored by casting replacements in molds taken from existing ornament. Decor was recreated by comparing samples found at the site with early descriptions of the building. Dressing rooms and other service spaces were completely modernized. The restoration of what Frank Lloyd Wright called "the greatest room for music and opera in the world—bar none," is a striking example of adaptive reuse and historic preservation.

Naturally, the upper floors that contain classrooms were modernized for safety but pleasantly designed and planned. The Michigan Avenue stairways have been painted to simulate the original copper-plated iron finish on the balustrades; and the stained glass windows were restored with artificial lighting behind. The stairways now face the new Walter Heller Center instead of the former light well.

Because Roosevelt University's downtown campus consists primarily of the former Auditorium complex, any expansion had to be within or adjacent to the confines of the property. This planning dilemma was turned into a challenge that was met head on by the architects and planners. The tower was remodeled and modernized. This was once the tallest tower in the city. Originally, the tower had 7 floors and now it has 8, and the new 16th floor houses the air conditioning, heating, and other mechanical equipment for the tower offices of the Labor Education Division, the Walter E. Heller College of Business Administration, and the English and Psychology departments. Within the main building, facing Michigan Avenue, there were sixteen classrooms, thirty offices, and five laboratories—all remodeled.

A fantastic piece of architectural squeezing was accomplished by constructing the Walter E. Heller Center within the former light and ventilation court. An 11-story and mezzanine structure, 100 feet long and 25 feet wide, was the answer. This structure now has classrooms, laboratories, a business office, and language laboratory. The connections at each floor to the main building are unobtrusive.

10

The Herman Crown Center, built on a land site 80 feet by 180 feet on Wabash Avenue just north of the Auditorium, is indeed a well-planned and well-conceived child of Louis Sullivan. The simple concrete facade with the typical Chicago school windows relates well to its parent building next door. The interior design carries the spirit of Sullivan into the later 20th century, to Roosevelt University's credit.

For free tours of the University call 341-3623, weekdays only. Tours of the Auditorium Theatre may be arranged by calling 922-4049. Groups of 10 preferred: general admission, adults, $3; students, $2.

North of the Auditorium is the Fine Arts Building.

◉ FINE ARTS BUILDING
410 S. Michigan Avenue
Architect: S. S. Beman (1885, 1898)

The Fine Arts Building has been a center of musical and dramatic events for years, and at one time—along with the Auditorium Theatre and the Orchestra Hall—was the performing arts center of Chicago. The facade is rugged and is a good companion for the Auditorium. The 1885 building was 8 stories. In 1898, the top floor was demolished and the upper stories, the terra-cotta with the copper cornice, were added. The building now contains four theaters and, on the upper floors, high-ceilinged studios and recital halls—from which sounds of hopeful artists can be heard scaling the heights.

Continue north to the corner.

THE CHICAGO CLUB BUILDING
81 E. Van Buren Street
Architects: Granger and Bollenbachker (1929)

The site was once occupied by the original Art Institute building designed by Burnham and Root, which was demolished in 1929. The building fronts 90 feet on Van Buren Street and 75 feet on Michigan Avenue. (The original Burnham and Root entrance was reused on the Van Buren Street side.) The building is 95 feet high, including 4 stories and basement, and is made of steel, Connecticut brownstone, and brick. The Italian Romanesque style of the exterior lends dignity to this section of Michigan Avenue.

Continue north.

318 S. MICHIGAN AVENUE
ARCHITECT: UNKNOWN (1885);
FOR THE RESTORATION: NAGLE HARTRAY AND ASSOCIATES (1982)

This building originated as the Hotel Richilieu in 1885. In 1911 a major renovation of the front facade and an addition occurred, which converted the building to office use. It is a heavy-framed timber building with cast-iron columns and masonry exterior. The building has 7 stories plus a basement, and an 8th story penthouse.

The 1982 renovations included refacing the first 2 floors in cut limestone, a material compatible with the terra-cotta of the upper floors and with the other architecture on the street. The windows were set deep for shadow to give the stone more massiveness, and jointing was revealed for more rustication. The five bays of the building were carried to the ground, with changes in scale and proportion creating a base, middle, and top, representing a conscious continuity of scale and form. The interior was entirely replaced, bringing the building in compliance with the latest building code.

Continue north.

318 S. Michigan
(Hedrich-Blessing courtesy
Nagle, Hartray & Associates)

CONTINENTAL NATIONAL AMERICAN CENTER
BUILDING 1: 310 S. MICHIGAN AVENUE
ARCHITECTS: GRAHAM, ANDERSON, PROBST AND WHITE (1924)
BUILDING 2: 55 E. JACKSON STREET
ARCHITECTS: C. F. MURPHY AND ASSOCIATES (1962)
BUILDING 3: 325 S. WABASH AVENUE
ARCHITECTS: GRAHAM, ANDERSON, PROBST AND WHITE (1972)

The three CNA buildings are connected and demonstrate the growth and progressive attitude of this large corporation. Building 1 is representative of the architecture of the 1920s. Building 3, designed by the same architectural firm some 50 years later, reflects the strength of the sleek steel-and-glass structures. Its 45-story steel structure stands high above its two predecessors and is virtually the tallest building in the southeast portion of the Loop. The steel-and-glass facade is of the Chicago school of architecture. The facade has a deep sculptured appearance. Here the 1/4-inch-thick steel plates that sheath the building reflect the shape of the structural members. The windows, which are twice as wide as those in the adjacent building, are set back and free from all metal surrounds. The window mullions are bold, and the structural columns exposed on the exterior clearly express the large uninterrupted interior spaces. The two later buildings (around the cor-

12

ner on Jackson Boulevard, and on Wabash Avenue), which were designed by different architectural firms, are painted a rich red color which helps unite them and brings color into the downtown area.

Cross Jackson Boulevard and walk north on Wabash Avenue. The fourth building on the west side of the street is the McClurg Building.

Santa Fe Center
(Olga Stefanos)

◉ McCLURG BUILDING
218 S. Wabash Avenue
Architects: Holabird and Roche (1900)

This landmark building was completed in 1900 and is 9 stories on pile foundations. The famous Chicago windows can be seen along with the terra-cotta facing of the facade. It is an excellent early example of a simple, straightforward, steel-cage design for an office building. Though the owners and the name of the structure have changed several times, it is still best known as the McClurg Building.

Return to Jackson Boulevard and walk east to Michigan Avenue. On the corner is the Santa Fe Center.

◉ SANTA FE CENTER
224 S. Michigan Avenue
Architects: D. H. Burnham and Company (1903);
for the renovation: Metz, Train and Youngren;
Frye, Gillan and Molinaro (1984-7)

The building is 17 stories with a white terra-cotta facing. There is one basement and the structure rests on hardpan caissons. Daniel Burnham maintained his office here on the 14th floor during preparation of the Chicago Plan, completed in 1909. His planning associate, Edward Bennett, also worked with him there.

The renovation and restoration has complied with the National Preservation Act while modernizing services, facilities, and office and commercial spaces to attract new tenants. This building's unobstructed view, neighboring cultural institutions, and historical significance have made it a prominent anchor worth preserving. Higher quality office space, competitive cost per square foot, and a better public image are some of the benefits of the renovation.

The 1st floor and the 2nd floor gallery are restored to their original elegance. A light court, originally designed for lighting and ventilation, used to run through the building's center. Modern

13

Santa Fe Center
(Olga Stefanos)

Santa Fe Center lobby
(courtesy Frye Gillan
Molinaro Architects)

technology makes this court unnecessary and energy inefficient, so it has been converted to an atrium. Open from the second floor to the roof, it is a focal point for all floors and creates a visual continuity. Three restaurants are being added on the ground floor. The SSC Grille's murals are being restored. Canopies over the garage entrance to the Grant Park underground garage are being added; they will be bronze and glass to compliment the adjacent storefronts. The work is a certified rehabilitation project by the National Trust for Historic Preservation.

14

● ORCHESTRA HALL BUILDING
220 S. MICHIGAN AVENUE
ARCHITECTS: D. H. BURNHAM AND COMPANY (1904);
FOR THE RESTORATION: HARRY WEESE (1969);
FOR THE REHABILITATION AND REMODELING:
SKIDMORE, OWINGS AND MERRILL (1982)

The building is 10 stories with one basement. The world-famous Chicago Symphony Orchestra, founded by Theodore Thomas in 1898, occupies most of the 9 stories, and the Orchestral Association, a not-for-profit citizens organization, owns the property. The facade is composed of Indiana limestone and red brick in a style derivative of the Italian Renaissance. The names of Bach, Mozart, Beethoven, Schumann, and Wagner are made a part of the design over the entrance.

The 1982 rehabilitation and remodeling by Skidmore, Owings and Merrill included new seating, improved acoustics, and increased stage depth. The basement was remodeled, including the women's locker rooms and the addition of a new rehearsal hall.

BORG-WARNER BUILDING
200 S. MICHIGAN AVENUE
ARCHITECTS: A. EPSTEIN AND SONS,
WILLIAM E. LESCAZE, ASSOCIATE ARCHITECT (1958)

This steel-cage building was the first contemporary structure on Michigan Avenue. It replaced the old Pullman Building that was erected in 1884 for which S. S. Beman was the architect.

Now cross Adams Street and then Michigan Avenue to view one of Chicago's most prized possessions, the Art Institute of Chicago—the entrance guarded by two large, sculptured lions.

ART INSTITUTE OF CHICAGO
MICHIGAN AVENUE AT ADAMS STREET
ARCHITECTS: SHEPLEY, RUTAN AND COOLIDGE (1892);
FOR MCKINLOCK COURT: COOLIDGE AND HODGDON (1924);
FOR NORTH WING: HOLABIRD AND ROOT (1956);
FOR MORTON WING: SHAW, METZ AND ASSOCIATES (1962);
FOR EAST WING: SKIDMORE, OWINGS AND MERRILL,
WALTER A. NETSCH, PARTNER IN CHARGE (1976)

The original part of the building is French Renaissance in spirit, a style considered appropriate for art museums at the time but quite at variance with the trend of the Chicago school.

15

Art Institute of Chicago
(Olga Stefanos)

The Art Institute houses a theater and an art school, in addition to its art collections. A section of special interest to architects is the Burnham Library of Architecture Gallery, created to provide space for exhibits from the Burnham Library Collection—established in 1912 in memory of the great architect and city planner, Daniel H. Burnham. In the center of McKinlock Court, which is classical rather than Renaissance, is a fountain with sea creatures sculptured by Carl Milles—a duplicate of one in his native Sweden.

To celebrate its centennial, the Art Institute added 216,500 square feet to its quarters—in a wing along Columbus Drive—and remodeled another 46,000 square feet. The building program included an east entry, dining facilities, auditorium, galleries around McKinlock Court, and an expanded facility for the school of art. The entry arch of the old Stock Exchange Building was re-erected in a garden on Columbus Drive. Also on the Columbus Drive side stands Isamu Noguchi's bicentennial sculpture.

A prominent part of the 1976 expansion was the reconstruction of the Trading Room of the former Chicago Stock Exchange building which stood at 30 N. LaSalle Street from 1894 to 1972. One of the foremost interior spaces created by the architectural partnership of Adler and Sullivan, the original room was reconstructed, using original salvaged materials and carefully duplicated missing elements, based on historical photographs and contemporary descriptions. Reopened in 1977, the Trading Room is a masterpiece of architectural form and color, the decorations of which were created by Louis Sullivan in close collaboration with master colorist Louis J. Millet. The stencil patterns on the walls and ceiling contain up to fifty-two colors each.

The Art Institute is open Monday, Wednesday, Thursday, and Friday from 10:30 a.m. to 4:30 p.m.; Tuesday, 10:30 a.m. to 8 p.m.; Saturday from 10 a.m. to 5 p.m.; Sunday from noon to 5 p.m. Suggested admission fee, $4.50 for adults, $2.25 for children, senior citizens, and students. Tuesdays free.

On the west side of Michigan Avenue at Adams Street is the Peoples Gas Company Building.

⦿ PEOPLES GAS COMPANY BUILDING
122 S. Michigan Avenue
Architects: D. H. Burnham and Company (1911)

This gray granite and terra-cotta building is 20 stories, with two basements on hardpan caissons. The exterior walls on the two street fronts, above the monolithic granite columns, are supported on steel cantilever girders. It was once the temporary quarters of city offices while City Hall was being built.

Continue north.

◉ LAKE VIEW BUILDING
116 S. MICHIGAN AVENUE
ARCHITECTS: JENNEY, MUNDIE AND JENSEN (1906, 1912);
FOR THE RESTORATION: PAPPAGEORGE HAYMES (1985)

The building was originally known as the Municipal Court Building. It was first built as a 12-story structure to which 5 stories were added in 1912. The facade has three bays for windows with white terra-cotta as the exterior material. In 1985 the lobby and facade were restored, the mechanical systems were upgraded, and a roof deck was added.

CHARLIE CLUB
112 S. MICHIGAN AVENUE
ARCHITECTS: HAYNES AND BARNETT OF ST. LOUIS, MISSOURI (1907);
FOR THE ADDITION AND RENOVATIONS: SWANN AND WEISKOPF (1985)

The Illinois Athletic Club was the original occupant of this building when it was completed in 1907 as 12 stories with two basements on hardpan caissons. The facade of the original building is Indiana limestone with a base of gray granite. Step to the curb and look up to the sculptured frieze at the 11th-floor level, just under the original cornice. The figures portray mythological characters in action. Also note the three heroic figures at the 2nd-floor level. These friezes add luster to the facade and to this section of Michigan Avenue.

The 6-story addition and major renovations, completed in 1985, increased the number of hotel rooms from 83 to 180, and added 16,000 square feet of commercial space. The newer construction is of cut limestone and glass, intended to complement the older structure. The club facilities include the most advanced exercise equipment, weight training equipment, and other amenities. The 4-story restaurant/lounge has a spectacular view of the lakefront.

MONROE BUILDING
104 S. MICHIGAN AVENUE
ARCHITECTS: HOLABIRD AND ROCHE (1912)

This building is 16 stories with a beige-colored, granite facade on the first 2 stories and white terra-cotta above, in a simplified eclectic Gothic and Italian Romanesque design. It not only has a pleasing appearance, but a well-planned series of office floors. Note the way the fluting is carried the full length of the building. The lobby is an excellent example of architectural faience produced by the famed Rookwood pottery.

Around the corner on Monroe Street is a building that extends along the east side of Wabash Avenue between Adams and Monroe streets.

MID-CONTINENTAL PLAZA BUILDING
55 E. MONROE STREET
ARCHITECTS: ALFRED SHAW AND ASSOCIATES (1972)

Look up at the 50-story structure, where the eye follows the vertical lines of the aluminum skin over the steel and concrete columns. There is a secondary horizontal series of lines that mark the floors and add rhythm to all three facades. The interior ground floor has been well planned for large pedestrian movements from the garage, street, and elevators to the upper floors. The striking lobby has gray marble floors and walls that set off the aluminum escalators.

This building and plaza in the heart of the Loop has been well conceived for the convenience of the public and tenants and, in addition, provides automobile parking for guests of the Palmer House.

To the east of the plaza at the northwest corner of Monroe Street and Michigan Avenue is the University Club.

UNIVERSITY CLUB
76 E. MONROE STREET
ARCHITECTS: HOLABIRD AND ROCHE (1909)

The Indiana limestone structure of Tudor Gothic design is 14 stories, with 1 basement on pile foundations. If you step to the curb on Michigan Avenue, you can see the great cathedral dining hall which occupies 2 stories of the top floors.

Walk around the corner from the University Club and north on Michigan Avenue and you come to the Gage Building.

● GAGE BUILDING
18 S. MICHIGAN AVENUE
ARCHITECTS: HOLABIRD AND ROCHE;
FOR THE DECORATIVE FACADE: LOUIS SULLIVAN (1898)

The citation of the city's first Landmarks Commission speaks of

18

"the imaginative use of original ornament." Although the two buildings to the south of it, at 30 and 24 S. Michigan Avenue (both completely the work of Holabird and Roche) seem more modern in their lack of ornament, they do not equal the quality of design in the Gage Building. The entire citation from the Commission reads:

In recognition of the fine relations established between piers, windows, and wall surfaces; the excellence of proportions throughout; and the imaginative use of original ornament.

CHICAGO ATHLETIC ASSOCIATION
12 S. Michigan Avenue
Architect: Henry Ives Cobb (1893);
for the addition at 71 E. Madison Street:
Schmidt, Garden and Martin (1906, 1925)

The building at 12 S. Michigan Avenue was completed in 1893 after experiencing a disastrous fire. It is 10 and 11 stories, with 1 basement, on spread foundations. The adjoining addition at 71 E. Madison is 12 stories (the top 2 of which were added in 1925 by the same architect) with three basements, steel columns, and rock caissons. Step to the curb on Michigan Avenue and note the fascinating way in which Cobb designed the facade in a Venetian Gothic theme. Note also that the top floors contain a great 2-story dining hall. Limestone and red brick are the materials used.

WILLOUGHBY TOWER
8 S. Michigan Avenue
Architect: Samuel N. Crowen (1929)

Replacing the 8-story Willoughby Building, this 36-story structure on caissons has a gray granite base with an Indiana limestone facade on Michigan Avenue as well as on Madison Street.

2

1. Tower Building
   6 N. Michigan Ave.

2. 20 N. Michigan Ave.

3. 30 N. Michigan Avenue Building

4. Garland Building
   111 N. Wabash Ave.

5. Pittsfield Building
   55 E. Washington St.

6. Chicago Public Library
   Cultural Center
   78 E. Washington St.

7. Associates Center
   150 N. Michigan Ave.

8. Doral Plaza
   155 N. Michigan Ave.

9. One Prudential Plaza
   130 E. Randolph Dr.

10. Two Prudential Plaza
    180 N. Stetson Ave.

11. Amoco Oil Building
    200 E. Randolph St.

12. Buckingham Plaza
    360 E. Randolph St.

13. Outer Drive East
    400 E. Randolph St.

14. Harbor Point
    155 N. Harbor Dr.

15. 175 N. Harbor Dr.

16. Maremont Building
    168 N. Michigan Ave.

17. Boulevard Towers North
    225 N. Michigan Ave.

18. Boulevard Towers South
    205 N. Michigan Ave.

19. Carbide and Carbon Building
    230 N. Michigan Ave.

20. Old Republic Building
    307 N. Michigan Ave.

21. 320 N. Michigan Ave.

22. 333 N. Michigan Avenue Building

23. One Illinois Center
    111 E. Wacker Dr.

24. Two Illinois Center
    233 N. Michigan Ave.

25. Hyatt Regency Chicago
    151 E. Wacker Dr.

26. Columbus Plaza
    233 E. Wacker Dr.

27. Three Illinois Center
    303 E. Wacker Dr.

28. Fire Station CF-21
    Columbus Dr. and South Water St.

29. Fairmont Hotel
    200 N. Columbus Dr.

WABASH MICHIGAN BEAUBIEN STETSON COLUMBUS FIELD BLVD. HARBOR DR. LAKE SHORE DR.

Chicago River

WACKER

LAKE

RANDOLPH

WASHINGTON

MADISON

MONROE

Lake Michigan

N

WALK • 2

MICHIGAN AVENUE: MADISON STREET TO CHICAGO RIVER

WALKING TIME: About 2 hours. HOW TO GET THERE: Walk south on State Street to Madison Street; walk 2 blocks east to Michigan Avenue and start at the northwest corner.

TOWER BUILDING
6 N. MICHIGAN AVENUE
ARCHITECTS: RICHARD E. SCHMIDT (1899);
FOR THE ADDITION: HOLABIRD AND ROCHE (1922);
FOR THE REMODELING: LOEBL, SCHLOSSMAN AND BENNETT (1955)

The building was formerly known as the Montgomery Ward and Company Building with a frontage of 86 feet on Michigan Avenue and 163 feet on Madison Street. This building of steel-frame construction is 12 stories with a tower and 1 basement on wood-pile foundations. Four stories were added later, thus reducing the original scale of the tower.

The street facade of the lower 3 stories was originally of carved Georgia marble. The upper part of the facade is of umber-colored brick and terra-cotta. A. Montgomery Ward, who occupied the original tower office, was victorious for all Chicagoans in obtaining an opinion from the Supreme Court of Illinois that no building other than the Art Institute be permitted in Grant Park.

20 N. MICHIGAN AVENUE
ARCHITECTS: BEERS, CLAY AND DUTTON (1885, 1892);
FOR REHABILITATION AND ADAPTIVE REUSE:
NAGLE HARTRAY AND ASSOCIATES (1985)

This building was originally a Montgomery Ward catalogue warehouse. It was built in three stages; the first, a 5-story building 3 bays wide, the second, an addition of the same size, and in 1892 a third, an 8-story addition 2 bays wide and an added 3 stories to the extant structure. The building has masonry walls and cast-iron beams and columns at each window.

Overleaf:
Chicago Public Library
Cultural Center
(Olga Stefanos)

23

Preston Bradley
Hall, Chicago Public
Library Cultural Center
(Kathy Richland, courtesy
Marshall Holleb)

Long the John M. Smyth Building, it has recently undergone major renovations. The exterior has been restored. A limestone base was added, and the building was gutted and all mechanical systems were upgraded with computer-monitored equipment. The windows were replaced. New elevator cabs were installed. A cut-out entry 50 feet into the building added an arcaded entrance, and an 8-story atrium and skylight were added.

30 N. MICHIGAN AVENUE BUILDING
ARCHITECT: JARVIS HUNT (1914)

This was originally named the Michigan Boulevard Building when it was 15 stories high. Five stories were added in 1923, making it 20 stories with two basements on rock caissons. The exterior design is a modified Gothic. The base is granite and the facade is terra-cotta. Many medical offices are located here.

Walk west on Washington Street. On the northeast corner of Washington Street and Wabash Avenue is the Garland Building.

GARLAND BUILDING
111 N. WABASH AVENUE
ARCHITECTS: C. A. ECKSTROM (1915, ADDITION 1925);
FOR THE REMODELING:
SOLOMON, CORDWELL AND BUENZ (1982-85)

This is a representative brick skyscraper with double-hung windows, typical of its period. With a change in occupancy of the store, the lobby was remodeled, and a new lobby to serve the new office space and the second floor stores was added on Washington Street. Show windows were put on the second floor level.

On the south side of Washington Street is the Pittsfield Building.

PITTSFIELD BUILDING
55 E. WASHINGTON STREET
ARCHITECTS: GRAHAM, ANDERSON, PROBST
AND WHITE (1927)

The building is 21 stories with a 17-story tower. A black granite base and terra-cotta facade give this structure a pleasing effect. Medical personnel are the principal occupants of the building.

Across the street, east of the Garland Building is the Chicago Public Library Cultural Center.

⊙ CHICAGO PUBLIC LIBRARY CULTURAL CENTER
78 E. WASHINGTON STREET
ARCHITECTS: SHEPLEY, RUTAN AND COOLIDGE (1897);
FOR THE RENOVATION: HOLABIRD AND ROOT (1977)

Extending a full block along Michigan Avenue from Washington to Randolph streets is the former main building of the Chicago Public Library, which is now the Chicago Public Library Cultural Center. Though the structure is not at all in the style of the Chicago school of the time in which it was built, it is an impressive example of revivalist architecture, not only on the outside but throughout the interior as well. The broad marble staircases and the many beautifully colored mosaics that decorate both the walls and the ceilings are a magnificent sight for any period. The lighting fixtures and mosaics are the work of Louis Tiffany.

The blue Bedford stone, granite, and limestone exterior with large arches and columns is not unlike a Roman gateway. The colonnade is Ionic, with solid piers interspersed. The frieze bears the names of historic authors. The Washington Street entrance is treated in the Roman style with coffers and ornament, while the Randolph Street entrance is in the Grecian style with Doric columns and entablature. A stone balustrade surmounts the walls. An enormous Soldiers Memorial Hall with Civil War mementos occupies the entire second floor north.

The Cultural Center includes a Popular Library, an exhibition hall, a theater, a Fine Arts Division (music and art), and a children's center. After years of obscurity, the two Tiffany domes are now revealed in their full beauty by means of artificial lighting placed outside the stained glass. The lighted south dome now arches above a Civic Reception Center.

Open daily 9 a.m. to 7 p.m.; Fridays 9 a.m. to 6 p.m.; Saturdays 9 a.m. to 5 p.m.; closed Sundays and holidays.

Across Randolph Street from the Cultural Center is a building best viewed from a distance in Grant Park.

ASSOCIATES CENTER
150 N. MICHIGAN AVENUE
ARCHITECTS: A. EPSTEIN AND SONS (1983)

Oriented to the southeast in a way that makes it prominent on Chicago's skyline, the Associates Center has a curtainwall of alternating bands of glass and metal. The entrance is arranged on

Associates Center
(Harr, Hedrich-Blessing
courtesy A. Epstein and Sons)

27

an angle, with a passage inviting the pedestrian to cut through the building, or into the shops of the arcade, as he turns the corner. The design was conceived to have the base of the building follow the grid of the city, while the top is sliced off at an angle to face the park and lake. This device also makes the structure very noticeable along the skyline. The sculpture, by Israeli artist Yaacov Agam, titled *Communication X9* (1983), changes as you walk around it.

On the east side of Michigan Avenue is Doral Plaza.

DORAL PLAZA
155 N. MICHIGAN AVENUE
ARCHITECTS: MARTIN REINHEIMER AND ARCHITECTS (1982)

This multi-use building has alternating Chicago bays with flat areas of metal and glass wall systems, sympathetic with the neighboring buildings to the north. The concrete structure is clearly expressed on the exterior in bands between the bays of the apartments. The base of the building is a 2-floor enclosed arcade. There are offices above, and apartments on the upper levels.

Walk east on Randolph Street. This 40-story building occupies a square block of choice property facing Grant Park.

ONE PRUDENTIAL PLAZA
130 E. RANDOLPH DRIVE
ARCHITECTS: NAESS AND MURPHY (1955);
FOR THE REMODELING: LOEBL, SCHLOSSMAN
AND HACKL (1985-6)

This was the first major office building built in Chicago in the twenty years after the Depression and World War II. Unlike buildings of the Chicago school of architecture, the gray Bedford limestone Prudential Building presents the appearance of a huge monolith. The Prudential's trademark, the Rock of Gibraltar, is used as the theme for a sculptured west wall of the east wing by Alfanso Ianelli. There is an observation tower which has a very commanding view of the city if the weather is clear.

In 1985, in connection with the addition of Two Prudential Plaza, the building underwent complete cleaning of its exterior, lobby renovations, the construction of new parking facilities, and a connection with the Underground Walkway system (see WALK 7). The Annex (to the north of the building) is to be torn down, and the new office tower will rise on that site.

TWO PRUDENTIAL PLAZA
180 N. Stetson Avenue
Architects: Loebl, Schlossman and Hackl (1988)

This 64-story office building, planned at this writing, will be the fourth tallest building in Chicago (after the Sears Tower, the John Hancock Center, and the Amoco Oil Building). It will have retail space and restaurants on the ground floor, and an indoor winter garden will overlook the one-acre outdoor plaza.

East of the Prudential Building is the Amoco Oil Building.

AMOCO OIL BUILDING
200 E. Randolph Street
Architects: Edward D. Stone and the
Perkins & Will Partnership (1974);
for the addition: Perkins & Will (1985)

Just east of the Prudential Building is the Amoco Oil Building, containing the corporate headquarters of the Amoco Oil Company of Indiana. The 80-story, steel structure with a light-gray marble exterior finish is the third tallest in the city. Facing Grant Park on the south, the building can be seen for miles around.

The slender structure occupies 25 percent of the site. The tower design is based on the tube principle. The design incorporates an outside wall of 5-foot windows separated by 5-foot triangular sections which are part of the building frame. This permits the bulk of mechanical services such as utilities and air conditioning to be supplied through the triangular sections. This design permits flush window walls inside the structure.

Facing Grant Park, the tower is 194 by 194 feet and set back 140 feet from Randolph Street. The tower rises 80 stories above street level to a height of 1,136 feet. The gross area of the tower is 2.7 million square feet.

An addition to Chicago's major public art work is situated in the reflecting pool of the plaza. It is entitled *Sounding Sculpture* by sculptor Harry Bertoia. The sculpture consists of eleven separate units. Each unit is composed of tall clusters of hard alloy copper rods welded to a naval brass plate and mounted on 18-inch pedestals of black granite in the reflecting pool. The pool, which is lined with 2-inch-thick slabs of the same polished granite, is surrounded by honey locust trees and a 190-foot long waterfall.

In 1985 a formal entrance was added at the north end of the

building, off Columbus Drive. A pedestrian entrance was added at the northwest corner of the building, at Stetson and Lake streets.

Continue east on Randolph Street.

BUCKINGHAM PLAZA
360 E. RANDOLPH STREET
ARCHITECTS: FUJIKAWA JOHNSON AND ASSOCIATES (1982)

This 44-story building has 375 apartments. It is a concrete structure with infilled glass panels. At the top of the building, the pool is covered by a skylight with outdoor decks on both sides. Eventually, it will connect to the concourse system.

The next building to the east, still called Outer Drive East is, of course, no longer east of the Outer Drive since the new section of highway opened.

OUTER DRIVE EAST
400 E. RANDOLPH STREET
ARCHITECTS: MARTIN REINHEIMER AND ARCHITECTS (1962)

This "T"-shaped apartment building has its major facade oriented south. It has infill panels of glass contrasting with white brick curtain walls. Note the domed recreation area containing the swimming pool.

Continue east to Harbor Drive.

HARBOR POINT
155 N. HARBOR DRIVE
ARCHITECTS: SOLOMON, CORDWELL AND BUENZ (1978)

Because of the advantages of its site, the architects wanted to design a tower, instead of a slab building. Influenced by the design of their recently built Edgewater Plaza triangular building, which provides exceptional views in all directions, this building started with the same inner design. The freer form of the articulated multi-curved bays of the exterior glass curtainwall (possibly influenced by Lake Point Tower in WALK 14, which can be seen to the north), provides both spectacular views in all directions and interesting reflections of light and of the city to the observer on the ground. The building is 50 stories tall. Its structure is evident at the first floor arcade.

175 N. HARBOR DRIVE
ARCHITECTS: FUJIKAWA JOHNSON AND ASSOCIATES (1988)

This apartment complex, under construction at this writing, will be 55 stories, containing 600 apartments. It is scheduled for completion in 1988.

Walk west on Randolph Street, back to Michigan Avenue. Turn north.

MAREMONT BUILDING
168 N. MICHIGAN AVENUE
ARCHITECTS: MARSHALL AND FOX (1916);
FOR THE REMODELING: CASRIEL HALPERIN (1964)

This structure was originally known as the Federal Life Building. With one basement on caissons, the building rises 12 stories. When the exterior and base were remodeled in 1964, the base was created of white marble.

The 8-foot metal sculpture by Theodore Roszak in the lobby fascinates and puzzles viewers who are no more enlightened when they read the title *206—H and R*. The actual title is *Invocation-Variation #3*, and was executed by this eminent modern sculptor in nickel, silver, and stainless steel. The work is the third in a series called *Invocation* which represents an ambitious attempt to translate and interpret fundamental ideas concerning the meaning of life.

Cross to the east side of Michigan Avenue.

BOULEVARD TOWERS NORTH
225 N. MICHIGAN AVENUE
ARCHITECTS: FUJIKAWA JOHNSON AND ASSOCIATES (1981)

BOULEVARD TOWERS SOUTH
205 N. MICHIGAN AVENUE
ARCHITECTS: FUJIKAWA JOHNSON AND ASSOCIATES (1985)

Boulevard Towers function as an entranceway from Michigan Avenue to the Illinois Center complex. The complex is of steel with glass curtainwalls, a continuation of the original Illinois Center buildings' design. The complex was built in stages. First was the 24-story north tower and the 19-story link between the towers. When the 44-story south tower was added in 1985, the complex was connected, and the link gave it structural strength as well as providing various options in tenant space. Under the north tower is the Illinois Central Gulf commuter station. It serves about 15,000 riders each day. There is parking underneath, and retail space on the concourse level and on the plaza. This is also the Michigan Avenue entrance to the Underground Walkway system

(see WALK 7). With the completion of these buildings, the concourse extends from Lake Street to Wacker Drive.

CARBIDE AND CARBON BUILDING
230 N. MICHIGAN AVENUE
ARCHITECTS: BURNHAM BROTHERS (1929)

The structure is 40 stories with two basements on rock caissons. It is distinguished for the gold and very dark green terra-cotta tower, dark green terra-cotta facade, and black granite and gold base. The gold, of course, is glazed on the terra-cotta and metal. The Burnham brothers were the sons of the distinguished architect and city planner Daniel H. Burnham.
Continue north.

OLD REPUBLIC BUILDING
307 N. MICHIGAN AVENUE
ARCHITECTS: VITZHUM AND BURNS (1925)

Left: One Illinois Center and 333 North Michigan (Architectural Camera)

Right: Tower of the Carbide and Carbon building (Allen Carr)

The original name of this structure was the Bell Building. This building is 24 stories on hardpan caissons. The base is a beige-colored granite and a light gray, terra-cotta facade—typical of the commercial school of architecture of the 1920s—otherwise undistinguished.

320 N. MICHIGAN AVENUE
ARCHITECTS: BOOTH/HANSEN AND ASSOCIATES (1983)

This very narrow building makes the best use of a small site. Note how all the windows face east and west, because of the close property lines on both sides. It is a highly articulated concrete structure with an arcade and entrance marked by two round columns and an interesting penthouse structure on top.

333 N. MICHIGAN AVENUE BUILDING
ARCHITECTS: HOLABIRD AND ROOT (1928)

This building is representative of the distinguished work of the equally distinguished firm of architects for the golden period of the late 1920s. The building can be seen from the full length of Michigan Avenue north of the Chicago River. The entrance was remodeled in 1969, but the balance of the building retains that fascinating design quality of the 1920s—sometimes referred to as Art Moderne. The elevator doors carry sculptured figures in relief by Edgar Miller. The building's base is a gray marble and the entire facade is a gray limestone.

Walk east on Wacker Drive.

ILLINOIS CENTER, also known as the Illinois Central Air Rights Development, is constructed on air rights over the Illinois Central railroad yards. The Center's business and residential towers, hotels, and parks, with below-plaza shopping concourse and parking facilities, have been developed on 83 acres of land. The Center extends east of Michigan Avenue to the lake, south of the Chicago River to Randolph Street.

ONE ILLINOIS CENTER
111 E. WACKER DRIVE
ARCHITECT: LUDWIG MIES VAN DER ROHE (1970)

One Illinois Center is an office tower consisting of 29 office floors and a lobby floor on a landscaped plaza overlooking the Chicago River. Lobby escalators lead below plaza level to a concourse bordered by retail shops and restaurants. Below the concourse are 3 levels of parking for more than 300 cars. The building contains approximately 1 million square feet of rentable office space and 35,000 square feet of retail shops. The structure is reinforced concrete. The curtainwall is dark bronze aluminum and bronze-tinted glass.

Walk through the plaza to the east of One Illinois Center to view Two Illinois Center.

TWO ILLINOIS CENTER
233 N. MICHIGAN AVENUE
ARCHITECT: LUDWIG MIES VAN DER ROHE (1973)

A twin of the One Illinois Center building, its concourse and parking areas are an extension of the levels provided under the other. The buildings function as a unified development. Two Illinois Center is built partially over the lower and intermediate levels of E. South Water Street.

The next building east on Wacker Drive is the Hyatt Regency Chicago.

HYATT REGENCY CHICAGO
151 E. WACKER DRIVE
ARCHITECTS: A. EPSTEIN AND SONS (1974, 1980)

Directly east of One Illinois Center is the Hyatt Regency Chicago. This hotel of more than 2,000 rooms is built of brick and glass.

The addition, in the same style and materials as the original building, is joined by a glass-enclosed, covered, pedestrian bridge. The hub of the complex is a glass winter garden. Above the first floor is a tilted, mirrored surface which creates an unusual reflection of the cars and pedestrians below. The brick of the complex stands in pleasant contrast to the glass and steel of the surrounding structures and bespeaks the privacy of it being a hotel.

Walk east on Wacker Drive.

COLUMBUS PLAZA
233 E. WACKER DRIVE
ARCHITECTS: FUJIKAWA JOHNSON AND ASSOCIATES (1980)

This 47-story building has 552 apartments. It is of exposed reinforced concrete, with an infill of dark bronze aluminum, and tinted double-insulated glass. There are two parking levels below and a solarium and sundeck on the penthouse level. It is connected to the concourse system.

On the southeast corner of Wacker Drive and Columbus Drive is Three Illinois Center.

THREE ILLINOIS CENTER
303 E. Wacker Drive
Architects: Fujikawa Johnson and Associates (1980)

This 28-story building has a refined bronze-painted aluminum and tinted glass curtainwall in the Miesian tradition and a reinforced concrete frame. Note the restrained use of materials. There are 40,000 square feet of retail space. It is also connected to the concourse level.

Attached to the south is a fire station.

FIRE STATION CF-21
Columbus Drive and South Water Street
Architects: Fujikawa Johnson and Associates (1981)

This fire station sits on a very tight site, partially tucked beneath Three Illinois Center. It is clad in dark aluminum and glass harmonizing with the neighboring building. It is 14,000 square feet on 2 stories. It has an apparatus room for the fire engines and equipment, drying rooms, hose tower, exercise room, offices, kitchen, lounge, and dormitories for both men and women. The station serves all levels of the Illinois Center complex and the adjoining Loop area.

Walk south.

FAIRMONT HOTEL
200 N. Columbus Drive
Architects: Hulmuth, Obata and Kassabaum (1987)

This hotel, under construction as we went to press, is scheduled for completion in 1987.

3

1. One Congress Center
   403 S. State St.

2. Central Chicago Public Library
   333 S. State St.

3. 14 East Jackson Boulevard

4. Home Federal Savings and
      Loan Building
   201 S. State St.

5. Singer Building
   120 S. State St.

6. Amalgamated Bank Building
   100 S. State St.

7. Palmer House
   17 E. Monroe St.

8. Mid-Continental Plaza Building
   55 E. Monroe St.

9. Carson Pirie Scott Store
   1 S. State St.

10. Chicago Building
    7 W. Madison St.

11. State-Madison Building
    22 W. Madison St.

12. Wieboldt's Department Store
    1 N. State St.

13. Stevens Store Building
    17 N. State St.

14. 32 N. State St.

15. Marshall Field Store
    111 N. State St.

16. 140-144 N. State St.

17. Chicago Theater
    175 N. State St.

18. ABC Building
    190 N. State St.

19. United Insurance Building
    1 E. Wacker Dr.

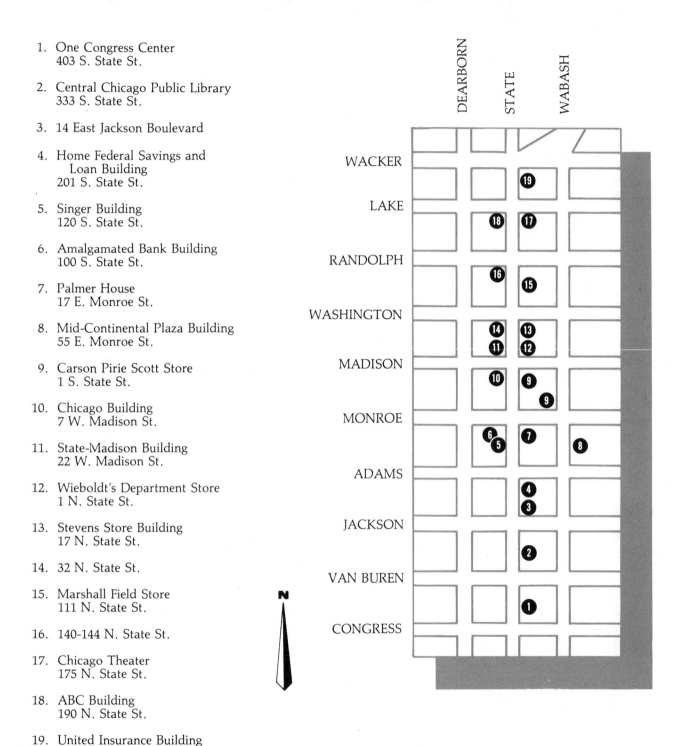

WALK • 3

STATE STREET: IN THE LOOP

WALKING TIME: About 1½ hour. HOW TO GET THERE: Walk to Congress Parkway, 7 blocks south of Randolph Street; or take any southbound CTA bus on State Street south of Randolph Street, and get off at Congress [500 S]. [Check with the driver to be sure the bus will not leave State Street before it reaches Congress Parkway.]

State Street—"That Great Street," as the song goes!—is a part of Chicago's central business district. State Street offers economic advantages provided nowhere else in the entire Midwest. It has been a market for buyers and sellers from all over the nation and the world, and this fact alone gives it special distinction. But, in addition, State Street displays some architectural gems along the way as it stretches through the Loop from the Congress Parkway to the Chicago River—the extent of this WALK.

In the last decade there has been a repositioning of State Street. No longer a mile-long shopping district, it has escaped the fate of other major urban downtown areas plagued by disinvestment. Since the establishment of the State Street Mall, there has been some major investment in older buildings, converting them from retail to office space.

Nowhere in the nation was there such a concentration of retail department stores. Starting at the south end with the former Sears store, there was one large building after another. The main entrances were on State Street, augmented by the former carriage entrances on the side streets as well as on Wabash Avenue. The linear relationship of the buildings made it convenient for the shopper to go on foot from store to store—or be driven to the nearest side street. Sears, Wiebolts, and the Montgomery Ward stores have been lost, and there has been downsizing of some of those that remain, but there is also healthy investment in the area. At the center of the street, Carson Pirie is spending 11 million dollars on a major renovation plan. The Dearborn Center, a 72-story office tower to be built at State and Adams Streets, will continue this growth.

Overleaf: State Street
(Olga Stefanos)

Marshall Field
(Olga Stefanos)

Once a theater and entertainment strip, at night State Street was Chicago's Great White Way, with its unusually large and brilliant lights. Now, with the rehabilitation and reopening of the Chicago Theater, State Street will again be able to attract people in the evening.

Starting the WALK at Congress Parkway, you come first to the former Sears Roebuck Store. It is on the northeast corner of State Street and Congress Parkway.

◉ ONE CONGRESS CENTER
403 S. STATE STREET
ARCHITECT: WILLIAM LeBARON JENNEY (1891);
FOR THE RENOVATION: LOUIS ARTHUR WEISS (1985-6)

The building extends a whole block—from Congress north to Van Buren Street. At the time it was built it was among the largest steel frame construction buildings in the world. In its very early days it was known as the Leiter Building II. Levi Z. Leiter, once a partner of Marshall Field, had already done business on his own at another location. The first Leiter Building, also designed by Jenney, stood at Wells and Monroe streets and later became the Morris Building. Although the building at Congress Parkway and State Street was originally constructed as an investment property for still another company, Leiter took it over after a very short time. In later years, it was operated as a cooperative store as Leiter Shops. Just under the cornice of the State Street facade remains this inscription: L. Z. LEITER, MDCCCXCI.

This 8-story building, with three facades of white Maine granite, was designed by one of the pioneers in the Chicago school of architecture, William LeBaron Jenney. He had produced the first example of typical Chicago construction in his Home Insurance Building of 1885 (no longer standing), and he continued the development of the Chicago school in the second Leiter Building. Jenney allowed the steel skeleton, only recently introduced at that time, to determine the outward characteristics of the building—its division into enormous square sections, each filled with many large windows. During renovation, it was found that Jenney had intended two open light wells, which were never built.

A plaque attached to the building on the State Street side quotes a citation from the Chicago Dynamic Commission, dated October 27, 1957 (two months before the Architectural Landmarks Commission was formed):

Former Goldblatt's building, planned as the new central Chicago Public Library (Howard Kaplan, courtesy Holabird & Root)

Bold, vigorous and original design expresses the light and open character of this building. One of the nation's most impressive early works of commercial architecture.

During the recent renovations, all windows were replaced, the electrical and mechanical systems were upgraded, and the elevators were rehabilitated. The fire escapes on the north and south sides were removed to improve the building's appearance. The lower level will be retail space; the first floor will be retail and a restaurant; mezzanine will be retail space; floors 2-8 will be offices. The building is now a national landmark.

Cross over now to the northeast corner of State and Van Buren streets.

CENTRAL CHICAGO PUBLIC LIBRARY
333 S. State Street

ARCHITECTS: HOLABIRD AND ROCHE (1912);
FOR THE ADAPTIVE REUSE: LESTER B. KNIGHT AND ASSOCIATES,
SUPERVISING ARCHITECTS/ENGINEERS, IN ASSOCIATION
WITH HOLABIRD AND ROOT (1988)

It was hoped that this would be the site for a world-class library in Chicago. However, the decision making process has been so long and tedious, and fraught with various dissensions, that it was unclear at this writing if this will indeed be the final selection.

This building was first known as Rothschild's, then as a subsidiary of Marshall Field and Company as the Davis Store, then as the Goldblatts Store. The building is 10 stories, with three basements. At this writing, plans are underway to open an atrium space through floors 1-3 in the center of the building, install new elevators, and replace all windows in a style in keeping with the original design. Probably the most significant part of the design is the use of columns throughout the building to provide a vertical counterpoint to the vertical stacks.

Continue north to the northeast corner of State Street and Jackson Boulevard.

14 E. JACKSON BOULEVARD
ARCHITECTS: MARSHALL AND FOX (1913)

This building contains the Lytton Store. The building is 19 stories with 3 basements on caissons—a graceful, well-designed structure for its time. The first three floors are retail; the rest of the building is now office space.

Continue north to the corner.

HOME FEDERAL SAVINGS AND LOAN BUILDING
201 S. STATE STREET
ARCHITECTS: SKIDMORE, OWINGS AND MERRILL (1966)

State Street has few skyscrapers. It was historically a street lined with multi-story buildings of moderate height, occupied by stores of long-established companies.

The principal exception is the Home Federal Savings and Loan Building, on the southeast corner of Adams and State streets. In this handsome structure the vertical lines are accented by the stainless steel mullions. The entire building is enveloped in dark glass panels. To make way for this building, an earlier one of considerable architectural merit—the Republic Building designed by Holabird and Roche (1905)—was demolished.

Continue north.

● SINGER BUILDING
120 S. STATE STREET
ARCHITECTS: MUNDIE AND JENSEN (1926);
FOR THE RESTORATION:
HASBROUCK HUNDERMAN ARCHITECTS (1986)

This 10-story building was built for the Singer Sewing Machine Company in 1926. At this writing it is being restored to its original grandeur. It will be an office building with a restaurant on the ground floor.

Continue north.

AMALGAMATED BANK BUILDING
100 S. STATE STREET
ARCHITECTS: A. EPSTEIN AND SONS (1972)

This steel-cage, 7-story bank building is a remodeled former department store structure.

Walk east on Monroe Street.

PALMER HOUSE
17 E. MONROE STREET
ARCHITECTS: J. M. VAN OSDEL, THEN C. M. PALMER (1874);
HOLABIRD AND ROCHE (1925)

On the east side of State Street just south of Monroe Street is the west entrance to the popular shopping arcade of the Palmer House. The arcade connects State Street with Wabash Avenue, and the Monroe Street entrance of one of the most distinguished hotels in Chicago. The Palmer House preceding this building was a real Chicago pioneer, for it was erected only a few years after the Great Fire of 1871—a still earlier Palmer House having been opened just two weeks before the fire and then completely destroyed. The 1875 building is said to have been the first fireproof hotel and the first to provide its residents with electric lights, telephones, and elevators. It was built at a time when the Chicago school of architecture was making great strides in improving the construction and facilities of hotels and apartment buildings.

Continue east.

MID-CONTINENTAL PLAZA BUILDING
55 E. MONROE STREET
ARCHITECTS: ALFRED SHAW AND ASSOCIATES (1972)

44

If you decide to walk through the Palmer House Arcade, be sure to step out at Wabash Avenue and look across the street at this 50-story office structure of tinted glass and aluminum that soars 572 feet. The spandrels, comprising the section between the gray-glass windows and the floors, match the glass and give a striking vertical appearance.

Backtrack west to State Street and turn north. At State and Madison streets, the intersection that is famed as the "World's Busiest Corner," stands the most notable of Chicago's department stores architecturally, and the one always most noticed by the infrequent visitor to State Street—the Carson Pirie Scott Store.

Left: Entrance to
Carson Pirie Scott
(Allen Carr)

Carson Pirie Scott
(Olga Stefanos)

● CARSON PIRIE SCOTT STORE

1 S. STATE STREET
ARCHITECTS: LOUIS SULLIVAN (1899, 1903);
D. H. BURNHAM AND COMPANY (1905);
HOLABIRD AND ROOT (1960);
FOR THE RESTORATION: JOHN VINCI (1979)

What you see today is the result of several stages of construction, so that the total building is probably less unified than it would otherwise have been. Fortunately, however, the architects of 1905 and 1960 had such deep respect for Sullivan's original design that they followed the pattern closely in their additions. Here you have one of the best illustrations of the effectiveness of the horizontally elongated Chicago window. The ornamentation decorating the windows of the first 2 stories is in pleasant contrast with the clean, unadorned precision of the window lines above them.

Originally occupied by the Schlesinger and Mayer Company, for whom it had been constructed in 1899 and enlarged in 1903, it was purchased later in 1903 by Carson Pirie Scott. The first and easternmost section, of only 3 bays and 9 stories, faced only Madison Street. The 1903 enlargement was made possible by the demolition of two older buildings next to this site. The addition, which rose 12 stories instead of 9, included 3 more bays on Madison Street and extended around the corner, with 7 bays on State Street. Sullivan was the architect for both the original building and the extension. His love of incorporating ornamentation even in the designs of commercial buildings is expressed here in the intricate intermingling of leaf and flower designs that decorate the main entrance at the corner, as well as the windows of the lower stories. This rich but delicate pattern gives an unusually luxurious effect to an entrance already distinguished by its semicircular shape and its location at the corner of the building.

The third unit, extending the building still farther on State Street, was designed by Burnham in 1905; and the extension of that long facade was by Holabird and Root in 1960, still following Sullivan's original plan. The result is therefore a true Sullivan masterpiece, no matter what other architects were involved before the building reached its present proportions.

Sigfried Giedion says of this building (*Space, Time and Architecture*, Sixth Edition. Cambridge: The Harvard University Press, 1946, p. 311):

46

The front is designed to fulfill its indispensable function, the admission of light. Its basic elements are the horizontally elongated "Chicago windows," admirably homogeneous and treated to coincide with the framework of the skeleton. The whole front is executed with a strength and precision that is matched by no other building of the period.

And Frederick Koeper remarks (*Illinois Architecture*. Chicago: The University of Chicago Press, 1968, p.64):

In this design Sullivan has afforded us those dual pleasures of architecture: an involvement with decoration as well as the satisfaction of discipline and order.

The recent restoration work included the stripping of layers of paint from the ornamental iron on the base of the building to restore it to its original red and green finish, which simulated patinated bronze. The terra-cotta on the upper stories was cleaned and repaired. The corner entrance vestibule was stripped and later alterations (the dropped ceiling and the formica paneling) were removed, and all was restored to the original mahogany finish.

On the southwest corner of State and Madison streets is the Chicago Building.

◉ CHICAGO BUILDING
7 W. Madison Street
Architects: Holabird and Roche (1905)

This building is 15 stories with 2 basements on rock caissons. It is an excellent example of Chicago school commercial architecture with large windows dominating the storefronts. The projecting bays give it a prismatic look.

ONE NORTH DEARBORN BUILDING
22 W. Madison Street
Architects: Holabird and Roche (1905-1917)

This building occupies the north side of Madison Street from State to Dearborn streets, comprising nearly a half block. It was first occupied by the Boston Store—an operation of the Netcher family and of the well-known Mollie Netcher who became the matriarch of the family in the 1920s. She was part of the colorful merchant families of Chicago. The building is 17 stories with 3 basements and was converted into an office building in 1948.

Continue north.

WIEBOLDT'S DEPARTMENT STORE
1 N. STATE STREET
ARCHITECTS: HOLABIRD AND ROCHE (1900, 1905, 1912);
FOR THE REMODELING: BARANCIK AND CONTE (1978)

Another colorful character of the 1920s was Colonel Leon Mandel, the titular head of an old Chicago merchant family. Formerly Mandel Brothers Store Building, this structure at 1 N. State Street was built in three main sections and today is divided into two main sections. The Wabash Avenue building is 12 stories and the State Street building is 15 stories.

Cross to the east side of the street and continue north.

STEVENS STORE BUILDING
17 N. STATE STREET, 16 N. WABASH AVENUE
ARCHITECTS: D. H. BURNHAM AND COMPANY (1912)

This building is 19 stories over 2 basements on hardpan caissons. Chas. A. Stevens and Company, a women's specialty store, occupies the lower floors and basements. Small shops and offices occupy the balance of the building.

Cross back to the west side of State Street. On the southwest corner of State and Washington streets is 32 N. State Street.

◉ 32 N. STATE STREET
ARCHITECTS: FOR GROUND FLOOR: BURNHAM AND ROOT (1890);
FOR THE REST OF THE BUILDING: D. H. BURNHAM AND COMPANY,
CHARLES ATWOOD, DESIGNER (1894-95)

This Architectural Landmark once was known as the Reliance Building. The original granite base was replaced by the terra-cotta and limestone base which contrasts markedly with the glass and white terra-cotta of the towering, 15-story structure above. About the Reliance Building, Sigfried Giedion comments ". . .although its glazed white tiles have become encrusted with dirt, its airiness and pure proportions make it a symbol of the Chicago school." He continues, pointing out that the Reliance was built nearly three decades before Mies van der Rohe envisioned his glass-and-iron skyscraper as a kind of fantasy in 1921, "But it may be that this Chicago building is something more than an incentive for fantasy: an architectonic anticipation of the future" (*Space, Time and Architecture*, Sixth Edition. Cambridge: The Harvard University Press, 1946, p. 310). The citation by the Architectural Landmarks Commission reads:

48

In recognition of the early and complete expression, through slender piers, small spandrels, and the skillfully restrained use of terra-cotta with large areas of glass, of the structural cage, of steel that alone supports such buildings.

The North Loop Development Program will soon rebuild the block on the west side of State Street between Randolph and Washington streets. The plans are to include a huge atrium running east and west to bring people from the west into State Street.

Cross the street diagonally. The WALK up State Street should include the interior of Marshall Field's. You can walk through from State Street to Wabash Avenue or from Washington Street to Randolph Street for the building occupies the entire block.

◉ MARSHALL FIELD STORE
111 N. State Street
Architects: D. H. Burnham and Company
(1892, 1902, 1904, 1906-7, 1914)

The original Marshall Field Store was built at the corner of State and Washington streets, the site of three previous buildings that had been used by the Field and Leiter partnership. The first building was destroyed by the Chicago Fire a few years after it was erected. The rest of this famous store was constructed in sections—between 1902 and 1914—and the former Marshall Field men's store, at the southwest corner of Wabash Avenue and Washington Street was added in 1914.

At the Washington and Randolph street ends of the store are open courts, surrounded by grilled railings at each floor and covered by skylights. The skylight at the south end of the store (Washington Street) is a slightly arched dome of colored mosaic at the level of the fifth floor ceiling. The other (Randolph Street) is a plain glass skylight at the top of the building. The Randolph Street court is a perfect setting for the enormous Christmas tree that has delighted Marshall Field's customers for years.

On the southwest corner of State and Randolph streets is a building in disrepair, but notable.

The Marshall Field
clock at State and Randolph
(Philip A. Turner)

140-144 N. STATE STREET
Architects: Carter, Drake and Wight (1872);
for the addition: Adler and Sullivan (1887)

This was originally the Bay State Building designed in 1872 by Carter, Drake and Wight. It was originally 4 stories tall. It is the

Chicago Theater
(Olga Stefanos)

only surviving High Victorian Gothic building designed by Peter B. Wight (who designed the National Academy of Design in New York City) still standing in the country. In 1887 Adler and Sullivan added the top 2 floors and the bay windows.

Cross to the east side of State Street and walk north past the alley. You are now standing in front of the Chicago Theater. The Marquee (the symbol of the theater) in many eyes is also considered the symbol of the City.

◉ CHICAGO THEATER
175 N. State Street
Architects: Rapp and Rapp (1921);
for the restoration: Daniel Coffey
and Associates, Ltd. (1986)

◉ PAGE BROTHERS BUILDING
Architects: J. M. Van Osdel (1871);
for the adaptive reuse: Daniel Coffey
and Associates, Ltd. (1986)

The landmark Chicago Theater and the Page Brothers Building are being tied together into a single, multi-use complex. The theater reopened on September 10, 1986 with a gala performance by Frank Sinatra, who opened his show singing *My Kind of Town.* There will be a major restaurant on the second floor of the Chicago Theater. The ground floor will be commercial space; there will be two floors of offices in the Chicago Theater and all of the Page Brothers Building will be office space. The entrance is through the Grand Lobby of the Chicago Theater—which will be open to the public. The Grand Staircase has been restored, as was the Grand Promenade which leads to the Lake Street entrance.

The facade of the Chicago Theater is ornamental terra-cotta; the Grand Arch exhibits a Tiffany stained glass window with the Balaban and Katz crest. B & K was the original builder, and this was their national headquarters. The Marquee (the symbol of the theater, and in many eyes the symbol of the City) has been restored with slightly lowered side panels so as not to obscure the view of the arch.

The Page Brothers Building is on the National Register of Historic Places because the cast iron facade on its Lake Street side is reputedly the last surviving example in the Loop. Through an innovative structural system, the entire interior is being replaced with new fireproof concrete construction. Interestingly, this is in keeping with the history of the building, because the State Street facade was replaced in the early 1900s when Potter Palmer redirected Chicago's major commercial street from Lake Street to State Street. Both structures have achieved landmark status.

On the southwest corner of State and Lake streets is the ABC Building.

ABC BUILDING
190 N. STATE STREET
ARCHITECTS: RAPP AND RAPP WITH G. ALBERT LANSBURGH (1917); FOR THE REMODELING: SKIDMORE, OWINGS AND MERRILL (1982-7)

This was formerly the State-Lake Building. Starting in 1982, the building underwent major upgrading. The entry was relocated one bay to the south; the terra-cotta facade was refurbished and cleaned; all windows were replaced; and a new storefront was installed. An interior atrium and penthouse were added, and the interior office space was reorganized.

On the west side of State Street, between Wacker Drive and Lake Street, is another part of the North Loop Redevelopment Program. At this writing plans call for the inclusion of a hotel, to be developed by Jerrold Wexler, Edward Ross, and J. J. Marken and an office building to be developed by the John Buck Company and the Leo Burnett Company. Cross to the northeast corner of State and Lake streets. If you look west, you will have an excellent view of the new State of Illinois Center (featured in WALK 6). Walk north to the corner.

UNITED INSURANCE BUILDING
1 E. WACKER DRIVE
ARCHITECTS: SHAW, METZ, AND ASSOCIATES (1962)

The marble-faced tower of the United Insurance Company of America was once the tallest marble-faced commercial structure in the world. The strongly vertical lines of this 41-story structure contrast sharply with the circular towers of Marina City, just across the river. (Marina City is a feature of WALK 4.)

4

1. Manhattan Building
   431 S. Dearborn St.

2. Old Colony Building
   407 S. Dearborn St.

3. Monadnock Building
   53 W. Jackson Blvd.

4. Standard Club
   321 S. Dearborn St.

5. Union League Club
   65 W. Jackson Blvd.

6. Everett McKinley Dirksen Building

7. John C. Kluczynski
   Federal Building
   219 S. Dearborn St.

8. Marquette Building
   140 S. Dearborn St.

9. Dearborn Center
   Dearborn and Adams St.
   (NE corner)

10. Inland Steel Building
    30 W. Monroe St.

11. Xerox Center
    55 W. Monroe St.

12. First National Bank Building and
    Plaza
    One First National Plaza

13. Three First National Plaza
    70 W. Madison St.

14. Citicorp Savings Building
    7 S. Dearborn St.

15. Connecticut Mutual Life Building
    33 N. Dearborn St.

16. Brunswick Building
    69 W. Washington St.

17. Richard J. Daley Center and Plaza
    55 W. Washington St.

18. Delaware Building
    36 W. Randolph St.

19. Dearborn Cinemas
    170-186 N. Dearborn St.

20. Ryan Insurance Building
    222 N. Dearborn St.

21. Marina City
    300 N. State St.

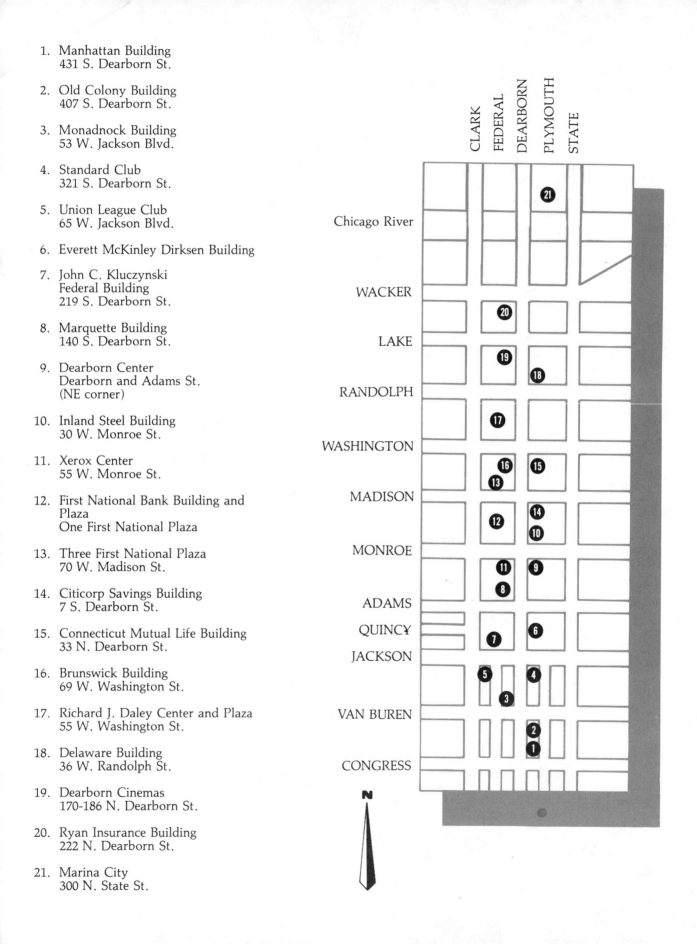

WALK • 4

DEARBORN STREET

*WALKING TIME: About 1½ to 2 hours. HOW TO GET THERE:
Take a southbound CTA bus No. 29 on State Street and get off at
Van Buren Street [400 S]. Walk west across Plymouth Court to
Dearborn Street [36 W], which runs parallel to State Street.
Street.*

This WALK offers a virtual history of the modern skyscraper,
which had its beginnings here in Chicago—one of the results of the
tremendous architectural development that rebuilt the city after its
almost total destruction by fire in 1871.

Located at the south end of the walk—in fact 1 block farther
south than Van Buren Street—is the Manhattan Building.

◉ MANHATTAN BUILDING

431 S. DEARBORN STREET
ARCHITECTS: JENNEY AND MUNDIE (1889-91);
FOR THE REHABILITATION: WILBERT R. HASBROUCK (1981)

Designed by the man who has often been called the father of the
steel skyscraper, William LeBaron Jenney, the Manhattan is now
the oldest tall office building in the world to have used skeleton
construction throughout. At the time it was built, it was also the
tallest building in the world. The second Rand McNally building,
designed by Burnham and Root in the same year, also used
skeleton construction throughout but was demolished in 1911.

The building has recently been restored to its original condition.
The ground floor is now retail space. The interior has been
adapted into 105 apartments. At the time of the conversion, it was
the largest commercial building in Chicago converted to residential use.

Next, please walk south to Congress Parkway to see the giant
sculpture *Arris* by sculptor John Henry and a gift to Chicago by
the Amalgamated Trust and Savings Bank.

Walk north to the southeast corner of Dearborn and Van
Buren streets.

Overleaf: Marina City
(Philip A. Turner)

55

Top left:
Manhattan Building
(Tom Yanul courtesty
Hasbrouk/Hunderman)

Bottom left:
Fisher Building
(Allen Carr)

Right: Monadnock
Building (Richard Nickel)

⊙ OLD COLONY BUILDING

407 S. Dearborn Street
Architects: Holabird and Roche (1893)

This building is 210 feet high, with 17 stories and a basement. It fronts on three streets—Plymouth Court and Dearborn and Van Buren streets. It is built with tower bays at the corners and presents a well-designed appearance. The first 4 stories are of light-blue Bedford stone and the upper part pressed brick and white terra-cotta. The building has received an architectural award as noted by a plaque at the entrance.

Cross Van Buren Street. On the northeast corner stands the Fisher Building, an Architectural Landmark.

⊙ FISHER BUILDING

343 S. Dearborn Street
Architects: D. H. Burnham and Company (1896);
for the addition: Peter J. Weber (1907)

The steel frame skeleton, which was also used here, is by no means disguised by the rather elaborate Gothic ornamentation. The architect for this building was the same Daniel Burnham who is world-famous for his Chicago city plan. His frequently quoted admonition, "make no little plans; they have no magic to stir men's minds," seems to have been heeded by Chicago architects, and Dearborn Street is one of the results. The 1907 addition is taller than the original part of the building, but follows the style of the older building.

Across the street from the Fisher Building, between Van Buren Street and Jackson Boulevard, is another Architectural Landmark.

⊙ MONADNOCK BUILDING

53 W. Jackson Boulevard
Architects: north half, Burnham and Root (1891);
south half, Holabird and Roche (1893)

This is the Monadnock Building, internationally famed as the world's largest office building at the time of construction and still known as the highest commercial building (16 stories rising 197 feet high) with outside wall-bearing construction. Some of the walls at the base are 6 feet thick to support the tremendous weight. The north half of the building, however—the only part that has outside walls of masonry only—does use steel for the interior columns and floor supports; and the south half, built two years later, used a full steel frame.

57

Originally this building had 4 separate entrances to 4 separate sections, each named after a New England mountain, according to the fancy of the four branches of the New England family that owned it. Jackson Street was the original entrance. When the south half of the building was added, a more impressive entrance was put on Van Buren Street. From the time of its opening, the building was popularly known as the Monadnock (although each section had a name) and over the years the separation of the entrances and the other names were forgotten.

The Monadnock's files tell of an early test of the building's ability to withstand Chicago's winds despite its unusual height and lack of wind braces. When a near-hurricane, with winds reaching the velocity of 88 miles per hour, struck Chicago a few years after the Monadnock was completed, experts in engineering rushed to the building with some trepidation and conducted a pendulum experiment from the top floor. A plumb bob that was swung down through the stairwell to the lobby floor, to measure the structure's vibrations at the height of the storm, marked a small pattern not more than 5/8" by 3/8"—an experiment that reassured everyone who had feared what high winds might do to this building!

The citation of the Monadnock Building as an Architectural Landmark reads:

In recognition of its original design and its historical interest as the highest wall-bearing structure in Chicago. Restrained use of brick, soaring massive walls, omission of ornamental forms, unite in a building simple yet majestic.

Continue north.

STANDARD CLUB
321 S. DEARBORN STREET
ARCHITECT: ALBERT KAHN OF DETROIT, MICHIGAN (1926)

This 10-story elegant private club building was constructed in 1926 and follows a general design pattern of the Italian Renaissance. Bedford limestone and pressed brick are the materials used on both the Dearborn Street and the Plymouth Court facades.

Walk north to Jackson Boulevard and turn west.

UNION LEAGUE CLUB
65 W. JACKSON BOULEVARD
ARCHITECTS: MUNDIE AND JENSEN (1926)

Just to the west of the Monadnock Building is this 22-story club building with a granite base and pressed-brick facade in the style of the late Italian Renaissance. The club still maintained a separate entrance and elevator "for the ladies" until the board of directors voted a rules change on February 15, 1972, and marked the end of an era. This private club was once famous as the citadel of the Republican party of Chicago.

Crossing Jackson Boulevard on Dearborn Street, going north, means jumping from the late 19th to the middle 20th century. The Chicago Federal Center has two buildings which share an address.

EVERETT McKINLEY DIRKSEN BUILDING
JOHN C. KLUCZYNSKI FEDERAL BUILDING
219 S. DEARBORN STREET
ARCHITECTS: LUDWIG MIES VAN DER ROHE;
SCHMIDT, GARDEN, AND ERIKSON;
C. F. MURPHY AND ASSOCIATES;
A. EPSTEIN AND SONS (1964; 1975)

On the east side of Dearborn Street stands a spectacularly modern 27-story structure of steel and glass, the Everett McKinley Dirksen Building, part of a complex of buildings in Chicago's Federal Center. The Center extends from Jackson Boulevard north to Adams Street, occupying both sides of Dearborn Street and extending west to Clark Street. The equally striking John C. Kluczynski Building of more than 40 stories is at the south end of the complex, and adjacent is a post office in a low-rise building. These two structures, completed in 1975, are actually one building; they share the same basements. All three structures face a large open plaza—the entire design being a strong statement of the genius and influence of the great architect Mies van der Rohe.

A stabile by Alexander Calder, 53 feet in height, made of carbon steel and painted a special shade of red has been placed at the center of the Federal Center Plaza, making Dearborn Street a great area of plazas, architecture, and sculpture. Calder's bright red steel *Flamingo* is a worthy addition to the Picasso, in the Richard J. Daley Plaza, and the Chagall, in the First National Bank Building Plaza.

Continuing north on this WALK, you will see these two other great plazas surrounded by first-rate buildings. The trend toward more open space around city skyscrapers is in marked contrast with the canyon effect so often developed in the past.

Walk north 1 block. At the northwest corner of Dearborn and Adams streets is the Marquette Building.

59

Marquette Building
(Howard Kaplan
courtesy Holabird
& Root)

Inland Steel Building
(Allen Carr)

◉ MARQUETTE BUILDING
140 S. DEARBORN STREET
ARCHITECTS: HOLABIRD AND ROCHE (1894);
FOR THE RESTORATION: HOLABIRD AND ROOT (1980)

The influence of Louis Sullivan can be noted in the ornamental design, which marks off the bottom 2 stories and the top 3, distinguishing these clearly from the rest. The wide windows and the obvious response of the pattern to the skeleton structure are characteristic of the Chicago school.

60

In 1980 major restoration work was done. The exterior terra-cotta was restored and cast aluminum storefronts, replicating the original work, were made. A new corridor, connecting the interior storefronts between the Edison Building and the Marquette lobby was created with the same cast aluminum. The earlier "re-modeling" of the lobby was removed. The bronze plaques over the entrance doors (designed by well-known sculptor, J. A. MacNeil) were restored; they commemorate Marquette's journey in the Mississippi River Valley. The Tiffany mosaics that decorate the mezzanine balcony, unquestionably the best in the city, are being restored and properly lighted for the public's enjoyment. They were designed by J. A. Holzer, who was Tiffany's chief mosaicist; he came to Chicago to execute the Tiffany Chapel at the World's Columbian Exposition of 1893. The mosaics depict scenes from Chicago history. You will want to go inside this building to see them.

Continue north.

DEARBORN CENTER
NORTHEAST CORNER OF DEARBORN AND ADAMS STREETS
ARCHITECTS: SKIDMORE, OWINGS AND MERRILL (1987)

Under construction at this writing, Dearborn Center is to be a 72-story, 2.5 million-square-foot multi-atria office tower. It will have a 5-story, arched entrance. The design has developed as a clear expression of the building's structural systems and programmatic functions. Eleven stacked atria are the primary organizing feature of the design.

Continue north 1 block. At the northeast corner of Dearborn and Monroe streets is the Inland Steel Building.

INLAND STEEL BUILDING
30 W. MONROE STREET
ARCHITECTS: SKIDMORE, OWINGS AND MERRILL (1957)

The Inland Steel Building is appropriately constructed of stainless steel and glass. In the lobby is a stunningly unique piece of wire sculpture by Richard Lippold.

This 19-story building was one of the first to use only external steel columns for support, also one of the first to build a separate structure (to the east) for elevators and stairs, and to use steel and glass as the chief building materials. The result is a striking, first-rate design.

Walk west on Monroe Street.

61

First National
Bank Building
(Philip A. Turner)

62

XEROX CENTRE
55 W. Monroe Street
Architects: Murphy/Jahn (1980)

This most elegant, straightforward design is a 40-floor office building with 900,000 square feet of rental space and commercial space on the ground floor and mezzanine level. Originally designed for a bank, it continues the development along the urban corridor between Dearborn and Clark streets.

The architects emphasized an optimum relationship to the First National Bank and Plaza, the historic Marquette Building, and the remaining structures along Monroe Street. The building is set back on Dearborn, curved at the corner, and slightly slanted toward the existing structures. The lower level fits the existing urban fabric and continues the plantings of trees from the First National Plaza. The curved front facade of the building turns the two planes into a single expanse. The west facade sets the building back from the property line, anticipating future development of the adjacent site.

Xerox Centre has concrete construction with columns based on 20-foot by 20-foot bays. The exterior wall is enameled aluminum painted white and the varying amounts of double glazed clear glass, responding to the views and orientation, are floor-to-ceiling on the north facade and cover 50 percent of the surface on the rest of the building. The single-story-high glass at street level is in scale to the pedestrian, and the paving at the corner invites the pedestrian to cut through the building as he travels on his way.

Cross Monroe Street and walk through the Plaza.

Xerox Centre
(Keith Palmer and
James Steinkamp
courtesy Murphy/Jahn)

FIRST NATIONAL BANK BUILDING and PLAZA
One First National Plaza
(between Monroe and Madison streets,
Dearborn and Clark streets)
Architects: Perkins & Will Partnership and
C. F. Murphy and Associates
(Building 1969, Plaza 1973)

This is one of the great plazas in the Loop—that of the First National Bank of Chicago. The first object to capture the eye is the building itself. The sweeping lines of this A-shaped, 60-story structure creates an exhilarating sight. The steel frame has a light-gray granite skin. The granite there is carried out, not only on the sidewalks and plaza, but in the 2-story banking room and mezzanine as well.

63

The upper floors contain not only the offices of the bank but distinguished works of art from all over the world. This excellent collection was made under the direction of Katherine Kuh, former Curator of Modern Art at the Art Institute of Chicago.

The exciting 2-level plaza covering a half a city block has restaurants, landscaping, and a major work of Marc Chagall called *The Four Seasons.* The massive architectural mosaic, measuring 70 feet long, 14 feet high, and 10 feet wide, has more than 3,000 square feet of bright glass murals, especially designed as a gift to the people of Chicago by the world-renowned artist, who personally supervised each step of its realization. The donors for the cost of construction were Mr. and Mrs. William Wood Prince of Chicago. The Chicago Chagall occupies an open terrace at the east end of the plaza and overlooks an illuminated fountain of changing water columns in a park-like setting of trees, plants, and flowers.

A large number of vehicles can park on underground levels reached by tunnels from spiral ramps and a port-of-entry located across Clark Street. From the existing subway under Dearborn Street, a station provides direct access to lower levels of the building.

The architects have explained that the form of the building evolved quite naturally from the bank's space-need program. From a broad base, where the lower floors accommodate all the bank's equipment and staff, the tower tapers upward in a sweeping curve to narrower tenant floors. Thus, form follows function. The bank's address is One First National Plaza. The bank's second building, across the street, is described in WALK 5 on Clark Street. Its address is Two First National Plaza. It follows that the next building on the WALK is Three First National Plaza.

Free tours of the bank building and plaza are available. Call 732-6037 for reservations, or inquire at the Information Desk on the main banking floor.

Walk through or around the bank, heading north, and cross to the north side of Madison Street.

THREE FIRST NATIONAL PLAZA
70 W. Madison Street
Architects: Skidmore, Owings and Merrill (1982)

This 75-story office tower has commercial space on the first two levels. There is a 9-story glass-enclosed lobby, designed to respond to the heavy pedestrian traffic in the area. The bay windows were chosen to pay homage to Chicago's architectural heritage. There is a Henry Moore sculpture, *Large Upright Internal/External Form* (1982), in the lobby. There is a sky bridge to the First National Bank Building. This building also connects to the underground walkway system.

Before continuing north, look back across Dearborn Street to the former Tribune Building now used by Citicorp Savings.

CITICORP SAVINGS BUILDING

7 S. Dearborn Street
Architects: Holabird and Roche (1902);
for the south wing: Holabird and Root (1958)

This structure housed the Chicago Tribune before the newspaper moved to its present location on North Michigan Avenue. The building is 17 stories high and reputed to be the first in Chicago with 2 basements (another first for the city).

Walk north on Dearborn Street 1 block. On the southeast corner of Dearborn and Washington streets is the Connecticut Mutual Life Building.

Three First
National Plaza
(Merrick, Hedrich-Blessing
courtesy Skidmore, Owings
and Merrill)

Brunswick Building
(Philip A. Turner)

Top right:
Richard J. Daley
Center
(Philip A. Turner)

Bottom right:
Picasso sculpture
in Daley Plaza
(Ira J. Bach)

CONNECTICUT MUTUAL LIFE BUILDING
33 N. DEARBORN STREET
ARCHITECTS: SKIDMORE, OWINGS AND MERRILL (1966)

This glass structure stands light and lean on its steel frame. Though this was designed by the same firm of architects as the Brunswick Building, the two are in striking contrast with each other. They are a tribute to the versatility of the architects' inventiveness and illustrate the wide variety of modern building materials and forms.

Walk west on Washington Street to view an utterly different type of building, the massive Brunswick Building.

BRUNSWICK BUILDING
69 W. WASHINGTON STREET
ARCHITECTS: SKIDMORE, OWINGS AND MERRILL,
PARTNER IN CHARGE: MYRON GOLDSMITH (1964)

Though more recently constructed, the heavy concrete wall surfaces of the Brunswick are reminiscent of the Monadnock Building. From the lower concourse of this building you can reach other downtown buildings by an underground walkway.

On the north side of Washington Street is the great plaza of the Richard J. Daley Center, a focal point of city and county government activity. This immense open space offers the visitor an exciting visual treat and a chance to sit and rest in the midst of otherwise crowded city streets.

RICHARD J. DALEY CENTER and PLAZA
BETWEEN WASHINGTON AND RANDOLPH STREETS,
DEARBORN AND CLARK STREETS
ARCHITECTS: C. F. MURPHY AND ASSOCIATES;
LOEBL, SCHLOSSMAN AND BENNETT;
SKIDMORE, OWINGS AND MERRILL (1964)

The Daley Center, 31 stories of offices and courtrooms, covers the north half of the plaza. This building was highly controversial at first, especially before the steel of its walls had oxidized to its present russet brown. Cor-Ten steel was chosen as the material for the building because it requires no upkeep and becomes more beautiful as it ages. (A special virtue of Cor-Ten steel is its resistance to atmospheric corrosion, so that it is not worn away by weathering, even though its color is changed.) The horizontal bays are 89 feet wide which makes this distinguished building one of great strength and vigor.

The power and the scale of this contemporary structure are overwhelming; the older, smaller buildings around the plaza come into focus only later, though many were most impressive when erected. They are a phenomenon of contrasts, one with another.

With fountain, flags, and trees, the plaza is dominated overwhelmingly by the huge Picasso sculpture also in Cor-Ten steel. The design of Chicago's Picasso was a gift to the city from the sculptor himself, and the original model is in the Art Institute of Chicago. Like most of Picasso's creations for many years, this was the subject of much controversy. There was disagreement about whether it represents the great head of a woman, the soaring wings of an enormous bird, a strange composite animal, or—as one facetious newspaper columnist would have it—the head of Picasso's pet basset hound! Controversy aside, however, this is a powerful work of art. It has been erected in an especially appropriate setting, which allows viewers to walk around it freely and consider it from all angles and various distances—from each of which it represents a different effect.

Free tours of City Hall, the City Council, the Mayor's office, the Daley Center courts, and the State of Illinois Center are available through the Mayor's Office of Inquiry and Information, Room 100 in City Hall. Tours take 1½ hours. Reservations are required. Phone 744-6671 for information.

Cross to the northeast corner of Randolph and Dearborn streets.

◉ DELAWARE BUILDING
36 W. Randolph Street
Architects: Wheelock and Thomas (1871);
for the addition: Holabird and Roche
(1889, 1894, 1904);
for the restoration: Wilbert R. Hasbrouck;
base building architects: Bernheim, Kahn
and Lozano (1982)

This is the oldest building in the Loop, and the first built after the Chicago Fire that still survives. Built as the Bryant Building (it was later known as the Real Estate Board Building), and designed by Wheelock and Thomas in 1871, the structure was 6 stories tall. Two stories added before 1890, and later changes by Holabird and Roche, gave it the appearance it has today. The facade of the first 2 stories is glass and cast iron; the next 4 stories are pre-cast concrete; and the top 2 floors are of pressed metal.

68

Delaware Building
(Ron Gordon courtesy
Hasbrouck Hunderman)

The building has recently undergone major rehabilitation. The exterior was restored exactly to its appearance in 1900. The interior public spaces, including the interior atrium, were restored; the office space was rehabilitated.

Cross to the west side of Dearborn Street and continue north.

● DEARBORN CINEMAS
170-186 N. DEARBORN STREET
ARCHITECTS: CRANE AND FRANZHEIM (1923);
FOR THE RENOVATION: BERTRAND GOLDBERG
AND ASSOCIATES (1956)

Originally the Harris and Selwyn, these twin theaters represent the best of their time. The exterior design is English Renaissance of the Edwardian period when many similar small theaters were built in London. The exterior skin is a white terra-cotta. The wood paneling and spacious proscenium arches of both auditoriums

69

created just the right climate for good, live performances and appreciative audiences.

Continue north past Lake Street.

RYAN INSURANCE BUILDING
222 N. Dearborn Street
Architects: C. F. Murphy and Associates (1968)

On the west side of Dearborn Street is the building originally erected for the Blue Cross-Blue Shield groups, which they occupied until 1972. This all beige-colored concrete structure has a rugged, heavy quality; it gives an effect of tremendous mass, especially in the upper section extending by cantilever construction beyond the lower part.

Across the river is Marina City.

MARINA CITY
300 N. State Street
Architects: Bertrand Goldberg and Associates (1964)

Although the official address of Marina City is State Street, you have an excellent view of these twin towers from Dearborn Street and Wacker Drive. This exciting, world-famous complex has included its many functions in a highly concentrated space—apartments, garages, restaurants, offices, bank, television theater, ice-skating rink, and marina. The parking space is a continuously rising circular slab throughout the first 18 stories of each tower, the apartments taking up the rest of the 62 stories. The cantilevered balconies of the apartments give these cylindrical towers their scalloped forms. Apartments are pie-shaped.

Marina City marks a departure from the glass-and-steel skeletons that have been so popular in recent years. The tallest concrete buildings in Chicago, 62 stories rising more than 580 feet in the air, use virtually no structural steel. These are towers of slab construction, circular disks resting on columns. Marina City also demonstrates excellent application of core-and-cantilever construction which was first used by Frank Lloyd Wright.

As you cross the Dearborn Street drawbridge, read the plaques. They summarize the history of the bridge and quote the citation presented to it as the "Most beautiful steel bridge movable span," by the American Institute of Steel Construction in 1963-64. (Also see information on the Ira J. Bach Walkway at the beginning of WALK 8—Ed.)

5

1. County Building
   118 N. Clark St.

2. City Hall
   121 N. LaSalle St.

3. Chicago Temple Building
   77 W. Washington St.

4. Chicago Title and Trust Building
   111 W. Washington St.

5. Avondale Centre
   20 N. Clark St.

6. St. Peter's Church and Friary
   110 W. Madison St.

7. Chicago Loop Synagogue
   16 S. Clark St.

8. Two First National Plaza
   20 S. Clark St.

9. Bell Savings and Loan Association
   Building
   79 W. Monroe St.

10. Edison Building
    72 W. Adams St.

11. Bankers Building
    105 W. Adams St.

12. Continental Illinois National Bank
    and Trust Building
    231 S. LaSalle St

13. Trans Union Building
    111 W. Jackson

14. William J. Campbell
    United States Courthouse Annex
    Van Buren and Clark St.

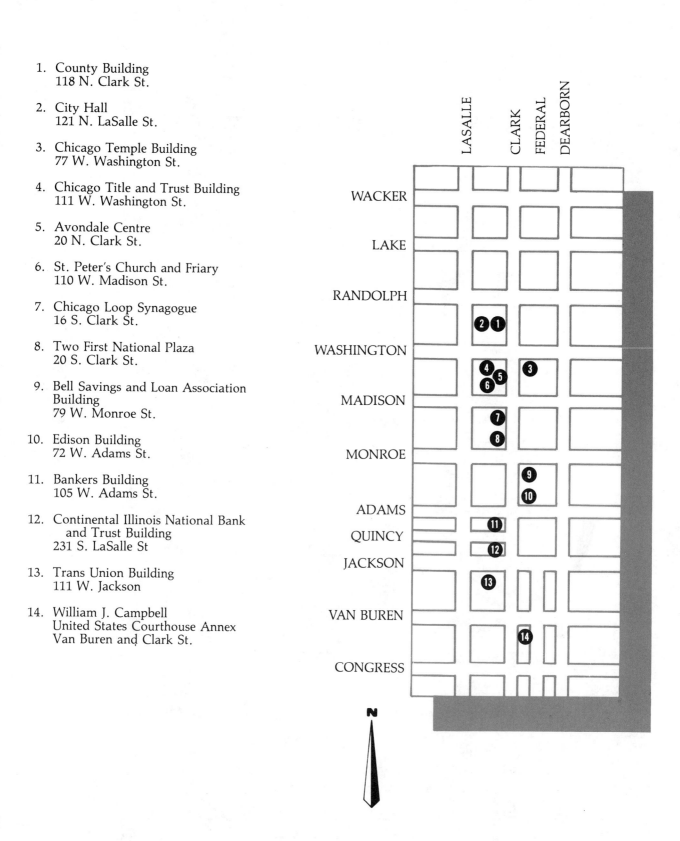

WALK • 5

CLARK STREET

WALKING TIME: 1 to 1½ hours. HOW TO GET THERE: Walk west on Washington Street to Clark Street [77 W] 2 blocks west of State Street.

This WALK starts at the west side of Clark Street, just opposite the Daley Center Plaza.

◉ **COUNTY BUILDING**
118 N. CLARK STREET
ARCHITECTS: HOLABIRD AND ROCHE (1907)

◉ **CITY HALL**
121 N. LaSALLE STREET
ARCHITECTS: HOLABIRD AND ROCHE (1911)

These twin buildings are the City Hall-County Building, dating back to the early 1900s. The County Building and City Hall cover an entire city block. The lobbies are connected and appear as one. City Hall, a duplicate of the County Building, was completed several years after its twin. Both buildings are built on sturdy classic revivalist lines with heavy Corinthian columns across the facade. In the County Building lobby is an entrance to the Underground Walkway system.

Free tours are available through the Mayor's Office of Inquiry and Information, Room 100, or phone 744-6671. Reservations are required. Tours include the City Hall, City Council, Mayor's office, Daley Center courts, and the State of Illinois Center. Tours take 1½ hours.

On the southeast corner of Clark and Washington streets is the Chicago Temple Building.

CHICAGO TEMPLE BUILDING
77 W. WASHINGTON STREET
ARCHITECTS: HOLABIRD AND ROCHE (1923)

This 21-story church stands 550 feet high, including an

Overleaf:
St. Peter's Church
(Allen Carr)

73

elaborate 8-story spire and a basement on rock caissons. This provides space for offices and a downtown Methodist church. Except for a short time after the Great Fire of 1871, this site has been occupied continuously for more than 100 years by a downtown church. The gray Indiana limestone, French Gothic style structure offers an interesting pattern of intricate design as opposed to the bold, plain design of the Brunswick Building to the east.

We will soon visit two additional religious structures—a Roman Catholic church and an Orthodox Jewish synagogue. These three major churches representing the Protestant, Catholic, and Jewish faiths are located within a 1-block radius, making it convenient for Loop workers to worship during daytime hours.

Now cross to the west side of Clark Street to a building that houses nearly all of abstract and real estate property insurance for metropolitan Chicago and many other regions of the U.S.A.

◉ CHICAGO TITLE AND TRUST COMPANY BUILDING
111 W. Washington Street
Architects: D. H. Burnham and Company (1913);
for the remodeling: Holabird and Root (1947);
for the renovations: Jack Train and Associates (1983)

County Building
and City Hall
(Philip A. Turner)

74

Known as the Conway Building when it was first constructed, the structure was purchased in 1947 and remodeled under the direction of Holabird and Root. At that time, the interior court was filled to a height of 6 stories. An indoor pedestrian walkway system connects with the adjacent American National Bank Building and One North LaSalle Street Building.

This white terra cotta building is 21 stories and is completely modernized and commands a strategic location near the City Hall-County Building and the Daley Center. Probably more business deals are made in its lobby than in all the offices above.

The 1983 work included updating the building without destroying the original design. The original effect of the light court was recaptured, and it was brightened substantially with the installation of bay windows. The utilization of the building was improved, including the roof terrace, which will come as an interesting surprise to anyone who receives an invitation to see it.

Walk south.

AVONDALE CENTER
20 N. Clark Street
Architects: A. Epstein and Sons (1980)

This 36-story office building on the corner of Clark and Madison streets has a smooth-planed facade that allows for the maximum utilization of interior floor space and gives the structure a clean look. The building has a curtainwall of flame-cut Aswan red granite, bronze aluminum, and reflective glass. The spacious lobby of marble and wood is enhanced by a vividly colored sculpture created by Israeli artist Yaacov Agam.

Walk west on Madison Street.

ST. PETER'S CHURCH and FRIARY
110 W. Madison Street
Architects: K. M. Vitzhum and J. J. Burns (1953)

St. Peter's Church is a 5-story, marble-covered Roman basilica, consisting of the main church, two chapels on the 2nd floor, and living quarters on the other 3 floors for the Franciscan priests in charge. The facade is overwhelmingly dominated—as the designers intended it to be—by a gigantic crucifix Christ of the Loop, 18 feet high, weighing twenty-six tons. This extraordinarily expressive figure of Christ, the work of the Latvian sculptor Arvid Strauss, hangs above the entrance in front of the only window of

75

Chicago Loop
Synagogue
(Olga Stefanos)

the building—a Gothic arch of stained glass. The church, built on the site of the old LaSalle Theatre, was planned as a religious center for Catholic visitors to the city and the many thousands of Catholics who work in the Loop.

Backtrack east across Clark Street and turn south.

CHICAGO LOOP SYNAGOGUE
16 S. CLARK STREET
ARCHITECTS: LOEBL, SCHLOSSMAN
AND BENNETT (1957)

As you approach the Loop Synagogue, just a few doors south of Madison, on Clark Street, you will be struck by the unique metal sculpture above the entrance—*The Hands of Peace*, by the Israeli sculptor Henri Azaz. Symbolically outstretched hands are surrounded by irregularly spaced letters, in both English and Hebrew, spelling out a Biblical benediction.

From the visitors' balcony inside you can see the interesting, well-conceived plan of this structure, which has made optimum use of the narrow city lot on which it is constructed. The seating arrangement, running at right angles to what might be expected, achieves a special effect of spaciousness. And the entire wall opposite the street entrance is composed of a gloriously colored stained-glass design on the theme "Let there be light!"—the work of Abraham Rattner of New York.

TWO FIRST NATIONAL PLAZA
20 S. CLARK STREET
ARCHITECTS: C. F. MURPHY AND ASSOCIATES
AND THE PERKINS & WILL PARTNERSHIP (1971)

This is the second structure of the First National Bank complex that faces on the First National Bank Plaza (see WALK 4). There are 30 stories above grade, as well as basement levels largely occupied by service ramps and tunnels extending under the plaza level and bank building.

The exterior columns and spandrels are fireproofed with poured-in-place concrete and faced with pointed steel panels. Enclosures at street level are clear glass in steel frames with bronze doors. Upper floors have solar bronze double glazing in steel frames with plastic thermal break for air circulation.

The granite paving on the sidewalks and interior floor areas at street level match the One First National Plaza. Note the pedestrian walkway through the center of the building that connects with LaSalle Street and the Barrister's Building. The walkway has been in this location for many years and continues the tradition of connecting the "First with the Barrister's."

Cross to the southeast corner of Clark and Monroe streets.

BELL SAVINGS AND LOAN ASSOCIATION BUILDING
79 W. MONROE STREET
ARCHITECTS: JARVIS HUNT (1906);
FOR THE SOUTH ADDITION: HOLABIRD AND ROCHE (1924)

This 13-story and 1 basement structure was formerly known as the Chicago Title and Trust Building and is now the home of the Bell Savings and Loan Association. Up-to-the-minute weather reports are available in the lobby. Also, monthly construction reports covering the Chicago metropolitan area are produced here.

Continue south to the northeast corner of Clark and Adams streets.

EDISON BUILDING
72 W. ADAMS STREET
ARCHITECTS: D. H. BURNHAM AND COMPANY (1907)

Located at the northeast corner of Clark and Adams streets, this 18-story structure has two basements and contains the principal offices and control center of this important utility company. Although the executive offices are located nearby in the First National Bank Building, nearly all of the consumer services are located here. There is a pedestrian walkway connecting the adjacent Marquette Building that contains shops, restaurants, and Edison service facilities.

Walk west.

BANKERS BUILDING
105 W. ADAMS STREET
ARCHITECTS: BURNHAM BROTHERS (1927)

Located at the southwest corner of Clark and Adams streets, this structure was designed by the Burnham brothers, who followed in the footsteps of their illustrious father, Daniel H. Burnham. The building is 41 stories with 1 basement on rock caissons.

78

Left:Lobby of
Two First
National Plaza
(Olga Stefanos)

Right: Two First
National Plaza
(C.F. Murphy
Associated
and the Perkins and
Will Partnership)

At this point it should be worth looking across the street to one of the three great open plazas that you encountered in WALK 4—the Federal Center Plaza. Note the low post office structure at the corner in contrast with the two tall structures and the excellent site plan that provided the open area for the plaza.

Backtrack to Clark Street and turn south.

CONTINENTAL ILLINOIS NATIONAL BANK AND TRUST BUILDING
231 S. LaSalle Street
Architects: Graham, Anderson, Probst and White (1924)

On Clark Street is the eastern facade of this huge bank building that is included on WALK 6. It was formerly known as the Illinois Merchant's Trust Building. After several bank mergers the name was changed to the present one. The building is 19 stories with 2 basements on rock caissons.

Continue south to the southwest corner of Clark and Jackson streets.

79

TRANS UNION BUILDING
111 W. Jackson Boulevard
Architects: A. Epstein and Sons (1961)

This 24-story building with marble-and-glass facade is the last stop on this WALK. There is a 2-story lobby of marble, wood, and bronze. The generous set back and plaza show off the building to good advantage.

Continue south to Van Buren Street.

(WILLIAM J. CAMBELL) UNITED STATES COURTHOUSE ANNEX
Van Buren Street, between Clark
and Federal streets
Architects: Harry Weese and Associates (1975)

This skyscraper detention center stands on a square block. The 27-story triangular tower and 7-story garage recognize the Loop in scale, geometry, and form. The triangular tower plan maximizes perimeter space for exterior windows, and minimizes corridor lengths. Corners function as stairwells and elevator service cores. One of three Metropolitan Correctional Centers in the United States, this federal correction center is an approach to more humanitarian prison conditions. Administration and social services comprise the lower half; federal detainees awaiting trial and prisoners are housed in the upper half which includes a rooftop landscaped exercise yard.

Based on program guide lines, each multi-purpose core space serves forty-four people. Each module contains inmates' rooms, exercise, lounge, kitchenette, dining, and visitor's space. The size of each module allows for separation of men from women, old from young, and first-time offenders from repeaters. The 5-inch vertical windows are the maximum opening allowed by the Bureau of Prison Standards, and also permit no bars to be seen from the outside.

WALK • 6

LaSALLE STREET

*WALKING TIME: 1 to 1½ hours. HOW TO GET THERE: Walk
west on Randolph Street to LaSalle Street [140 W], 3 blocks west
of State Street.*

Be sure to take this WALK on a weekday during business hours,
when the rhythm of Chicago at work is best felt. LaSalle Street in
the Loop is the Wall Street of the Midwest. From Randolph Street,
the street looks like a canyon, with skyscraper office buildings and
banks along each side and the 45-story Board of Trade Building
like a towering mountain at the south. Here, in the 4-block area
between Madison Street and Jackson Boulevard, are clustered
Chicago's major banks; here is the Midwest Stock Exchange; and
here, at the end of the 4 blocks, stands the overpowering Board of
Trade Building with the statue of Ceres at its top. Activities inside
some of these buildings send political and economic waves across
the country, affecting in fact the world economy.

This WALK starts at the northeast corner of LaSalle and Lake
streets. This is the cornerstone of the North Loop Redevelopment
Project (see p. 49).

LOOP TRANSPORTATION CENTER
203 N. LaSalle Street
Architects: Skidmore, Owings and Merrill (1986)

The 27-story Loop Transportation Center is designed to
integrate the most complete concentration of transportation and
travel services in Chicago with office and retail facilities. The
multi-use structure consists of two distinct elements: the Loop
Transportation Center is composed of travel and retail services
and 10 levels of self-parking spaces; the office portion of the
building (known as 203 N. LaSalle) rises from the 13th through the
27th floor.

The building exterior is painted precast concrete with silver
reflective glass on the north and south facades and a combination
of silver reflective and green tinted insulated glass on the east and

Overleaf: View of
LaSalle Street and the
Board of Trade Building
(Allen Carr)

83

west facades. The atrium, with a distinctive stepped back design, provides expansive views of Lake Michigan and the surrounding city as well as a variety of floor configurations. This is also a gateway to the Underground Walkway system.

200 N. LaSALLE STREET
ARCHITECTS: PERKINS & WILL,
WOJCIECH MADEYSKI, PARTNER IN CHARGE (1984)

This is one of a new generation of office buildings which break from the stereotype of the box, making the building more open to the environment. The impressive serrated plan opens the corners and steps back to create corner offices (ten to the floor) allowing views of neighboring buildings. The curved access from the corner leads to a monumental 4-story lobby. It is clad with insulated clear glass panels to break the claustrophobic feeling of some buildings, and to allow the occupants to feel a participation in city life.

Walk south on LaSalle Street.

LaSALLE PLAZA
180 N. LaSALLE STREET
ARCHITECTS: HARRY WEESE AND ASSOCIATES (1972)

This plainly rugged and distinguished 38-story reinforced concrete building has a 2-story lobby. The trees and brick plaza give a new human scale to this cavernous LaSalle Street thoroughfare. The handsome structure is truly in the tradition of the Chicago school.

STATE OF ILLINOIS BUILDING
160 N. LaSALLE STREET
ARCHITECTS: HARRY WEESE AND ASSOCIATES (1972)

This building is 20 stories with 1 basement and was originally known as the Burnham Building until its purchase by the State of Illinois in 1946. The building contains many branch offices of the state government.

On the northeast corner of LaSalle and Randolph streets is the State of Illinois Center.

STATE OF ILLINOIS CENTER
100 W. RANDOLPH STREET
ARCHITECTS: A JOINT VENTURE OF MURPHY/JAHN
AND L. B. KNIGHT & ASSOCIATES (1980)

State of
Illinois Center,
exterior and interior
(James R. Steinkamp
courtesy of
Murphy/Jahn)

The State of Illinois Center was designed to make several statements about the building's own use as well as its relationship to the surrounding buildings. The southeast portion of the block is sliced away to form a sloped, setback configuration and open the space at the corner to the Dearborn-Clark corridors, the City Hall-County Building, and the Civic Center, without losing the spatial closure of the street. The continuous, but stepped-back, west facade of the building rises from the street line to reinforce its relationship to LaSalle Street. An indentation of the skin at the lowest two floors creates a covered arcade which continues along both LaSalle and Clark streets as well as along the curved southeast wall. The arcade provides a zone of spatial transition into the rotunda.

Along Randolph and Clark streets, the granite screen wall of the arcade continues to define the open space, but diminishes gradually in deference to the entry. The plaza thus created is a free composition of water, paving, and trees. The Lake Street elevation is a straight wall along the building line which plays up the setbacks on the other exposures.

85

The building is also a statement of the importance and the dignity of state government in its large scale and urban monumentality. A truncated glass cylinder projects above the building's mass, creating a top and making a clearly identifiable shape on the city's skyline. This cylinder suggests the tradition of domed government buildings throughout the history of the building arts. The State of Illinois Center breaks with tradition by making the central space visible from the outside. This openness is continued along the curved facade by the 5-story atriums which follow the setbacks.

The abstract form of the building comes from conceptual, historic, and urban references and from their synthesis with today's materials and techniques. This synthesis of many influences surpasses any attempt to use geometry or historical references for form in architecture.

A glazed skin encloses all surfaces of the building. Opaque glasses, colored blue-gray-white are used with silver and clear glass to create various amounts of transparency and reflection, and to give the monumental shape a painted quality on the surface.

Free tours are available through the Mayor's Office of Inquiry and Information, Room 100 in City Hall, or phone 744-6671. Reservations are required. Tours include the City Hall, City Council, Mayor's office, Daley Center courts, and the State of Illinois Center. Tours take 1½ hours.

Cross to the southwest corner.

BISMARCK HOTEL
171 W. RANDOLPH STREET
ARCHITECTS: RAPP AND RAPP (1926)

The hotel is the focus of a well-planned complex that contains an office building, theater, and the hotel. The hotel lobby and Walnut Room are well-designed and worth a visit.

Across from the hotel on the east side of LaSalle Street, between Randolph and Washington streets, looms the bulky, massive City Hall-County Building with its heavy pillars, designed under the old belief that government buildings should be monumental in size and style. (See WALK 4.) The interior has been renovated and modernized. The terrazzo floor in the lobby has been well preserved.

On the northwest corner of LaSalle and Washington streets is 100 N. LaSalle Street.

86

100 N. LaSALLE STREET
ARCHITECTS: GRAVEN AND MAYGEN (1929);
FOR THE REMODELING: JOEL SCHÉCKERMAN (1985)

This 25-story brick and steel building was constructed in 36 days in 1929. It has undergone changes over the years, the most recent in 1985. At that time the first 40 feet of the facade were refaced in granite, and the interior was remodeled.

Continue south past Washington Street.

30 N. LaSALLE BUILDING
ARCHITECT: THOMAS E. STANLEY OF
DALLAS, TEXAS (1975)

This 43-story blue paneled and glass office building is located on the site of the old Stock Exchange Building designed by Adler and Sullivan, completed in 1894 and demolished in 1972.

The trading room of the old Chicago Stock Exchange Building has been incorporated in the Columbus Drive wing (completed in 1976) of the Chicago Art Institute. The entry arch of the famous old building now stands in the Art Institute's Grant Park Garden (see WALK 1).

Cross to the east side of the street.

AMERICAN NATIONAL BANK BUILDING
33 N. LaSALLE STREET
ARCHITECTS: GRAHAM, ANDERSON, PROBST
AND WHITE (1929)

The building was originally known as the Foreman National Bank Building. It is 38 stories with 2 basements on rock and hardpan caissons. A granite base and Bedford limestone comprise the exterior materials. The lower floors, occupied by the bank, were completely remodeled in 1971 in the Williamsburg style.

Continue south.

ONE N. LaSALLE STREET BUILDING
ARCHITECTS: VITZHUM AND BURNS (1930)

This Bedford limestone building is 49 stories on rock caissons. The majority of tenants are law firms as are those in the American National Bank Building, both buildings representing the powerful growth of the banking business just prior to the Great Depression.

Cross to the northwest corner of LaSalle and Madison streets.

Madison Plaza
(Gregory Murphy
courtesy Skidmore,
Owings & Merrill)

2 N. LaSALLE STREET
Architects: Perkins & Will (1979)

This 27-story contemporary office building was designed and built in only twenty-three months. The light gray aluminum paneled structure provides retail space at street level and offices above. The attractive lobby is finished with glass, marble, and mirrored stainless steel.

Continue south.

10 S. LaSALLE STREET
Architects: Holabird and Roche (1909);
Holabird and Root (1985)

This building is built atop the partially-demolished 1909 structure. The bottom two floors remain. The ground floor space includes the lobby, retail space, public toilets, and service functions; the upper floors contain office space. The exterior is of granite with tinted glass.

Turn west on Madison Street to the northwest corner of Wells Street.

MADISON PLAZA
200 W. Madison Street
Architects: Skidmore, Owings and Merrill (1982)

This 45-story office building has a glass front elevation in a sawtooth form which rises from the entrance plaza to the sloped roof of the 39th and 44th floors. The steel tube structure is clad with bands of silver reflective glass and light gray polished granite. By setting the building back from the street, a triangular elevated entry plaza was formed as a buffer from the heavy street traffic and the adjacent elevated rapid transit tracks. This plaza also provides an appropriate setting for a major public sculpture by Louise Nevelson. The lobby is finished in statuary Bettogi marble with polished stainless steel trim. Stainless steel elevator doors are etched with a subtle grid. The elevator interiors are mahogany wood paneled with a custom ceiling of stainless steel and luminous panels. Madison Plaza was chosen as the winner of the 1981 ASHRAE Energy Award for new commercial buildings. The building envelope contains highly reflective glazing to minimize winter heat losses and summer solar heat gains, while maintaining acceptable office window area.

Walk south on Wells Street. Look at the refreshing change from the city canyon of LaSalle Street—an open space landscaped with fountains, providing a drive-in section for hurried or late customers.

NORTHERN TRUST COMPANY
50 S. LaSalle Street
Architects: Frost and Granger (1906);
for the addition: Frost and Henderson (1928);
for the addition: C. F. Murphy Associates (1967)

At the northwest corner of Monroe and LaSalle streets is the Northern Trust Company and its adjoining structure to the west, which extends almost to Wells Street.

Walk east on Monroe Street to the southeast corner of LaSalle Street.

HARRIS TRUST AND SAVINGS BANK
111 W. Monroe Street
Architects: Shepley, Rutan and Coolidge (1911);
for the additions: Skidmore, Owings and Merrill (1957, 1975)

The original 20-story building is now framed by two stunning additions. The first is to the east and is at the southwest corner of Monroe and Clark streets and the second at the southeast corner of Monroe and LaSalle streets. All three buildings are connected at the banking floor levels and constitute a complex of buildings 1 block in length.

An unusual feature of the building farthest east is its recessed floor halfway up, which holds mechanical equipment usually found on the roof or in the basement. The stainless-steel mullion and the tall, narrow window pattern are especially effective.

The third building, which extends west from the original bank building to LaSalle Street, is 38 stories. Completed in 1975, it is a combination bank and office building; the bank occupies the ground floor level from Clark to LaSalle Street.

A 6½-foot-high bronze sculpture fountain by Russel Secrest is located at the bank's public plaza at Monroe and LaSalle streets. Water flows over the seven petal-like pedestals.

Walk south.

EXCHANGE NATIONAL BANK BUILDING
120 S. LaSalle Street
Architects: Graham, Anderson, Probst and White (1926-29)

On the southwest corner of Monroe and LaSalle streets is the Exchange National Bank Building. The bank occupies most of the

Harris Trust and
Savings Bank
(courtesy
Harris Bank)

89

LaSalle Bank Building
(Allen Carr)

lower floors. The building also provides space for various other financial concerns. It faced many difficulties in its early years, for it was completed just at the beginning of the Depression of the 1930s.

Continue south.

LaSALLE BANK BUILDING
135 S. LaSalle Street
Architects: Graham, Anderson, Probst
and White (1934)

The LaSalle Bank Building, formerly known as the Field Office Building, was carried out in two sections—one on Clark Street and the second facing LaSalle Street. The building is 23 stories with a 19-story tower and 3 basements on rock caissons.

This is the site of the famous Home Insurance Building (demolished in 1931) which was the world's first skeleton steel-and-iron building, designed in 1884 by the father of such construction—William LeBaron Jenney.

190 S. LaSALLE STREET
Architects: John Burgee Architects with
Philip Johnson of New York City (1986)

This 42-story office tower has 900,000 gross square feet. It is a concrete core, steel framed building with cladding of Spanish pink granite in a flame finish and grey tinted glass. The building has two different window systems, both punched and the more typical glass curtainwall windows. There is an extruded bronze framing around the clear glass at the entry points. The granite on the 5-story base is a flame finish, and the accent bands around the entrance and horizontal bands around the windows are a honed finish. The building is topped by a copper roof and six gables topped by an ornate bronze cresting.

All buildings on South LaSalle Street from 190 south to the Board of Trade are from 50 to 100 years old. The design for the gabled rooftop and for the base of the building drew on elements of design seen in John W. Root's Masonic Temple (built in the early 1890s) which stood at State and Randolph streets. Johnson and Burgee also drew on design elements of the nearby Rookery and paid homage to it in their design of this building.

There are 5-story lobbies off both LaSalle and Adams streets. The handsome LaSalle Street lobby is 180 feet long, 40 feet deep, and 55 feet tall and has a floor of a black and off-white botticino

90

marble; the walls are clad in the same botticino marble and a red alicante marble up to a height of 33 feet. The fluted columns with Corinthian capitals are in matching red alicante marble. The recessed lighting in the red alicante marble crown molding, which wraps around the entire lobby, shines onto the gold leaf painted barrel-vaulted ceiling. The 4-foot-high wainscotting is of the same alicante marble; the rest of the walls are in the botticino. The lobbies are retail-free, an unusual occurrence in today's buildings. Major artworks will be in each lobby.

Walk west on Adams Street.

200 W. ADAMS STREET
ARCHITECTS: FUJIKAWA JOHNSON AND ASSOCIATES (1985)

The structural design of this 30-story building is new to Chicago. To facilitate construction, the concrete core was poured in its entirety, with steel erection following. The steel provides large spans and the concrete core braces the high-rise structure. The exterior is of silver metallic aluminum cladding with blue tinted reflective insulating glass. The lobby is made of a variety of granites with stainless steel hardware and trim. The lobby level includes retail space fronting on both Adams and Wells streets, with entrances from both the interior and the exterior of the building.

Backtrack east to LaSalle Street and turn south.

◉ THE ROOKERY BUILDING
209 S. LaSalle Street
ARCHITECTS: BURNHAM AND ROOT (1885-8);
FOR THE INNER LOBBY: FRANK LLOYD WRIGHT (1905);
FOR THE ELEVATORS AND LOBBY: WILLIAM DRUMMOND (1932);
FOR THE REMODELING OF GROUND FLOOR:
GRAHAM, ANDERSON, PROBST AND WHITE (1972);
FOR THE RENOVATIONS:
BOOTH/HANSEN AND ASSOCIATES (1986-7);
FOR THE RESTORATION: HASBROUCK
AND HUNDERMAN (1986-7)

Just across from the LaSalle Bank Building on Adams Street is an architectural landmark—an extraordinary building called The Rookery. This quaint name is a heritage from the temporary city hall located here from 1872 to 1884, which had been nicknamed The Rookery because it seemed to be the favorite gathering place of downtown pigeons! The city hall had been built around an iron

190 S. LaSalle
(courtesy John Buck)

91

water tank, the only remnant of the previous occupant of this site—a city reservoir building serving the south side of Chicago, which was destroyed in the Fire of 1871. While the temporary city hall was here, Chicago's first public library stored its books in the old water tank—surely the only library in the world to have been housed in such a container.

The present Rookery, one of the oldest precursors of the modern skyscraper, is distinguished in its own right. The Rookery was designed to be the most modern and amenable office building of its day. The architects used masonry bearing walls for the exterior facades of the building and iron framing for the walls of the interior light court and atrium. Through this design, both inner and outer offices received a maximum amount of natural light. The public spaces of the building were also carefully designed and ornamented with marble, glass, and cast iron. Its sturdy yet ornamental exterior is partly of skeleton structure, partly wall-bearing, and the building as a whole has the appearance of enormous vitality. The powerful columns, alternating with piers, arches, and stonework, which characterize the exterior, make a dramatic contrast with the lobby inside—unique in its elaborate but delicate ornamentation. The glass-and-iron tracery of the domed skylight above the second floor of the lobby court (recently restored) harmonizes with the extensive grille work used below around the first- and second-floor balconies and along the sides of the two-part suspended stairway at the west side. The main stairway, unconnected with this one, starts at the second floor and runs to the top of the building. A cylindrical staircase, it projects beyond the west wall of the building, requiring an additional, semicircular tower to enclose it.

The gold-and-ivory decorations of the lobby court are the work of Frank Lloyd Wright, who remodeled this part of the building in 1905. The result was a splendid integration of new materials carefully blended with the lobby design of Frank Lloyd Wright. The citation from the Landmarks Commission reads:

In recognition of its pioneering plan in providing shops and offices around a graceful and semi-private square and further development of the skeleton structural frame using cast iron columns, wrought iron spandrel beams, and steel beams to support party walls and interior floors.

Starting in 1986, the building is to undergo major restoration of the exterior and public spaces under the direction of architects Hasbrouck and Hunderman. Plans for the restoration of the

Opposite: overall view and details of the Rookery (Allen Carr, left; Philip A. Turner, right)

92

Rookery were made in two phases: the cleaning, repairing and restoration of the exterior facades; and the design, restoration and rehabilitation of the interior public and tenant spaces. Work began with a complete inspection of the exterior facades, documented with written and illustrative data and video photography. Sample material was removed and laboratory tested to assist in the development of the long-term masonry repairs. This led to the cleaning of the brick, terra-cotta, and granite facades, including appropriate repairs. The second phase of the project involved the restoration and preservation of the designated historic features of the building, and the rehabilitation of the tenant spaces. The historic areas of the building include the light court, lobbies, entrances, and stairways. The base building architects for the renovation work are Booth/Hansen and Associates. The Rookery is now on the National Register of Historic Places, and also a Chicago Historic Landmark.

Continue south.

CONTINENTAL ILLINOIS
NATIONAL BANK AND TRUST BUILDING
231 S. LaSalle Street
Architects: Graham, Anderson, Probst
and White (1924, 1975);
for the remodeling: Skidmore, Owings
and Merrill (1981)

In the giant, block-square building of the Continental Illinois National Bank and Trust company, you have revivalist architecture again. The design is said to have been taken from some early Roman baths. Inside, you take an escalator to the enormous open banking floor, where tall Ionic columns stress again the pseudo-classic style. In 1981, the lobby was redesigned.

The Continental Illinois claims to be Chicago's oldest bank, the result of many mergers and changes of name dating back to 1857. It became officially the Continental Illinois National Bank and Trust Company, with a national charter, in 1932.

Cross to the west side of LaSalle Street and walk back north a few feet.

208 S. LaSALLE STREET BUILDING
Architects: D. H. Burnham and Company (1914)

This building, formerly known as the Continental Bank Building, is 20 stories with 2 basements on rock caissons. A huge

94

monolith extends west to Wells Street, from Adams to Quincy streets. It has a Bedford limestone base with terra-cotta above and adds to the canyon-like quality of LaSalle Street.

Now directly south on LaSalle Street is another bank building.

FEDERAL RESERVE BANK
230 S. LaSalle Street
Architects: Graham, Anderson,
Probst and White (1922);
for the addition: C. F. Murphy and Associates (1960)

This bankers' bank for the entire Midwest has 3 basements on rock caissons and faces on LaSalle, Jackson, and Quincy streets. The original structure's entrance on LaSalle Street has Roman Corinthian columns and pediment. All facades are of a light Bedford limestone. The addition faces on Jackson and Quincy streets and is 25 stories.

Continue south.

◉ BOARD OF TRADE BUILDING
141 W. Jackson Boulevard
Architects: Holabird and Root (1929);
for the addition: Murphy/Jahn;
Shaw and Associates;
Swanke, Hayden and Connel (1979-82)

The focal point of this entire WALK has been the Board of Trade Building, with its commanding location at the foot of LaSalle Street, on Jackson Boulevard. From Randolph Street this towering structure seems to block LaSalle Street at its southern end, but at Jackson Boulevard you discover that the north-south street merely jogs a bit to the east and continues southward beyond the Board of Trade. At the top of the 45 stories in this building stands—appropriately—a statue of Ceres, Greek goddess of grain. The 32-foot figure topping the 526-foot skyscraper is by John Storrs.

Step into the lobby and enjoy the interior Art Deco design by Gilbert Hall, former chief designer of Holabird and Root. The school of design known as Art Deco flourished briefly from the mid-1920s to the outbreak of World War II. The style was forceful and direct, emphasizing rectilinear rather than voluptuously curving lines. It was an upbeat, inspiring type of art, featuring sunrays, rainbows, large leafy plants, and well-muscled young people at work or at some athletic pursuit.

Board of Trade
with addition in
foreground
(Keith Palmer
courtesy
Murphy/Jahn)

The lobby, upper lobby, trading room, elevator doors, and lighting fixtures are exceptionally high caliber Art Deco. The contrasting of the black and light color marbles is fascinating and pleasant to view. The enormous room of the grain exchange, which was the largest in the world, has been divided horizontally into two trading rooms.

If you are fortunate to be here before 1 p.m. on a weekday, you will be admitted to the visitors' gallery of the Trading Room. Presentations are made at 9, 10, 11, noon, and 12:30, Monday through Friday. Call 435-3620 for information. To the uninitiated, the sights and sounds from the trading pit seem like bedlam. Fortunately, however, visitors are given a leaflet explaining the rules of the game (which indeed is a game with far-reaching economic consequences). Here are several pits, each a circle of traders interested in buying or selling a particular commodity—wheat, soybeans, soybean oil and meal, oats, rye, and several other commodities, such as cotton, lard, and beef. Shouts and hand signals in the bidding are clear to those involved, and the constantly changing prices are recorded on a big board immediately for all to see. Messengers run back and forth between the bidders with messages telephoned or wired from firms or individual customers from all parts of the world. The men and women trading here represent more than 1400 members of the Board of Trade. Traders, messengers, and staff of the exchange are distinguished by the color of the jackets they wear. The Board of Trade is indeed a tremendous marketplace, although the actual commodities that change hands here are miles away.

A mural, Ceres, named for the goddess of food grains and patroness of the corn trade (there's also a statue on top of the building) once decorated the trading room. After the addition, it was moved to the 12th floor atrium.

The addition provides over a half million more gross square feet to the Chicago Board of Trade, including a new trading floor, support spaces for the trading floor, and office space for exchange members and staffs. The addition was designed to function with the existing building as one unit.

The building responds functionally and formally to the existing Art Deco landmark structure. The first twelve floors are large bulk spaces housing the trading floor and support spaces corresponding to similar spaces in the existing structure. Above floor twelve, the office floors are designed as U-shaped spaces around a central atrium which adjoins the existing structure. To provide the required trading floor area, the building projects 20 feet beyond

96

Board of Trade
addition interior
(Keith Palmer and
James Steinkamp
courtesy
Murphy/Jahn)

the existing structure to the street curb, creating a covered
pedestrian arcade at street level.

The addition derives its formal characteristics from an
abstracted, literal duplication of the Art Deco style of the existing
building. The device used is a glass wall, wrapping the highly
articulating planes of the wall and the roof. This taut membrane
slips behind limestone "screen walls" on both sides, recalling the
dominant expression and the material of the old building. An
atrium on the 12th floor is reached by all elevators, and acts as a
major transfer point for all spaces in both buildings. The glass
elevators in the atrium provide orientation and reference to the

97

existing structure. Through their movement, they add a dynamic element to the central open space.

Note the bridge crossing over at the 4th floor level. It connects the two buildings.

Turn east, then walk south on LaSalle Street to Van Buren Street.

◉ TRADERS BUILDING
401 S. LaSalle Street
Architects: Holabird and Roche (1914);
for the restoration: Booth/Hansen
and Associates (1983-5)

This 17-story building once housed the Fort Dearborn Hotel. Recently restored and transformed into office space, the masonry and terra-cotta exterior and the mahogany-laden lobby are restored to their original grandeur. The original decorative plaster ceiling, ornate bronze and iron work, murals, and marble floors were also restored, and the upper 16 floors regutted and transformed into modern business facilities. A skylighted atrium extends from the lobby to the roof, surrounded on all sides by office space. The newly restored old Fort Dearborn Hotel stands in pleasant contrast along the mostly modern street.

Continue south.

EXCHANGE CENTER
440 S. LaSalle Street
Architects: Skidmore, Owings
and Merrill (1983-4)

Exchange Center is a complex composed of three elements: the Chicago Board Options Exchange, the Midwest Stock Exchange, and the One Financial Place office tower. The first uses a separate address of 400 S. LaSalle Street. The exterior cladding on the buildings is Imperial red polished granite with reflective, bronze-tinted, double pane, insulating glass.

Two covered exterior arcades and a ground-level interior concourse link the three elements of the complex. The pedestrian concourse, part of the Underground Walkway system (see WALK 7) joins the three structures to the Chicago Board of Trade Building and Annex. Beneath the complex is a CTA subway station, which provides connections to other rapid transit lines and to the Northwestern commuter station. There is also a Rock Island commuter station incorporated with the Exchange Center complex.

CHICAGO BOARD OPTIONS EXCHANGE

This is a 7-story building with a 44,000-square-foot trading floor, including an electronic display system. It also contains one of the largest in-house computer facilities in the city of Chicago. The trading floor has a raised floor system to allow for the cabling requirements between the trading posts. The building was planned to place all core elements at the perimeter so the center is an open and uninterrupted space. The building is designed to permit an equally large trading floor to be installed on the 6th level at a later date. The central area is a high clerestory-lit space which will serve as open offices until becoming a future trading room. There is a bridge linking this building to the Chicago Board of Trade.

ONE FINANCIAL PLACE

This 40-story office tower, a steel frame structure with cladding to match the other structures in the complex, is joined to the Midwest Stock Exchange building. It is one of the first "intelligent" office buildings in the world. It provides special communication equipment to serve the modern business tenant. It also contains one of the largest in-house computer facilities in the city of Chicago.

MIDWEST STOCK EXCHANGE

This building is 6 stories tall and houses the 19,000-square-foot trading floor. It also contains a lunch and sports club. Free tours of the Midwest Stock Exchange are available. Call 663-2742 for information.

WALK • 7

UNDERGROUND WALKWAYS

WALKING TIME: 2 hours or more [if you don't stop along the way to shop]. HOW TO GET THERE: Start at State and Madison streets.

7

An all-weather underground walkway system, which is being planned for Chicago's Loop, is partially completed and available for a walking tour. When finished, the walkways will connect the majority of the Loop buildings. Mail will be delivered by postmen with pushcarts starting from the underground section at the new Loop post office, which is in the Federal Center (see WALK 4). Because of the outdoor connotation of the term "walking tour," this suggestion for a subterranean walk may seem odd. Yet one of Chicago's fascinations is this underground walkway system, on a scale that is rare today even in great urban centers like Chicago.

There are several segments available for walking at this time. To begin, enter the subway at State Street north of Madison Street. From the Howard subway terminal you can enter the Wiebolt's Building at 1 N. State Street, then the State and Madison Building at 7 W. Madison Street, the Woolworth's store at 18 N. State Street, and the Walgreen's store at 4 N. State Street. You can then walk west to the Congress-Douglas subway station on Dearborn Street between Washington and Madison streets, and Three First National Plaza at 70 W. Madison Street.

At this point there are two options: you can walk south to the First National Bank at One First National Plaza, which leads to Two First National Plaza at 20 S. Clark Street, and then to the Congress-Douglas station at Monroe and Dearborn streets; or you can walk north from Three First National Plaza to the Brunswick Building at 69 W. Washington Street, and the Daley Center Concourse between Washington and Randolph streets and Dearborn and Clark streets. If you have taken the second option, you have two more choices: you can walk west and north through the Daley Center, to the County-City Hall Building at 118 N. Clark Street and 121 N. LaSalle Street, to the State Of Illinois

Opposite: Subway entrance, under the Richard J. Daley Center (Allen Carr)

101

1. JH / EH Subway
State & Madison St.

2. Wiebolt's Building
ONE N. State St.

3. ONE North Dearborn Building
ONE N. Dearborn St.

4. Woolworths
18 N. State St.

5. Walgreens
4 N. State St

6. CD Subway
Washington & Dearbron

7. Three First National Plaza
70 W. Madison St.

8. First National Bank
One First National Plaza

9. Two First National Plaza
20 S. Clark St.

10. CD Subway
Monroe & Dearborn St.

11. Brunswick Building
69 W. Washington St.

12. Richard J. Daley Center
50 W. Washington St.

13. County / City Hall Building
118 N. Clark St.

14. State of Illinois Building
100 W. Randolph St.

15. CD Subway
Clark & Lake St.

16. Transportation Center
203 N. LaSalle St.

17. JH / EH Subway
Washington & State St.

18. Marshall Field Building
111 N. State St.

19. Marshall Field Annex
25 E. Washington St.

20. Chicago Public Library Cultural Center
78 E. Washington St.

21. Avondale Centre
150 N. Michigan Ave.

22. Illinois Central Gulf Terminal
Randolph & Michigan Ave.

23. North Grant Park Underground Garage

24. One Prudential Plaza
130 E. Randolph Dr.

25. Two Prudential Plaza
180 N. Stetson Ave.

26. Amoco Oil Building
200 E. Randolph St.

27. Fairmont Hotel
200 N. Columbus Dr.

28. Hyatt Regency Chicago Annex
151 E. Wacker Dr.

29. Three Illinois Center
303 E. Wacker Dr.

30. Columbus Plaza
233 E. Wacker Dr.

31. Hyatt Regency Chicago
151 E. Wacker Dr.

32. One Illinois Center
111 E. Wacker Dr.

33. Two Illinois Center
233 N. Michigan Ave.

34. Boulevard Towers North
225 N. Michigan Ave.

35. Boulevard Towers South
205 N. Michigan Ave.

36. Monroe Drive
Underground Parking Lot

37. Buckingham Plaza
360 E. Randolph St.

38. Outer Drive East
400 E. Randolph St.

39. Harbor Point
155 N. Harbor Dr.

40. 175 N. Harbor Dr.

41. South Grant Park
Underground Garage

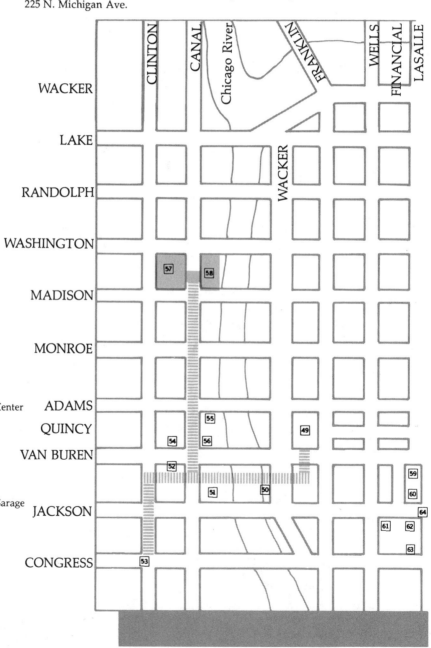

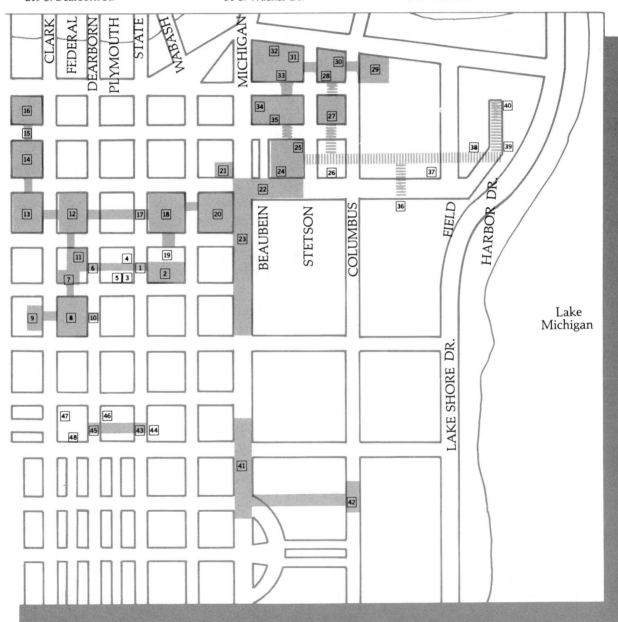

Outside entrance
to the Daley Center
Concourse
(Olga Stefanos)

Building at 100 W. Randolph Street, to the new concourse level to the Lake Street Congress-Douglas subway terminal at Lake and Clark streets, and to the Transportation Center at 203 N. LaSalle Street; or you can walk east from Daley Center through the Dearborn Congress-Douglas subway tunnel, to the Howard subway station, and then to the Marshall Field building at 111 N. State Street. At this point you again have two options: you can walk south into the Marshall Field Annex at 25 E. Washington Street, where it dead ends; or you can continue east, through the Marshall Field building to the 139 N. Wabash Building (the old Blackhawk restaurant), to the Chicago Public Library Cultural Center at 78 E. Washington Street, to Avondale Center at 150 N. Michigan Avenue, and to the Illinois Central Gulf Terminal.

At this point you again have two options: you can enter the North Grant Park Underground Garage; or you can walk east to One Prudential Plaza at 130 E. Randolph Drive, then to Two Prudential Plaza at 180 N. Stetson Avenue. Although not yet connected at this writing, it will be possible to continue east to the Amoco Oil Building at 200 E. Randolph Street, into Illinois Center to the Fairmont Hotel at 200 N. Columbus Drive, and the Hyatt Regency Chicago Annex at 151 E. Wacker Drive. Connections already exist in Illinois Center from the Hyatt Regency Chicago Annex to Three Illinois Center at 303 E. Wacker Drive (from which you can also reach Fire Station CF-21 at Columbus Drive and South Water Street), and Columbus Plaza at 233 E. Wacker Drive. You can then walk to the Hyatt Regency Chicago at 151 E. Wacker Drive (which is also connected to the Hyatt Regency Annex), and from there you can continue to One Illinois Center at 111 E. Wacker Drive, Two Illinois Center at 233 N. Michigan Avenue, Boulevard Towers North at 225 N. Michigan Avenue, and Boulevard Towers South at 205 N. Michigan Avenue.

There is a proposed Walkway which will link the Amoco Oil Building at 200 E. Randolph Street (and also to One Prudential Plaza at 130 E. Randolph Drive) with the Monroe Drive Underground parking lot, Buckingham Plaza at 360 E. Randolph Street, Outer Drive East at 400 E. Randolph Street, Harbor Point at 155 N. Harbor Drive, and 175 N. Harbor Drive.

There is another underground segment along South Michigan Avenue. If you enter the South Grant Park Garage at Adams and Jackson streets, you can reach the Illinois Central-Southshore station at Van Buren Street east of Michigan Avenue.

Another segment begins at the Howard subway station at State and Adams streets. From there, it connects with the Woolworth's

Store at 18 N. State Street (although not accessible at this writing), and continues through a tunnel to the Congress-Douglas Adams Street station, which connects to the Dirksen Federal Building at 219 S. Dearborn Street, the Post Office at Adams and Clark streets, and the Kluczynski Federal Building at 219 S. Dearborn Street (although none of the three was accessible at this writing), which are in line—but not yet linked—with the proposed West Loop Pedway, 3 blocks away.

The proposed West Loop Pedway will start at the Sears Tower at 233 S. Wacker Drive, and is likely to connect with a building directly south of Sears Tower (not even proposed at this writing), then to the 300 S. Wacker Drive Building. The route will continue under the river to 300 S. Riverside Plaza, and the Union Station Garage at 310 S. Canal Street. From the garage, there will be two options: you will be able to walk south to the Clinton Station of the Congress-Douglas El; or walk north to Union Station at 210 S. Canal Street, the Marsh & McLennan Plaza at 222 W. Adams Street, the Chicago Mercantile Exchange at 10 and 30 S. Wacker Drive, and to the Northwestern Atrium Center at 500 W. Madison Street (which currently connects with the Riverside Plaza Building at 2 N. Riverside Plaza).

Another segment has part of its connection above street level. Start at Jackson and LaSalle streets. The Board of Trade Building at 141 W. Jackson Boulevard is connected to the Board of Trade Annex (which shares its address), from there you can walk over the bridge to the Chicago Board Options Exchange at 400 S. LaSalle Street, and though the lower levels of the rest of the Exchange Center at 440 S. LaSalle Street, which includes the Midwest Stock Exchange, the One Financial Place office tower, the LaSalle Street Station, and the Ravenswood station at LaSalle Street.

8

1. Stone Container Building
   360 N. Michigan Ave.

2. Lincoln Tower Building
   75 E. Wacker Dr.

3. Executive House
   71 E. Wacker Dr.

4. Seventeenth Church of Christ, Scientist, Chicago
   55 E. Wacker Dr.

5. North American Life Insurance
   35 E. Wacker Dr.

6. United Insurance Building
   1 E. Wacker Dr.

7. Combined International Insurance Building
   222 N. Dearborn

8. 333 W. Wacker Dr.

9. Apparel Center and Holiday Inn Mart Plaza

10. Merchandise Mart
    350 N. Wells St.

11. City of Chicago, Central Office Building
    325 N. LaSalle St.

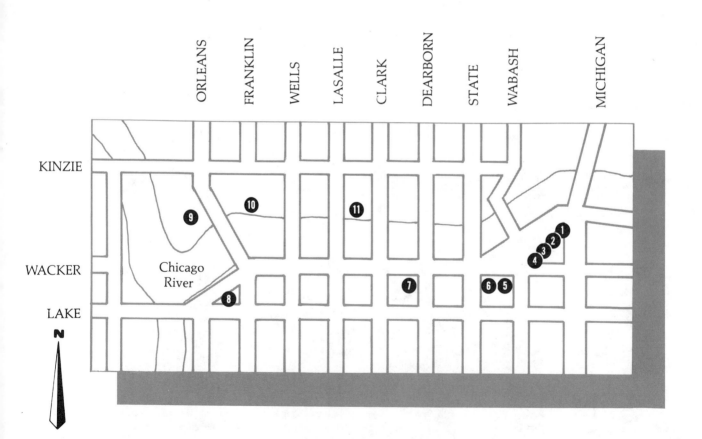

WALK • 8

WACKER DRIVE: EAST-WEST

WALKING TIME: 1½ hours.   HOW TO GET THERE: Take a northbound CTA bus No. 11, No. 146, No. 147, or No. 151 on State Street. Get off at Michigan Avenue and Wacker Drive [300 N]. Or walk east to Michigan Avenue, turn left and walk north to Wacker Drive.

This WALK begins at the intersection of East Wacker Drive and North Michigan Avenue, the spot where once stood Fort Dearborn, one of the military outposts established by President Thomas Jefferson. Plaques on both sides of the street are the only things to remind you of this historic fact. If you stand near the Michigan Avenue bridge and look west, you can see an exciting panorama of today's Chicago along the banks of the Chicago River, where that primitive fort was once the only settlement. The array of contemporary architecture—vertical, horizontal, round, and square—would surely have astonished those early settlers, no matter how ambitious their visions for the future may have been.

The Chicago River, along which you walk, is famed as the river that runs backwards. In order to make it serve more adequately the commercial and sanitary needs of metropolitan Chicago, engineers reversed its current in 1922, so that it now flows from Lake Michigan to the Mississippi River, rather than into Lake Michigan as nature intended. With the opening of the St. Lawrence Seaway in June 1959, the character of the boats seen on the river has changed. In addition to the barges and pleasure boats that always used it, seagoing vessels from distant ports are sometimes anchored here—from England, Denmark, Sweden, Italy, and other far countries.

Wacker Drive, named for Charles Wacker, first chairman of the Chicago Plan Commission, was constructed in 1925, following up the Burnham Plan of 1909. The cluttered old South Water Street produce market was demolished to make way for this vast improvement.

Overleaf: View of Wacker Drive, with the Stone Container Building in center and the Ira J. Bach walkway along the bottom (Robert Thall courtesy Commission on Chicago Landmarks)

109

Wacker Drive and North Michigan Avenue, along with the Michigan Avenue bridge, are double-decked, with a seemingly different life going on at the lower level. A double-decked ring road around the Loop had been proposed as part of the Burnham Plan of 1909. But the Wacker Drive segment was the only portion to be completed. Traffic on this lower level moves freely.

(Ira would not have mentioned the following, but the people who share his WALKS with him will want to note the name of the walkway followed here—Ed.) As you walk along the river bank on Upper Wacker Drive, you will be on the Ira J. Bach Walkway.

IRA J. BACH WALKWAY
South bank of the Chicago River along
Upper Wacker Drive from
Franklin Street to Michigan Avenue

A resolution adopted from the City Council of the City of Chicago reads:

Whereas, the City of Chicago has been the beneficiary of the dedication, expertise and commitment of Ira J. Bach for many years; and

Whereas, Ira J. Bach started his distinguished career in the public sector in 1946 when he was appointed Director of Planning for the Chicago Housing Authority; and

Whereas, Ira J. Bach has continually served the public as Executive Director of the Cook County Housing Authority, Executive Director of the Chicago Land Clearance Commission, the first Commissioner of Planning for the City of Chicago, Executive Director of the Chicago Dwellings Association, Administrator of the Illinois-Indiana Bi-State Planning Commission, Senior Projects Advisor and then Director of City Development for the Mayor Byrne administration and presently was reappointed Director of City Development by Mayor Harold Washington; and

Whereas, he has voluntarily participated in numerous organizations such as the Northeastern Illinois Planning Commission, the Commission on Chicago Historical and Architectural Landmarks; and

Whereas, he is a noted author having written numerous books on the architecture and landmarks of the Chicago metropolitan area . . . (which) have greatly improved our understanding of the beauty and importance of our City; and . . .

110

Dedication of the Ira
J. Bach Walkway
(Peter Schulz courtesy
Elizabeth Hollander)

Whereas, Ira J. Bach has always been a person of quite
unassuming humility, he has also been a very meticulous public
servant; . . .

Be it resolved that the Mayor of City of Chicago and the
Members of its Council duly assembled on this 25th day of April,
1984 hereby designate the walkway along Upper Wacker Drive
between Franklin Street and Michigan Avenue bordering the
Chicago River the "Ira J. Bach Walkway," a permanent expression
of the city of Chicago's appreciation, acknowledgment, and
gratitude to Ira J. Bach for his past, present and future contributions to our City . . .

111

The Stone Container Building, at the southwest corner of East Wacker Drive and North Michigan Avenue, is the first building to be noted on this WALK.

STONE CONTAINER BUILDING
360 N. MICHIGAN AVENUE
ARCHITECT: ALFRED S. ALSCHULER (1923)

Formerly the London Guarantee Building, it is especially well known for the replica of a Greek temple on its roof. Obviously, the designers were not following the standards of indigenous art that were developed by the late 19th century architects of the Chicago school.

A few hundred feet west is the 24-story Lincoln Tower Building (formerly known as the Mather Tower), with its pseudo-Gothic ornamentation in terra-cotta.

LINCOLN TOWER BUILDING
75 E. WACKER DRIVE
ARCHITECT: HERBERT H. RIDDLE (1928)

This narrow structure is distinguished primarily by the fact that it has the smallest floor space per story of any commercial building in Chicago!

⦿ HEALD SQUARE
EAST WACKER DRIVE, SOUTH WATER STREET, AND NORTH WABASH AVENUE

A block west of Michigan Avenue lies Heald Square, with sculpted figures of American Revolutionary War heroes in the center—George Washington, Haym Salomon, and Robert Morris. The square was named for Captain Nathan Heald, ill-fated commandant of Fort Dearborn at the time it was ordered evacuated. He was advised that the Indians would permit safe passage of the soldiers and their families. But as the group of ninety-five left the fort on August 15, 1812, they were attacked. Only forty-five survived.

Incidentally, this is an excellent place from which to view the area—and take pictures if you are a camera fan.

Just to the east of Heald Square you will see the stainless steel balconies of the striking high-rise Executive House.

EXECUTIVE HOUSE
71 E. WACKER DRIVE
ARCHITECTS: MILTON M. SCHWARTZ AND ASSOCIATES (1960)

This was designed as a high-quality hotel with special appeal to the business traveler—an appeal that has proved highly successful.

To the west of Executive House is the handsome Seventeenth Church of Christ, Scientist.

SEVENTEENTH CHURCH OF CHRIST, SCIENTIST, CHICAGO
55 E. WACKER DRIVE
ARCHITECTS: HARRY WEESE AND ASSOCIATES (1968)

This is a travertine marble church—semicircular-shaped to fit the wedge of land it occupies on a prominent corner of Heald Square. The bronze and glass street level lobby, which leads to the auditorium one level above and the Sunday School one level below, serves as an important gathering place, sheltered from passersby and traffic by a sunken garden which admits natural light to the Sunday school. The auditorium, seating 925, is the dominant element of the structure, and its semi-circular geometry, with seats encircling the reader's platform, is expressed on the exterior in the curved travertine facade which turns the corner. The convex curve of the ceiling defuses organ sounds, and rises to a domed lantern directly over the platform. The adjacent office

Seventeenth Church of Christ, Scientist (Olga Stefanos)

113

wing accommodates spaces for meetings and committee work, reader's studies, and mechanical equipment.

South of Heald Square is the former Jewelers Building, now the North American Life Insurance Building.

NORTH AMERICAN LIFE INSURANCE BUILDING
35 E. WACKER DRIVE
ARCHITECTS: GIAVER AND DINKELBERG, WITH
THIELBAR AND FUGARD AS ASSOCIATES (1926)

This building is topped with a neoclassical temple on each of the four corners, surrounding a huge central tower. Not following any single architectural style, the designers, it may be said, have used an eclectic design, though the term Baroque would be more appropriate.

Next to the North American Life Insurance Building is the white marble tower of the United Insurance Company of America Building.

UNITED INSURANCE BUILDING
1 E. WACKER DRIVE
ARCHITECTS: SHAW, METZ, AND ASSOCIATES (1962)

This 41-story structure was the world's tallest marble-faced commercial building when it was built. It is also featured in WALK 3.

Continue west to Dearborn Street.

COMBINED INTERNATIONAL INSURANCE BUILDING
222 N. DEARBORN STREET
ARCHITECTS: C. F. MURPHY AND ASSOCIATES (1969)

This was formerly the Blue Cross-Blue Shield Building, and then the Ryan Insurance Building. This heavy, beige-colored concrete structure, with its cantilevered floors, is described in WALK 4.

Continue west 3 blocks.

333 W. WACKER DRIVE
ARCHITECTS: KOHN, PEDERSEN AND FOX OF NEW YORK
AND PERKINS & WILL (1983)

This 36-floor granite and glass office building is one of the finest recent additions to Chicago's downtown area. It has a lobby with retail spaces and a colonnade at the bottom and office space above. The base is marble and granite, richly detailed with

Combined International
Insurance Building
(Allen Carr)

Opposite:
333 Wacker Drive
(Barbara Karant
courtesy Perkins and Will
and Kohn Pederson Fox
Associates)

114

333 Wacker Drive,
street level detail
and interior
(Gregory Murphy
courtesy Kohn
Pederson Fox
Associates)

stainless steel. The well-detailed, reflective glass curtain wall, granite, marble, and stainless steel exterior creates a striking view from the street. The interior of the lobby is granite, marble, stainless steel, and terrazzo. The curved facade reflects the bend in the river; the other facades, which are geometric, reflect the grid of the Loop.

Across the Chicago River is the Apparel Center and Holiday Inn.

APPAREL CENTER and HOLIDAY INN MART PLAZA
50 N. Orleans Street
Architects: Skidmore, Owings and Merrill (1976)

This complex was built as an addition to the Merchandise Mart, and is in scale with the extant building. The complex is of steel construction with a pre-cast concrete cladding. There are two connected towers, which rise from a 4-story masonry podium, which has a lobby serving the complex, a 140,000-square-foot exhibition hall, tenant space, and a mechanical equipment area.

The complex has parking for 900 cars. The taller, 23-story tower is the 526-room Holiday Inn Mart Plaza; a 9-story, skylighted and landscaped atrium highlights the hotel lobby. The 13-story tower is the addition to the Merchandise Mart, which is the next building to the east.

MERCHANDISE MART
MERCHANDISE MART PLAZA (ABOUT 350 N. WELLS STREET)
ARCHITECTS: GRAHAM, ANDERSON, PROBST AND WHITE (1930);
FOR THE RESTORATION: GRAHAM, ANDERSON, PROBST
AND WHITE (1986-8)

On the north side of the Chicago River, between Wells and Orleans streets, where the CTA elevated lines cross the river, looms the massive Merchandise Mart. Although its architectural design is hardly as distinguished or praiseworthy as it was thought to be at the time of construction, this building is nevertheless not to be missed. For many years the largest building in the world, the Merchandise Mart is still the world's largest wholesale marketing center and one of its largest commercial buildings. Its floor space amounts to about 4 million square feet, where more than 5,000 manufacturers and designers display their products, chiefly furniture and other home furnishings. Twice a year wholesale buyers from all across the country come to Chicago to the home furnishings show that is held here.

Opposite the entrance to the Merchandise Mart on the river side of the plaza stand tall columns with the busts of those who have been selected as the "Merchandise Mart Hall of Fame": Julius Rosenwald, Frank Winfield Woolworth, Marshall Field, John Wanamaker, George Huntington Hartford, Edward A. Filene, Robert E. Wood, and A. Montgomery Ward.

The Mart is owned by the Joseph P. Kennedy family, who bought it in 1945 from the Marshall Field family. At this writing a major cleaning and restoration project is underway. The building is being cleaned; there will be restoration of the stone work and the roof ornament, and terra-cotta repairs; and about 4,000 new windows will be installed. The entrance ramps will be redone, and future commercial development will take place along the lower level at the river front.

Although not all floors of the mart are open to the public, there are tours of the building. The tours are given on Tuesdays and Thursdays at 10 a.m. and last approximately 1½ hours. The fee

117

is $3.75 (children under 17 years old are not allowed on the tours). Call 527-7606 for information.

Walk east along the river bank.

◉ CITY OF CHICAGO, CENTRAL OFFICE BUILDING
325 N. LaSalle Street
Architect: George C. Nimmons (1913)

West of Clark Street, still on the river front, is the City of Chicago Central Office Building, operated by the city of Chicago as a Traffic Court, with offices for city departments. Formerly the Reid, Murdoch and Company Building, it was leased, then sold, to the city. This is a clean, straightforward structure in red brick—its 320-foot-long facade of 8 stories topped off at the center with a prominent clock tower of 4 more stories. The brick work and contrasting terra-cotta accents give this structure a pleasing effect.

To return to Michigan Avenue, cross to the south bank of the Chicago River and walk east on the Ira J. Bach Walkway.

9

1. 300 Wacker Building
   300 S. Wacker Dr.

2. Mid-American Commodity Exchange
   444 W. Jackson Blvd.

3. Union Station
   210 S. Canal Street

4. 222 Riverside Plaza Building

5. 150 S. Wacker Drive Building

6. 200 S. Wacker Drive

7. Sears Tower
   233 S. Wacker Dr.

8. The Northern Building
   125 S. Wacker Dr.

9. U.S. Gypsum Building
   101 S. Wacker Drive

10. Harris Trust And Saving Bank
    111 W. Monroe St.

11. The Chicago Mercantile Exchange
    10 and 30 S. Wacker Drive

12. Hartford Building
    100 S. Wacker Drive

13. 120 S. Riverside Plaza Building

14. 10 S. Riverside Plaza Building

15. Illinois Bell Telephone and
    American Telephone and
    Telegraph Building

16. Presidential Towers
    555, 575, 605, and
    625 W. Madison Street

17. Social Security Administration
    Great Lakes Program Service Center
    600 W. Madison St.

18. Northwestern Atrium Center
    500 W. Madison St.

19. 2 N. Riverside Plaza Building

20. **Civic Opera Building**
    20 N. Canal St.

21. 1 S. Wacker Dr.

22. 101 S. Wacker Dr.

23. Morton Thiokol Building
    110 N. Wacker Dr.

24. 123 N. Wacker Dr.

25. Illinois Bell Telephone Building
    225 W. Randolph St.

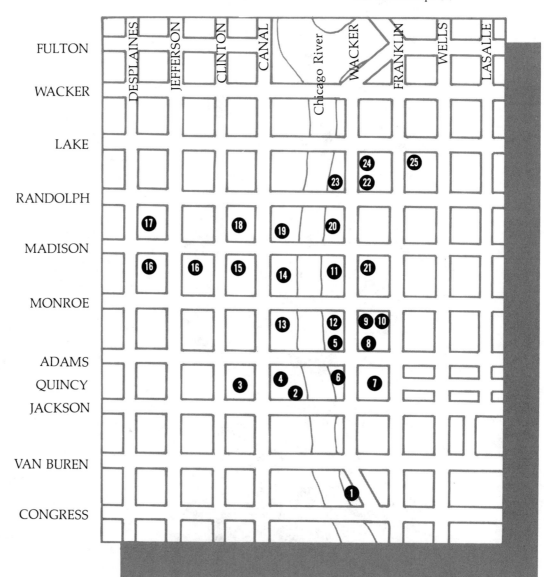

WALK • 9

GATEWAY AREA: SOUTH BRANCH OF CHICAGO RIVER

WALKING TIME: About 1½ hour. HOW TO GET THERE: Walk east 2 blocks to Michigan Avenue. Take a southbound CTA bus No. 1. Get off at Wacker Drive [348 W].

Wacker Drive, which here runs north and south, intersecting Van Buren Street, is the same street you followed from east to west in WALK 8. The change in direction took place just after the end of that WALK, where Wacker Drive follows a bend in the Chicago River and then turns directly south, at Lake Street, to follow the South Branch of the river.

Daniel Burnham, in his plan for Chicago back in 1909, saw Wacker Drive as part of a ring of roads surrounding the Loop. Incidentally, Burnham also anticipated the need for a highway comparable to the Eisenhower Expressway. With this plan in mind, the architects constructed the Central Post Office building with a large opening in the center at street level. Consequently, the Eisenhower Expressway passed through and under the building with a minimum of inconvenience to the Post Office.

This section of the city is sometimes referred to as the Gateway area, since Wacker Drive and the South Branch of the Chicago River are in fact a gateway to the near west. South Wacker Drive, formerly the wholesale garment section of the city, lost hundreds of tenants to the Merchandise Mart when that building was constructed, in 1930 (see WALK 8). This change forecast in a way the Drive's redevelopment. The city government and area businessmen are now carrying out a gigantic urban renewal program in this area, extending to the Kennedy Expressway on the west.

300 WACKER BUILDING
300 S. WACKER DRIVE
ARCHITECTS: A. EPSTEIN AND SONS (1971)

The design of this unusually long and narrow structure was dictated by a narrow site on the Chicago River. The 36-story office

Overleaf: Sears Tower
(Ezra Stoller
courtesy Skidmore
Owings & Merrill)

121

Mid America
Commodity Exchange
(Philip A. Turner)

tower is of reinforced concrete, with a bronze anodized aluminum curtain wall with bronze-tinted glass.

Walk west on Jackson Boulevard.

MID AMERICA COMMODITY EXCHANGE
444 W. JACKSON BOULEVARD
ARCHITECTS: SKIDMORE, OWINGS AND MERRILL (1972)

Supported by four huge columns over air rights of the Union Station, this distinctive dark green glass building is well-engineered. A combination of columns, crisscross girders and walls transfer the entire load of the roof and trading floor to the four main columns to make the column-free interior possible. The visitors' gallery is open on weekdays from 9 a.m. to 1:15 p.m. By all means, go inside and see the exciting trading floor. The dimensions are 225 feet facing Jackson and 100 feet facing the Chicago River. The height of the room is 60 feet. The brokers can be seen

122

trading in such items as live cattle, pork bellies, eggs, live hogs.

Walk west to Canal Street and turn north.

UNION STATION
210 S. CANAL STREET
ARCHITECTS: GRAHAM, ANDERSON, PROBST
AND WHITE (1925)

The Union Station formerly covered two square blocks instead of one. The eastern section was razed and replaced by the 222 Riverside Plaza and 444 W. Jackson buildings. The lower level of that building serves as the main corridors for entering and departing passengers. The cavernous, high-pillared waiting room still remains. It is one of the few remaining enormous railway terminals still in existence. The closing of the three south Loop railway terminals resulted in bringing several railway lines into Union Station. This concentration of terminal facilities leaves three operating terminals in Chicago. They are the Illinois Central and Chicago Northwestern in addition to Union.

Continue north.

Union Station
interior
(Michael J. Schawal)

222 RIVERSIDE PLAZA BUILDING
ARCHITECTS: SKIDMORE, OWINGS AND MERRILL (1972)

This 35-story building—constructed on air rights of the railway tracks—is the third office building of the Gateway Center com-

Union Station
(Olga Stefanos)

123

plex. The project's 80,000 square-foot plaza provides all pedestrian and vehicular entrances to the office tower and railroad. Below the plaza, a concourse level accommodates a new passenger terminal area and space for commercial development. The super-structure was a composite structural system consisting of structural steel interior framing and reinforced-concrete, exterior-bearing wall. The exterior of the building has a light-colored architectural concrete finish, complementing the steel buildings of the Gateway Center.

Continue north to the corner. Walk east on Adams Street to Wacker Drive.

150 S. WACKER DRIVE BUILDING
ARCHITECTS: SKIDMORE, OWINGS AND MERRILL (1971)

The Hartford Plaza has been extended to form a platform for this 33-story office building by the same owners and architects as the Hartford Building. The lower concourse connects the two structures and provides space for a complex of restaurants and shops.

This building's reinforced concrete bearing walls are clad in black granite. From the 10th floor down, alternate columns transfer vertical loads to spandrels of increasing depth to form the major column system at plaza level.

200 S. WACKER DRIVE
ARCHITECTS: HARRY WEESE AND ASSOCIATES (1981)

This 38-story building has an unusual plan, designed to fit the small site and the angle of the river. The building is a four-sided polygon comprised of a right triangle joined at the hypotenuse with its mirror image. The 3-story, glass enclosed lobby is set back from the building's perimeter to create a pedestrian arcade at street level and along the river. Two partial mezzanines, which float within the lobby, provide commercial space. The extensive use of glass brings natural light to these spaces. There is a 2-story health club below street level. The facade is of reinforced concrete and glass; the tower is sheathed in a curtainwall of painted aluminum panels and tinted insulating glass and reflective spandrel glass.

200 S. Wacker Drive
(Bill Hedrich, Hedrich-
Blessing courtesy
Harry Weese & Associates)

SEARS TOWER
233 S. WACKER DRIVE
ARCHITECTS: SKIDMORE, OWINGS
AND MERRILL (1974, 1984-5)

124

Upon completion in 1974, Chicago's Sears Tower became the largest private office complex in the world. The total development contains a gross area of 4.4 million square feet with 101 acres of floor space. The daily population is 16,500 people.

Sears Tower itself is the world's tallest structure, enclosing 3.9 million gross square feet of floor area rising 109 stories or 1468.5 feet above Chicago City datum. It occupies a full city block of approximately 129,000 square feet—bounded by Wacker Drive, Jackson Boulevard, Franklin and Adams streets.

The tower consists of a structural-steel frame bolted in place on the site. The fireproofed frame is clad in a black aluminum skin and bronze-tinted, glare-reducing glass. The exterior sloping plaza has a granite surface. The space below the plaza has three full levels, including a cafeteria and tenant storage space.

The Sears Tower is 100 feet higher than the twin towers of the New York World Trade Center and approximately 325 feet higher than the roof of the John Hancock Center.

Starting in 1984, there were major renovations, also by Skidmore, Owings, and Merrill. A striking 4-story glass-enclosed, domed entrance has been added on Wacker Drive; extending from the street, it shelters visitors from the weather. A new entrance, with domed skylights, was added on Jackson Boulevard. There was a major upgrading to all public areas on five floors: Franklin Concourse, Wacker Plaza Level, Lower Level I, Lower Level II, and to the 103rd-floor Skydeck. Many changes were made to make the building more accessible to the handicapped. New commercial areas were added at the ground level and below. A Sears Business Systems Center was added, and new restaurants opened.

The observation platform, near the top of the tower, which affords spectacular views of Chicago and environs, is open every day from 9 a.m. to midnight. Adults: $3; children: $1.50; includes "The Chicago Experience" a 6½ minute slide show about Chicago, and a 5-minute light and sound show about the Sears model. Call 875-9696 for information.

THE NORTHERN BUILDING
125 S. Wacker Drive
Architects: The Perkins & Will Partnership (1974)

This 30-story structure, on the northeast corner of Wacker Drive and Adams Street, has an attractive exterior that consists of granite-faced columns with an infill of anodized aluminum that frame the dark glass windows. The floor plan has an off-center

U.S. Gypsum Building
(Philip A. Turner)

utility core that is not visible from the street as is the similar floor plan of the Inland Steel Building.

The ground floor consists of drive-in bank facilities with an interior service area for pedestrians.

Walk north on Wacker Drive.

U.S. GYPSUM BUILDING
101 S. WACKER DRIVE
ARCHITECTS: THE PERKINS & WILL PARTNERSHIP (1961)

In the southeast corner of Monroe Street and Wacker Drive is the U.S. Gypsum Building. Its placing on the building lot—at a 45-degree angle from the street lines—caused some consternation among the adherents of the Chicago school of architecture. Many of them felt this departure from the usual procedure insulted the unity of the buildings that Chicago school architects had developed in the Loop over more than half a century. Many others, however, admired the arrangement and the building itself, designed as a trademark to symbolize the company and the materials the company mines. For example, the triangular character of the plazas and the shape of the building itself (note that each of the 19 stories has 8 corners!) were designed to represent the crystalline mineral in gypsum. Thus the building and its placement were intended to suggest the corporate image of the company that owns it. The soberness of the slate panels and gray glass is offset by the columns of white Vermont marble, which also give the building a sweeping vertical effect.

Walk east on Monroe.

HARRIS TRUST AND SAVINGS BANK
111 W. MONROE STREET
ARCHITECTS: A. EPSTEIN AND SONS (1973)

Just east of the U.S. Gypsum Building, on the southwest corner of Franklin and Monroe streets, is this 15-story structure that houses the bank's data processing and computer departments. There is a complete banking facility on the main floor. The structure is a modular design with a tinted-glass and granite exterior facade.

Backtrack west to Wacker Drive and turn north.

THE CHICAGO MERCANTILE EXCHANGE
10 AND 30 S. WACKER DRIVE
ARCHITECTS: FUJIKAWA JOHNSON AND ASSOCIATES (1984-86)

Chicago Mercantile Exchange
(courtesy Fujikawa and Johnson)

127

The Chicago Mercantile Exchange trading floors form a focal point and connecting base for twin towers, each containing 1.1 million square feet of office space. The exteriors of the buildings are clad in Carnelian granite and solar-gray tinted glass. The trading floors of the south tower were completed in 1984 and the north tower is scheduled for completion in 1986.

In order to achieve the required amount of floor space in the office towers, without infringing on the clear spanned space of the two trading floors, the top 34 stories of each tower had to be cantilevered 32 feet over the low-rise building. Site constraints led to the design of the serrated corners, which allow sixteen corner offices per floor.

The two trading floors contain a total of 70,000 square feet. The main trading room measures 215 feet by 90 feet by 30 feet high and contains 40,000 square feet of clear span trading space. The expansion trading floor is located immediately above the main floor and has 30,000 square feet of clear span space.

The facility also has 24,000 square feet of retail space and a 4-level parking garage below for 500 cars. A public promenade along the Chicago River, connecting Madison and Monroe streets, will be available at the completion of the second tower.

Cross to the south side of Monroe Street.

HARTFORD BUILDING
100 S. WACKER DRIVE
ARCHITECTS: SKIDMORE, OWINGS AND MERRILL (1961)

On the southwest corner of Wacker Drive and Monroe Street is the Hartford Building—of the Hartford Fire Insurance Company. Here the architects exaggerated the old Chicago school belief that the facade of a building should disclose its interior structural composition. The 21-story concrete skeleton here becomes more than a framework: it serves as sunshades for the interior and gives the building a constantly changing pattern of light and shadow during the day.

Walk west on Monroe Street.

10 S. RIVERSIDE PLAZA BUILDING
ARCHITECTS: SKIDMORE, OWINGS AND MERRILL (1968)

120 S. RIVERSIDE PLAZA BUILDING
ARCHITECTS: SKIDMORE, OWINGS AND MERRILL (1974)

Union Station and its concourse has given way to development of nearby Gateway Center. The first two buildings, just north of

128

Hartford Building
(Ezra Stoller
courtesy Skidmore,
Owings and Merrill)

the station's concourse exit ramp at West Adams Street, were built on air rights over the tracks leading to Union Station. They were the first buildings in the continuing style of the Chicago school of architecture and extend the business center west of the Chicago River. The tinted glass and russet beams used in the buildings give them the functional exterior framework of the old school.

129

Surrounded by wide plazas, these two buildings look somewhat squat and bulky, despite their 20-story height—a characteristic dictated by construction over the tracks. The wide architectural spans, similar to those used by the same architects in the Richard J. Daley Center, were made possible by the omission of any columns between the center service core and the exterior columns.

From Gateway Center Plaza along the river bank you have a distant view of two markedly different architectural neighbors back on the east side of the river—the Hartford Building, a contemporary expression of the still vibrant Chicago school of architecture, and its sculptured neighbor, the U.S. Gypsum Building, sitting gracefully askew on its site at south Wacker Drive and west Monroe Street. You had a close-up view of these buildings earlier in the WALK.

Walk west to Canal, and turn north.

ILLINOIS BELL TELEPHONE AND
AMERICAN TELEPHONE AND TELEGRAPH BUILDING
10 S. CANAL STREET
ARCHITECTS: HOLABIRD AND ROOT (1971)

This 25-story building contains eighteen floors of equipment and seven floors of office space. The architects had a problem designing and planning a structure that called for radiation protection, as well as added structural strength to meet high lateral loads. Telephone equipment heat loads required special fan rooms on each floor.

The non-public building has enclosed equipment floor panels. The office floors have glazed infill panels that are replaceable with a continuation, when necessary, of the equipment floor-panel system.

The exterior colors are smooth buff concrete, matching hammered precast concrete infill panels, solar bronze glazing, and bronze anodized-aluminum louvers and glazing sections. It is noteworthy that this building has received two merit awards.

Walk west on Madison.

PRESIDENTIAL TOWERS
555, 575, 605, AND 625 W. MADISON STREET
ARCHITECTS: SOLOMON, CORDWELL AND BUENZ (1985-86)

Presidential Towers consist of four 49-story apartment towers. Each has a 3-story base. The main entrance is through a 40-foot skylit atrium. The atrium connects the 80,000-square-foot

130

shopping mall with a winter garden and a third level pedestrian arcade. The arcade bridges the street at two locations, linking the enclosed shopping mall with a winter garden and a third level pedestrian arcade. The arcade bridges the street at two locations, linking the towers and the enclosed parking garage. The third level also contains laundry facilities, tenant storage, commercial space, a fully equipped health club with an enclosed swimming pool, basketball court, a one-seventh mile running track, and access to the outdoor recreation deck. The tower floor plans are designed for maximum efficiency, with short corridor lengths and well proportioned apartments ranging from 461 to 1,140 square feet. Chamfered corners allow eight corner units per floor. The towers' exteriors are painted and rusticated cast-in-place concrete and tinted glass. The ground level is extensively landscaped to provide a park-like setting.

Every effort was made to attract tenants to this previously nonresidential location in an area that had been blighted and is, at this writing, undergoing major upgrading.

Continue west.

SOCIAL SECURITY ADMINISTRATION
GREAT LAKES PROGRAM SERVICE CENTER
600 W. Madison Street
Architects: Lester B. Knight & Associates (1976)

This 10-story structure sits on a 2.3 acre site, a complete city block. It was a pioneer in the redevelopment of the Near West Side. The design is an early example of the modular systems approach to open planned office space. The utility cores are placed at the building perimeter and are expressed as solid shafts of precast concrete intercepting the silvery glass curtain wall around the office areas. The same warm toned exposed aggregate concrete is used for the plazas and sidewalks surrounding the building and on the lobby walls of the first floor. The transparent glass used around the recessed first floor is set in mirror finish stainless steel frames to complement the concrete finish, giving the building a distinctive high-tech image.

Three significant works of art augment the building design. On the exterior, the superscale *Bat Column* by Claes Oldenburg is positioned to interplay with the silver reflective glass curtain wall. An extensive porcelain enamel mural by Ilya Bolotowsky surrounds the first floor lobby. In the employees' cafeteria, several large terra-cotta panels designed by Louis Sullivan in 1894 for the

Social Security
Administration Program
Service Center
(Bill Engdahl,
Hedrich-Blessing
courtesy Lester
B. Knight)

Scoville Building, formerly on the site, are used as a decorative screen.

Walk east on Madison Street.

NORTHWESTERN ATRIUM CENTER
500 W. MADISON STREET
ARCHITECTS: MURPHY/JAHN (1987)

This 40-story combined commuter terminal and office building has replaced the Chicago and Northwestern Commuter Station. The 1.6-million-square-foot building forms a major gateway between the Loop to the east and the urban renewal area to the west. A bridge crosses from the Northwestern Center to the Riverside Plaza Building to the east (at 2 N. Riverside Plaza).

The steel building has a curtainwall of blue enameled aluminum and blue and silver glass in a pattern of setbacks reminiscent of a railroad streamliner.

A continuous arcade along Madison Street leads to a sequence of multistory atria, creating a commuter walkway full of light and spatial excitement.

Opposite: Northwestern
Atrium Center
(James Steinkamp
courtesy Murphy/Jahn)

132

The office tower above the commuter train facilities is served from a sky-lobby one floor above track level. Floors vary in size from roughly 30,000 to 50,000 square feet, and the large floor areas are broken up by the shifting shapes of the building.

Continue east.

RIVERSIDE PLAZA BUILDING
2 N. RIVERSIDE PLAZA
ARCHITECTS: HOLABIRD AND ROOT (1928)

With its setbacks and angles, this building is an excellent example of the Chicago skyscraper of the 1920s. A colorful remnant of the building's original occupancy by the Chicago Daily News can be seen in the excellent murals on the lobby ceiling. The work of noted Chicago muralist John Norton, the scenes depict newspaper production.

As you cross the bridge over the river at West Madison Street, you can see the Riverside Plaza Building more fully, sitting sphinx-like as it was designed. Continue east to Wacker.

Civic Opera House
(Olga Stefanos)

CIVIC OPERA BUILDING
20 N. WACKER DRIVE
ARCHITECTS: GRAHAM, ANDERSON, PROBST,
AND WHITE (1929)

Another example of the Chicago skyscraper of the 1920s is this 45-story building for a time known as the Kemper Insurance Building. The immense structure was erected—at a cost of some $20 million—by Samuel Insull in 1929. Such an investment in that year by even the most sound and upright financier would have been a gamble; in this case it proved a disaster. The subsequent ruin of Insull's financial empire, to say nothing of the dubious methods he had used in building it up, unfortunately wiped out whatever pleasant associations Chicago might have had with the name of a man who loved opera. And the fact that the construction of this building led to the closing of the Auditorium Theatre (see WALK 1) seemed to many Chicago opera lovers a cause for resentment rather than gratitude. Herman Kogan has expressed this harsh but understandable judgment of Sam Insull (Kogan, Herman, and Wendt, Lloyd, *Chicago: A Pictorial History*. New York: E. P. Dutton and Company, 1958, p. 203):

More than any one man, he was responsible for the abandonment of the glorious Auditorium as a center of music and opera, because he had built, in an illogical place and with inferior acoustics, his own Civic Opera House at Wacker Drive and Madison Street.

Whatever may be the sentiments toward Insull, however, his building has not gone empty. The current Lyric Opera of Chicago uses its auditorium, seating 3,500 people, just as two other opera companies did before the Lyric was formed. Hundreds of offices are available in the remainder of this mammoth structure.

1 S. WACKER DRIVE
ARCHITECTS: MURPHY/JAHN (1982)

The design of the building sets back twice to create three typical floor areas of 38,000, 32,000, and 26,000 gross square feet. This corresponds to the three elevator groups serving the building. Another setback occurs at the mechanical penthouse. The variety of possible floor arrangements has been further increased by a 3-story atrium, located above and below the setbacks. This creates U-shaped floor areas which increase the perimeter and daylight exposure without an added exterior wall and result in an energy

135

savings. This is essentially an adaptation of the typical office tower of the early 1920s to today's standards and requirements.

At the ground floor, the atrium extends into a multilevel commercial galleria which serves as a civilized public throughway between the Wacker Drive and Madison Street entrances to the building. This arrangement puts the public space inside the building and keeps the commercial space on the exterior along the street. The facade is on a 5-foot module to reinforce the articulated shape and reduce the bulk of the tower. The facade is completed by filling in the abstract grid with silver and gray reflective glass.

Walk north on Wacker Drive.

101 N. WACKER DRIVE
ARCHITECTS: PERKINS & WILL (1980)

This 24-story office building was built with energy conservation in mind. Heat-absorbing, insulated glass is on all four sides of the building and a special reflective coating on the inside face of the glass on the west and south sides. Horizontal bands of light and dark gray glass create a lively exterior.

Continue north. Located on the west side of Wacker Drive is the Morton Thiokol Building, extending between Washington and Randolph streets.

MORTON THIOKOL BUILDING
110 N. WACKER DRIVE
ARCHITECTS: GRAHAM, ANDERSON, PROBST
AND WHITE (1961)

This Indiana limestone structure, housing the main offices of the Morton Salt Company, affords all its offices and dining rooms a splendid view of the river.

123 N. WACKER DRIVE
ARCHITECTS: PERKINS & WILL (1986)

This 30-story office tower with commercial space on the ground floor, under constructions at this writing, is relatively small compared to other recent Loop high-rises. It is located on one of the widest streets in Chicago, with this portion of Wacker Drive claiming a wide range of building styles and architectural types, everything from the world's tallest building (Sears Tower) to the art deco Civic Opera House.

The developer required a dignified and elegant building, marketable as a corporate headquarters. The principal tenant is to

136

be Combined Insurance. The design challenge has been to give this relatively small building a dignified prominence on the street.

Since it will not have the size to overpower the surrounding buildings, the designer has used other means. The height is accentuated by a series of setbacks, together with strong vertical stripes of alternating dark and light gray reflective glass.

The uppermost three floors of the building form a transparent pyramid. This construction allows an atrium and very dramatic views from the corporate headquarters suite atop the building.

Walk east on Randolph Street to Franklin Street.

ILLINOIS BELL TELEPHONE BUILDING
225 W. Randolph Street
Architects: Holabird and Root (1967)

This building of the Illinois Bell Telephone Company, one block east of Wacker Drive on Randolph Street makes an effective use of vertical lines of marble and glass, dramatized at night by the interior lighting. This is a first-rate modern building.

This concludes the WALK. To return to State Street, walk east on Randolph Street.

123 North Wacker Drive
(Jess Smith, photosmith,
courtesy Perkins & Will)

137

10

1. Franklin Building
   525 S. Dearborn St.

2. Terminals Building
   537 S. Dearborn St.

   The Morton Hotel
   538 S. Dearborn St.

3. Duplicator Building
   530 S. Dearborn St.

4. Morton Building
   538 S. Dearborn St.

5. Pontiac Building
   542 S. Dearborn Street

6. Mergenthaler Building
   531 S. Plymouth Ct.

7. Moser Building
   621–631 S. Plymouth Ct.

8. Pope Building
   633 S. Plymouth Ct.

9. Transportation Building
   600 S. Dearborn St.

10. Printer's Square
    600–732 S. Federal Ave.

11. Grace Place
    637 S. Dearborn St.

12. Donohue Building
    701–721 S. Dearborn St.

14. Rowe Building
    714 S. Dearborn St.

15. Franklin Building
    720 S. Dearborn St.

16. River City
    800 S. Wells St.

17. Dearborn Street Station
    South Dearborn St. at West Polk St

18. Lakeside Press Building
    731 S. Plymouth Ct.

19. Two East Eighth

20. The Terraces

21. The High-Rises

22. The Mid-Rises

23. The Gardenhomes

24. The Townhouses

25. The Townhomes

26. The Oaks

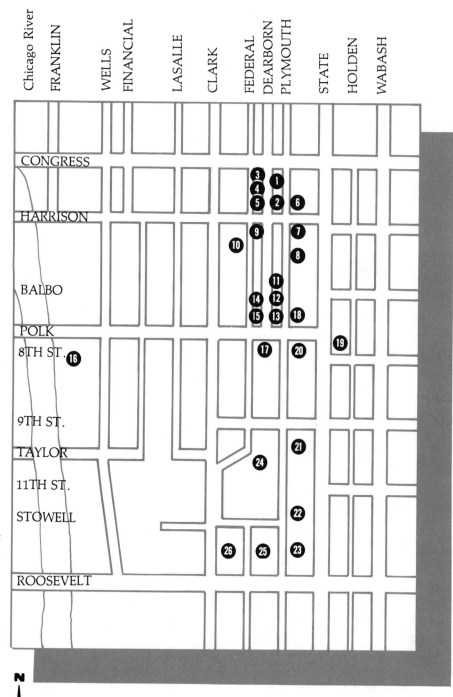

WALK • 10

BURNHAM PARK: THE SOUTH LOOP

WALKING TIME: About 1½ hours. HOW TO GET THERE: Take a southbound CTA bus No. 29 on State Street and get off at Congress Street [500 S]. Walk west across Plymouth Court, to Dearborn Street [36 W], which runs parallel to State Street.

Printing House Row is a 2-block area on both sides of Dearborn Street between Congress Parkway and Polk Street, consisting of historic structures, once involved in the printing industry, and vacant land on which new development may take place in the future, but which now provides parking. This WALK did not appear in earlier editions of this book because the area wasn't a neighborhood until 1977. Here are the true urban pioneers living in one of Chicago's best kept secrets.

The five general co-partners for the development were Baird and Warner, Ivan Himmell Companies, Theodore Gaines, Larry Booth, and Harry Weese. Development in the area began with the Donohue Building in 1976, and continues at this writing. The majority of projects along Dearborn Street were developed by members of the Community Resources Corporation partnership.

Harry Weese took a lead role in the revitalization of the area, including taking equity positions in individual projects and risking his own capital. He advocated the continued use and preservation in this benignly neglected section of the city after the train station closed. He prepared the 1976 nomination petition to place the South Loop Printing House District on the National Register of Historic Places.

Begin the WALK on the east side of Dearborn Street. Look at the clock tower on Dearborn Station at the south end of the street. It will be described later in the WALK. After the Dearborn Street Station opened in 1885, many printers and publishers built plants in this area because of the proximity of the railroads. The architects of virtually every building in Printers Row have taken some features from the Dearborn Station and incorporated them in the later buildings.

Overleaf: River City
(Barry Rustin
courtesy River
City Developers)

141

Old Franklin
Building
(courtesy Booth
Hansen and
Associates)

(OLD) FRANKLIN BUILDING
525 S. DEARBORN STREET
ARCHITECT: UNKNOWN (1888);
FOR THE ADAPTIVE REUSE: BOOTH/HANSEN
AND ASSOCIATES (1983)

   Called the Old Franklin Building after the newer one was built
in 1912, this and the Duplicator Building across the street are the

oldest on the block. The red brick, 7-story building will have fifty-four apartments above a commercial ground floor. The exterior has been cleaned and restored and new windows have been installed. The interior has been completely renovated.

TERMINALS BUILDING
537 S. Dearborn Street
Architects: John Mills Van Osdel (1892);
for the adaptive reuse: Harry Weese and
Associates (1986)

This was the last building of Van Osdel (completed after his death), who was responsible for all of Chicago's major buildings built before and shortly after the Chicago Fire. The oldest remaining building is the McCarthy Building of 1872. The Terminals Building has a heavy rusticated base with an arched entrance and two very prominent oriels. The sandstone faces of many heritages above the door are sadly fading away.

The 14-story building has recently undergone exterior cleaning and the windows have been replaced. The interior was completely rehabilitated. It will have fifty-two apartments above a commercial ground floor.

Across the street is a unique and unexpected idea; a hotel created by splicing two buildings together.

THE MORTON HOTEL
538 S. Dearborn Street

DUPLICATOR BUILDING
530 S. Dearborn Street
Architect: Unknown (1886)

MORTON BUILDING
538 S. Dearborn Street
Architects: Jenney and Mundie (1896);
for the adaptive reuse: Booth/Hansen
and Associates (1986-7)

The Duplicator Building was built in 1886. Its design reflected the functional requirements of the printing industry. The innovative metal frame design was the result of the latest developments of the Chicago school of architecture.

143

The Morton Building was erected in 1896 to house small companies that needed to display wares to the public. Designed by the eminent architectural firm of Jenney and Mundie, the building reflects the influence of classicism from the World's Columbian Exhibition of 1893.

Here a hotel is being created by joining together the floors of two older buildings. The Duplicator, a 7-story building, uses red brick like the Old Franklin Building, but is plainer. The Morton has polygonal bays like the Terminals Building across the street. Supporting the bays are remnants of the neoclassical revival—two "Atlas" figures. The building is made of a light brick, and has segmental keystone lintels, an almost Georgian detail.

The first phase of the Morton Hotel development will have 113 rooms, to be completed this year. At least fifty more will be added next year. The Morton is planned to be a first-class hotel catering to the financial district, and to include an appropriately impressive restaurant. Its up-to-date interior design features reminders to the visitor of the history of Chicago.

On the northwest corner of Harrison and Dearborn streets is a reddish building with two huge sweeping bays.

● PONTIAC BUILDING
542 S. DEARBORN STREET
ARCHITECTS: HOLABIRD AND ROCHE (1891);
FOR THE ADAPTIVE REUSE: BOOTH/HANSEN
AND ASSOCIATES (1986)

This is Holabird and Roche's oldest surviving building in Chicago. One of the great pioneering efforts of the Chicago school, the 14-story Pontiac Building is listed on the National Register of Historic Places. Sparse in decoration, its liveliness is based on its window treatments. The massive bays are trimmed with red terra-cotta.

This 14-story fireproof riveted steel frame building of dark brown masonry has tile arch floor slabs, ornamental red terra-cotta and a sandstone base. Projecting bays above the second floor level (Chicago windows) run continuously from the 3rd to 13th floor.

Now in adaptive reuse as an office building, it has a commercial ground floor. At this writing, the building is being completely renovated. The exterior will be cleaned; new windows will be installed; new storefront detail (to match the original cast iron) will be made; and a new lobby with mahogany paneling, granite

144

flooring, and brass fittings and fixtures will be installed. The original brass plate cage of the elevators will be refurbished.

The short dark green building on the northeast corner has the offices of Booth/Hansen and Associates. This firm has the most rehabilitation projects underway in Printer's Row, including three on this block. Turn left on Harrison Street and continue 1 block. The building on the northeast corner was originally known as the Mergenthaler Linotype Building.

MERGENTHALER BUILDING
531 S. Plymouth Court
Architects: Schmidt, Garden and Martin (1886);
for the addition and remodeling: Schmidt, Garden and Martin, Samuel N. Crowen associate architect (1917);
for the adaptive reuse: Ken Schroeder and Associates (1981)

This 6-story structure is one of the most clever examples of adaptive reuse on a tour consisting of many ingenious examples. Into the original entrance Ken Schroeder has inserted a new post and lintel (the most basic of all architectural structures), consisting of two red pillars supporting a bright blue beam. As if further proof were necessary that this is no longer an old factory building, there is a neon address sign above the door. At the building's northeast corner are the remnants of Tom's Grill. The entire building is gone except for this framework. Plants grow where the floor used to be; ivy grows up the columns; a barbeque testifies to its past. This structure is also a post and lintel construction as is the wacky parking entrance on the south side of the building. Like a suburbanite returning home, the residents here use an automatic garage door opener to enter through a roll-up door, but this is a free-standing door with no enclosed space behind it!

Also on the south side is one of the building's most notable additions—the wedge-shaped bays added onto the wall. These bays, with their multi-paned windows, function on the outside to make people stop and gape; on the inside they create a beautiful small area with a south-facing view. Mirrors form a "trick reveal"—looking like a glass wall.

Continue ½ block south on Plymouth Court.

MOSER BUILDING
621-631 S. Plymouth Court
Architects: Holabird and Roche (1909);
for the adaptive reuse: Lisec and Biederman (1986-7)

145

This was originally the Moser Paper Company, a supplier to the printing businesses of the area. The 9-story building has recently been cleaned and all windows have been replaced with reproductions of the original windows. The interior has been totally redone with only the octagonal columns with their conical octagonal capitals retained. There will be eighty-eight apartments above a commercial ground floor.

POPE BUILDING
633 S. PLYMOUTH COURT
ARCHITECTS: H.G. HODGKINS (1904);
FOR THE ADAPTIVE REUSE: LISEC AND BIEDERMAN (1986)

This 12-story building originally housed a printing company. It is now in adaptive reuse as apartments with retail space on the ground floor. The exterior, including the terra-cotta, was restored. The building boasts a lively combination of windows. Starting with large picture windows, it rises through bays containing three windows each, followed by a story with Chicago windows, then multi-paned windows whose narrow spaces create a definite vertical emphasis. All windows are replacements, conforming to the original designs. The mullions and window frames are painted an attention-getting green, also a restoration to the original, which conforms with the requirements of the National Register of Historic Places. The floors, vaulted ceilings, and elevator doors were preserved while the rest of the interior was completely redone.

Walk west through the parking lot back to Dearborn Street. The huge building on the west side is called the Transportation Building.

TRANSPORTATION BUILDING
600 S. DEARBORN STREET
ARCHITECTS: FRED V. PRATHER (1911);
FOR THE ADAPTIVE REUSE: HARRY WEESE
AND ASSOCIATES (1983)

Originally serving as offices for many small non-printing companies that needed close contact with Chicago rail lines, this building was aptly named. The reinforced concrete building, with a pragmatically buff-colored brick facade, almost overwhelms the street. It is a very shallow building, but very wide along Dearborn Street, and tall enough to sway in Chicago's winds. The 22-story building now has 294 apartments above a commercial ground floor.

During the recent work, the original integrity of the container was respected; the windows were replaced; the interior was completely remodeled, maintaining the original circulation which was fortunately up to current code requirements. At this writing the exterior is being cleaned. The tall ceilings and wide windows provide wonderful views to the lake on the east and the expanse of the city to the west.

Cross Dearborn Street and walk west through the small park.

PRINTER'S SQUARE
600-732 S. FEDERAL AVENUE
ARCHITECTS: FROST AND GRANGER (1909);
CHARLES S. FROST (1912);
CHARLES S. FROST AND CHARLES C. HENDERSON (1928);
FOR THE ADAPTIVE REUSE: LOUIS ARTHUR WEISS (1983)

Printer's Square is the adaptive reuse of five older buildings (known as the Borland buildings) tied to the newest one. The three north structures were built in 1909, with additions following to the south in 1912 and 1928. Designed as manufacturing buildings, they have as high a floor load capacity as any in the city at 250 pounds per square foot.

The conversion to Printer's Square was one of the largest privately financed redevelopment projects in the country. Covering 600,000 square feet, the development includes 356 apartments in a total of twenty-six floor plans, an 180-car garage, 90,000 square feet of offices, and 70,000 square feet of retail space. The interiors were completely redesigned and all mechanical systems were replaced. All windows were replaced with ones in a compatible design. The addition was designed with compatible masonry and a glass curtainwall.

Walk east back through the park. On the east side of the street is a small 3-story building.

GRACE PLACE
637 S. DEARBORN STREET
ARCHITECTS FOR THE ADAPTIVE REUSE:
BOOTH/HANSEN AND ASSOCIATES (1985)

Here in a town of lofts and rehabilitations is the Grace Episcopal Church—a loft church. This small printing building, whose architect is unknown, was built about 1915. It has been converted into a community meeting hall with a chapel on the second floor. It also has a newly-installed dance floor.

The whole is a conglomeration of shapes and textures. The coat room and adjoining wall have cut-out openings in the shape of gabled churches. There is also a slight nautical feel with doors having porthole windows. The columns supporting the floors are unadorned rough-hewn timber. The newly installed ductwork is left exposed and painted gray in true high-tech fashion.

The second floor is the sanctuary. At the entrance, you look through more gabled church openings, toward the seating area which is surround by a circular wall. When you enter this space your attention is focused on the pulpit, behind which a piece of sheet metal does double duty—as a bracket holding a post and beam together, and as the congregation's cross. Talk about melding form and function!

DONOHUE BUILDING
701-721 S. Dearborn Street
Architect: Julius Speyer (1883)

DONOHUE BUILDING ANNEX
727 S. Dearborn Street
Architects: Alfred S. Alschuler (1913);
for the adaptive reuse of both buildings:
Harry Weese and Associates (1976)

Built for Donohue and Hanneberry Company, this was one of the first printing houses in the area. This was also one of the first buildings to be converted to condominium lofts. The building is architecturally responsive both to Dearborn Street and to Plymouth Court (which for years was unfortunately treated as an alley) with equally nice facades on each side. The annex was designed by the same architect as the Stone Container Building. It is sympathetic in style, but more subdued.

In the recent adaptive reuse, the buildings' exteriors were preserved in-situ. The original windows were repaired (not replaced, as in many other projects) down to the glass panes. Since this was an industrial loft building, it has large expanses of clear space which in many cases were maintained and enhanced by each tenant. Considered a democratic conversion, each owner was free to define and use his large open space as he saw fit. Some are business condominiums; some are apartments. The ground floor is all condominium businesses, the first such use of that new concept.

Located here is the Prairie Avenue Bookstore, with the largest collection of architectural books in the country, and the Printer's Row Printing Museum. Open weekends: Saturday 9 a.m. to 5 p.m.; Sunday 10 a.m. to 3:30 p.m. During the summer months only: Tuesday through Friday 10 a.m. to 4 p.m. Admission is free.

ROWE BUILDING
714 S. DEARBORN STREET
ARCHITECTS: (POSSIBLY) WILLIAM LeBARON JENNEY (c. 1892);
FOR THE ADAPTIVE REUSE: KEN SCHROEDER,
GEORGE HINDS AND PHILIP KUPRITZ (1980)

This 8-story building was originally a printing loft. It is in the style of other Dearborn Street structures and similar to the Donnelly Building. The top originally contained a proofreading room, which was skylit. The building has a cast iron front and cast iron window mullions on the upper floors. It is of heavy timber construction with brick exterior. The window proportions vary from floor to floor.

One of the first conversions in the area, each unit in this office condominium is a full floor. The interior was sandblasted, the floors sanded, and a new bath core was added.

FRANKLIN BUILDING
720 S. DEARBORN STREET
ARCHITECT: GEORGE C. NIMMONS (1912);
FOR THE ADAPTIVE REUSE: LISEC AND
BIEDERMAN (1987)

This building once housed printing and printing-related businesses. At this writing work was about to begin on a major program of restoration and adaptive reuse. The 13-story building will have eighty-one apartments. The building has been cleaned and will have restoration of the masonry, lintels, and terra-cotta, and of the parapet. Some new openings will be punched in the 13th story (to match the windows below), which had none, but boasts skylights that run from 15 to 30 feet above the level of the floor.

An amazing array of colored tiles forming many different mosaics cover the building from top to bottom. They will be cleaned and restored. There is an interesting illusion created with

Dearborn Station
(Olga Stefanos)

terra-cotta. You almost see tapered, two-story columns with unadorned, pentagon-shaped capitals. Near the top of each are strange images. Above the first floor are a series of small pictures of men working on the first printing press. These pictures culminate in a much larger picture entitled *The First Impression.*

Continue south to Polk Street. If you stand on the northwest corner and look west you will see River City. If you wish a closer look, walk west on Polk Street to Wells Street.

RIVER CITY
800 S. WELLS STREET
ARCHITECTS: BERTRAND GOLDBERG AND ASSOCIATES (1984-)

Bertrand Goldberg designed the twin towers of Marina City over twenty-five years ago, Chicago's first "city within a city"—a

150

combination of apartments, garages, restaurants, offices, a bank, ice-skating rink, commercial space and a marina—from which residents could walk to work in the Loop.

In River City, Goldberg continues this idea. The curvilinear buildings, completed at this writing, have 446 rental units and 240,000 square feet of commercial space in 10- to 17-story poured concrete towers. There is also a seventy-slip marina. The development is planned to be expanded toward the south, with three additional residential structures adding over 2,500 units to complete the "city." Inside is a winding, skylit, atrium walkway called River Road, meant to convey a sense of community.

The developers envision stores, shops, and theaters extending north along the river bank on a site now occupied by a sculpture park. Every year from mid-August to mid-September six sculptors are chosen, from over two hundred applicants, to participate in the event. Call 987-1980 for information. As River City expands, the site will be moved.

Return to Dearborn Street.

◉ **DEARBORN STREET STATION**
South Dearborn Street at West Polk Street
Architects: Cyrus L. W. Eidlitz (1885);
Project architects for Dearborn Street Station Mall:
Kaplan, McLauglin, Diaz of San Francisco;
consulting architects for the restoration: Hasbrouck
and Hunderman (1986)

Dearborn Station, the oldest surviving railroad terminal in Chicago, is the focal point of the WALK. The station is an exuberant mass of arches, string and belt courses, and applied terra-cotta decoration. It is missing many parts, including a huge cupola (originally on the clock tower), a steeply pitched roof that was lost during a fire in 1922, and its shed which was removed in the 1960s. Notice that the clock tower is not set into the middle of the building. This was to center it on Dearborn Street.

The landmark was in danger of being demolished, when the plan for a shopping mall rescued it. At this writing the facade facing Dearborn Street is being restored with minor changes, including the glass arcade on the east. The 60,000 square foot, 3-story addition is being built behind the station. The 120,000 square foot project is roughly half rehabilitated space and half a new addition. There will be 88,000 square feet of rentable space of which 28,000 square feet will be office space and 60,000 square feet will be retail. You will see the addition later in the WALK.

Walk east on Polk Street to Plymouth Court. On the northeast corner is the Lakeside Press Building.

◉ LAKESIDE PRESS BUILDING
731 S. PLYMOUTH COURT
ARCHITECTS: HOWARD VAN DOREN SHAW (1897, 1901);
FOR THE ADAPTIVE REUSE: LISEC AND
BIEDERMAN (1985-6)

Originally the Lakeside Press Building of the R.R. Donnelley Company (note the Indian chief in the Donnelley seal on the front), this 8-story brick structure was later the Racing Form building. It has recently undergone exterior restoration, major interior rehabilitation, and the replacement of all windows as part of its conversion into apartments. The original 12-foot ceilings and columns were retained in all apartments. The building is on the National Register of Historic Places.

Walk east to State Street.

TWO EAST EIGHTH
2 E. 8TH STREET
ARCHITECT: SEYMOUR GOLDSTEIN (1984)

This 27-story apartment building has a commercial ground floor. There are 330 apartments, two sundecks, and an indoor pool.

Backtrack west on Polk Street.

DEARBORN PARK

When you cross over into the area known as Dearborn Park you feel as if you've entered another town. Here, built over the former railway tracks of Dearborn Station is a variety of housing: high-rises, town houses, "garden apartments," senior citizen housing, and even a grade school. As late as 1977 none of this existed. Yet there is already a feeling of a community. The amazing thing about Dearborn Park, and the revitalized South Loop, is that its spectacular growth has been accomplished without the usual preliminary of throwing out of less privileged people. This is because there were no people!

To the east of Dearborn Street Station is a building consisting of many terraces. It is appropriately called "The Terraces." To enter

152

The Terraces
(Gregory Murphy
courtesy Skidmore,
Owings, & Merrill)

Dearborn Park, take the path between the station and the Terraces.

THE TERRACES
801 S. Plymouth Court
Architects: Skidmore, Owings and Merrill (1983)

These buildings, located on a 2-acre site, consist of twenty-one garden homes and an 11-story building with 198 one- and

two-bedroom apartments. The 11-story building, located on top of a garage podium is an L-shaped, terraced structure adjoining the two-story garden homes. The garden homes are U-shaped to create a courtyard which provides security as well as privacy for residents. Individual entrances to the garden homes and the main entry to the mid-rise building are from the raised courtyard.

A warm red brick was used for the apartments. This color is complementary to the other masonry buildings in Dearborn Park. Masonry was chosen because it has a residential quality and is a traditional Chicago building material.

Walk south on Plymouth Court.

THE HIGH-RISES
901 S. PLYMOUTH COURT AND 899 S. PLYMOUTH COURT
ARCHITECTS: EZRA GORDON, JACK M. LEVIN AND
ASSOCIATES (1978-79)

These 21-story and 26-story apartment buildings with commercial ground floors are the two tallest structures in Dearborn Park. Although they are cast-in-place concrete, in keeping with the motif of the area they are faced with red brick. They also have polygonal bays reminiscent of the earlier buildings of Printer's Row.

Continue south.

THE MID-RISES
1115, 1143, 1169 S. PLYMOUTH COURT

THE GARDENHOMES
1001, 1121, 1153 S. PLYMOUTH COURT
ARCHITECTS: BOOTH, NAGLE AND HARTRAY (1977-81)

On your left is a grouping of three 7-story "mid-rises." These have terraces which the architects describe as "backyards in the sky." Each mid-rise wraps around a courtyard containing a three-story building. These are the town houses known as "The Gardenhomes." There are 238 units and 144 parking spaces.

On your right are the Townhouses.

THE TOWNHOUSES
933-971, 1040-1080, 1122-1158 S. PLYMOUTH COURT
836-888, 960-996, 1061-1097 S. PARK TERRACE
ARCHITECTS: HAMMOND BEEBY AND BABKA;
THOMAS H. BEEBY, DESIGNER (1978)

Opposite:
The High-Rises
(David Clifton
courtesy
Ezra Gordon)

155

The exteriors of these plain gray brick buildings contain no hint of the architectural flair that has since become the trademark of Thomas Beeby. Yet, a closer examination reveals a site plan that effectively shuts out the city and creates a place of public and private spaces. A tree-lined walkway runs through the center of the complex. Intersecting this "car-less" boulevard are parks and playgrounds. As you walk through you'll have to remind yourself that you are only minutes from the heart of the downtown of a major city.

Continue south on Plymouth Court.

THE TOWNHOMES
1160-1182 S. Plymouth Court
Architect: Michael Realmuto (1986)

These strikingly modern buildings are a sharp contrast to the other buildings of Dearborn Park. The first floor contains the red brick seen on Printer's Row, but then a wild vernacular of colors and shapes comes into play. This includes cream-colored stuccoed walls and deep blue "streamlined" pipe rails. There are references to houses of the 19th century: oversized quoins, keystones, and window lintels, and a hint of gabled roofs.

Backtrack on Plymouth Court until you get to the sidewalk running along the south of the Townhouses. (Just to the south of 1156 S. Plymouth Court.) Turn west and walk ½ block. Enter through the black gates on your right. This is the interior walkway of the Townhouses.

Continue walking north and exit through the gates at the end. You will now be on Park Terrace. Continue north. The building west of the train station is called The Oaks.

THE OAKS
820 South Park Terrace
Architects: Dubin, Dubin, Black
and Moutoussamy (1978)

This 8-story, 190-unit apartment building was built as senior citizen housing with Section 8 funds from HUD. It has a reinforced concrete frame on caissons with a masonry exterior. There are protruding bays at the ends, and a nice glass atrium entrance. It is developed in two wings with elevators in a glazed bridge connecting link.

Walk north between the Oaks and Dearborn Street Station to return to Printer's Row.

11

1. Chicago Sun-Times Building
   401 N. Wabash Ave.

2. One IBM Plaza
   330 N. Wabash Ave.

3. Downtown Court Club
   441 N. Wabash Ave.

4. 420 N. Wabash Plaza
   420 N. Wabash Ave.

5. Tree Studios Building
   4 E. Ohio St.

6. Medinah Temple
   600 N. Wabash Ave.

7. Nickerson Mansion
   40 E. Erie St.

8. American College of Surgeons
   55 E. Erie St.

9. Episcopal Cathedral of St. James
   65 E. Huron Street

10. American Library Association
    50 E. Huron St.

11. National Congress of Parents and Teachers
    700 N. Rush St.

12. Catholic Cathedral of the Holy Name
    730 N. Wabash Ave.

13. Lewis Towers
    820 N. Michigan Ave.

14. James F. Maguire S. J. Hall
    1 E. Pearson St.

15. Chestnut Galleria
    1–15 E. Chestnut Street

16. Quigley Preparatory Seminary–North
    103 E. Chestnut St.

17. Newberry Library
    60 W. Walton St.

18. 2 E. Oak St.

19. Newberry Plaza
    1000–1050 N. State St.

20. Esquire Theatre
    53 E. Oak Street

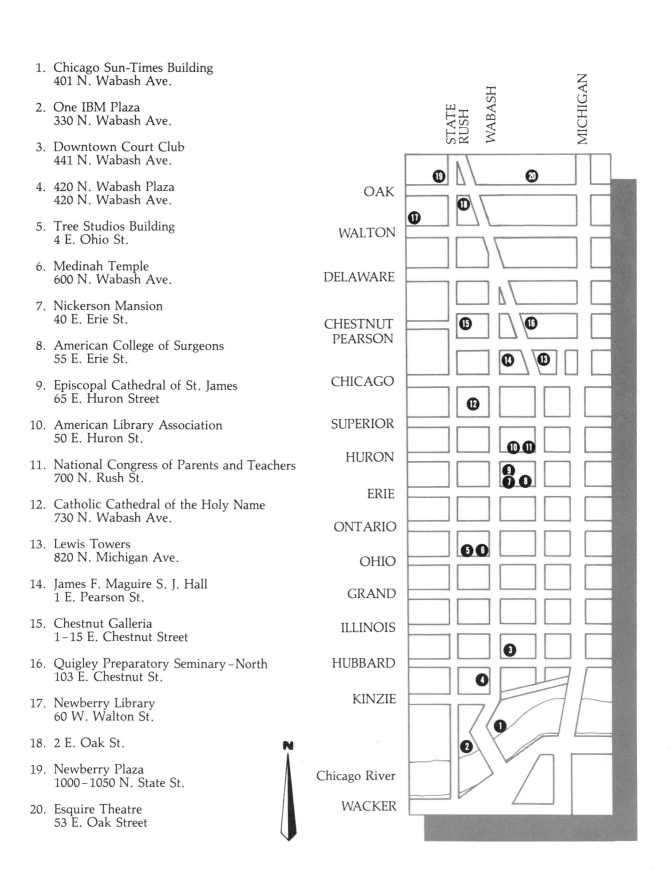

WALK • 11

NORTH WABASH AVENUE

WALKING TIME: About 2 hours. HOW TO GET THERE: Walk 1 block east of State Street at Randolph Street, then turn left on Wabash Avenue and walk 3 blocks north, crossing the Wabash Avenue bridge over the Chicago River.

If you are a lucky sightseer, you may arrive at the Chicago River just in time to see one or more of the bridges split in two and rise, permitting tall boats to pass by. These are bascule bridges, or—as they are sometimes called— "jackknife" bridges. Don't be in a hurry; both bridges and boats move slowly!

The WALK starts at the Chicago Sun-Times Building on the north bank of the Chicago River at Wabash Avenue.

CHICAGO SUN-TIMES BUILDING
401 N. WABASH AVENUE
ARCHITECTS: NAESS AND MURPHY (1957)

This modern newspaper plant is housed in a long, low building that faces the river the full length of its facade. The horizontal emphasis in the building's architecture contrasts with the many skyscrapers on all sides. As you walk inside to the main corridor, you will see the enclosed presses on one side of the building. Through the glass partition you can generally watch one of the newspaper editions going to press—a fascinating process to the uninitiated. Free tours through this busy modern newspaper plant are available at 10:30 a.m. weekdays. Call 321-2032 for reservations and information.

A pleasant open effect is achieved by the river beside the building and the Wrigley Building Plaza, which gives easy access to Michigan Avenue. The landscaped plaza on the east and a pedestrian walkway on the riverside contribute to making the building and its environs a pedestrian's delight. Take a short side trip to the plaza and over to the pedestrian walk from Wabash Avenue along the north bank of the river. On the way, note the charming small landscaped terrace built and maintained by Field Enterprises.

Overleaf: Tree Studios (Olga Stefanos)

159

ONE IBM PLAZA
330 N. WABASH AVENUE
ARCHITECTS: THE OFFICE OF MIES VAN DER ROHE
AND C. F. MURPHY ASSOCIATES (1971)

IBM's office building was designed to consolidate the offices of the International Business Machine Company's branches in downtown Chicago. The 52-story, steel-and-glass structure is sheathed in a curtain wall of bronze aluminum and tinted glass. The granite plaza is on a 1.6 acre site overlooking the Chicago River between Wabash Avenue and State Street.

At first glance the building may seem pristine or plain. A second glance will reveal the richness of the travertine marble lobby, the glass expanses, and the gray granite floor of the lobby and plaza. This is truly a great work of architecture. More than that, it is a final statement of one of the 20th century's most distinguished architects, Ludwig Mies van der Rohe. Chicago is indeed fortunate to have been the home, for over thirty years, of this superb interpreter of the machine age. He used the precision of the machine to make clean, sculptured monuments. Appropriately, the stunning lobby is enhanced by a bust of Mies van der Rohe.

There are 51 floors above the lobby. Of these, 46 are for office space. Two floors contain major computer facilities tied into a network of IBM computers across the country and available to other tenants in the building.

The building's special curtain wall and heating-cooling system were designed to meet the stringent humidity and temperature requirements of the computer areas. The building's power is all electric. Directly north, note the striking garage structure of Cor-Ten steel designed by George Schipporeit in 1972.

Before returning to Wabash Avenue, look west across State Street and see the gigantic home of the American Medical Association. Walk north.

DOWNTOWN COURT CLUB
441 N. WABASH AVENUE
ARCHITECTS: SOLOMON, CORDWELL AND BUENZ (1978)

Downtown Court Club is a fully equipped health facility located on a small urban site. The club's seven levels contain sixteen racketball and four tennis courts, a swimming pool, exercise rooms, lockers, saunas, lounges, pro-shop, restaurant, and self parking for 225 cars. The building's exterior is of simple ribbed-metal industrial siding.

160

420 N. WABASH PLAZA
420 N. WABASH AVENUE
ARCHITECTS: J. SPEYER AND SON (1908);
FOR ADAPTIVE REUSE: PAPPAGEORGE HAYMES (1983)

Originally the Great Western News Company Building, this 7-story structure with one basement on a wood pile foundation is a typical Chicago industrial building with heavy timber interior and a brick and terra-cotta exterior. The exterior has been restored, and the main entrance of the building was moved from Hubbard Street to Wabash Avenue. To dramatize the entrance, a glass curtainwall was set back to create a 5-story entry, which leads into a symmetrical axial hallway into the center of the building where the elevators have been relocated. The walls are detailed with aluminium reveals and there is a marble floor. All mechanical systems have been replaced. The building now has 100,000 square feet of office space and a restaurant on the Hubbard Street side.

Continue north to Ohio Street. Turn west.

◉ TREE STUDIOS BUILDING
4 E. OHIO STREET
ARCHITECTS: FOR STATE STREET SIDE:
PARFITT BROTHERS (1894);
FOR ADDITIONS ON ONTARIO AND OHIO STREETS:
HILL AND WOLTERSDORF (1912, 1913)

Walk west on Ohio Street to the other half of this block for a glimpse of the Tree Studios building. Though rather drab in outward appearance, this is nevertheless a unique structure, devoted to spacious artists' studios with high ceilings and large window areas. Judge Tree, whose wife was an artist, donated the building. Be sure to walk through the Ohio Street entrance, marked rather oddly "4-Tree Studios-6" for a pleasant surprise: on the other side of a small vestibule a door leads you again outdoors, into a delightful, hidden bit of park—with trees, flowers, and benches —which runs the length of the building. Since the park is enclosed on all sides, this gives special privacy to the studio entrances.

Walk back to Wabash Avenue.

MEDINAH TEMPLE
600 N. WABASH AVENUE
ARCHITECTS: HUEHL AND SCHMID (1912)

Now note the very large Medinah Temple at the northwest corner of Ohio Street and Wabash Avenue and extending to Ontario Street. The building with its Moorish style of architecture resembles a mosque, as of course the designer intended (it is the headquarters for the Chicago area Shriners). Inside are drill halls, offices, and an auditorium seating about 2,000, which is used for circus performances and other spectaculars as well as for the Medinah Shriners drill teams and bands.

Continue north 2 blocks on Wabash Avenue. On the northeast corner of Wabash Avenue and Erie Street is what was once one of the most opulent homes in Chicago, the Nickerson residence.

◉ NICKERSON MANSION
40 E. Erie Street
Architects: Burling and Whitehouse (1883)

This 3-story stone mansion of some 30 rooms was built for the Nickerson family more than 10 years after their previous home on the North Side had been destroyed by the Great Fire of 1871.

For more than 40 years the building was occupied by the American College of Surgeons (see the next stopping place). Nickerson himself, an active financier and one of the founders of the first bank in Chicago to become a national bank, enjoyed the mansion for many years, selling it only in his last years, when he returned East. In his day it was referred to as Nickerson's Marble Palace, and the richness of the interior certainly merits the name.

Fortunately, those who have used the building since Nickerson's day have cherished its original elegance and kept it in good condition. The mansion is a property of the American College of Surgeons and used by the college for special functions.

Walk east.

AMERICAN COLLEGE OF SURGEONS
55 E. Erie Street
Architects: Skidmore, Owings and Merrill (1963);
for addition: Graham, Anderson, Probst and White (1983)

From 1919 until the completion of this building in 1963, the College of Surgeons occupied the Nickerson Mansion just described. At 50 E. Erie Street, across the street immediately east of the Nickerson Mansion is the Auditorium used by the American College of Surgeons, the John B. Murphy Memorial. The ground on which the auditorium stands was once the side yard of the Nickerson Mansion.

162

St. James Cathedral reflected in the windows of the office headquarters and parish house. (Allen Carr)

Backtrack west to Wabash Avenue. Turn north to Huron Street.

EPISCOPAL CATHEDRAL OF ST. JAMES
65 E. Huron Street
Architects: Edward Burling (1856);
for the reconstruction: Burling and Adler
(possibly with Clarke and Faulkner) (1875);
Civil War Memorial Tower: Calvert Vaux and
Frederick Law Olmstead (1867);
St. Andrew's Chapel: Bertram Goodhue
and Ralph Cram (1913);
Office Headquarters and Parish House:
James Hammond and Peter Roesch (1968-9);
for the restoration: Holabird and Root (1985)

This structure is typical of a number of churches built shortly before and after the Great Fire of 1871, for which architects followed the Gothic style in a free, somewhat inventive manner. These churches were often built of local limestone, called Joliet stone or Lemont limestone, which is seen in this building. To the east of the church is a stunning office headquarters and parish house of contemporary design.

163

In 1985, the church underwent extensive restoration. The roof was redone, and the stonework (especially of the east side of the tower) was restored. On the interior, the basement and main floor were remodeled; the ornamental windows and the nave floor were replaced. The spectacular 1888 interior finishes (an Arts and Crafts Movement stencil project, of twenty-six different colors, with stylized plant motifs as the central theme, the work of New York architect E. J. Neville Stemt) were restored under the direction of project architect Walker Johnson and paint consultant Robert Furhoff.

On the north side of Huron Street are two buildings dedicated to educational purposes.

AMERICAN LIBRARY ASSOCIATION
50 E. Huron Street
Architects: Holabird and Root (1961-63)

McCormick House—the home of Cyrus H. McCormick II until 1889 or so—was on this site. That structure was used as the headquarters of the ALA from 1945 until it was razed prior to the construction of this building.

Both the ALA and the PTA have expanded their headquarters by the purchase of property on Rush Street. The PTA owns the building just north of its 700 N. Rush Street headquarters and the ALA is at work in a building at 716 N. Rush.

On the northwest corner of Huron and Rush streets is the headquarters building of the PTA.

NATIONAL CONGRESS OF PARENTS AND TEACHERS
700 N. Rush Street
Architects: Holabird and Root (1954)

Funds to meet the expenses of constructing the National PTA building came largely from individual or PTA donations of anywhere from ten cents to ten dollars. "Quarters for Headquarters" was the slogan, and PTA members all across the country contributed whatever they could to provide a home of their own, where the national staff might work in more space and better conditions than had been possible previously in their rented offices. PTAs may well be proud of the result, for the building was cited for excellence of design soon after it was completed.

Walk west on Huron Street to Wabash Avenue. Turn north. In the next few blocks you will come to a variety of buildings representing the Roman Catholic Archdiocese in Chicago.

164

CATHOLIC CATHEDRAL OF THE HOLY NAME
730 N. WABASH AVENUE
ARCHITECTS: P. C. KELLY (1874);
HENRY J. SCHLACKS (1915);
FOR RENOVATION: C. F. MURPHY AND ASSOCIATES (1969)

The cathedral and the immediately related buildings occupy the entire block between Wabash Avenue and State Street, Superior Street and Chicago Avenue. School buildings, parish houses, convent and church are all built in a similar style—the neo-Gothic used so widely for places of worship.

To the north, on the east side of Wabash Avenue and extending to Rush Street and then Michigan Avenue, are buildings used by the Loyola University of Chicago graduate school.

Walk north to Chicago Avenue. Turn east and walk on the north side of the street. The sign before Michigan Avenue also says "Michigan Avenue," but don't get confused—yet. Turn north before the Water Tower (which is featured in WALK 12). The third building on your left is Lewis Towers.

LEWIS TOWERS
820 N. MICHIGAN AVENUE
ARCHITECTS: SCHMIDT, GARDEN AND ERIKSON (1925)

The structure that gives this complex of buildings its name is a converted office building on Rush Street (though the official address of the complex is North Michigan Avenue) donated by the late Frank Lewis, Chicago philanthropist. A newer building on the west side of Rush, connected with Lewis Towers at the 2nd floor by a covered walkway over the street, carries the name "Pere Marquette Campus."

Walk west on Pearson Street to State Street. The next building is at the Loyola University School of Law.

JAMES F. MAGUIRE S. J. HALL
1 E. PEARSON STREET
ARCHITECTS: GRAHAM, ANDERSON, PROBST AND WHITE (1979)

This 5-floor brick and steel frame building has a courtroom and lecture hall on the first floor; classrooms, seminar rooms, and a lounge on the second floor; a law library on the third and fourth floors; and administration offices on the top floor.

Walk north on State Street to Chestnut Street. Turn east.

Cathedral of the
Holy Name
(Philip A. Turner)

CHESTNUT GALLERIA
1-15 E. Chestnut Street
Architects for the adaptive reuse: Booth/Hansen
and Associates (1984-85)

Chestnut Galleria is the renovation of four turn-of-the-century apartment buildings into a new retail and business complex. The design unifies the original four buildings with a common curtainwall system and a new plaza, but uses a different color for each building to keep them separate. New retail space was established at the basement, ground, and second floors throughout the project by punching through existing party walls. Upper floor tenants share a new atrium entry with elevators and stairs in what was once an exterior rear courtyard.

Continue east. On the southeast corner of Rush and Chestnut streets, you will find the imposing buildings of a seminary where youngsters start their training for the priesthood.

QUIGLEY PREPARATORY SEMINARY—NORTH
103 E. Chestnut Street
Architect: Gustav Steinbeck of New York City (1918)

Archbishop James E. Quigley in 1905 had established what was then called Cathedral College. He died before his plans for an expanded school could be carried out, but his successor—Cardinal George Mundelein—fulfilled his aims. Many of the funds came as gifts from children of the archdiocese, and the school's name was changed to make it a memorial to the man who had originally planned it.

At Quigley Seminary you feel that you are standing before a great French Gothic municipal hall of the 12th century. Various Gothic features combine to give the effect of an authentic medieval structure: the rose window over the chapel entrance, the sculpture on either side, the high-pitched roofs, the buttresses on the Chestnut Street side, and the medieval courtyard. They almost make you expect to see knights in armor ride in on horseback—until you catch a glimpse of the 20th century cars parked inside the courtyard! Whatever Louis Sullivan might have thought of the architecture, this is a most impressive complex of buildings.

At this point, you are at Rush and Chestnut streets, and it is suggested that you include in your WALK a particularly rewarding structure—the Newberry Library. Walk north on Rush Street to Delaware Street, then walk west to Dearborn Street. Now you are at Washington Square on which the Newberry Library faces from the north.

167

NEWBERRY LIBRARY

60 W. Walton Street
Architect: Henry Ives Cobb (1892);
for renovations: Harry Weese and Associates (1960-)

Washington Square is precisely the amount of open space necessary to properly view the Newberry Library. A few other institutional buildings line the east and south perimeters. Together, they form the classic relationship of low structural mass and open space to give the viewer the delightful experience of enjoying architecture in a way that was afforded pedestrians during the Classic and Renaissance periods in Europe.

This library of splendid Spanish Romanesque design stands on the site of the Mahlan Ogden house, a wooden mansion that miraculously escaped the Great Fire of 1871 but was later razed to make way for this building. Newberry Library was created by a bequest from Walter Loomis Newberry, an early Chicago businessman. The Newberry Library houses outstanding collections of reference materials—both bound and unbound matter—that are used by scholars working on advanced research projects in the humanities.

The Newberry Library, with its Cyclopean granite stonework, St. Giles portico and powerful cornice, has been a landmark on the north side of Chicago's Washington Square since 1893. The renovations to the Newberry Library have been an ongoing process of over twenty years, as the needs and demands of that institution have grown and changed. When a decision was made to update the facility, the Board of Trustees was faced with a difficult choice—to restore a structurally sound but mechanically obsolete, 19th-century Romanesque Revival building, or to demolish it in favor of new construction. The spacious rooms, mosaic tile, oak paneling, and marble floors and wainscots would be far too difficult and costly to replace. The loss would have been great if the Board had opted for a new facility. It was discovered that restoring the original building was significantly more economical than constructing a new library of equivalent size and grace.

The first phase of the renovation began in 1960. In order to safeguard the library's renowned collection, air conditioning was installed to maintain 50 percent relative humidity at 70 degrees F. The existing 16- to 20-foot ceilings allowed for the addition of an air circulation system contained in trapezoidal enclosures. Due to their shape, these enclosures minimized the impact of the mod-

168

Newberry Library
(courtesy Harry
Weese & Associates)

ernization efforts upon the existing architectural detail. Supply
ducts and return plenums distribute air through nozzles between
corridors and adjacent reading rooms. Other restorative changes
include the replacement of the original wood sash with insulated
aluminum windows and the addition of new elevators and
mechanical rooms located on either side of the existing monumental staircase. Throughout all phases of construction and
renovation, utmost care was taken to insure the safety of the
collections.

Before leaving, note that Washington Square during warm
weather is a resting place for people of the neighborhood and
vagrants. In the 1920s—and until as recently as the 1950s—it
served as a forum for any radical or far-out speaker who chose to
lend his oratory to the crowds that gathered each night in
anticipation.

If you desire, return to Michigan Avenue by walking east on
Oak Street. You will see a variety of chic stores, shops, galleries,
and restaurants for several blocks.

Esquire Theater
(Olga Stefanos)

To continue the WALK, walk east on Walton Street to State Street, and turn north. On the northeast corner of State and Oak streets is 2 E. Oak Street.

2 E. OAK STREET
Architect: Joel R. Hillman (1972)

The narrow but striking triangular concrete apartment building is bounded by Oak, State, and Rush streets. Also housed here are a theater and a restaurant.

Continue north. On the west side of State Street between Oak and Maple streets is a stunning concrete tower apartment building.

NEWBERRY PLAZA
1000-1050 N. State Street
Architects: Ezra Gordon and Jack Levin (1972-4)

A unique feature of the complex is the town houses on the south roof. Also note the striking entrance.

Backtrack south to Oak Street and turn east.

170

ESQUIRE THEATRE
53 E. Oak Street
Architects: William and Hal Pereira (1937)

This building was one of the first attempts at producing a modern theme for the motion picture theater, which up to then had been completely wallowing in "borax" architecture. Also in the area are several high-rise apartment buildings.

12

1. Wrigley Building
   400 N. Michigan Ave.

2. Equitable Building
   401 N. Michigan Ave.

3. Mandel Building
   425 N. Michigan Ave.

4. Tribune Tower
   435 N. Michigan Ave.

5. Uptown Federal Savings and
   Loan Association Building
   430 N. Michigan Ave.

6. 444 N. Michigan Ave.

7. 500 N. Michigan Avenue Building

8. The Hotel Continental
   505 N. Michigan Ave.

9. Michigan Terrace Apartments
   535 N. Michigan Ave.

10. Time-Life Building
    303 E. Ohio St.

11. McClurg Court Center
    333 E. Ontario St.

12. Museum of Contemporary Art
    237 E. Ontario St.

13. 625 N. Michigan Avenue Building

14. Arts Club of Chicago
    109 E. Ontario St.

15. Woman's Athletic Club
    626 N. Michigan Ave.

16. Saks Fifth Avenue Building
    669 N. Michigan Ave.

17. Allerton Hotel
    701 N. Michigan Ave.

18. Sheraton Plaza Hotel

19. Barclay Chicago Hotel
    166 E. Superior St.

20. Olympia Centre
    737 N. Michigan Ave.

21. Arby's
    115 E. Chicago Ave.

22. American Dental Association Building
    211 E. Chicago Ave.

23. Water Tower
    800 N. Michigan Ave.

24. Water Tower Pumping Station
    163 E. Pearson St.

25. I. Magnin Store Building
    830 N. Michigan Ave.

26. Water Tower Place
    845 N. Michigan Ave.

27. 111 E. Chestnut Street

28. Fourth Presbyterian Church
    126 E. Chestnut St.

29. John Hancock Center
    875 N. Michigan Ave.

30. 110 E. Delaware Pl.

31. 900 N. Michigan Ave.

32. The Westin Hotel
    909 N. Michigan Ave.

33. Playboy Building
    919 N. Michigan Ave.

34. Knickerbocker Hotel
    163 E. Walton Pl.

35. Walton Colonnade Apartment Building
    100 E. Walton St.

36. One Magnificent Mile
    950–980 N. Michigan Ave.

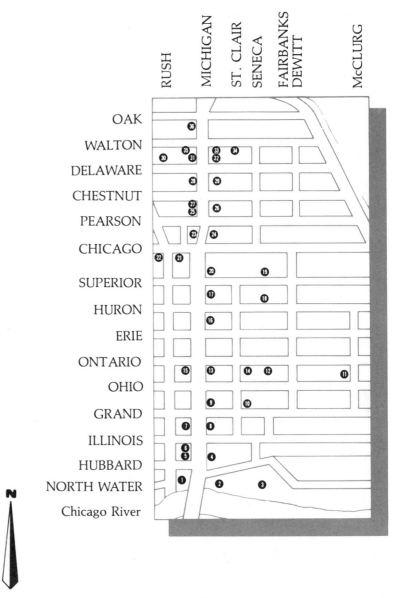

WALK • 12

MICHIGAN AVENUE: THE MAGNIFICENT MILE

WALKING TIME: About 2½ hours. HOW TO GET THERE: Take one of the following northbound CTA busses on State Street: No. 11, No. 146, No. 147, or No. 151. Get off at the Michigan Avenue bridge, Michigan Avenue and East Wacker Drive [300 N].

Where Chicago's Magnificent Mile begins, just north of the Chicago River, are buildings of contrasting architecture. The development of this part of Michigan Avenue, featuring both revivalist and contemporary styles, might be said to date from the 1920s, when both the street and underground levels of the Michigan Avenue bridge were completed.

During the growing season, trees, flowers, and shrubbery give this part of North Michigan Avenue color, texture, and beauty. It is a pleasure to stroll here and view these outdoor attractions as well as the enticing window displays of jewelry, books, and wearing apparel. At Christmastime, tiny Italian bulbs strung on the branches of all the trees on the Avenue create an air of enchantment.

WRIGLEY BUILDING
400 N. MICHIGAN AVENUE
ARCHITECTS: GRAHAM, ANDERSON, PROBST,
AND WHITE (1921, 1924)

The gleaming white Wrigley Building (named for the family of chewing-gum fame) with its finger-like clock tower rises from the northern edge of the Chicago River. The white terra-cotta with which the building is covered and the powerful floodlights focused on it every night make this always a conspicuous part of the Chicago skyline. Featuring baroque terra-cotta ornamentation, the building is an architectural link to Chicago's earlier days. Between the main building and its annex (built in 1924) is an attractive small plaza.

Overleaf: John Hancock Center
(Philip A. Turner)

175

Wrigley Building
(Bill Engdahl,
Hedrich-Blessing)

Equitable Building
(Philip A. Turner)

EQUITABLE BUILDING
401 N. MICHIGAN AVENUE
ARCHITECTS: SKIDMORE, OWINGS, AND MERRILL;
ALFRED SHAW AND ASSOCIATES (1965)

The Equitable Building stands like another sentinel on the east side of the avenue. Set far back from the street, it is approached through a spacious plaza called Pioneer Court, which includes an attractive fountain with the names of early Chicago leaders—its pioneers—inscribed around the base. From Pioneer Court a stairway leads down to the lower level of the building and to the restaurant and shops which overlook the river bank.

The building itself, a 40-story structure of metal and glass, is clearly a product of the 20th century, with a variation in the window arrangement that gives it special character. The slender external piers that separate the regular groups of 4 windows each have supportive value and are more than ornamental. They also contain pipes for pumping hot or cold air into the offices as needed—from machinery located at the top and bottom of the building.

Directly to the east, at 425 N. Michigan Avenue, is the red brick 13-story Mandel Building.

MANDEL BUILDING
425 N. MICHIGAN AVENUE
ARCHITECTS: GRAHAM, ANDERSON, PROBST
AND WHITE (1926);
FOR REHABILITATION: HOLABIRD AND ROOT (1976)

Originally the Hibbard Spencer Bartlett Building, the Mandel Building now contains the stacks and main reference center that were formerly housed in the main building of the Chicago Public Library. This is a temporary facility until the new structure is completed (see pp. 42-3).

The library is open Monday through Thursday 9 a.m. to 7 p.m.; Fridays 9 a.m. to 6 p.m.; Saturdays 9 a.m. to 5 p.m.

TRIBUNE TOWER
435 N. MICHIGAN AVENUE
ARCHITECTS: HOOD AND HOWELLS (1925)

The Tribune Tower, a Gothic revival skyscraper, has long been a Chicago landmark. North Michigan Avenue would not be the same without the Wrigley Building, Water Tower, and the

Tribune Tower
(Philip A. Turner)

Tribune Tower. They are synonymous with the growth and strength of Chicago.

In 1922, the Tribune's publisher, the late Robert R. McCormick, for whom McCormick Place was named, held an international competition for the design of the building. Architects from all over the world responded and out of the many designs, the winners selected were Raymond Hood and John Mead Howells, prominent New York architects.

The great Gothic arch entrance is quite impressive as are the pieces of stone set around the base of the building. The small pieces of stone are from famous buildings around the world, such as Westminster Abbey, Cologne Cathedral, the Arch of Triumph in Paris, the Holy Door of St. Peter's in Rome, and even the Taj Mahal.

You must step across the street to see the crowning glory of this unusual building, the great flying buttresses, like those on the exterior of European Gothic cathedrals. To see the sunlight piercing the buttresses is a remarkable sight and most rewarding to all photographers.

Along the south side of the building located just east of Tribune Tower are displayed oversized reproductions of the front pages of eighteen issues of the Tribune with headlines of great national events dating back to the last century. The pages are in the form of copper etchings. The brick-fronted building, now refaced in limestone to match the adjoining tower, was designed by architect Jarvis Hunt in 1920.

WGN radio recently moved its offices and studios to Tribune Tower. The public will be able to watch local radio personalities doing their shows through a glass-fronted studio on the southwest corner of the building.

Just north of the Tower is the Annex, used for Tribune offices. This is a 4-story Gothic structure with an Indiana limestone skin, like the Tower. There is a statue of Revolutionary War hero Nathan Hale in the courtyard.

Cross to the west side of Michigan Avenue.

UPTOWN FEDERAL SAVINGS AND LOAN ASSOCIATION BUILDING
430 N. MICHIGAN AVENUE
ARCHITECT: FRED H. PRATHER (1963);
FOR REMODELING: HAGUE RICHARDS (1972)

This white marble structure is a fine example of a well-planned institution. As a part of the original design, a plaza was designed to represent all the flags of the nations in this hemisphere. Named "The Plaza of the Americas," it features a flagpole and flag for each nation, with the exception of Cuba. There are lunchtime presentations in the summertime.

Walk north.

444 N. MICHIGAN AVENUE
ARCHITECTS: PERKINS & WILL (1976)

Though not originally designed for commercial purposes, this striking all-reinforced concrete structure is now an office building. It is 36 stories, with about 500,000 square feet.

Continue north.

500 N. MICHIGAN AVENUE BUILDING
ARCHITECTS: SKIDMORE, OWINGS AND MERRILL (1970)

This efficiently designed travertine marble structure expresses the steel-and-concrete construction it conceals. This handsome building was expressly designed for office use.

THE HOTEL CONTINENTAL
505 N. MICHIGAN AVENUE
ARCHITECTS: FOR SOUTH TOWER,
WALTER W. AHLSCHLAGER (1929);
FOR NORTH TOWER, QUINN AND CHRISTENSEN (1961)

The hotel includes two towers and a below-level parking garage. The south tower was once the Medinah Athletic Club and still carries the ornament of its earlier function, including the Oriental turret and onion-shaped dome at the top.

Continue north.

MICHIGAN TERRACE APARTMENTS
535 N. MICHIGAN AVENUE
ARCHITECTS: RICHARD A. RAGGI AND
GUENTER MALITZ (1962)

Here is a fine example of the urban center living with amenities that include an indoor swimming pool, lower level garage and restaurant. The building is 33 stories and contains 480 apartments. The exterior is white glazed brick with yellow glazed brick spandrels. The bay windows and tinted glass as well as the marble base combine to make an inviting structure.

Next, walk north to Ohio Street. Turn east and walk about 2 blocks to the Time-Life Building.

TIME-LIFE BUILDING
303 E. Ohio Street
Architects: Harry Weese and Associates;
Jerry Shlaes (1968)

Time-Life Building
(Daniel Bartush
courtesy Harry Weese
& Associates)

The Chicago Time-Life Building has entrances on East Ohio Street and North Fairbanks Court. The building is a 30-story structure that rises to a height of 400 feet with a gross floor area of 700,000 square feet. The building is a rectangular tower 3 bays wide by 7 bays long. Each bay is 30 feet square.

The structure is concrete with a metal curtain wall of weathering steel which will gradually weather to a deep brown. The windows are of gold, mirrored glass; the elevator shafts and lobby walls are covered with granite. The same granite is used in the sidewalk paving and the floors of the lobby. Typical floors begin 87 feet above the sidewalk. The typical floor has no exposed columns.

The regular bay spacing, exposed structure, and horizontal emphasis of windows is in the tradition of the Chicago school, the early office buildings of Louis Sullivan, Carson Pirie Scott and Company department store, as well as the past period inspired by Mies van der Rohe. This superbly designed building is well worth your spending more time here than you originally anticipated.

Time Incorporated Subscription Services is one of the largest mailing operations in the country. Operations require that the 1,800 employees begin at the same time. For this reason, the 12-passenger elevators employ tandem cabs. The 2-story elevator cabs were first used in the United States in this building. During peak hours the 1,800 employees can be handled most efficiently, with those wishing to go to odd-numbered floors entering the cabs at the lower level, and those wishing to go to even-numbered floors entering from the upper lobby. After the peak has subsided, the system can be switched to normal service in which only the upper half of the 2-story cab is used, stopping at each floor in the conventional manner. On the upper lobby level is the Time Library, containing all past copies of Time, Incorporated publications. The Time Gallery, located in the lower level of the arcade, is used for public exhibitions.

Now walk 1 block north, then 1 block east on Ontario Street to a large city within a city.

McCLURG COURT CENTER
333 E. Ontario Street
Architects: Solomon, Cordwell
and Buenz (1971)

McClurg Court Center
(Philip A. Turner)

McClurg Court Center covers most of the city block between Ontario and Ohio streets, Fairbanks and McClurg courts. It is a fascinating example of the trend in inner-city living towards obtaining maximum security for all the tenants. In this case when a tenant enters the Center, he has at his disposal all the necessities of life that make it unnecessary to step out after dark.

These twin 46-story apartment towers were built with economical rectangular construction with curved columnless corners. Exposed concrete shear walls create a visual counterpoint to the exterior bronze, metal, and glass curtainwall. They also serve to restrain the buildings against the wind and offer the viewer a dramatic demonstration of power and strength. The towers were located to maximize apartment views and free the remaining site for the many facilities.

The project was conceived as a total in-city living center. Besides covered parking facilities, McClurg Court Center contains 1,028 dwelling units, a 1,250-seat movie theater, and three tennis courts enclosed in the metal pavilion at the west end of the Center. There are also complete health club facilities, including a swimming pool. There are shops for the convenience of the tenants that service their needs.

Walk west on Ontario Street.

MUSEUM OF CONTEMPORARY ART
237 E. Ontario Street
Architect: Unknown (1915);
for remodeling: Brenner, Danforth
and Rockwell (1967);
Larry Booth (1979)

In October, 1967, the Museum of Contemporary Art opened in a building previously used by Playboy Magazine, remodeled (by one of its founding members) for its present purpose. The 1979 remodeling added a connection to the neighboring building. Although the Museum had no permanent collection when it opened, now there are collections of artists' books, prints, sculpture, and drawings reflecting contemporary art trends. The Museum continues its support of avant-garde art by presenting a new show periodically. If you are one who thinks that art consists only of oil paintings on canvas or representational statuary, you may find this museum disturbing. But you can't fail to find it exciting, and you shouldn't miss it. The Museum is open Tuesday through Saturday from 10:00 a.m. to 5:00 p.m.; Sunday from noon to 5:00 p.m.; closed Monday.

Walk west to Michigan Avenue. Turn left.

625 N. MICHIGAN AVENUE BUILDING
ARCHITECTS: MEISTER AND VOLPE ARCHITECTS (1971);
FOR REMODELING: MURPHY/JAHN (1984-5)

The exterior of the building is of exposed, smooth, formed architectural concrete. Special aggregate, sand, and cement were used to achieve the building's distinctive buff color. The lower portion of the building was sandblasted to give the concrete an even more textured appearance.

This 27-story reinforced-concrete office building was the winner of the 1971 first prize from the Concrete Contractors Association of Greater Chicago. Among the building's unusual architectural features is its corner treatment. Structural corner columns were eliminated to provide open corner windows for executive offices.

In 1985, the entrance was remodeled by Murphy/Jahn. A new glass atrium entrance was added at street level. The handsome design has forest green marble and ivory terrazzo floors.

Cross Michigan Avenue and walk west on Ontario Street. An indispensable inside visit for this WALK is the Arts Club of Chicago, on the 2nd floor of 109 E. Ontario Street.

ARTS CLUB OF CHICAGO
109 E. ONTARIO STREET
ARCHITECT FOR THE CLUB'S INTERIOR:
LUDWIG MIES VAN DER ROHE (1955)

Quite aside from any exhibit there, the interior of the club is worth seeing, since it was designed by Mies van der Rohe. Though private, the club opens all its exhibits to the public. Over the years it has a history of most distinguished exhibits, many of them the first in Chicago—or even in the country—of works by artists later recognized as of world importance. Rodin, Picasso, Toulouse-Lautrec, Vlaminck, Utrillo, and Brancusi, for instance, were given early one-man showings by the Arts Club of Chicago.

Across the street is the Woman's Athletic Club.

WOMAN'S ATHLETIC CLUB
626 N. MICHIGAN AVENUE
ARCHITECTS: PHILIP B. MAHER AND
ASSOCIATES (1928)

183

This low-key, carefully designed structure is representative of some of the best work by architects in the 1920s. The structure is 9 stories on pile foundations. The Bedford limestone and pressed-brick exterior articulate the air of quiet elegance of the interior.

Now, cross to the east side of Michigan Avenue.

SAKS FIFTH AVENUE BUILDING
669 N. MICHIGAN AVENUE
ARCHITECTS: PHILIP B. MAHER AND
ASSOCIATES (1925);
FOR THE REMODELING AND ADDITION:
HOLABIRD AND ROOT (1966)

The North Michigan Avenue branch of this nationally known department store chain is housed in a complex of three elegant buildings. The two oldest, 669 and 671-75 N. Michigan Avenue, were originally the Blackstone Shop. Remodeling of these two structures and the addition of the third, 11-story, building was done by Holabird and Root.

Walk north on Michigan Avenue.

ALLERTON HOTEL
701 N. MICHIGAN AVENUE
ARCHITECTS: MURGATROYD AND OGDEN (1924)

This 25-story, famous hotel includes the equally famous Gucci shop. As you walk north on Michigan Avenue, you will pass Tiffany's and the Elizabeth Arden Building.

Before you continue north, look directly east of the Allerton Hotel at the striking Sheraton Plaza Hotel.

SHERATON PLAZA HOTEL
160 E. HURON STREET
ARCHITECT: JOEL R. HILLMAN (1973)

This reinforced concrete, 24-story, multi-use structure was formerly the Knott Hotel and Office Building.

Continue north to Superior Street. Turn east.

BARCLAY CHICAGO HOTEL
166 E. SUPERIOR STREET
ARCHITECT: JOEL R. HILLMAN (1965);
FOR THE REMODELING: LOUIS ARTHUR WEISS
AND GERALD O'HARA (1982)

184

This 28-story building originally had offices on the lower seven floors and apartments above. Now the 7th floor has the private Barclay Club and floors 8-27 are remodeled into 120 hotel suites, with meeting rooms above. The ground floor, originally set back 20 feet for the entrance, has been filled in to increase the lobby, and round bay windows and a canopy have been added to enhance the entrance.

Walk back to Michigan Avenue.

OLYMPIA CENTRE
737 N. MICHIGAN AVENUE
ARCHITECTS: SKIDMORE, OWINGS AND MERRILL (1984)

Olympia Centre combines a 63-story tower with a 4-story Nieman Marcus department store. The design was chosen to preserve the low-to-middle-rise retail character of Michigan Avenue and Superior Street, and to reinforce the open space edge already existing along Chicago Avenue. It also provides better views for the condominiums in the tower. The tower's tube structure is articulated by highlighting portions of the columns and window sills. At the top 6 floors the enclosed area is stepped inward from the corners, leaving a skeletal frame which provides a sense of enclosure for the interior terraces. The building is clad in granite in varying finishes. Windows are glazed with tinted and insulated glass in coated aluminum frames. Patterns of granite jointing and storefront articulation carry through from the north

Olympia Centre, street level and tower (Hedrich-Blessing courtesy Skidmore, Owings and Merrill)

185

Water Tower
(Philip A. Turner)

to south side, unifying the visual impression of the base and tower and the low-rise retail store. Note the magnificent arch, where a light fixture occupies the place usually reserved for a keystone—unnecessary with today's structural technology.

Continue north to Chicago Avenue. Turn west.

ARBY'S
115 E. Chicago Avenue
Architects for the remodeling: Stanley Tigerman,
David Woodhouse, associate in charge (1979)

This is a major remodeling and renovation of an existing 20-foot wide, 4-story structure. The facade as infill is clad in stucco and glass with straight and curved sections of both transparent and opaque materials. The envelope is effectively detailed as a flush precise white and transparent skin, almost as "non-architecture."

Walk east on Chicago Avenue, past Michigan Avenue.

AMERICAN DENTAL ASSOCIATION BUILDING
211 E. Chicago Avenue
Architects: Graham, Anderson, Probst
and White (1966)

In marked contrast with the historic Water Tower is the 23-story building just east of Michigan on Chicago Avenue, a slender, stately structure used as the headquarters of the American Dental Association.

On both sides of Michigan Avenue at Chicago Avenue, stands one of Chicago's most famous—though by no means its most beautiful—landmarks, the Water Tower and Pumping Station.

Return to Michigan Avenue.

◉ WATER TOWER
800 N. Michigan Avenue

◉ WATER TOWER PUMPING STATION
163 E. Pearson Street
Architect: W. W. Boyington (1867-69);
for the interior renovations: Lloyd van Meter,
Loebl, Schlossman and Hackl (1978);
for restoration of park: City of Chicago (1978);
for adaptive reuse: Michael Arenson
and Associates (1983)

The oldest structure in the city, the elaborate tower symbolizes Chicago's historic growth. When it was built two years before the

Great Fire, this fantastic, pseudo-Gothic creation, with its many turrets rising around the central tower like a section of a medieval castle, was considered a most artistically satisfactory disguise of the standpipe it concealed.

Its design is far removed from what was developed later in the century by the Chicago school of architecture—except that in a sense its form did follow function (or at least originated in function) as those later builders insisted a building should. Within the tower was an iron standpipe 3 feet in diameter and nearly 150 feet high that stored the water supply for the Near North Side.

In the recent restoration the park was restored with the railing and light fixtures obtained from the public viewing galley of the Lake View Pumping Station, which was scheduled for demolition at the time. Five Kennedy hydrants from before the turn of the century were obtained for the Department of Water and brought to the site. The drinking fountain, a "3-level" design (for people at the top, horses in the middle, and dogs at the bottom), was obtained from the Chicago Park District. The north stairs were replaced with limestone from Valders, Wisconsin; the stone, equal in color and texture to Joliet limestone but more dense, was chosen because it should last longer.

Call the Visitor's Center at 225-5000 for more information. The Center also has a 24-hour event line (225-2323) with information on sports, theater, museums, events in the City's plazas, etc.

Across the street is the pumping station—still in use!— built of the same Joliet limestone but with less elaborate ornamentation. In 1867 it was noteworthy that the then new station could pump as much as 18 million gallons a day. Historic notes on the back of a menu for the Water Tower Cornerstone Centennial Luncheon in March, 1967 (sponsored by the Greater North Michigan Avenue Association) pointed out that the 1967 capacity of Chicago's water system was then 3 billion gallons a day. It still supplies 40 percent of Chicago's water today.

Though long ago the Water Tower ceased to be of any use as a standpipe, the City cherishes its presence in the midst of Michigan Avenue traffic. For all its antiquated style of architecture, it seems strangely appropriate here among the beautiful modern structures. By its very contrast in style, it is a reminder of Chicago's triumph over the Great Fire of 1871, which destroyed practically everything else in this part of Chicago but was followed by a period of unprecedented building and architectural progress.

In 1983 the old boiler rooms in the Pumping Station were redesigned into theaters which show *Here's Chicago*. The workshops were converted into a lobby and gift shop. There is also a display by the Chicago Historical Society. The interior, which had been covered or destroyed over the years, was restored. Now you can see the Gothic terra-cotta detailing in the interior. The tower was designated as an Historic Landmark by the City Council in 1971.

Here's Chicago is a dazzling sound and sight show, a must for any visitor to Chicago. Shows are every half hour, starting at 9:30 a.m. Adults: $3.75; children and senior citizens: $2. Call 467-7114 for information.

Walk north.

I. MAGNIN STORE BUILDING
830 N. MICHIGAN AVENUE
ARCHITECTS: SHAW, METZ AND ASSOCIATES (1958);
FOR REMODELING AND ADDITION: SOLOMON, CORDWELL
AND BUENZ (1971)

I. Magnin Building
(Howard N. Kaplan
courtesy Solomon,
Cordwell and Buenz)

The building was originally occupied by Bonwit Teller, who then moved into the lower floors of the John Hancock Building when it was built. A floor was added to the top, increasing the height to 5 stories, and a 5-story, 52-foot section was added at the west end of the store building. The fifth floor preserved the vertical street scale, and the slightly projecting panels below that floor strengthen the linear scale of the structure and lower the apparent building height.

A large parking garage and apartment building are immediately adjacent to the west. Across Pearson Street, to the west and south, are the Park Hyatt on Water Tower Square and the Lewis Towers of Loyola University of Chicago.

WATER TOWER PLACE
845 N. MICHIGAN AVENUE
ARCHITECTS: LOEBL, SCHLOSSMAN, BENNETT AND DART
AND C. F. MURPHY AND ASSOCIATES (1976)

This complex covers the area bounded by Michigan Avenue and Pearson, Seneca and Chestnut streets. This multiple-use all marble structure is an astounding combination of commercial and residential uses. The 12-story base contains a shopping complex and office space.

The unique urban shopping complex on the first seven floors is constructed around a grand atrium and five courts. With more than 610,000 square feet of floor space, the shopping center

Fourth Presbyterian
Church
(Chicago Plan
Commission)

accommodates some 100 stores, shops, and boutiques. Marshall Field and Company and Lord and Taylor, the major tenants, occupy nearly half the retail space.

The 8th and 9th floors provide more than 200,000 square feet of office space. The 10th and 11th floors include the health spa facilities of the Ritz-Carlton Hotel and mechanical system. The 12th floor contains the hotel restaurant facilities.

Rising from the southeast corner, 162 E. Pearson Street, is a 62-

story tower with the Ritz-Carlton Hotel and luxury condominium residences.

Walk west on Chestnut Street.

111 E. CHESTNUT STREET
ARCHITECTS: SOLOMON, CORDWELL AND BUENZ (1971-72)

This 57-story residential tower, placed at the back of the property which includes the I. Magnin store in the front, was built to make maximum use of the site. The cast-in-place concrete tower was designed to harmonize with the extant limestone store. The existing store building was expanded and totally remodeled. A 6th floor was added to the top and a 6-story addition was added along one side of the existing building. The building was given a limestone facade to unify the old and new parts and relate to the neighboring stone structures. The apartment tower provides 444 apartments over a 7-story parking garage.

Return to Michigan Avenue.

◉ FOURTH PRESBYTERIAN CHURCH
126 E. CHESTNUT STREET
ARCHITECTS: RALPH ADAMS CRAM (1912);
FOR PARISH HOUSE: HOWARD VAN DOREN SHAW (1925)

Providing a diametric contrast is the Fourth Presbyterian Church, famed for its modified Gothic style. The architect designed many other Gothic revival buildings. The modifications executed here can be seen in such things as the narrowness of the side aisles and the placement of a balcony in the transept space. The building, and a connecting arcade, are of carved Bedford stone and surround a grass plot. The stained glass windows were designed by Charles Connick.

Across Michigan Avenue, you will be overwhelmed by the 100-story John Hancock Center, towering more than 1,000 feet in the air. It dominates the vicinity and the skyline much as the Eiffel Tower does in Paris. This characteristic, however, is the only one the two structures have in common.

JOHN HANCOCK CENTER
875 N. MICHIGAN AVENUE
ARCHITECTS: SKIDMORE, OWINGS AND MERRILL,
PARTNER IN CHARGE: BRUCE GRAHAM (1969)

The modern steel building, surrounded by much open space at its base, is a combination commercial-residential project, with

191

apartments limited to the uppermost 50 stories. Black anodized aluminum and tinted glass are the materials used in the exterior. To cope with Chicago's winds (it is said that the top of the building may sway anywhere from 10 to 15 inches—though those inside would not be aware of it!) the John Hancock has huge cross-bracing steel members that make several giant Xs on each side. These produce an interesting ornamental effect as the Xs become gradually smaller with the tapering of the building from foundation to top, a perfect blending of form and function.

The 95th Restaurant occupies the 95th and 96th floors. On the 94th floor is an observatory and it is open to the public. There is a fee for the observatory.

Walk west on Delaware Place.

110 E. DELAWARE PLACE
ARCHITECTS: SOLOMON, CORDWELL AND BUENZ (1981)

Because of the limitations of the site, an irregularly sized lot as narrow as forty-three feet, this building has windows only on its front and back facades. The facade is of precast concrete and glass. There are sixty-seven units in the building, the maximum number allowed on the site.

Return to Michigan Avenue.

900 N. MICHIGAN AVENUE
ARCHITECTS: PERKINS & WILL;
KOHN, PEDERSEN AND FOX OF NEW YORK
ASSOCIATED ARCHITECTS;
FOR PARKING STRUCTURE: WALKER AND ASSOCIATES;
PERKINS & WILL (1989)

This 66-story mixed-use development is just beginning construction at this writing. The site is 133,000 square feet; the building will be 2.7 million square feet; there will be 200,000 square feet of retail space, and an additional 250,000 square feet for Bloomingdale's department store; office space will take another 500,000 square feet.

The building will have steel construction though the office floors and concrete construction above that. The cladding is to be a combination of French limestone (used to recall the traditional use of limestone on Michigan Avenue), glass, and metal. The base of the building will be ornate with the use of granite and marble.

Plans call for the basement and first 6 stories to be retail, with a multi-theater complex (not defined at this writing) and half that space to be used by Bloomingdale's. The 7th floor will be the public level of the Four Seasons Hotel. Floors 8-27 will be 20 levels of office space. Above that will be 19 floors of guest rooms for the 246-room Four Seasons Hotel and its health club facilities. The top of the building will be 125 condominium units. There will be 260 parking places under the building.

The basement and 7 commercial levels will stand about 150 feet, the approximate height of the old 900 N. Michigan Avenue building and the traditional cornice line of the older buildings along Michigan Avenue. After that, the building will set back from the lot line and the tower will rise from that point. The set-back, to the western line of the One Magnificent Mile building, will allow views from both buildings.

The architecture of the tower recalls the style of Chicago buildings of the 1930s and 1940s and has a strong relationship to 333 N. Michigan Avenue, thus unifying the stretch of Michigan Avenue's Magnificent Mile from the River to Oak Street. This design uses many similar devices including the solid corners which have the windows punched into the masonry. The center sections of the tower become more vertical and more open. The top of the building is unique, giving it a special signature along the skyline.

The entrance to the commercial space, from Michigan Avenue, the retail street, will be into a 6-story galleria with escalator systems to the shopping levels; the entrance to the apartments, and the separate entrance to the hotel will be on Delaware Place, a residential street; and the entrance to the offices will be on the more appropriate Walton Street. The parking structure, for 1,450 cars, on Ernst Court will have retail space on the Rush Street side, and 2 levels of office space above that. At this writing there was the possibility of a health club in the building. There will be a bridge between the buildings at the 3rd floor level.

THE WESTIN HOTEL
909 N. MICHIGAN AVENUE
ARCHITECTS: ALFRED SHAW AND ASSOCIATES (1963, 1975)

Directly north of the Hancock is this very busy hotel containing many shops and restaurants. A new west wing was completed in 1975.

Continue north to Walton Place.

PLAYBOY BUILDING
919 N. Michigan Avenue
Architects: Holabird and Root (1929);
for remodeling: Ron Dirsmith and
A. Epstein and Sons (1972);
for renovations: Skidmore, Owings and
Merrill (1979-82);
for the Mark Shale Store remodeling:
Solomon, Cordwell and Buenz (1981)

Formerly the Palmolive Building, this structure is now part of the Playboy Center that includes the Playboy headquarters and magazine offices. Architect Ron Dirsmith designed the Playboy offices in this building. Splendid lighting, colors, and curved wall surfaces with dropped ceilings make each of the several floors of offices unique and quite handsome.

The latest renovations, begun in 1979, included the restoration and redevelopment of the lobby and the renovation of the facade at grade level and 2nd-story level. The original cast iron and nickel bronze storefronts of the 1929 Palmolive Building by Holabird and Root were replaced by a black aluminum and dark glass facade during the early 1970s. The present owners of the building wanted to revitalize the basement, ground, and second floors with a new commercial tenancy on the prime corner location and believed it necessary to replace the existing character with a conservative, sophisticated facade more in keeping with the building itself. The basic goal was to complement the original architectural vocabulary within a budget that would not permit full restoration.

The new facade is composed of large lights of glass suspended in a steel structural framework applied to the building shell. Bays of sheer glass and steel mullions, varying from 8 to 10 feet, are framed by ribbed lintels and fluted columns above a black granite base. The fluted columns of extruded aluminum replicate the remaining second-level cast iron columns and lanterns. Detailing allows the eventual additions of pediments and medallions similar to the original Art Deco ornaments.

The commercial arcade of the original Palmolive Building was designed to accommodate many small shops. As the new commercial tenants occupied larger, often 2-story spaces, a continuous 2-story expression was chosen for the projected bays. Soffits are set back and the bay is a single open volume where the same tenant occupies both floors. The office lobby was refurbished with black-painted glass, patterned terrazzo and Tennessee pink mar-

194

ble. The original elevator cabs, carved wooden elevator doors, and a nickel bronze mailbox cover were preserved.

The Mark Shale Store remodeling, by Solomon, Cordwell and Buenz was designed with the intention to provide a relaxing environment for customers, conducive to looking, trying, and buying. The fixtures, lighting, materials, and spatial design are all tuned to making shopping a pleasant experience.

Walk east on Walton Place.

KNICKERBOCKER HOTEL
163 E. WALTON PLACE
ARCHITECTS: RISSMAN AND HIRSCHFELD (1926);
FOR THE REMODELING: LOUIS ARTHUR WEISS;
FOR INTERIOR DESIGN: GERALD O'HARA (1980)

Originally built for the Davis hotel chain, and now renamed the Knickerbocker (it had been the Playboy for many years), the hotel's grand ballroom was once the most famous in the city. At one time gold leaf, it was later sprayed white. The 14-floor hotel had 360 rooms, but in the recent remodeling this was reduced to 256. It has now been restored as closely as possible to the general character and original grandeur of the building.

Walk west, past Michigan Avenue.

WALTON COLONNADE APARTMENT BUILDING
100 E. WALTON STREET
ARCHITECTS: DUBIN, DUBIN, BLACK AND
MOUTOUSSAMY (1972)

This is a 256-unit, 44-story apartment building of reinforced concrete. The building employed a poured-in-place, reinforced concrete, strut exterior wall system. The exterior is infilled with darkened glass and aluminum fenestration.

The apartments, rooftop pool, and solarium are serviced by 3 high-speed elevators. Each floor contains 8 apartments. Also included are a 7-level parking garage, and a ground-level and lower-level concourse which contain 23,000 square feet of commercial space. The lower-level concourse has an open terraced court as its focal point.

Return to Michigan Avenue. The name of the last building personifies the WALK.

ONE MAGNIFICENT MILE
950-980 N. Michigan Avenue
Architects: Skidmore, Owings and Merrill (1983)

Three hexagonal concrete tubes rise 57, 49, and 21 stories and are joined together to resist wind loads as a bundled tube. A 5-story hexagonal entrance pavilion in front of the highest tower has a glazed roof sloping northeast toward the Oak Street beach. The same motif is repeated on top of the 57-story tower. The bottom three levels contain commercial space; office space is on floors 4 through 19; and the rest of the building is condominiums. A 2-story mechanical floor tops the twenty-first story level and is carried across the entire tower floor area dividing the offices levels and residential floors by a broad horizontal line. Fenestration is also treated in a different manner below and above this visual division. The towers are clad in granite with clear windows at the commercial level and gray reflective glass for the condominiums.

The Magnificent Mile comes to an end just beyond the Drake Hotel where Michigan Avenue loses its identity by merging with Lake Shore Drive. If the weather permits, take the underpass pedestrian walkway to the Oak Street Beach. Here at Oak Street Beach is a glorious view of Lake Michigan and the pedestrian walkway and bicycle path will take you north with Lake Michigan on your right and many handsome apartment buildings facing you on the left. This is indeed a glamorous section of Lake Shore Drive and is part of the Gold Coast of Chicago.

The Drake Hotel, on the east side of Michigan Avenue, is included in WALK 13, East Lake Shore Drive. You may chose to take that WALK or WALK 15, The Gold Coast at this point.

196

13

1. Drake Hotel
   140 E. Walton St.

2. Drake Tower Apartments
   179 E. Lake Shore Dr.

3. Mayfair Regent Hotel
   181 E. Lake Shore Dr.

4. 199 E. Lake Shore Dr.

5. 209 E. Lake Shore Dr.

6. 219 E. Lake Shore Dr.

7. 229 E. Lake Shore Dr.

8. 999 N. Lake Shore Dr.

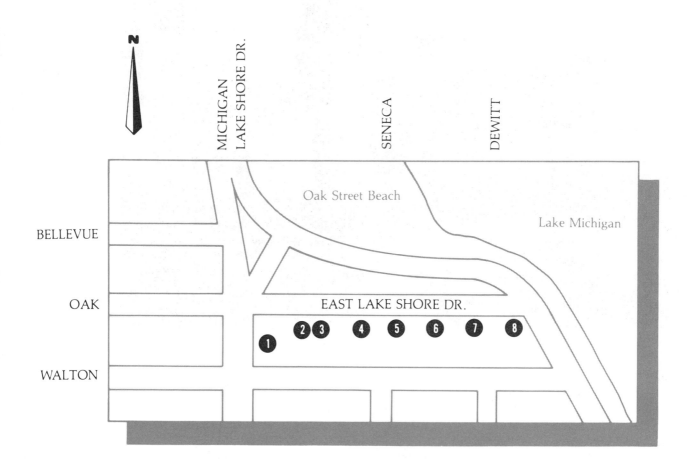

WALK • 13

EAST LAKE SHORE DRIVE

WALKING TIME: About ½ hour.   HOW TO GET THERE: Take a northbound CTA bus No. 151 or 116 at State and Washington streets, and get off at Walton Street [900 N]. [Ask the driver if he stops there; you may have to get off a stop earlier, at Water Tower Place, in which case you walk north, 1 block on Michigan Avenue, to the Drake Hotel.]

East Lake Shore Drive belongs to both Streeterville (see WALK 14) and to the Gold Coast (see WALK 15). It is suggested, since this is a short walk, you might want to start with WALK 14, and/or follow with WALK 15, if time permits.

The street developed in the second and third decades of this century, a period of significant growth in Chicago. These buildings typify the elegant urban lifestyle of that time. Architectural styles during this period fell into two categories. While the designs of Frank Lloyd Wright and Louis Sullivan did not find wide public acceptance in residential application, historical eclecticism—a return to the American Georgian, English Gothic, Italian Renaissance, or French Baroque—was deemed appropriate for the residential structures along this desirable stretch of real estate.

These buildings share a gracious appearance. East Lake Shore Drive provides an intimate streetscape in a congested area. At eye level, the street appears, for a moment, to be one of grand mansions. The entrances are all grand, Beaux Arts, mostly 3-and 4-story, and most of the buildings are relatively plain above. The entrances and all the fenestration and the landscaping make one of the finest pedestrian areas in the city. Take note of the elaborate wrought iron doors, lamps, and hardware of the entranceways.

Begin your WALK at the Drake Hotel, on the northeast corner of Walton Street and Michigan Avenue.

◉ DRAKE HOTEL
140 E. WALTON STREET
ARCHITECTS: MARSHALL AND FOX (1920)

This is truly one of the last of the "grand hotels" of this city. It is 13 stories on pile foundations. The exterior is Bedford limestone.

Overleaf: View of
East Lake Shore Drive
(Robert Thall
courtesy Commission
on Chicago Landmarks)

The fenestration is generous, affording excellent views for the fortunate guests whose rooms face Lake Shore Drive and the Oak Street Beach. The hotel is well-maintained and has retained its air of gracious living. The great fireplace in the center of the lobby is a pleasant sight at all times of the year.

Walk around to view the west and north sides of the building, then walk east on East Lake Shore Drive.

◉ DRAKE TOWER APARTMENTS
179 E. Lake Shore Drive
Architect: Benjamin H. Marshall (1929)

This is a simple brick tower above a decorated two-story limestone base. Note the top, where apartments are set back to accommodate the penthouse, and the steeply pitched, standing seam, metal roof and the elevator equipment penthouse is formed into a pseudo-chimney in proportion with the rest of the building. Marshall was an important theater architect at the turn of the century. He was the designer of the Iroquois Theater (remembered, unfortunately, because of the fire).

◉ MAYFAIR REGENT HOTEL
181 E. Lake Shore Drive
Architects: Fugard and Knapp (1924)

This building was described in *Architectural Forum* in November, 1924:

The exterior design follows the style of the Georgian and Adam periods. The three lower floors are of Indiana limestone, conservatively enriched with small pilasters above the first floor. The shaft of the building is of reddish face brick with light joints, while the upper portion is relieved with simple quoins and cornices of stone, and parapets which have balustrades and urns to create an interesting skyline.

The attention given to the lower few floors of the facade set off the grand entranceway, while the simplicity of the floors above were intended to detract from the building's height. This building shares with others on the block the feature of a particularly handsome entranceway and lobby. The rooftop restaurant was added in 1979.

◉ 199 E. LAKE SHORE DRIVE
Architects: Marshall and Fox (1915)

200

This building is of brick with limestone trim above a 2-story limestone base. It has one tier of square bays and one of round bays. Note its similarity to 999 N. Lake Shore Drive, designed three years earlier by the same architects.

● 209 E. LAKE SHORE DRIVE
ARCHITECTS: MARSHALL AND FOX (1924)

This limestone building shows the influence of the Renaissance style. The building is broken into three bands of design, becoming more simple as it rises.

● 219 E. LAKE SHORE DRIVE
ARCHITECTS: FUGARD AND KNAPP (1922)

The first three floors suggest a limestone Georgian mansion, topped at the third floor level with an elaborate carved stone cornice. Above that are nine floors of simple brick construction with token decoration at the top.

● 229 E. LAKE SHORE DRIVE
ARCHITECTS: FUGARD AND KNAPP (1919)

This building, with a limestone facade, again takes the form of a mansion at the lower levels. That is topped by more apartments and a cornice.

● 999 N. LAKE SHORE DRIVE
ARCHITECTS: MARSHALL AND FOX (1912)

This building was designed in the Second French Empire style. It is capped by a distinctive mansard roof. The wall surface is broken by round and rectangular oriels; red brick spandrels interplay with white limestone trim.

14

1. Navy Pier
   East Grand Ave.
   and Streeter Dr. at Lake Michigan

2. Jardine Water Purification Plant
   1000 E. Ohio St.

3. Lake Point Tower
   505 N. Lake Shore Dr.

4. Onterie Center
   446 E. Ontario St.

5. 666 N. Lake Shore Dr.

6. Northwestern University
   Chicago Campus
   710 N. Lake Shore

7. Northwestern University Law School/
   American Bar Center
   375 E. Chicago Ave.

8. American Hospital Association
   840 N. Lake Shore Drive

9. Lake Shore Center
   850 N. Lake Shore Dr.

10. 860 N. DeWitt Place

11. 860 and 880 N. Lake Shore Dr.

12. 900 and 910 N. Lake Shore Dr.

13. 990 N. Lake Shore Dr.

14. Chess Pavilion
    North end of Oak St. Beach

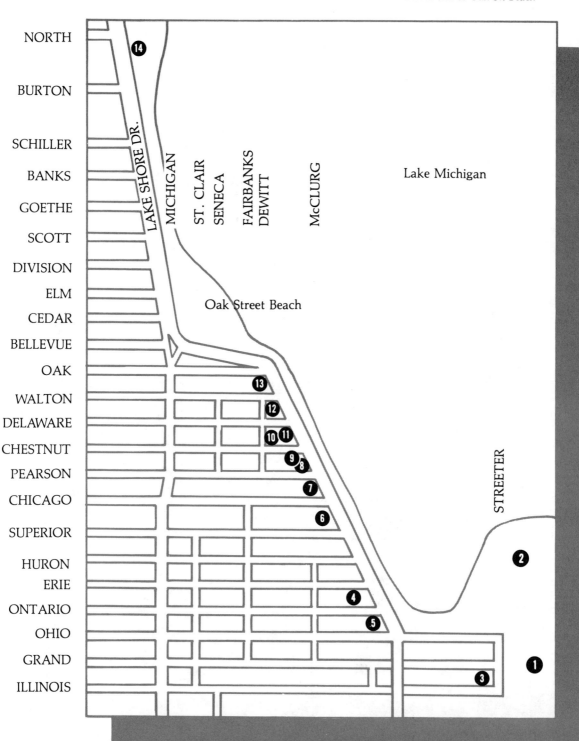

WALK • 14

LAKE SHORE DRIVE: NEAR NORTH

WALKING TIME: 1½ hours. HOW TO GET THERE: Take a northbound CTA bus No. 29 [State Street] [weekdays only] and get off at Navy Pier. Or take a No. 151 or 147 bus on State Street [ask for a transfer] and get off at Michigan and Grand avenues [530 N]. Walk down the steps. Transfer [at the lower level] to an eastbound bus No. 65 [Grand Avenue], which will take you to Navy Pier, the end of the line.

This WALK starts at Navy Pier, 1 block to the east and 1 block north of the Outer Drive/Lake Shore Drive bridge.

◉ **NAVY PIER**
EAST GRAND AVENUE AND STREETER DRIVE,
AT LAKE MICHIGAN
ARCHITECT FOR WEST ENTRY BUILDINGS
AND EAST END BUILDINGS:
CHARLES S. FROST (1916);
FOR RESTORATION OF NAVY PIER:
JEROME R. BUTLER, JR. (1976)

A 25-acre peninsula on which commercial, cultural, and recreational activities are provided, Navy Pier was built in 1916 as a port facility for commercial shipping and Great Lakes excursion boats. Although not usually open to the public, perhaps a special event will be underway, to allow your visit.

The Pier's east promenade, lying nearly a mile out in the lake, offers unparalleled views of Chicago's maritime activity and its spectacular skyline and provides a park-like haven in which to enjoy a refreshing pause from city activity. On the promenade is the East End Recreational Facility, a complex of 3 connected structures—the opulent Auditorium, the Shelter, and the Terminal buildings—plus vintage street lights and park benches, roof-top terraces, trees, and landscaping.

Returning to the mainland along the Pier's north promenade, you will see the Navy Pier murals. A colorful series of wall paintings done by youthful artists from Chicago's public and parochial

Overleaf:
North Lake Shore Drive
from the Chess Pavilion
looking south to Oak
Street Beach
(Allen Carr)

schools, the murals depict the city's skyline, parks, and waterfront in rich patterns and colors from east to west along the promenade.

Streeter Drive, a curving street at the foot of Navy Pier, is a reminder of the colorful, controversial shantytown which once occupied this 180-acre site stretching north from Grand to Chicago avenues and west to St. Clair Street. Streeterville got its name from George Wellington Streeter, who for more than 30 years claimed squatter's rights to the area, insisting that neither Chicago nor Illinois laws had any jurisdiction over it. Other squatters who bought real estate from Streeter backed him in his lawsuits with the city.

This sea captain turned real estate con man seems to have been the first to redeem land from Lake Michigan and make a profit on it—a procedure that made possible the lakefront skyscrapers today! The story goes that Streeter and his wife, Maria, started this fantastic real estate project in 1886 after running their excursion boat aground on a sandbar in Lake Michigan somewhat south of Chicago Avenue. Freeing the boat proved difficult, so they decided to fill up the lake around it instead. With the help of nearby residents who contributed dirt from construction sites and whatever lay at hand, this is exactly what they did. Streeter defied all attempts by the law to oust him from his property until someone was killed in one of the many confrontations with the police. He was then imprisoned on a charge of manslaughter. Out on parole months later, he returned to his battle with the law. Finally, in 1918, court orders were actually carried out: Streeter was removed and the shanties of Streeterville burned to make way for later development.

Walk north. Out in the lake, just north of Navy Pier, spreads the James W. Jardine Water Purification Plant.

JARDINE WATER PURIFICATION PLANT
1000 E. OHIO STREET
ARCHITECTS: C. F. MURPHY AND ASSOCIATES
AND THE CITY ARCHITECT (1966)

This purification plant with its 51 acres of buildings is the largest facility of its kind in the United States. It is considered one of the country's waterworks show places. Thousands of people visit this plant each year. Tours of the plant are permitted by appointment only. Call 744-3692 for reservations.

A sculpture in the lobby of the main building, by Chicagoan Milton Horn, represents the history of the various uses of water.

206

At the west end of the plant site, over the filtered water reservoirs, is a 10½ acre public park, Milton Lee Olive Park, with fountains, beautiful landscaping, and a promenade. There is a splendid view of the Chicago skyline from this park.

Walk south on the west side of the street toward the black highrise.

LAKE POINT TOWER
505 N. LAKE SHORE DRIVE
ARCHITECTS: SCHIPPOREIT-HEINRICH;
GRAHAM, ANDERSON, PROBST AND WHITE (1968)

The most prominent building on the shoreline to the north of the Chicago River is Lake Point Tower. This 70-story, cloverleaf-shaped, glass-sheathed apartment building is indeed a beautiful sight. In 1921 a similar building was designed by Ludwig Mies van der Rohe in Berlin, but it was never built. The young architects who designed Lake Point Tower, former colleagues of Mies, were

Navy Pier
(Bill Engdahl,
Hedrich-Blessing)

207

Central District
Filtration Plant
and Olive Park
(Orlando R. Cabanan)

obviously influenced by the master. Much of the building's sweep and fluidity, its even sensuous quality, has to do with its hidden columns, all enclosed by the bronze-tinted glass. It is almost mirror-like at times, and in the setting sun's reflection it looks like a golden shaft.

Walk west on Grand Avenue, under Lake Shore Drive, to McClurg Court. Turn north 2 blocks. Turn east on Ontario Street.

ONTERIE CENTER
446 E. ONTARIO STREET
ARCHITECTS: SKIDMORE, OWINGS AND MERRILL (1985)

Onterie Center is composed of a 58-story multi-use tower and an adjacent 10-story office tower. A 5-story, triangular, glazed atrium connects the two structures and leads to a pedestrian galleria for easy communication with both major streets. The apartment lobby off Erie Street is independent of the two distinct office lobbies with entries from Ontario Street. Twin elevators in each of these spacious lobbies give access to the office space on floors six through ten. A unique structural system of diagonal framed tubes with diagonal concrete infill panels was developed for this building. This original and highly economical system creates a rhythmic architectural expression which lends visual strength to the building image. Dual thermal glazing and specially prefabricated exterior panel system with incorporated insulation contribute to the buildings' exceptional energy efficiency. Retail space and a restaurant are found on the first floor.

Continue east to Lake Shore Drive. Turn north.

208

666 N. LAKE SHORE DRIVE
ARCHITECTS: HENRY RAEDER AND
GEORGE NIMMONS (1924, 1926);
FOR THE ADAPTIVE REUSE: FRANK LAROCCA (1980-3)

This 16-story structure with its 29-story tower on the west was designed in 1924 to provide large showrooms for the former occupant, the American Furniture Mart, one of the two major Chicago marts used by leading furniture manufacturers to display their latest creations. (The other is the Merchandise Mart. See WALK 8, Wacker Drive: East-West.) By the 1970s, many of the tenants had relocated, leaving the building more than half empty despite its prime lakefront location. In 1979 the joint venture of Fujikawa, Conterato, and Lohan with Larocca Associates redesigned the 2,000,000-square-foot building as the largest known "adaptive reuse" project to date. Half the space was devoted to residential units; a quarter of it to office use; and the rest to retail, common areas, parking, and loading uses. An effort was made to preserve, restore, and enhance the character of the building through its classic lobbies, cast plasterwork, terra-cotta and stone work, all as a commitment to the building's established image.

The original building had been developed in two phases. Built in 1924, the main facility is of reinforced concrete with round columns at 20-foot centers on wood pilings. In 1926, the 29-story section was added on the west. It is steel framed with concrete fireproofing on concrete caissons. The only structural mod-

ifications in the rehabilitation work was cutting out of floor sections for new concrete ramps, stairs, and shafts for the elevators.

Continue north.

NORTHWESTERN UNIVERSITY CHICAGO CAMPUS
710 N. LAKE SHORE DRIVE
ARCHITECTS: JAMES GAMBLE ROGERS (1926-32);
HOLABIRD AND ROOT (1929-67);
SCHMIDT, GARDEN AND ERIKSON (1968);
BERTRAND GOLDBERG AND ASSOCIATES (1974)

The Chicago campus of Northwestern University (bounded by Chicago Avenue, Lake Shore Drive, Erie and St. Clair streets) includes the graduate schools of medicine, dentistry, management, law, and the evening divisions—in various buildings along the 300 block of East Chicago Avenue, with administrative offices at 710 N. Lake Shore Drive. It also is the main site of the McGaw Medical Center of the university which includes, in this location, Northwestern Memorial Hospital, Prentice Women's Hospital and Maternity Center, the Passavant Pavilion and Wesley Pavilion, the Veterans Administration Research Hospital, and the Rehabilitation Institute of Chicago. The Institute of Psychiatry, a

210

part of the Northwestern Medical School, shares a building with Prentice.

A walking tour of this exciting urban campus is most rewarding. For information, call the Chicago campus personnel office at 908-8481 or Northwestern Memorial Hospital public relations office at 908-2030.

Left: Lake Point Tower (Philip A. Turner)

Right: 860-880 Lake Shore Drive, by Mies van der Rohe, with 860 DeWitt just behind (Mart Studios, Inc.)

NORTHWESTERN UNIVERSITY LAW SCHOOL/ AMERICAN BAR CENTER

375 E. Chicago Avenue and
750 N. Lake Shore Drive
Architects: Holabird and Root (1984)

This handsome addition to the law school was built in 1984. The architect's challenge was to design a building which served its

211

Northwestern University
Law School
(Timothy Hursley, courtesy
The Arkansas Office)

occupants while still relating to the university architecture on one
side and the neighboring 666 N. Lake Shore Drive and the Mies
buildings along the Drive. The steel structure has an aluminum
skin with glass and granite. The building is 13 stories tall. It has
300,000 square feet of space, almost 100,000 of it for the library.
The 1st floor has classrooms, the 800-seat Thorne Hall, and a
moot court. The 2nd and 3rd floors are library space with some
faculty offices. Floors 4 and up are the American Bar Association's
space.

Continue north on Lake Shore Drive.

AMERICAN HOSPITAL ASSOCIATION
840 N. LAKE SHORE DRIVE
ARCHITECTS: SCHMIDT, GARDEN AND ERIKSON (1961-70)

These two pleasant-looking structures house this enormously important association.

LAKE SHORE CENTER
850 N. LAKE SHORE DRIVE
ARCHITECT: JARVIS HUNT (1929)

This 18-story building is a quiet and dignified reminder of the 1920s. Formerly the Lake Shore Club, it is now a dorm for Northwestern University students.

Continue north to Chestnut Street. Turn west to DeWitt Place. Turn north.

860 N. DeWITT PLACE
ARCHITECTS: SKIDMORE, OWINGS AND MERRILL (1966)

Directly west of the 860-880 Lake Shore Drive buildings, at DeWitt and Chestnut streets, is another apartment building—a handsome structure of reinforced concrete covered with travertine marble. The contrast between this and "The Glass Houses" is a reminder that modern builders can use old-time building materials with effective results. Always present in the background of this WALK is the imposing John Hancock Building with its 100 stories, 2 blocks to the west on Michigan Avenue. (See WALK 12.)

Backtrack south to Chestnut Street. Turn east to Lake Shore Drive. Turn north.

860 and 880 N. LAKE SHORE DRIVE
ARCHITECTS: LUDWIG MIES VAN DER ROHE,
WITH ASSOCIATE ARCHITECTS P A C E AND
HOLSMAN, HOLSMAN, KLEKAMP AND TAYLOR (1952)

900 and 910 N. LAKE SHORE DRIVE
ARCHITECT: LUDWIG MIES VAN DER ROHE (1956)

The first pair of these to be constructed have been cited by the Architectural Landmarks Commission in these words:

In recognition of an open plan in a multistory apartment building where the steel cage becomes expressive of the potentialities of steel and glass in architectural design. The second pair were built four years later, in 1956. These buildings reflect the skill

213

of a great architect, engineer, and innovator. Nicknamed "The Glass Houses" because they seem to be made entirely of glass, they have been the inspiration for many buildings all over the world.

990 N. LAKE SHORE DRIVE
ARCHITECTS: BARANCIK AND CONTE (1973)

This stunning concrete structure with metal bay windows presents a powerful punctuation mark at the turn of the drive.

Around the corner of Lake Shore Drive, as it bends westward are several palatial apartment buildings that mark the beginning of that section of Chicago referred to as the Gold Coast. You may want to take WALK 13, East Lake Shore Drive, at this point. WALK 15, The Gold Coast, begins 1 block to the west at the corner of Oak Street and Lake Shore Drive (or the corner of Michigan Avenue and East Lake Shore Drive; it's the same corner).

If the weather permits, stroll along Oak Street Beach, which you can reach through a pedestrian tunnel on the northwest corner. Such a walk can be exhilarating, with Lake Michigan on one side and the prestigious apartment buildings of WALK 15 on the other.

CHESS PAVILION
NORTH END OF OAK STREET BEACH
ARCHITECT: MORRIS WEBSTER (1956)

The Chess Pavilion at the north end of Oak Street Beach (the south end of Lincoln Park) is a fitting terminal to this WALK, well worth the stroll north along Lake Shore Drive or the lakefront. This small building is beautiful in its unusual and simple design. The reinforced concrete roof appears to be floating in the air.

15

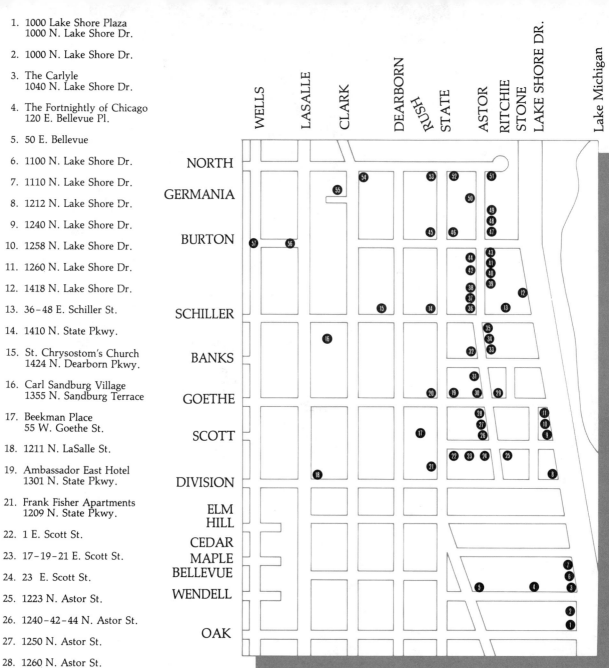

WALK • 15

THE GOLD COAST

WALKING TIME: About 2 hours. HOW TO GET THERE: Take a northbound CTA bus No. 151 or 146 at State and Washington streets, and get off at Walton Street [900 N]. [Ask the driver if he stops there; you may have to get off a stop earlier, at Water Tower Place.] Cross to the west side of the street and walk north to Oak Street.

In Chicago the term "Gold Coast" applies to the area bounded by Lake Michigan on the east, LaSalle Street (150 W) on the west, Oak Street (1000 N) on the south, and North Avenue (1600 N) on the north. The name was given many years ago, indicating that this section of the city was peopled by those with most of the city's gold. (Suburbs and country houses were still a thing of the future.)

This WALK starts with the lakefront high-rises, then focuses on another part of the Gold Coast, starting at State and Division streets and moving through Scott Street, Astor Street, and Burton Place. (It seems especially appropriate that the Gold Coast should include a street that carries the glittering name of John Jacob Astor!)

You will be struck by the beauty and tranquility of this residential area. What is unseen is the struggle to preserve these qualities in the face of change. At one time the section was zoned for single-family residences only, but as land values increased, zoning was changed to accommodate the economic forces. As in Kenwood (see WALK 19), most people could no longer afford to maintain such establishments—with rising taxes, increased cost of operation, and the dearth of household help. The choice for many was selling the property to high-rise developers or converting the interior into apartments. Wherever feasible, the latter was attempted. Fortunately, some of the homeowners have been able to keep their property as single-family dwellings.

⊙ Portions of this WALK are in the Gold Coast Historic District, roughly bounded by North Avenue, Lake Shore Drive, and Oak Street

Overleaf:
1418 N. Lake Shore Drive
(Howard N. Kaplan
courtesy Solomon,
Cordwell and Buenz)

1000 LAKE SHORE PLAZA
1000 N. LAKE SHORE DRIVE
ARCHITECTS: SIDNEY MORRIS AND ASSOCIATES (1964)

The Carlyle
(courtesy
Martin Reinheimer)

This is a 55-story steel and concrete condominium building.

On the face of the next building, at 1000 N. Lake Shore Drive, is a sculpture—by Bernard Rosenthal, of New York, formerly of Chicago—depicting the Gold Coast of Africa.

1000 N. LAKE SHORE DRIVE
ARCHITECTS: SIDNEY MORRIS AND ASSOCIATES (1954)

This 24-story condominium building has a concrete frame and a brick and glass exterior.

Cross Bellevue Place.

THE CARLYLE
1040 N. LAKE SHORE DRIVE
ARCHITECTS: HIRSCHFELD, PAWLAN
AND REINHEIMER (1966)

This condominium building has a concrete and steel frame with a masonry and limestone exterior wall with aluminum framed windows. Note that the entrance is not on the front, but from the driveway to the west. The Borden-Stevenson mansion formerly stood on this site.

Walk west on Bellevue Place.

● THE FORTNIGHTLY OF CHICAGO
120 E. BELLEVUE PLACE
ARCHITECTS: McKIM, MEAD AND WHITE (1892);
FOR REMODELING: PERKINS & WILL (1972)

This imposing 3-story mansion was originally the Brian Lathrop house. It is 3 windows wide at the center with wide bays on each side and was originally the home of the Lathrop family. The symmetry of the facade, which is in keeping with its 18th century classic style, is pleasantly relieved by having the entrance set in the left, not the center, of the three central arches. It can be compared with some of the fine 19th century mansions in Boston and New York City designed by this leading architectural firm of that period. It is probably the only remaining example in Chicago of the work of McKim, Mead and White.

The mansion has been restored and rehabilitated with structural, plumbing, and electrical changes. The entire structure has been modernized and functions as a gathering place for members of the club and their friends.

Continue west.

50 E. BELLEVUE
ARCHITECTS: SOLOMON, CORDWELL
AND BUENZ (1980)

Since the site does not back on an alley, this 27-story building was designed to provide all service activities through the front street facade. The building was set behind a paved courtyard. This created a pleasant entrance area with the courtyard providing for the service functions of the building. The street facade is designed to be elegant yet totally functional. The base of the building is limestone. The upper floors are concrete and glass.

Backtrack to Lake Shore Drive and walk north.

1100 N. LAKE SHORE DRIVE
ARCHITECT: HARRY WEESE (1980)

This 40-story luxury condominium tower was constructed of reinforced concrete with punched window openings. Windows are solar bronze-tinted glass and the exterior a warm gray concrete. The 38 apartment floors contain seventy-six three-bedroom condominium units, half of which are duplexes. The units are stacked in such a way that each two-floor layer contains two duplex units and two single level units.

1110 N. LAKE SHORE DRIVE
ARCHITECTS: HAUSNER AND MACSAI (1971)

This very attractive, 39-story, concrete, condominium building has a glass curtainwall facing the lake.

1212 N. LAKE SHORE DRIVE
ARCHITECTS: BARANCIK AND CONTE (1969)

This condominium is easily the most handsome and rugged of the newer structures on this portion of Lake Shore Drive. It is a 36-story, concrete and steel building with a glass curtainwall facing the lake.

1240 N. LAKE SHORE DRIVE
ARCHITECTS: HAUSNER AND MACSAI (1971)

This 33-story concrete and steel condominium building has a glass curtainwall facing the lake.

220

1258 N. LAKE SHORE DRIVE
ARCHITECTS: HOLABIRD AND ROCHE (1895)

This charming 3-story Venetian Gothic townhouse was designed in 1895 by architects Holabird and Roche. It was originally the Arthur Aldis house.

1260 N. LAKE SHORE DRIVE
ARCHITECTS: HOLABIRD AND ROCHE (1906)

There is a charming Georgian house at the corner. It was also designed by Holabird and Roche, but in 1906.

Continue north.

1418 N. LAKE SHORE DRIVE
ARCHITECTS: SOLOMON, CORDWELL AND BUENZ (1984)

The configuration of this 29-story building was dictated by the narrow site and the requirements of the City's Lake Front ordinance which required the approval of adjoining property owners and the necessity of not blocking views of the extant buildings. There is one large luxury unit on each floor. The unusual configuration of the front facade allows views of the lake, and north and south along Lake Shore Drive.

Backtrack to Schiller Street. Walk west.

◉ 36-48 E. SCHILLER STREET
ARCHITECT: POSSIBLY C. M. PALMER (c. 1889-91)

These red brick, 3-story, vine-covered townhouses, some with bay windows and each with a distinctive subtle design of its own, were built by Potter Palmer. It is likely they were designed by C. M. Palmer, who often worked on the other Mr. Palmer's projects.

Continue west to State Parkway. Turn north.

1410 N. STATE PARKWAY
ARCHITECTS: SOLOMON, CORDWELL AND BUENZ (1981)

This 27-story luxury high-rise was designed to give exposures in three directions to each of the two apartments on each floor. The exterior is finished in a warm brick with bronze tinted glass.

Return to Schiller Street. Walk west to Dearborn Parkway, then turn north.

Opposite:
1100 Lake Shore Drive
(courtesy Harry Weese
& Associates)

ST. CHRYSOSTOM'S CHURCH
1424 N. Dearborn Parkway
Architects: Clinton J. Warren (1894);
Clark and Walcott; Bennett, and Parsons
consulting architects (1923);
Chester H. Walcott; Bennett, Parsons and
Frost, consulting architects (1924)

This fine English Gothic church was built in 1894. In the early
1920s, one adjoining building was removed and the others were
incorporated into the complex you see today. The original facade
was changed, and interior changes made. Work was completed in
1925. The design of the church received a gold medal from the
American Institute of Architects in 1926. Walk inside to see a
mosaic replica of St. John, copied from a 10th century mosaic in
the Church of St. Sophia in Constantinople. The design of the
altar and sanctuary was the last commission of architect David
Adler.

Return to Schiller Street. Walk west to Clark Street. Walk south
along Clark Street, the western border of the old Gold Coast, for a
view of Carl Sandburg Village.

222

CARL SANDBURG VILLAGE
1355 N. Sandburg Terrace
Architects: L. R. Solomon and
J. D. Cordwell and Associates (1960-72)

This "village," named for Chicago's famous and well-loved poet Carl Sandburg, consists of high-rise apartment buildings, townhouses, studios, gardens, fountains, and shops. A landscaped central pedestrian mall covers the parking areas, an early use of this approach to land use.

The complex is between Clark and LaSalle streets, Division Street and North Avenue. An urban renewal plan referred to as the Clark-LaSalle Redevelopment Project cleared the slums to which the area had deteriorated.

Continue south to Goethe Street—pronounced "go-thee" with the "th" as in "thin," which may be necessary guidance if you come from outside Chicago. On the east side of Clark Street, between Goethe and Division streets, is the last parcel of land in the Carl Sandburg development project.

BEEKMAN PLACE
55 W. Goethe Street
Architect: Michael Gelick (1986)

Forty-three townhouses are arranged in nine buildings to maximize the number of end units. A four-level commercial/office structure comfortably bridges the transition from commercial space on the south to the townhouses of Sutton Place to the north. The exterior of the commercial building, brick and limestone with granite trim and an atrium entry, emphasizes its location and blends well with the brick and limestone trim on the townhouses. The private wing in the center of the development adds a sense of neighborhood and security.

Walk west on Goethe Street to LaSalle Street. Notice the mural on the building to your left.

1211 N. LaSALLE STREET
Architects for the renovation: Weese Seegers
Hickey Weese (1980-1)

This renovation changed a 1920s, 187-unit apartment hotel into a 68-unit apartment building. The original arched openings and concrete coffered ceilings were retained to unify the new space. Under the architects' direction, artist Richard Haas designed a mural to complete the three raw elevations. Entitled "Homage to the Chicago School of Architecture," the mural incorporates memories of Chicago's heritage—Sullivan's Transportation Building arch, Adolf Loos' 1922 Chicago Tribune competition entry, and three tiers of Chicago bay windows.

Backtrack east on Goethe Street to State Parkway.

AMBASSADOR EAST HOTEL
1301 N. State Parkway
Architect: Robert S. De Golyer (1926)

AMBASSADOR WEST HOTEL
1300 N. State Parkway
Architects: Schmidt, Garden and Martin (1919)

At the corner are the Ambassador hotels, home of the noted Pump Room, where so many famous people have dined and danced—or entertained those dining and dancing there.

Walk south on State Street. You will come to a brick apartment building painted white with glass block windows and small terra-cotta figures in the brickwork.

FRANK FISHER APARTMENTS
1209 N. State Parkway
Architect: Andrew Rebori (1936-37)

This was built around the time of the 1933-34 Century of Progress in the style of the time—Art Moderne. High ceilings, balconies, and terraces give this structure a handsome appearance. Architect Andrew Rebori and artist Edgar Miller closely collaborated to create this unique apartment building, planned to take maximum advantage of a narrow city lot. Skillful detailing of its painted white brick, glass block, and sculptured elements recall the Art Moderne style of the times.

Backtrack north to Scott Street.

1 E. SCOTT STREET
Architects: Dubin, Dubin, Black and Moutoussamy (1970)

The building's tower is a 24-story, reinforced-concrete structure which employs a poured-in-place, reinforced-concrete strut, exterior wall system. This exterior is infilled with glass-and-aluminum fenestration. The typical floors and rooftop pool

1211 N. LaSalle
(Paul Zakoian,
courtesy Weese
Hickey Weese)

225

are serviced by 3 high-speed elevators. Each floor contains 12 dwelling units.

Walk east on Scott Street.

◉ 17-19-21 E. SCOTT STREET

Note these delightful limestone-and-brick facades. The bay windows and individual entrances give each house a bit of Old World charm.

◉ 23 E. SCOTT STREET

This old townhouse has been handsomely remodeled. The below-grade entrance with the white limestone wall and black columns behind a black iron picket fence give it a modernized look. The yellow-painted facade of the upper three stories is quite striking.

Continue east to Astor Street. On the southeast corner is 1223 N. Astor Street.

◉ 1223 N. ASTOR STREET
ARCHITECT: UNKNOWN (c. 1893);
FOR THE RESTORATION: RALPH YOUNGREN (1980-1)

This house, which dates from about 1893, was recently converted to condominiums. The interior was gutted and split into three apartments. The exterior was restored.

Walk north on Astor Street.

◉ 1240-42-44 N. ASTOR STREET

Here are three charming townhouses built around 1890. The delightful 3-story structures have bay windows. The below-grade entrance and curved facade on the northern one give an 18th century character to the house.

◉ 1250 N. ASTOR STREET
ARCHITECT: UNKNOWN (1890)

This 3-story 1890 townhouse, with limestone facade, imitates an Italian Renaissance design.

◉ 1260 N. ASTOR STREET
ARCHITECT: PHILIP B. MAHER (1930)

This is a 10-story, limestone-faced apartment building in the Art

Moderne style of about 1930. Kitty-corner is a similar structure. These are two of the elegant cooperative apartment buildings which have replaced some of the earlier one-family residences, and they were designed for very much the same kind of homeowner.

◉ 1301 N. ASTOR STREET
ARCHITECT: PHILIP B. MAHER (1929)

See listing above. The Potter Palmers once occupied the top 3 floors here as their Chicago home.

ASTOR TOWER
1300 N. ASTOR STREET
ARCHITECTS: BERTRAND GOLDBERG
AND ASSOCIATES (1963)

The building was originally a hotel, designed by the architects of Marina City (see WALK 4).
Continue north on Astor Street.

◉ 1308-10-12 N. ASTOR STREET
ARCHITECTS: BURNHAM AND ROOT (1887)

Burnham and Root designed these three delightful rowhouses in 1887, and John W. Root chose the center house for his personal residence. After his death in 1891, the house continued to be occupied by his widow, and at times by his sister-in-law, Harriet Monroe, founder of the poetry magazine. The houses are of sandstone and red brick, with beautiful bay windows at the 2nd and 3rd floors.
Backtrack south to Goethe Street. Turn west to State Parkway. Turn north.

PLAYBOY MANSION
1340 N. STATE PARKWAY
ARCHITECT: JAMES GAMBLE ROGERS (1899)

This large Georgian mansion was originally built for surgeon George Isham. The famous multi-millionaire owner of the Playboy empire, Hugh Hefner, owned the building for years. The building is now owned by the Art Institute of Chicago and used as a residence dorm by students.
Walk south to Banks Street. Turn east to Astor Street, then turn north. On the east side of the street is the Court of the Golden Hands, a charming apartment complex with a delightful courtyard.

Astor Tower
(Philip A. Turner)

227

● COURT OF THE GOLDEN HANDS
1349-53 N. ASTOR STREET
ARCHITECT: HOWARD VAN DOREN SHAW (1914-15)

Originally the residence of lumberman William O. Goodman, donor of the Goodman Theatre, Howard Van Doren Shaw designed the home, as well as the theater and the family mausoleum at Graceland Cemetery (see pp. 419-20). Each of the golden hands at the entrance seems to be holding an apple. The Georgian facade and marble figure set in a niche make this a memorable sight.

● 1355 N. ASTOR STREET
ARCHITECT: HOWARD VAN DOREN SHAW (1910s)

Formerly the Goodman Mansion, this is a well-designed, large-scale English Georgian mansion copied from 18th century originals.

● CHARNLEY HOUSE
1365 N. ASTOR STREET
ARCHITECTS: ADLER AND SULLIVAN (1892);
FOR RENOVATIONS: JOHN VINCI (1980)

This 11-room, 3-story, single-family residence has fortunately been maintained as such. Although the official architects were

Charnley House
(Olga Stefanos)

228

Adler and Sullivan, this is understood to be a Frank Lloyd Wright design, drawn up by him for the famous partnership of architects, for whom he was then working as a young draftsman. The building's compactness contrasts with Wright's later rambling Prairie House style but is similar to other earlier works. Some see Sullivan's touch in the wooden balcony and copper cornice.

What is obviously an extension to the south was built at a later date. It detracts from the original symmetry of the design. The house underwent some renovations in 1980. At this writing, plans are underway to remove the addition and restore the house to its original condition.

Continue north.

● 1406 N. ASTOR STREET
ARCHITECT: DAVID ADLER (1921)

This house was built for Joseph T. Ryerson from plans by society architect David Adler. The house has a limestone facade and a mansard roof.

● 1412 N. ASTOR STREET

On the west side you come to a combination limestone and yellow-brick house. A pediment at the roof line and ornament on the facade gives it a Dutch quality.

● 1416 N. ASTOR STREET
ARCHITECT: ARTHUR HEUN (c. 1917)

Of Georgian design, this house was built for William McCormick Blair. It is the only house on Astor Street with a side yard and formal gardens.

● 1427 N. ASTOR STREET
ARCHITECT: WILLIAM LeBARON JENNEY (1889)

Across the street, a 4-story rusticated red brick house has a handsome, pristine look. Boldly fronted with red rough-faced brick and bandings of limestone, the facade of this significant work by skyscraper pioneer William LeBaron Jenney was recently cleaned and restored by its owners.

● 1431 N. ASTOR STREET

A curved facade embraces the brick of this building, with white Ionic columns supporting a pediment over the porch.

◉ 1435 N. ASTOR STREET

This house was built in two stages. It is another facsimile of a great Georgian mansion, a style so popular here at the turn of the century. The pilasters at the corners with their Ionic caps give the facade a somewhat heavy appearance. The pleasant ornamentation below the cornice somehow lends an air of authenticity. Black iron picket fences enclose the grounds.

◉ 1432 N. ASTOR STREET
ARCHITECT: JAMES EPPENSTEIN (1936)

Back on the west side of the street is a stunning remodeling of a townhouse, converting it into 3 apartments. Limestone and large horizontal glass areas give this daring design a contemporary look.

◉ 1443 N. ASTOR STREET
ARCHITECT: JOSEPH LYMAN SILSBEE (1891)

This is a fine Romanesque Revival composition, built in 1891 for the H. M. May family. Although usually credited to architect Joseph Lyman Silsbee, it may well have been designed by George W. Maher.

◉ 1444 N. ASTOR STREET
ARCHITECTS: HOLABIRD AND ROOT (1936)

230

This interesting 4-story house with a limestone facade and bay windows was built for Edward P. Russell. Designed by a firm famous for their Art Deco skyscrapers, it has some of the appearance of Art Moderne.

Continue north. Turn west on Burton Place across State Parkway.

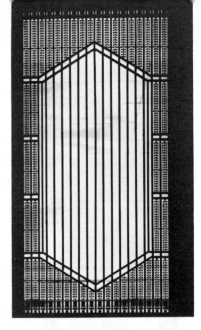

⦿ MADLENER HOUSE

4 W. Burton Place
Architects: Richard E. Schmidt,
Hugh M. G. Gardiner, designer (1902);
for interior remodeling: Brenner,
Danforth, and Rockwell (1963)

This is an architectural landmark. The noted Madlener House has been successfully restored by the Graham Foundation for Advanced Studies in the Fine Arts and is the home of the foundation. Note the Sullivan-like ornamentation around the door, relieving somewhat the severity of the design as a whole. At this writing, plans are underway to create an "architectural fragment" sculpture garden in the foundation's courtyard. Open Monday through Thursday 9 a.m. to 4:30 p.m. Call 787-4071 for an appointment.

Backtrack east to the northwest corner of Astor Street and Burton Place.

⦿ THE PATTERSON-McCORMICK MANSION

20 E. Burton Place
Architects: McKim, Mead and White,
Stanford White, designer (1893);
David Adler (1927);
for rehabilitation and conversion:
Nagle Hartray and Associates (1978-9);
for restoration: Wilbert R. Hasbrouck (1978-9)

Here stands another landmark residence. The building's historical associations are with Chicago's society life. It was built for Mrs. Robert W. Patterson, daughter of Joseph Medill (once mayor of Chicago and editor of the Chicago Tribune) by the ill-fated architect Stanford White. Another owner—Cyrus McCormick—had extensive alterations made in 1927.

This orange brick and terra-cotta building with marble columns —once a mansion of some forty to ninety rooms (the count

Patterson-McCormick
Mansion, full view
and detail (right,
Olga Stefanos; left,
Philip A. Turner)

depends on one's definition of a room)—was the scene of some of Chicago's most sumptuous social functions. Here, it is said, slept visiting kings and queens as guests. The interior of the house had a graceful winding staircase, 3-inch-thick doors, and marble bathrooms. A step into 20 E. Burton Place was a step into the glittering past.

It has been converted into condominiums. The base building architects for the project were Nagle Hartray and Associates. The architect for the restoration work was Wilbert R. Hasbrouck.

◉ Astor Street was designated a historic and architectural Landmark District in 1976 by the Commission of Chicago Historical and Architectural Landmarks and the Chicago City Council. This building is part of the Astor Street Landmark District.

Cross to the northeast corner of Astor Street and Burton Place.

◉ GREEK ORTHODOX DIOCESE OFFICE
40 E. Burton Place

This house was built for W. Beale in the 1910s. It is now the office of the Greek Orthodox Diocese of Chicago.

Walk north on Astor Street.

232

1505 N. ASTOR STREET
ARCHITECTS: JENNEY, MUNDIE AND JENSEN (1911)

This Georgian mansion has been converted to condominiums.

1511 N. ASTOR STREET
ARCHITECT: ARTHUR HEUN (1917)

This fine Georgian house was built in 1917 and designed by Arthur Heun. Note the alternating rows of common and Roman brick. It is in superb condition.

1518 N. ASTOR STREET
ARCHITECTS: JENNEY, MUNDIE AND JENSEN (1911); FOR THE RENOVATIONS: GRUNFELD AND ASSOCIATES (1986)

Built for Francis Dickenson, the building is a red-brick Georgian design with bay windows and a well-proportioned entrance. At this writing the building was undergoing renovations.

Continue to the north end of Astor Street.

1555 N. ASTOR STREET
ARCHITECTS: SOLOMON, CORDWELL AND BUENZ (1975)

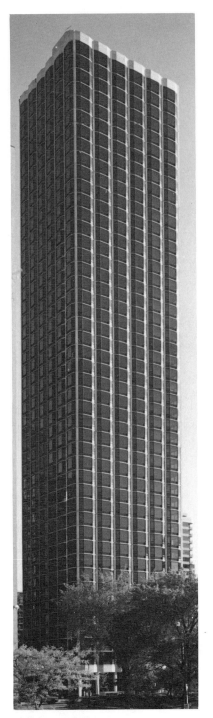

1555 N. Astor Street
(courtesy Solomon, Cordwell and Buenz)

This stunning 47-story condominium building overlooks Lincoln Park on one of the most desirable pieces of land in the Gold Coast neighborhood. The base of the building repeats the faceting of the tower in brick and contains the garage and necessary service functions. On top on the base is a private land-scaped deck with tennis court and enclosed pool. Bronze tinted glass bays highlight the tower's exterior and frame the spectacular views from each unit.

Walk west on North Boulevard.

RESIDENCE OF ROMAN CATHOLIC ARCHBISHOP
1555 N. STATE PARKWAY
ARCHITECT: ALFRED F. PASHLEY (1880)

Facing Lincoln Park is a large 19th century mansion. Many chimneys (you will count 19 if you see them all!), several roof peaks, and impressive facades make this building a distinctive landmark. This has been the home of Chicago's Roman Catholic Archbishop since the 1880s.

On the southwest corner of State Parkway and North Boulevard is 1550 N. State Parkway.

233

1550 N. STATE PARKWAY
ARCHITECTS: MARSHALL AND FOX (1912)

This magnificent building was designed by Marshall and Fox. It originally had a single, 15-room apartment on each floor. The enormous apartments and the dignified Beaux Arts facade made this a most desirable address.

Continue west.

THE LATIN SCHOOL OF CHICAGO
59 W. NORTH BOULEVARD
ARCHITECTS: HARRY WEESE AND ASSOCIATES (1969)

The Latin School of Chicago is one of the city's finest progressive private schools. This structure houses the upper grades and is one block west of the lower-grade school building at 1531 W. Dearborn Parkway.

The 5-story concrete frame and brick structure serves an enrollment of 400 pupils. Among the features of the building are an Olympic-size swimming pool at the lowest level and a theater-auditorium seating 450 on the ground level. The ground level also includes a large fully covered loggia at the entry and a two-level spacious gallery. A full-service cafeteria with an outdoor terrace for autumn and spring use is on the 4th level. There are, of course, classrooms, laboratories, and recreation areas. The urban renewal site and subsequent land use necessitated the inclusion of a rooftop recreation area allowing total reclaiming of the site. The music and art studios and the chemistry and physics laboratories are included at the top floor and receive generous amounts of natural light from the top glazed projections visible on the north and west sides. A roof-top botanical laboratory is connected by a spiral stair to the labs on the top floor. Before urban renewal, this site was occupied by the Plaza Hotel, constructed in 1892 and designed by architect Clinton J. Warren.

Cross Clark Street. Just south of North Avenue is Germania Place.

◉ THE GERMANIA CLUB
108 W. GERMANIA PLACE
ARCHITECT: AUGUST FIEDLER (1889)

The Germania was long the center of activity where many families of German ancestry gathered. The membership has dwindled since, today, as in so many other instances, the present generation has either moved to the suburbs or no longer feels tied to its roots.

Backtrack north to North Avenue. Turn west to LaSalle Street. Turn south to Burton Place.

BURTON PLACE

Between LaSalle and Wells streets, West Burton Place has a 1-block stretch of some of the most unusual do-it-yourself architecture in all of Chicago. Unique and imaginative remodeling and rehabilitation by the owners themselves make Burton Place fascinating. Tile mosaic, glass block, marble, terra-cotta, and old brick, garnered from nearby demolished structures, are some of the materials used in what is obviously self-help work without benefit of an architect.

Behind the brick walls you will find patios with marble walks, fountains, sculptured figures, flowers, and trees. A plaque on the wall at 155 Burton Place states that this building was restored in 1927 by Sol Kogen. Kogen was the first owner on Burton Place to attempt rehabilitation by himself. Working in close association with artist Edgar Miller, they produced a fascinating and delightful environment for living in the 1920s and 1930s. They were responsible for much of the Burton Place rehabilitation.

Walk through Burton Place, and through the small park to Wells Street.

OLD TOWN

You are now in the center of a 1½-mile strip known as Old Town. Besides the many restaurants, taverns, bookstores, boutiques, museums (yes, museums), there is Piper's Alley (1608 N. Wells Street), a completely covered shopping and entertainment mall. Next door, at 1616 N. Wells Street, is the famous Second City, nationally known for its high-quality satirical performances. Note the exterior ornament that was formerly a part of the facade of the Garrick Theatre Building designed by architects Adler and Sullivan. (That building, demolished in 1961, stood on the north side of Randolph Street opposite the Daley Center. A garage now occupies the site.)

This concludes the WALK. You will find a southbound CTA bus 1 block east, on Clark Street, to take you back to the Loop. This is also the starting point of WALK 24 (Old Town Triangle) and WALK 25 (Lincoln Park Museums, Zoos, and Conservatory), either of which you may want to take now.

● The Old Town Triangle Historic District is roughly bounded by North Avenue, the extension on Ogden Avenue north to Armitage Avenue

16

1. Amphitheatre

2. University Hall

3. Jane Addam's Hull-House Museum
   800 S. Halsted St.

4. Chicago Fire Academy
   558 W. DeKoven St.

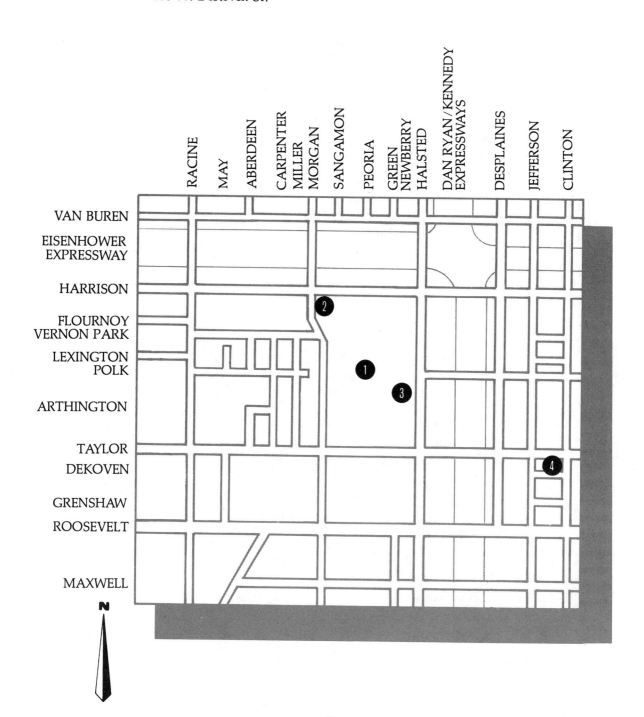

WALK • 16

UNIVERSITY OF ILLINOIS AT CHICAGO

WALKING TIME: 1 to 2 hours, depending on how much you "browse" among the buildings. HOW TO GET THERE: Walk south to Jackson Boulevard. Take a CTA bus No. 7 [Harrison] west and get off at Halsted Street [800 W]. Or walk to Dearborn and take the Congress-Douglas "El" to Halsted.

UNIVERSITY OF ILLINOIS AT CHICAGO

ARCHITECTS: SKIDMORE, OWINGS AND MERRILL,
WALTER A. NETSCH, JR., PARTNER IN CHARGE (1965, 1968, 1971);
FOR THE CHICAGO CIRCLE CENTER (STUDENT UNION BUILDING):
C. F. MURPHY ASSOCIATES

The modern, urban university has emerged to serve space-age students who live with speed, movement, and change. One of these is the campus of the University of Illinois at Chicago, less than a mile southwest of Chicago's Loop. Prior to the building of this campus the University's Chicago undergraduate division operated for nearly 20 years (1946-1965) at Navy Pier.

This new location is accessible to students from every part of the Chicago area. Featured specifically as a "commuter college," with no resident students, Chicago campus is easily reached by every kind of transportation—commuter railroads bringing passengers to different stations in Chicago, city subway and buses, and, of course, private cars. (The college provides extensive parking space.)

When first built, the campus was referred to as the University of Illinois Circle campus—from the Circle Interchange, where the Eisenhower, Kennedy, and Dan Ryan expressways exchange an unending flow of moving horsepower. But the name alone was not the only contribution of the freeways to the campus. In this constant stream of vehicles the architect, Walter A. Netsch, Jr. (a partner in Skidmore, Owings and Merrill, who had already designed the Air Force Academy in Colorado) must have seen the elements of his campus design—power, dash, energy, freedom of movement, and strength. He mixed these ingredients on his

Overleaf: Behavioral
Sciences Building
(Allen Carr)

239

drawing board and fit the entire campus plan around a centerpiece that epitomizes the university concept of all times—communications. There is a kiosk at the corner of Halsted and Harrison streets to direct you in the campus.

AMPHITHEATRE

This centerpiece is an open amphitheatre, surrounded by a powerful grouping of buildings in concrete, glass, and brick. Netsch planned this as an open forum, to be used for drama, debate, "outside classrooms," discussions, political rallies, or just socializing. The amphitheatre is especially spectacular because it descends from the center of the Great Court, which constitutes the common roof of six lecture buildings. Here are open elevated walkways from which students may enter the other major buildings of the campus at the 2nd-story level or go down to the lower-level walkways through the amphitheatre. The 2-level granite walkways give Circle Campus a character far removed from the green lawns of traditional college campuses. And so does the design of the campus buildings outside the Great Court—the Student Union, library, and engineering buildings with their strong concrete skeletons and skins of brick and glass.

240

UNIVERSITY HALL

Presiding over the Great Court with its forum and the surrounding group of buildings, garden courts, and lecture centers is University Hall, a 28-story administration and faculty office building. This high-rise structure spreads in width as it stretches skyward—it is 20 feet wider at the top than at the base—so that the upper floors provide more space. Narrow, almost Gothic windows squeeze between concrete channels to limit distracting outside views and unnecessary exterior light.

The campus, developed on a former slum that was Chicago's "Port of Entry" for thousands of immigrants, retains an important link to the past—the two buildings of the original Hull House, now a National Historic Landmark, resting quietly and with dignity near the main campus entrance on Halsted Street at Polk Street.

◉ JANE ADDAMS' HULL-HOUSE MUSEUM

800 S. Halsted Street
Architects: for Hull House: Unknown (1856);
for the Dining Hall: Alvin
and Irving K. Pond (1905)

These buildings perpetuate the saga of Jane Addams and her dedicated aides in helping the forefathers of many of today's students adjust to their new urban environment.

242

The University of Illinois has rehabilitated and restored the original two structures. Jane Addams' furniture and fixtures are in their proper places, so that here you have a delightful example of the architecture and furnishings of a late 19th-century Chicago residence, reflecting the individual qualities of the extraordinary, indomitable woman who once lived and worked there.

The Dining Hall contains an extensive exhibit of historical materials on the history of the near West Side. On the second floor, they show orientation slide shows on the history of Hull House and the surrounding neighborhood on request. As a museum, they now make a fitting memorial to Jane Addams.

The Museum is open Monday-Friday, 10 a.m. to 5 p.m., and Sunday (summers only) noon to 5 p.m. Admission is free. Call 996-2793 for information.

In some ways it is unfortunate that this beautiful restoration stands on its original site, for it is now dwarfed by the massive contemporary structures around it. But in the controversy about the siting of the University's campus (which necessitated taking over a whole block of the Hull House complex), sentiment for keeping the original Hull House at its original location was so great that respecting this wish of the area's residents became a necessary compromise.

Although the University of Illinois now occupies the site once used by the world-renowned Hull House, Jane Addams' work goes on in other parts of the city.

Jane Addams'
Hull House
(Philip A. Turner)

243

You can tour the campus by yourself at any time. Or you may arrange for guided tour service (on one or two day's advance notice) by calling 996-5000. There is no charge for tours. Parking lots with coin-operated gates, on the east, south, and west edges of the campus, are available to visitors.

Not only the architectural student will be fascinated with Chicago Campus. Anyone will be thrilled by the scale of this vast complex, reminiscent of the Mayas, yet definitely modern in design and function. Note the vast indoor shopping mall at Racine Avenue and Harrison Street.

In 1970, the campus was extended south of Roosevelt Road and north of Harrison Street. The total acreage was increased and now is 170 acres. The current enrollment is more than 25,000 students, making it the largest commuter campus in the nation. Students are offered a choice of more than 97 fields for undergraduate credit, master's degrees in 79 areas, and doctoral degrees in 44 specializations. It should be noted that just 1½ mile west are the University's Medical, Dental, and Pharmaceutical Colleges located on the West Side Medical Center Campus.

The southernmost building on campus is the Physical Education Building located on Roosevelt Road between Morgan and Newberry streets. Its primary feature is an Olympic-size swimming pool, complete with diving facilities and underwater windows for viewing swimming and diving. It is the largest indoor swimming pool in the Midwest. The basketball court holds more than 3,000 persons on the movable bleachers.

The Education and Communication Building is located on Harrison Street between Morgan and Congress Parkway. This structure houses the College of Education, departments of speech, theater, and music. The Jane Addams Graduate School of Social Work is also housed here. One feature is a small theater that can be converted for any type of show use—proscenium, theater-in-the round, or motion picture.

In contrast with these contemporary buildings is the Maxwell Street Market, only 2 blocks south of the south end of the campus. There is an Old World atmosphere about this outdoor marketplace, where almost anything can be purchased, especially on Sunday.

Another contrast is at the north end of the campus, just across the Eisenhower Expressway. A small section of shops clustered together and known as "Greek Town" has restaurants that feature belly dancers as well as those that provide other kinds of atmosphere in addition to the good food.

Opposite:

Architectural and Art Laboratories (Allen Carr)

245

Walk east on Polk Street, over the expressway, to Des Plaines Street. Turn south to Taylor Street, then east again 1 block. From this vantage, you have an excellent view of River City (featured in WALK 10) across the Chicago River to the east. On the southeast corner of Taylor and Jefferson streets is the Chicago Fire Academy.

⊙ **CHICAGO FIRE ACADEMY**
558 W. DeKoven Street
Architects: Loebl, Schlossman,
and Bennett (1960)

Several blocks to the east of the University of Illinois at Chicago campus is the Chicago Fire Academy. In front of the red brick Academy stands a large bronze sculptured flame, by Chicagoan Egon Weiner, expressing the fury of the Fire of 1871, which supposedly started on this very spot. The Fire Academy was built on the site of the old house and barn of the O'Leary family, whose famous cow is alleged to have kicked over a lantern and thus set off the whole catastrophe.

A 30-minute introduction to how our present-day fire fighters are trained for service in the Chicago Fire Department is available in a tour of the Academy—an experience that always has a fascination for everyone, especially young people, whether fire buffs or not. They also teach fire prevention and fire safety. Tours by appointment: 9 a.m. to 3 p.m.; call 744-6691 for reservations.

While you are at the Academy, don't miss the exhibit of photographs in the main lobby or the ancient (1835) horse-drawn hand-pumper fire engine.

Walk west to Halsted Street and turn north to return to your starting point.

17

1. Field Museum of Natural History
   Lake Shore Dr. at Roosevelt Rd.

2. John G. Shedd Aquarium
   1200 S. Lake Shore Dr.

3. Adler Planetarium
   900 E. Solidarity Dr.

4. Merrill C. Meigs Field
   15th St. at the Lakefront

5. Soldier Field
   425 E. McFetridge Dr.

6. McCormick Place-On-The-Lake
   2301 S. Lake Shore Dr.

7. McCormick Hotel
   451 E. 23rd St.

8. Donnelley Hall
   411 E. 23rd St.

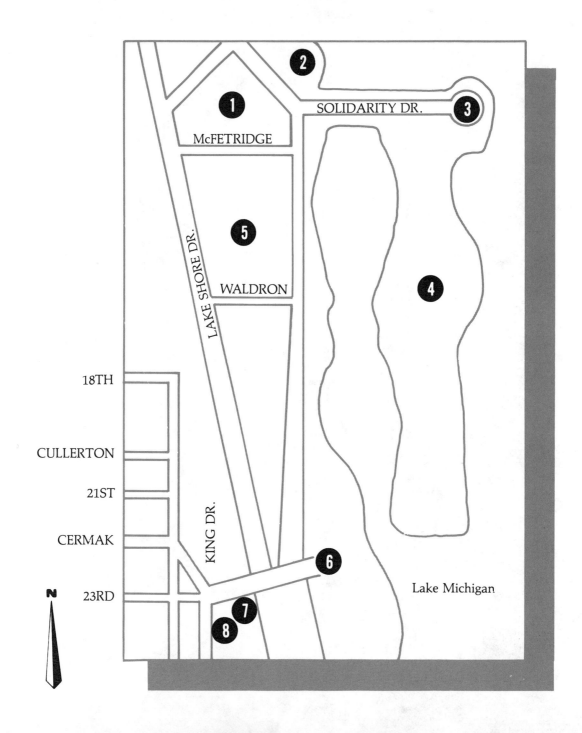

WALK • 17

BURNHAM PARK: MUSEUMS

WALKING TIME: 1 hour or less for outside viewing. [For inside visits: each museum rates a separate trip. You may want to spend at least one hour, say, at the Shedd Aquarium and whole days at the Field Museum. Hours when the museums are open vary somewhat and sometimes change from summer to winter. It is wise to consult each museum separately just before making your visit.] HOW TO GET THERE: You can reach the Burnham Park area over the foot bridges from Michigan Avenue at 11th Street, or through Grant Park along Columbus Drive and the adjacent formal gardens. Or you can take a southbound CTA "shuttle" bus, No. 149 [Michigan-State-Wacker], on State Street, which will take you directly to the Field Museum at the north end of Burnham Park. If you drive, you will find the best parking near Adler Planetarium or Soldier Field.

On Chicago's lakefront just south of Grant Park is a great concentration of museums and other public facilities. Still just a portion of Lake Michigan in 1910, it was filled with land and developed in accordance with the Burnham Plan of 1909. Construction of the Field Museum was started in 1911, Soldier Field in 1924, Shedd Aquarium in 1929, and Adler Planetarium in 1931. In 1933-34 this stretch of land reclaimed from the lake was the site of Chicago's Century of Progress exposition and a few years later of the city's Railroad Fair. Here, too, are Meigs Field airstrip and McCormick Place-on-the-Lake, one of the nation's busiest convention centers.

Just south of Grant Park, in the island of land formed when South Lake Shore Drive divides into separate southbound and northbound lanes, are the Field Museum and Soldier Field.

Start at the Field Museum, pausing on the long flight of steps for a glorious view of Chicago's downtown skyline.

Overleaf: Meigs Field looking toward Soldier Field across Burnham Harbor (Allen Carr)

249

◉ FIELD MUSEUM OF NATURAL HISTORY
LAKE SHORE DRIVE AT ROOSEVELT ROAD
ARCHITECTS: D. H. BURNHAM, AND COMPANY;
GRAHAM, ANDERSON, PROBST,
AND WHITE (1911-1920);
FOR THE INTERIOR OF STANLEY FIELD HALL:
HARRY WEESE AND ASSOCIATES (1968);
FOR THE RENOVATION: HARRY WEESE AND
ASSOCIATES (1975);
FOR THE RESTORATION: HARRY WEESE
AND ASSOCIATES (1986-7)

The Field Museum is regarded as the largest Georgia marble building in the world. It was built—and is partly maintained —with funds donated by Marshall Field I, the founder of Marshall Field and Company, then by other members of this family and Chicago families interested in its program. The huge structure is a variation of the Fine Arts Building in Jackson Park (now the Museum of Science and Industry—See WALK 21), which was built in 1893 for the Columbian Exposition and used as the Field Museum from then until 1920, when the Field collections were moved to their present quarters.

250

Field Museum
(Philip A. Turner)

Part of the celebration of the Field Museum's 75th anniversary, in 1968, was a redesigning of Stanley Field Hall—the tremendous entrance space on the first floor, named for a nephew of Marshall Field closely identified with the museum's development.

The effects of acid rain on the marble and terra-cotta exterior of the museum were studied at length over the last few years, and possible solutions were identified. In the process of restoration at this writing, the plan is to clean and restore the marble walls and base (on which the building sits), the terra-cotta cornice, and the caryatides. On the interior, the staircase network will be restored. The principle of the restoration is to be true to the designs of Daniel H. Burnham, and none of his elements will be altered.

The Field Museum is a distinguished showcase for prehistoric and recent cultures, with a staff of scholars behind the scenes who are constantly extending knowledge as the result of their investigations in the fields of anthropology, botany, geology, and zoology. Though they are classified according to these four areas of knowledge, the exhibits seem endless in variety—from the enormous stuffed African elephants and dinosaur skeletons in Stanley Field Hall, and corridor after corridor of dioramas showing hundreds of stuffed animals in their native habitats, to the life-sized figures of prehistoric man in his environment; from

251

Field Museum
(Merrick, Hedrich-
Blessing courtesy
Harry Weese
& Associates)

one of the world's finest collections of Oceanic art and of
American Indian art and artifacts, to displays of meteorites, rare
gems, and flowers. The museum is in fact filled with priceless
specimens.

The museum is open daily 9 a.m. to 5 p.m. except major
holidays. Adults $2; children 6-17 and students with I. D. $1;
senior citizens 50 cents; families $4; admission free on Thursday.

Directly east of the Field Museum, reached by a pedestrian tunnel under the South Outer Drive, is the Shedd Aquarium.

JOHN G. SHEDD AQUARIUM

1200 S. Lake Shore Drive
Architects: Graham, Anderson, Probst,
and White (1929);
for Coral Reef: Donal A. Olsen (1970);
for remodeling: Donal A. Olsen (1975, 1980);
for remodeling: FCL (1985, 1986);
for addition: Lohan Associates (1987-9)

Shedd Aquarium
(Chicago Association
of Commerce)

The aquarium was built with funds donated by John G. Shedd, former chairman of the board of Marshall Field and Company. Far smaller than the Field Museum, this is nevertheless one of the world's largest buildings devoted exclusively to living specimens of aquatic life. A white marble structure with bronze doors, it has a simple Doric design, another example of the neo-classical tendency that inspired the style of so many public buildings of the time.

253

In more than 130 tanks of water the Shedd Aquarium displays some 7,500 living specimens, representing 350 different species of marine and fresh-water creatures.

In the past few years many improvements have been made. In 1970 the Coral Reef, designed by Donal A. Olsen, was added. In 1975, the education center was added. During the 50th anniversary celebration there was major refurbishing of the Balanced Aquarium room and the main foyer, a new souvenir shop, the handicapped entrance, and offices were installed.

At this writing there are plans to create an addition to be located to the east of the extant building on land fill. The new building will be a 3-million gallon performing arena for killer whales and dolphins.

The aquarium is open daily except Christmas and New Year's Day from 10 a.m. to 5 p.m. Call 939-2438 for information. Adults $2; children 6-17 $1; senior citizens 50 cents; admission free on Thursday.

Directly east of the aquarium, about 2 city blocks away, is the Adler Planetarium.

ADLER PLANETARIUM AND ASTRONOMICAL MUSEUM
900 E. ACHSAH BOND DRIVE
ARCHITECT: ERNEST A. GRUNSFELD, JR. (1931);
FOR UNDERGROUND ADDITION: C. F. MURPHY
ASSOCIATES (1975)

Adler Planetarium
detail
(Allen Carr)

The planetarium is named for its donor, Max Adler, a former vice-president of Sears Roebuck and Company. It is located at the lakefront. The small granite structure with its planetarium dome is handsome and strong, devoid of all architectural superlatives.

The Astronomical Museum section contains one of the finest collections in the world of antique astronomical and mathematical instruments (second only to the collection in Oxford, England) as well as some of the most modern. Frequent 15-minute demonstrations of how some of these instruments work are given daily.

For anyone interested in stars and planets—and who of any age isn't?—the chief attraction of the Planetarium lies in its daily sky show inside the domed chamber in which the Zeiss projection instrument, also called a "planetarium," reproduces the natural night sky at any time or any place selected for fascinating explanations about what is going on up there. The lectures that accompany these projections of the sky make faraway scientific

254

Adler Planetarium
(Olga Stefanos)

information simple and clear for anyone. For this sky show, which varies from month to month, a small fee is charged.

Admission to the planetarium itself and the other exhibits is free. Admission to the sky show: adults, $2.00; children, $1.50. The building is open daily except Thanksgiving Day and Christmas Day 9:30 a.m. to 4:30 p.m.; Friday to 9 p.m. Call 322-0300 for information.

South of the planetarium on the lakefront is Chicago's "downtown airport."

MERRILL C. MEIGS FIELD
15TH STREET AT THE LAKEFRONT
ARCHITECTS: CONSDER AND TOWNSEND (1961)

The architects produced a delicate, well-planned building to serve as the passenger terminal for Meigs Field. This lakefront airstrip for light planes and helicopters is one of the largest downtown spaces of its kind in the country.

255

McCormick-Place-on-
the-Lake
(Hube Henry, Hedrich-
Blessing)

South of the Field Museum, in the area between the southbound and northbound lanes of South Lake Shore Drive, is Soldier Field.

⊙ SOLDIER FIELD

425 E. McFetridge Drive
Architects: Holabird and Roche (1922-26);
for remodeling: Chicago Park District (1939, 1971);
for sky boxes: Chicago Park District (1980-81)

The stadium, Soldier Field, with a seating capacity of about 106,000, was constructed as a war memorial. It is the site of the annual All-Star football game, political rallies, and various other activities. The 100-foot Doric columns that surround Soldier Field harmonize its architecture well with that of the Field Museum, just to the north. In 1939 the north end of the stadium was closed by the addition of the Administration Building for the Chicago Park District.

In 1971, the stadium was remodeled to accommodate the Chicago Bears, professional football team. The remodeling consisted primarily in improving the seating and in adding seating at the north end of the football field—replacing temporary stands that had been placed at the north end in order to give fans a closer view of the games. A synthetic turf was also placed on the field.

Between South Lake Shore Drive and the lake, south of Soldier Field parking area, is Chicago's premier convention center.

256

McCORMICK PLACE-ON-THE-LAKE

2301 S. Lake Shore Drive
Architects: C. F. Murphy Associates (1971);
for the addition: Lester B. Knight & Associates;
Skidmore, Owings and Merrill (1987)

McCormick Place was built on the site of the previous building which was destroyed by fire in 1969. This structure has out-stripped its predecessor as one of the world's busiest convention centers. Gene Summers was the architect in charge for C. F. Murphy Associates. He had previously been an associate of Mies van der Rohe and the design clearly shows Mies' influence.

The basic requirements submitted to the architects were 1) to reconstruct the severely fire-damaged building with expediency; 2) to enlarge the prime exhibition area to 600,000 square feet; and 3) to maximize the residual value of the existing structure. The increase in building area had to be accomplished without unduly removing valuable lakefront area. Special considerations con-sisted of a complete fire-protection system that included water reservoir, fire pumps, standpipe, sprinkler, and detection systems. The design concept was to contain the two dominant functions of exhibit and theater under a single unifying roof resting on a plat-form sheathed in masonry. A 75-foot cantilever of the roof affords protection to the pedestrian and vehicular passageways around the theater unit and to the truck dock area around the exhibit area.

257

Overall, the section of the convention center along the lakefront contains approximately 600,000 square feet of exhibition area, a 4,300 seat theater, 100,000 square feet of meeting rooms, a dignitary suite, and 42,000 square feet of restaurant and cafeteria facilities. A below-grade parking facility is located immediately south of the building for 2,000 cars.

Building materials consist chiefly of exposed face brick, painted concrete block, painted structural steel, terrazzo, and exposed concrete floors, plaster, and metal pan ceilings. The exterior curtain wall is made of painted steel framing with 7 x 8-foot polished gray plate glass. The building, or rather project, is a stunning and powerful statement that does credit to the distinguished firm of architects as well as the many city officials involved.

The new addition, designed by Skidmore, Owings and Merrill, provides another 1,150,000 square feet of space. If you walk far enough for a view of the roof, you will see the support system of the "hung roof," which allows for the creation of the largest column-free space in the world. It has an aluminum and glass window wall to blend with the extant structure. There is also a covered pedestrian mall to connect the structures.

If you are exhausted from walking by this time, a good idea might be to walk west over the 23rd Street bridge to the hotel.

McCORMICK HOTEL
451 E. 23RD STREET
ARCHITECTS: A. EPSTEIN AND SONS (1973)

This hotel is 25 stories, has 700 rooms, and parking for 500 cars. The tower is sheathed in bronze-tinted glass and has a brick base that houses the parking facilities. This stunning structure is well sited and is complementary to McCormick Place.

Just to the west of the hotel is Donnelley Hall.

DONNELLEY HALL
411 E. 23RD STREET
ARCHITECT: ALBERT KAHN OF DETROIT, MICHIGAN (1947);
FOR THE ADAPTIVE REUSE: C. F. MURPHY AND ASSOCIATES;
DUBIN, DUBIN AND MATOUSSAMY (1978)

Originally part of the Donnelley printing plant, Life Magazine was once printed here. It now adds 330,000 square feet of exhibit area to the McCormick Place complex.

18

1. Widow Clarke House
   1836 S. Prairie Ave.

2. Glessner House
   1800 S. Prairie Ave.

3. Kimball House
   1801 S. Prairie Ave.

4. Coleman House
   1811 S. Prairie Ave.

5. Elbridge Keith House
   1900 S. Prairie Ave.

6. Marshall Field, Jr. (or Schwartz) House
   1919 S. Prairie Ave.

7. William H. Reid House
   2013 S. Prairie Ave.

8. Edson Keith, Jr. House
   2110 S. Prairie Ave.

9. Charles D. Hamill House
   2126 S. Prairie Ave.

10. Second Presbyterian Church
    1936 S. Michigan Ave.

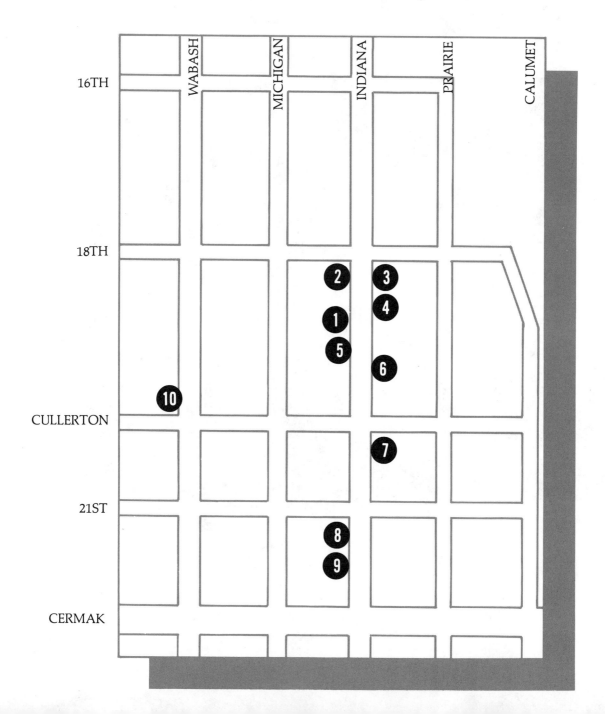

WALK • 18

◉ **PRAIRIE AVENUE HISTORIC DISTRICT**

WALKING TIME: About 1½ hours. HOW TO GET THERE: Take a CTA southbound No. 1, No. 3, or No. 4 bus on Michigan Avenue. Get off at East 18th Street. Walk 1 block east to South Prairie Avenue.

This historic district has been restored with 19th century gas lamps and cobblestones along with the renovation of 5 celebrated houses—Glessner, Kimball, Keith, Coleman, and the Widow Clarke House—around an architectural park that can be considered an outdoor museum. The Widow Clarke House, which was not part of the original Prairie Avenue district, has been relocated here.

◉ **WIDOW CLARKE HOUSE**
1836 S. PRAIRIE AVENUE
ARCHITECT: UNKNOWN (1836);
FOR RESTORATION: WILBERT R. HASBROUCK
AND JOSEPH CASSERLEY (1978-82)

The Widow Clarke House, believed to be the oldest in the city, was built in 1836 for Henry B. Clarke, a hardware businessman and banker, on Michigan Avenue near 16th Street. About 1871, shortly before the Great Fire, the house was moved to 4526 S. Wabash Avenue and finally to the east side of South Indiana Avenue, south of 18th Street.

This handsome Greek revival house is operated as a museum to interpret life in Chicago between 1836 and 1860 when the Clarkes occupied it. The basement (new space on the new foundation) is being developed as a museum of the history of the house itself from 1836 to 1977. The house has been restored to its appearance of about 1853.

Overleaf: Kimball House (Commission of Chicago Historical and Architectural Landmarks)

Widow Clarke House
(Olga Stefanos)

⚫ GLESSNER HOUSE
1800 S. Prairie Avenue
Architects: Henry Hobson Richardson (1886);
for the exterior cleaning: John Vinci (1984)

This masterwork of Henry Hobson Richardson is owned by the Chicago Architecture Foundation which was formed to rescue the house. For the last twenty years they have continued their commitment to its restoration. The Historic House museum now has the appearance and furnishings of the 1890s.

J. J. Glessner, a founder of the International Harvester Company, in 1885 commissioned the great architect Henry Hobson Richardson to design a fitting house for him on Prairie Avenue, referring to the street as the finest residential street in Chicago.

It is appropriate that an architectural foundation should be housed in the only remaining example in Chicago of a design by one of the earliest and greatest of American architects. Although this 35-room, massive, rough-hewn granite house seems a far cry from the delicate atrium houses of architect Y. C. Wong in Kenwood (see WALK 19), they have one feature in common: win-

Glessner House
(Olga Stefanos)

dow placement in both is designed for privacy and quiet. All main rooms of the Glessner house face a private courtyard, instead of the street.

The citation from the Architectural Landmarks Commission reads:

In recognition of the fine planning for an urban site, which opens the family rooms to the quiet serenity of an inner yard; the effective ornament and decoration; and the impressive Romanesque masonry, expressing dignity and power.

Tours are available of Glessner House, Clarke House, and the Prairie Avenue Historic District. Call 326-1393 for information. The Foundation also holds exhibits and conducts seminars and walking tours in the downtown area from the ArchiCenter. The time and starting place of these tours can be determined by telephoning 782-1776.

Walk south on Prairie Avenue.

◉ KIMBALL HOUSE
1801 S. PRAIRIE AVENUE
ARCHITECT: S. S. BEMAN (1890)

263

A "French chateau" which cost an estimated $1,000,000 when it was built in 1890 for W. W. Kimball (head of the piano company), the Kimball House was designed by Solon S. Beman, architect of the town of Pullman. The house is owned and used by R. R. Donnelley and Sons Company, the country's largest printers, under a protective agreement negotiated by the Historic District Committee.

COLEMAN HOUSE
1811 S. Prairie Avenue
Architects: Cobb and Frost (1886)

Joseph A. Coleman, a hardware manufacturer, built this stone-faced Romanesque-inspired house.

ELBRIDGE KEITH HOUSE
1900 S. Prairie Avenue
Architect: Unknown (c. 1870)

Elbridge Keith, a hat wholesaler and banker, built this 3-story gray sandstone and brick house with huge paneled rooms and parquet floors which reflected the Prairie Avenue lifestyle. It is a fine old mid-Victorian mansion, with mansard roof and classic columns.

MARSHALL FIELD, Jr. (or SCHWARTZ) HOUSE
1919 S. Prairie Avenue
Architect: Solon S. Beman (1887)

Although added to and reworked many times over the years, it is clear that Solon S. Beman was responsible for early work in the 1880s.

WILLIAM H. REID HOUSE
2013 S. Prairie Avenue
Architect: Unknown (c. 1905)

This is a 3-story Classical Revival house with a classic facade of brick and stone trim. Note the Palladian motif at the 3rd-floor window and the Ionic columns at the porch level.

EDSON KEITH, Jr. HOUSE
2110 S. Prairie Avenue
Architect: Unknown (c. 1889)

This is a 3-story house with a limestone facade in Romanesque style, and a large pediment at the roof—a design that suggests the influence of Richardson. Edson Keith, Jr., the original occupant, worked in the family millinery business.

CHARLES D. HAMILL HOUSE
2126 S. Prairie Avenue
Architect: Unknown (c. 1907)

Charles D. Hamill was president of the Board of Trade, a supporter of the Chicago Symphony Orchestra, and a founding trustee of the Art Institute of Chicago. The red brick house is Classical Revival with a center entrance. It is 5 bays wide.

This is all that remains of the once great wealth-laden avenue of fine houses and mansions. In 1890 one of the grandest mansions on this same Prairie Avenue was that of Marshall Field, built for the multimillionaire merchant by Richard Morris Hunt, the famous architect who had also designed the luxurious dwellings of such New York millionaires as William H. Vanderbilt and John Jacob Astor.

Nearly all the property in the area has been acquired by the Lakeside Press of R. R. Donnelley and Sons Company, who have constructed an enormous complex of buildings to print—among other things—Time magazine and many telephone directories.

Backtrack north to Cullerton Street. Walk west 1 block to South Michigan Avenue.

◉ SECOND PRESBYTERIAN CHURCH
1936 S. Michigan Avenue
Architects: James Renwick (1872-74);
for remodeling: Howard Van Doren Shaw (1900)

This fine old semi-Gothic South Side landmark church is a vestige of 19th-century Chicago, standing in what was then the city's finest neighborhood.

The congregation was a wealthy and powerful one. Robert Todd Lincoln was on the Board of Trustees. Many of the wealthy packinghouse millionaires, such as the Swifts and Armours, and undoubtedly some of the nearby residents such as the Glessners, Pullmans and Marshall Fields attended here. Howard Van Doren Shaw was responsible for the remodeling after a fire in 1900. After hitting a low point in membership in the 1960s, the membership is now growing. The Church now has city, state, and National Register of Historic Places landmark status.

Note the stained glass windows of green pastoral scenes, lavender irises or fields of thick glass lilies. Eight of the windows were designed by the Tiffany Studios and two were done by British artist-designer Sir Edward Burne-Jones.

Tours are available by advance reservation. The fee is $2. Call 225-4951 for information.

Before returning to Prairie Avenue, or boarding a northbound CTA bus on Michigan Avenue to return to the Loop, note the high-rise apartment buildings that house moderate-income families. These concrete towers were designed by Dubin, Dubin, Black and Moutoussamy and completed in 1971.

19

1. Heller House
   5132 S. Woodlawn Ave.

2. Madison Park

3. 1239-41-43 E. Madison Pk.

4. 1302 E. Madison Pk.

5. 1366-80 E. Madison Pk.

6. Farmer's Field

7. 1351-1203 E. 50th St.

8. 1243 E. 50th St.

9. 1220 E. 50th St.

10. 1229 E. 50th St.

11. 1207 and 1203 E. 50th St.

12. 4940 S. Greenwood Ave.

13. Magerstadt House
    4930 S. Greenwood Ave.

14. 4935 S. Greenwood Ave.

15. 4929 S. Greenwood Ave.

16. 4920 and 4906 S. Greenwood Ave.

17. 4906 S. Greenwood Ave.

18. 4900 S. Greenwood Ave.

19. 1222 E. 49th St.

20. 4850 S. Greenwood Ave.

21. 4819 S. Greenwood Ave.

22. 1126 E. 48th St.

23. 1125 E. 48th St.

24. 1144-1158 E. 48th St.

25. Lake Village

26. 1322 E. 49th St.

27. 4858 S. Kenwood Ave.

28. 4852 S. Kenwood Ave.

29. 4915 S. Woodlawn Ave.

30. 4912 S. Woodlawn Ave.

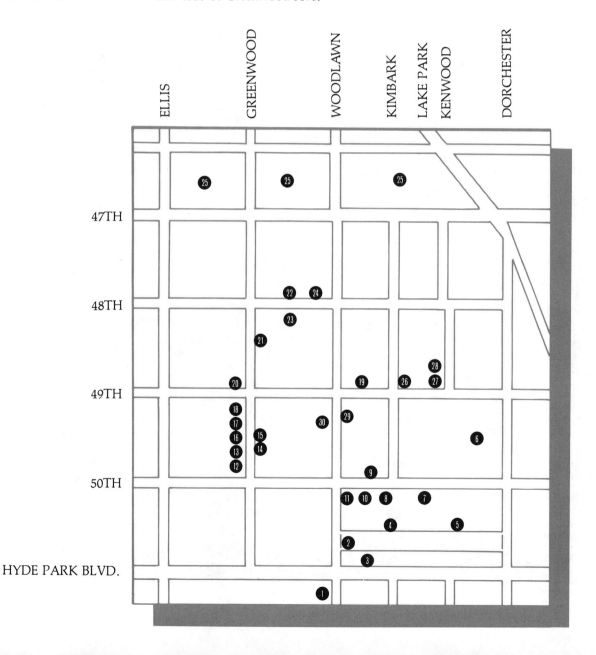

WALK • 19

KENWOOD-MADISON PARK

WALKING TIME: At least 2 hours. HOW TO GET THERE: Take a southbound CTA bus No. 1 [Indiana-Hyde Park] on Michigan Avenue. Get off at Hyde Park Boulevard [5100 S] and Woodlawn Avenue [1200 E].

You are now at the south end of Kenwood, which lies just north of the Hyde Park area. Here are some of the finest old mansions, wooded gardens, and boulevards in the city. Among the houses called to your attention here are a number that are famous because of the architects who designed them; these of course will be identified. On the whole, however, houses have been selected for their individual architectural quality, whether or not a well-known architect designed them.

At the turn of the century, Kenwood was actually a suburb of Chicago, where many of the wealthiest families built their estates. Residents have carried some of Chicago's most noted—and notorious—names: Julius Rosenwald, Max Adler, Ben Heineman, Harold Swift, and the tragically doomed families of Leopold and Loeb. As the depression of the 1930s struck some of the owners and later, when the return of prosperity only increased the costs of domestic help, as well as the difficulty of securing it, the expenses of maintaining such mansions often became too exorbitant to meet. Between much absentee ownership and neglect of property by some who still lived there, Kenwood was rapidly deteriorating. Houses were being sold indiscriminately, and the usual flight of white residents at the appearance of a few black families was threatening.

Citizens of Kenwood are to be thanked—and congratulated—for saving the neighborhood. An interracial committee of homeowners took the situation in hand. Dedicated to the conviction that character and ability to maintain property, not color of skin, determine whether or not a prospective purchaser will be a desirable neighbor, they worked with real estate dealers to establish a stable, well-integrated community. Naturally, because of the kind of houses available, most Kenwood

◉ Portions of this walk are included in the Hyde Park-Kenwood Historic District, roughly bounded by 47th and 59th streets and Cottage Grove and Lake Park avenues

Overleaf:
4935 S. Greenwood
(Allen Carr)

Heller House
(Allen Carr)

homeowners of both races have upper-middle or high incomes. For many years a local committee sponsored a "Kenwood Open House" weekend each spring, when outsiders were invited to call at a specified number of homes and witness the success of this undertaking.

In Kenwood, too, as in Hyde Park, urban renewal has been responsible for some effective rehabilitation and redevelopment. Two citizens' organizations that cooperated actively with the city government in recent changes are the Hyde Park-Kenwood Community Conference and the South East Chicago Commission. Other groups interested in Kenwood's redevelopment were the Amalgamated Clothing Workers Union and the Lake Village Development Corporation.

270

⊚ HELLER HOUSE
5132 S. Woodlawn Avenue
Architect: Frank Lloyd Wright (1897)

This 3-story brick house is an early example of Wright's work. At first it seems quite unlike the "Prairie House" that he designed 12 years later, for the compact upright lines of the first 2 stories contrast markedly with the widespreading horizontal lines of the Robie House (see WALK 20). Yet the widely projecting eaves and the openness of the 3rd story suggest some of the later design.

Note the molded plaster frieze at the top of the building—by the sculptor Richard Bock.

Cross Woodlawn Avenue at Hyde Park Boulevard (51st Street), and walk north about half a block to the entrance of Madison Park.

(Allen Carr)

MADISON PARK

Between Hyde Park Boulevard and East 50th Street, running from Woodlawn to Dorchester avenues, Madison Park is not a park in the usual sense of the word. It is, instead, a small residential section of Kenwood that seems to belong completely to itself. As you pass through the large iron gate that tells you the name and the fact that it is private, you see a long stretch of green, with trees and mounds, bordered on each side by a street with a continuing line of houses, occasionally an apartment building, in varying styles, most of them built probably three generations ago. The minute you are inside the gate, you are overwhelmed by the almost rural quiet of the place. Madison Park stretches from east to west 3 blocks with no north-south streets coming through, and east-west traffic from outside is minimal. The strip of park down the center is used only by the residents—usually a few children playing happily and perhaps an adult lounging on the grass reading. Despite the city-like rows of houses close together on each side, Madison Park does indeed have much of the small village atmosphere about it. It is populated by families of many races and ethnic origins, who have cooperated to maintain the beauty and serenity of this delightful area.

At the west end of Madison Park, stop on the south side of the street.

1239-41-43 E. MADISON PARK
Architect: Y. C. Wong (1967)

Here are three handsome townhouses, constructed in 1967 and

271

1302 E. Madison Park
(Allen Carr)

designed by Y. C. Wong. Although these are newer buildings in the Park, they seem to blend very well with their neighbors. A yellow brick wall shields lovely private gardens from the view of passersby. The horizontal lines of the stucco upper wall and glass windows give the north facade an appearance of strength. The south facade, which faces Hyde Park Boulevard, has garages conveniently located just below the living room terraces.

Across the street is a charmingly unconventional yellow brick apartment building.

1302 E. MADISON PARK

The pitched roof and garage below the main entrance suggest the style of many buildings in San Francisco. Other features that give this building individuality are stairs to the first-floor apartments on each side of the garage and attractive metal grillwork across the balcony of the main entrance.

Farther down on the same side you come to eight stunning townhouses well known in the Chicago area—architect Y. C. Wong's "Atrium Houses."

272

1366-80 E. MADISON PARK
Architect: Y. C. Wong (1961)

The exterior walls have no windows whatever, the outside light for all the rooms coming from an interior open court, or atrium. The complete privacy and quiet provided by this arrangement are considered a decided advantage in urban living.

With the Atrium Houses you have reached the east end of Madison Park, which is Dorchester Avenue. Walk north on Dorchester to East 50th Street. At the northeast corner, to your right, stands the Church of St. Paul and the Redeemer, two merged Episcopal churches, in a relatively new building constructed after the old St. Paul's was damaged by fire. To your left, at the northwest corner of Dorchester and 50th Street, you will see the sign "KENWOOD PARK." This stretch of plain green "pasture", covering an entire block, has long been known to Chicagoans as "Farmer's Field."

Walk out the east end of Madison Park and turn north to 50th Street.

FARMER'S FIELD
50th to 49th Street and
Dorchester to Kenwood Avenue

Although the history of Farmer's Field seems somewhat hazy, a house-owner on East 50th Street says that a resident of days gone by told him that a cow used to graze there every day as recently as the 1920s. A downtown bank is credited with having bought the property with the commendable intent of keeping it unchanged.

Now walk west on 50th Street and note the row of townhouses extending from 1351-1319 E. 50th Street.

1351-1203 E. 50th STREET

All are well-maintained houses of about the early 1900s.

1243 E. 50th STREET

This is an older house, built about 1875, a charming gray house with white trim, set in a garden.

1220 E. 50th STREET

This is an enormous red brick Georgian house with white door, shutters, and trim. The windows and entrance are in good scale.

273

1229 E. 50th STREET

Back on the south side of the street, is a gray frame house with very high ceilings, which has an appearance of great dignity and serenity.

1207 and 1203 E. 50th STREET
ARCHITECTS: GRUNSFELD AND ASSOCIATES (1965)

Look at these two red brick, 2-story townhouses. Set back from the street, they blend perfectly with their older neighbors.

Continue west to Greenwood Avenue and enjoy the beauty of the many old trees, fine shrubbery, and delightful front yards. These provide much of the charm of the area, and Kenwood homeowners are determined to keep it that way. The majority of the houses along Greenwood Avenue were built between 1910 and 1925.

Walk north on Greenwood Avenue and stop at 4940 S. Greenwood Avenue, on the west side of the street.

4940 S. GREENWOOD AVENUE

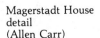

Magerstadt House
detail
(Allen Carr)

This 3-story red brick mansion is of collegiate Gothic design. Unusual Gothic ornamentation surrounds the front windows and doors. At the rear are a tremendously large yard and garden, and a garage with living quarters above.

Be sure to note the mansion across the street at 4939 S. Greenwood Avenue—an enormous red brick house with quoins at the corners and high-pitched roof. Doric pilasters adorn the entrance porch. This was the home built by Max Adler, of Adler Planetarium fame (see WALK 17).

Walk a bit farther north, and cross the street.

MAGERSTADT HOUSE
4930 S. GREENWOOD AVENUE
ARCHITECTS: GEORGE W. MAHER (1906);
FOR REMODELING: ARTHUR MYHRUM (1968)

The Magerstadt House was designed by a contemporary of Frank Lloyd Wright and quite naturally reflects to some extent Wright's style—the long plan and side entrance, for instance, and the wide overhang. On the other hand, Wright would surely not have used the two unnecessary pillars that pretend to support the

274

porch roof. And the building as a whole is more massive than most of Wright's. The present occupants of the house completed its rehabilitation in 1968. The interior lighting, bathrooms, and kitchen have been completely remodeled; the woodwork has been restored and repainted. In general, the interior has a new glow, making this a truly delightful home.

Magerstadt House (Allen Carr)

4935 S. GREENWOOD AVENUE

This is a heavy 3-story building with semicircular facade extending the entire height. Note the stone columns at the entrance porch and the ornament on the pediment at the roof line. At 4935½ S. Greenwood Avenue, to the rear, is a 2-story coach house of similar design and material. Remodeled in 1963, it contains a new kitchen, fireplace, and paneled study. It is typical of many of the old coach houses in the area.

Continue north.

4929 S. GREENWOOD AVENUE

This is a well-proportioned red brick house of the Georgian design. The white wood trim is in good scale with the rest of the facade.

Across, on the west side of the street, is a house of a different school of design.

4920 and 4906 S. GREENWOOD AVENUE

This 3-story limestone English Tudor house is worth viewing. Take particular note of the enormous grounds and gardens, and of the iron picket fence.

4906 S. GREENWOOD AVENUE

Here you will see a red brick symmetrical facade with a design similar to early Louis Sullivan houses.

4900 S. GREENWOOD AVENUE

The enormous, light gray limestone Doric columns give this structure an appearance of a large apartment building rather than a private residence. Constructed about 1900, it still dominates the corner of 49th and Greenwood.

Walk 2 blocks east—for a short detour—to a very charming former coach house built originally in 1906 and remodeled 40 years later. It is hidden behind much landscaping.

1222 E. 49th STREET
ARCHITECTS: UNKNOWN (1906);
FOR REMODELING: CROMBIE TAYLOR AND
EDWARD NOONAN (1946)

Although the exterior remodeling is at a minimum, concentrated primarily in the west wall and the entrance, it is characteristic of the quality and style exhibited in the interior remodeling. The stunning, all-glass west wall of the living room was formerly the coach entrance.

Back in the mainstream of the WALK, on Greenwood Avenue and 49th Street, you come to a 3-story neoclassic red brick mansion.

4850 S. GREENWOOD AVENUE
ARCHITECTS: GEORGE FRED AND
WILLIAM KECK (1967)

276

Here is a cluster of 3-story, red brick, freestanding townhouses, all with pitched roofs (one of them a mansard roof). They make a handsome addition to this section of Kenwood.

4819 S. GREENWOOD AVENUE

This stately Georgian mansion has red brick walls with quoins of the same material at the corners. The grand scale of the windows and the ceiling heights give the house an appearance of enormous dignity. The immense, well-landscaped grounds include a tennis court at the rear.

Walk north on Greenwood Avenue and then east on 48th Street until you come to a large gray brick house.

1126 E. 48th STREET
ARCHITECT: UNKNOWN (1888);
FOR REMODELING: JAMES EPPENSTEIN (1941);
ARTHUR MYHRUM (1963)

Originally constructed in 1888, this house has been remodeled twice, the major part taking place in 1963. By removing the original front staircase the architect was free to design a stunning 3-story entrance hall on the side of the building, facing a landscaped patio to the east. He set a library adjacent to the entrance hall, with a wall of grillwork between, and placed a large living room at the front of the building, facing 48th Street. Other alterations have provided this house with modernized kitchen, spacious rooms on the 2nd floor—including a splendid master bedroom, with separate "His" and "Her" dressing rooms, bathrooms, and studies—and guest rooms on both 2nd and 3rd floors.

Across the street is a 2-story gray frame house.

1125 E. 48th STREET
ARCHITECT: UNKNOWN (1895);
FOR REMODELING: ERNEST A. GRUNSFELD (1938)

The main house has an elegant entrance hall, dining room, and kitchen on the first floor, four bedrooms and two baths on the second. The living room is in a 1-story east wing, with windows to the south, facing a large landscaped garden and play area.

Farther east on 48th Street you come to a row of 8 townhouses that have been cited for architectural excellence.

277

1144-1158 E. 48th STREET
ARCHITECT: Y. C. WONG (1965)

The townhouses were designed by the same architect who planned the famous atrium houses in Madison Park. The 9-foot walls that encompass the gardens around these homes are characteristic of this architect's emphasis on privacy for the homeowner.

The WALK ends at this point, but you may wish to drive north to 47th Street and note the charming red brick townhouses, walk-up apartments, and high-rise buildings—all part of land cleared through urban renewal.

LAKE VILLAGE
EAST 47TH STREET, SOUTH ELLIS AVENUE TO
SOUTH LAKE PARK AVENUE
ARCHITECTS: HARRY WEESE AND ASSOCIATES;
EZRA GORDON AND JACK LEVIN (1971)

A number of these structures won architectural awards in 1971. The completed program will have approximately 500 dwelling units comprising a mix of social, ethnic, racial, and economic groups.

Just to the south and east of Lake Village are two striking high-rise buildings and the parking garage of the Amalgamated Clothing Workers Union development consisting of approximately 600 dwelling units. The architects were George Fred Keck and William Keck. The majority of the units are cooperative.

Drive east on 48th Street to Kimbark Avenue (1300 E). Turn south to 49th Street, then turn east.

1322 E. 49TH STREET
ARCHITECT: FRANK LLOYD WRIGHT (1907)

Here you will see a 2-story coach house, designed for the house below. The yellow Roman brick and the wide eaves clearly mark this small garage structure as the work of Frank Lloyd Wright. It was originally designed for insurance man George Blossom.

Continue east to Kenwood Avenue.

4858 S. KENWOOD AVENUE
ARCHITECT: FRANK LLOYD WRIGHT (1892)

This yellow frame, neoclassic house, at the corner of East 49th Street and South Kenwood Avenue, was built for insurance broker George Blossom in 1892. While "moonlighting" from his job as chief draftsman for Adler and Sullivan, Wright designed this and several other (now known as the "bootleg") homes in his off hours to help support his growing family. To avoid raising Louis Sullivan's ire, Wright designed these houses under the name of an architect friend, Cecil Corwin, but Sullivan found out in 1893, and abruptly launched Wright on his illustrious independent architectural career.

4852 S. KENWOOD AVENUE
ARCHITECT: FRANK LLOYD WRIGHT (1891, 1902)

Like the Blossom House next door, this brick and stucco residence was clandestinely designed by Frank Lloyd Wright while he was working for Adler and Sullivan. The client, Warren McArthur, also had Wright execute major alterations to the interior in 1902.

Drive west on East 49th Street to South Woodlawn Avenue, and then turn south to view the last two houses.

4915 S. WOODLAWN AVENUE

This is another red brick Georgian house, with an excellent formal facade. The two circular bays extend from grade to roof. The white wood trim is in good scale, and so are the slender white Ionic pilasters at the entrance.

Across the street is a modern house in the heart of this middle-aged group of homes—well set back from the sidewalk and shielded by trees and shrubbery.

4912 S. WOODLAWN AVENUE
ARCHITECT: JOHN JOHANSEN OF NEW YORK CITY (1950)

Although constructed in the 1950s, the house looks surprisingly contemporary. The base is of random-cut limestone and the overhanging balcony of wood. Painted sections of the base—large rectangles in yellow, blue, and green—give a splendid, light feeling to the house. The all-glass stairwell contributes a special quality to this excellent design.

There are many more homes in Kenwood that are beautiful and noteworthy, as those who continue exploring will discover.

20

1. University Apartments
1400–1450 E. 55th St.

2. St. Thomas Apostle Church
5472 S. Kimbark Ave.

3. Lutheran School of Theology
1100 E. 55th St.

4. Augustana Evangelical Lutheran Church
5500 S. Woodlawn Ave.

5. Stanley R. Pierce Hall
5514 University Ave.

6. 5551 S. University Avenue Building

7. Cochrane-Woods Art Center
5540–5550 S. Greenwood Ave.

8. Court Theater
5535 S. Ellis Ave.

9. Quadrangle Club
1155 E. 57th St.

10. Mitchell Tower
1131 E. 57th St.

11. Mandel Hall
1131 E. 57th St.

12. Cobb Gate and Hull Court

13. Joseph Regenstein Library
1100 E. 57th St.

14. Charles Hitchcock Hall
1009 E. 57th St.

15. Nuclear Energy

16. Laboratory for Astrophysics
and Space Research

17. High-Energy Physics Building
935 E. 56th St.

18. Snell Hall
5709 S. Ellis Ave.

19. Searle Chemistry Building
5715 S. Ellis Ave.

20. Kersten Physics Teaching Center
5720 S. Ellis Ave.

21. John Crerar Library
5730 S. Ellis Ave.

22. Henry Hinds Laboratory
E. 58th St. and Ellis Ave.

23. Cummings Life Science Center
950 E. 58th St.

24. Cobb Hall
5811 Ellis Ave.

25. University of Chicago Quadrangle

26. Julius Rosenwald Hall
1101 E. 58th St.

27. The Walker Museum

28. Albert Pick Hall for International Studies
5828 S. University Ave.

29. Oriental Institute
1155 E. 58th St.

30. Chicago Theological Seminary
5757 S. University Ave.

31. Woodward Court
5825 S. Woodlawn Ave.

32. Robie House
5757 S. Woodlawn Ave.

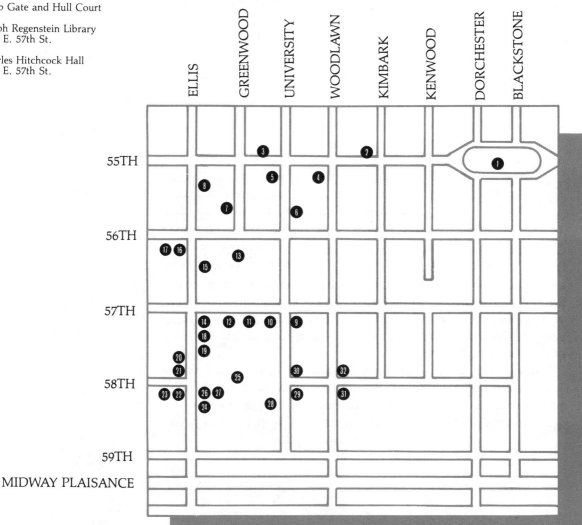

WALK • 20

HYDE PARK: NORTH OF THE MIDWAY

WALKING TIME: 2 hours. HOW TO GET THERE: Take an Illinois Central [I. C.] suburban train at its Randolph Street and Michigan Avenue underground station, and get off at 55th Street. [Check before buying your ticket and boarding the train to find out which train makes that stop.] Walk west on 55th Street. If you go by car, take the South Lake Shore Outer Drive south to 47th Street, turn west under the I. C. railroad's viaduct, and then south on Lake Park Avenue [1400 E] to 55th Street. Turn west.

HYDE PARK—UNIVERSITY OF CHICAGO

Hyde Park and the University of Chicago are practically inseparable. Faculty, university staff, married students, graduate and undergraduate students, alumni, and friends of the University are clustered about the campus in new and old houses, townhouses, and apartments. And a large percentage of the non-university residents of this interracial community are business and professional people.

⦿ This WALK is within the Hyde Park-Kenwood Historic District, roughly bounded by 47th and 59th streets and Cottage Grove and Lake Park avenues

Hyde Park families are civic-minded to a high degree and guard with real concern their parks, lakefront, and trees. They have sometimes been very much concerned about individual houses that were razed by recent urban renewal projects. At the same time, they recognize too that urban renewal has made many desirable changes in the neighborhood—removing some badly deteriorated apartment buildings, restoring many fine old homes, and constructing new buildings where land was cleared.

Because of the close relation between Hyde Park and the University of Chicago, no attempt has been made in this WALK to separate arbitrarily University buildings from others in the area (though of course each University building is identified as such). For anyone interested in making a more thorough tour of the university campus by itself, free tours are available Monday through Friday at 10 a.m., leaving from the Admissions Office in Harper Memorial Library, and Saturday at 10 a.m., leaving from Ida Noyes Hall. Call 962-8650 for information.

Overleaf:
John Crerar Library
(Hedrich-Blessing courtesy Loebl Schlossman and Hackl)

283

It has seemed desirable, however, to divide this area into two WALKS, 20 and 21. These WALKS must not be interpreted as a division between "town and gown." They are suggested only as a possible geographical division of an area that has no logical division, in the hope that each WALK will be more pleasurable and less tiring than both together would be.

Since a purely arbitrary separation was necessary, it has been made at the most obvious geographical dividing line—the Midway Plaisance. WALK 20 will take you to Hyde Park-University of Chicago buildings that lie definitely north of the Midway; WALK 21 will take you to the Midway and the buildings along both the north and south sides of it.

UNIVERSITY APARTMENTS
1400-1450 E. 55TH STREET
ARCHITECTS: I. M. PEI;
HARRY WEESE AND ASSOCIATES;
LOEWENBERG AND LOEWENBERG (1959-1962)

A part of the Hyde Park renewal is evident in the two 10-story apartment buildings in the middle of 55th Street. The street has been widely extended on each side to allow a continuing flow of east and west traffic. Known as the University Apartments, these buildings constitute one of the first large-scale urban renewal projects of its kind. Citizens committees and governmental agencies cooperated to bring about these first-rate results. The South East Chicago Commission and the Hyde Park-Kenwood Community Conference did outstanding work.

Built in an extremely simple form, these twin apartment towers have a forceful horizontal rhythm, resulting largely from the long stretches of closely positioned windows. Although the buildings are set in the midst of city traffic, the landscaping—with trees, flowers, pool, and fountain—softens the effect. The many townhouses that surround University Apartments, to the north and the south of 55th Street, were designed by the same architects.

Walk west on 55th Street to Kimbark Avenue.

⦿ ST. THOMAS APOSTLE CHURCH
5472 S. KIMBARK AVENUE
ARCHITECT: BARRY BYRNE (1922)

The influence of Frank Lloyd Wright on his former apprentice can be noted in the design of St. Thomas Apostle Church, at the corner of East 55th Street and Kimbark Avenue. The warmth of

St. Thomas Apostle Church
(Philip A. Turner)

color in the building material, the sculpture around the entrance, and the human scale on which all seems to have been constructed give this church an especially appealing effect. Inside, the fourteen Stations of the Cross, carved in bas-relief by the Italian sculptor A. Faggi, are justifiably famous for the sweep and rhythm of their design.

Two blocks west of St. Thomas, on the north side of a boulevard-like 55th Street, is the Lutheran School of Theology.

285

LUTHERAN SCHOOL OF THEOLOGY
1100 E. 55TH STREET
ARCHITECTS: PERKINS & WILL PARTNERSHIP (1968)

The school consists of 3 stunning sections with transparent enclosures of lightly tinted glass between sweeping curved steel columns that rest on sturdy pins, much like those in bridge construction.

Diagonally across 55th Street is a Lutheran church.

AUGUSTANA EVANGELICAL LUTHERAN CHURCH
5500 S. WOODLAWN AVENUE
ARCHITECTS: LOEBL, SCHLOSSMAN, BENNETT, AND DART (1968)

The low, spacious design of this church was planned by Edward D. Dart, of Loebl, Schlossman, Bennett, and Dart. Within the main entrance stands an impressively unconventional bronze statue of Christ, the work of Egon Weiner. The statue was cast in Norway.

On the southwest corner is a University of Chicago residence hall.

STANLEY R. PIERCE HALL
5514 UNIVERSITY AVENUE
ARCHITECTS: HARRY WEESE AND ASSOCIATES (1959-60)

This is a residence for undergraduate students. A high-rise tower, with an effective 2-story extension, this has become a distinguished addition to the University of Chicago campus. Tiers of bay windows—a feature restored by this architect, after years of disuse—accentuate the vertical lines of the structure. Actually the building is four separate residence halls—Henderson, Shorey, Thompson, and Tufts.

Now walk south on University Avenue and note the brick building on the east side of the street.

5551 S. UNIVERSITY AVENUE BUILDING
ARCHITECTS: GEORGE FRED AND WILLIAM KECK (1937)

This building is one of the earliest modern buildings in the area with cooperative apartments. Each of the three apartments extends over an entire floor. Across the front of the building at ground level are 3 garages, and the entrance is placed inconspicuously at the side, far back from the street. Contrast in

Opposite:
Pierce Hall
(Philip A. Turner)

286

the brick facade on the University Avenue side is provided by dark metal louvres, two at each floor level—for the two wide windows—with a stretch of contrasting brick between them. At the time this building was erected its design was considered quite extreme, though today it blends well with other architecture in the area and seems to meet naturally the needs of the city dweller.

Next walk west on 56th Street to Greenwood Avenue.

COCHRANE-WOODS ART CENTER
5540-5550 S. Greenwood Avenue
Architect: Edward Larrabee Barnes (1974)

The Center's 2-story limestone-faced contemporary structures face each other across a court. The Art Department, at the north, houses classrooms and offices. The two buildings are the first of an eventual University Visual Arts Complex. The David and Alfred Smart Gallery, south of the Art Department, was designed to contain sculpture. The university has an extensive collection of modern art pieces on display all through the campus. The interior exhibition space was designed for the permanent collection and temporary exhibits. On the mezzanine of the dramatic entrance hall are the Gallery offices, a conservation workshop, and a print and drawing study room.

The permanent collection includes representative works of art—paintings as well as sculpture—from Classical Greek through modern times, including Oriental art. Special exhibitions, an important part of the Gallery's activities, are geared to the interest and needs of the University students and are also of interest to the general public.

Admission to the Gallery is free. Hours: Tuesdays to Saturdays 10 a.m. to 4 p.m.; Sundays noon to 4 p.m.; closed Mondays. Closed during September and from mid-December through the first week in January.

The Court Theater can be reached two ways: on weekdays you can walk straight through the courtyard containing a figure by Henry Moore and a bronze by Arnaldo Pomodoro. Take note of the form that these artists use because you will see another sculpture by each later in the WALK. There is also a Richard Hunt sculpture, which used to be in the main quadrangle. If the entrance gates are locked, walk back to 56th Street, then continue west ½ block. Court Theater is visible up a pathway on your right.

288

COURT THEATER
5535 S. ELLIS AVENUE
ARCHITECTS: HARRY WEESE AND ASSOCIATES (1981)

The new home of Court Theater is a technically sophisticated 250-seat theater. The audience sits in three banks of upholstered seats wrapped around the front of the thrust stage. The thrust area of the stage has been designed so it can be shortened, altered, or eliminated altogether for conventional proscenium staging. The building's lobby has approximately the same dimensions as the stage so that rehearsals can be conducted there when necessary. State-of-the-art technology was used so that lighting equipment could be hung anywhere in the auditorium and lighting and sound cues for an entire production can be prerecorded. Note that the coursing of the stone blocks is a scaled-down version of the neighboring Cochrane-Woods building. The small John Henry sculpture is entitled "Forecast."

Backtrack to University Avenue, turn right, continue to 57th Street.

QUADRANGLE CLUB
1155 E. 57TH STREET
ARCHITECT: HOWARD VAN DOREN SHAW (1914)

On the southeast corner you will see the faculty club known as the Quadrangle Club. It contains a second-floor, cathedral-type

289

dining hall with great wood trusses that span this spacious room, and smaller dining and meeting rooms. There are tennis courts south of the club.

On the southwest corner is Mitchell Tower.

MITCHELL TOWER
1131 E. 57TH STREET
ARCHITECTS: SHEPLEY, RUTAN AND COOLIDGE (1903)

Mitchell Tower is the entrance to Mandel Hall and Hutchinson Commons, part of a complex of buildings at 57th Street and University Avenue. The exteriors of the English Gothic structures are Indiana limestone. The tower, copied from the tower of Magdalen College, Oxford University, houses the Alice Freeman Palmer Bells and campus radio station (WHPK-FM). It has no ground floor but sits atop Reynolds Student Clubhouse, north of Mandel Hall. Hutchinson Commons is a vaulted dining hall, with massive stone fireplaces and wood wainscoting, modeled on that of Christ Church College, Oxford.

● MANDEL HALL
1131 E. 57TH STREET
ARCHITECTS: SHEPLEY, RUTAN AND COOLIDGE (1903);
FOR REMODELING: SKIDMORE, OWINGS AND MERRILL (1978)

The exterior was modeled after the great hall of Crosby Place in England, built about 1450 as the home of Sir John Crosby. The donor was Leon Mandel, a prominent Chicago merchant. The auditorium seats about 1,000. There is a bronze tablet in the lobby by sculptor Lorado Taft that is a portrait of Senator Stephen A. Douglas.

This building, in the northeastern section of the Quadrangle, is not only a University landmark but one for the entire Chicago area as well. Named for the family of the donor, a retail merchant, the structure has been the showplace for years for drama, dance, ballet, musicals, and symphony concerts.

The entire building has been carried out in English Gothic and harmonizes with the other early member structures of the Quadrangle. The great hall, lounges, and theater are well worth a visit.

In 1978 the University began a program to upgrade the capabilities for continued viable use of Mandel Hall. On-going University arts activities over the years have required a level of

290

technology not available to the original architects. For decades, make-shift additions of lighting and sound equipment and control and projection facilities had been made. The renovation program developed a new, enlarged, and more appropriately shaped music platform at the audience side of the proscenium arch. This platform, which comfortably seats 100 musicians, is separated from the stage house at the back of the proscenium arch by a system of hard movable panels. This isolation of the absorbent stage house from the music environment allows music and theater activities to occur simultaneously without striking or resetting sets. A system of acoustical reflectors is suspended over the music platform. Sight lines and sound have been improved on the main floor by moving the side aisles to the outside wall and relocating the side seats closer to center.

Projection, sound, and light equipment in the balcony have been moved into new facilities constructed behind the hall which allowed the reinstallation of sixty center seats with excellent sight lines. New provisions for contemporary theater lighting and appropriate musicians' lighting were provided at the sides of the proscenium and in the ceiling. Between the backstage area and the neighboring Eckhart Hall to the south, a small building was inserted to provide loading and unloading capability, general backstage work space, and storage for musical instruments, risers, theater props, rigging, and costumes. Dressing room space for performers was created by redeveloping facilities below the stage, including three private dressing rooms and a small performers' lounge.

The interior of the hall was returned to much of its original, rich, Victorian-era palette. R. Lawrence Kirkegaard was the acoustical consultant, Lustig and Associates was the consultant on stage lifts and theatrical lighting, and John Vinci assisted in the determination of the original palette and techniques.

Walk west on 57th Street.

COBB GATE and HULL COURT
(Opposite the Regenstein Library)
Architect: Henry Ives Cobb (1897)

The great Gothic gate, in the spirit of those at Oxford and Cambridge universities, was constructed as a part of Hull Court of the Quadrangle. The court consists of the Anatomy, Botany (named the Ida B. and Walter Erman Biology Center), and Zoology buildings, and Cullver Hall. Notice how effectively this

Gothic courtyard shuts out the outside world. Return to 57th Street. Across the street is the Regenstein Library.

JOSEPH REGENSTEIN LIBRARY
1100 E. 57TH STREET
ARCHITECTS: SKIDMORE, OWINGS, MERRILL,
WALTER NETSCH, PARTNER IN CHARGE (1970)

The University's Graduate Research Library is an exceptionally popular addition to the intellectual life of the campus. Of the same gray limestone as its Gothic neighbors, it has a modern design that is impressive in scale.

Actually, it has 7 service floors and some 577,000 square feet. With a total volume capacity of 3.5 million books, it houses the University's 1.9 million-book collection in the social sciences and humanities, excluding law, art, and theology. It is a graduate research library, costing $21 million, and was built principally through the generosity of Chicago industrialist, Joseph Regenstein. The interior is highly functional. Each of the major service floors is divided into four areas; book stacks, offices, faculty studies, and reading areas. The architecture harmonizes well with the adjoining buildings. The vertical wall elements and narrow recessed bay windows relieve the structure's mass. Exterior walls are formed by deeply grooved, cut limestone slabs, which add nice texture to the service. This magnificent structure is a welcome addition to a campus of many distinguished buildings.

Continue west. On the southeast corner of Ellis Avenue and 57th Street is Hitchcock Hall.

CHARLES HITCHCOCK HALL
1009 E. 57TH STREET
ARCHITECT: D. H. PERKINS (1902)

This early residence hall was designed by Dwight Perkins, an early advocate of shedding old architectural trappings. This simplified Gothic style is representative of his approach. The structure houses 105 students and contains a club room, infirmary, and library. A "preacher's room" was furnished at one time. With its low pitched roof, shed dormers, and horizontal emphasis it really could be described as "Prairie Gothic".

Now walk north ½ block on Ellis Avenue.

◉ NUCLEAR ENERGY
ELLIS AVENUE BETWEEN 56TH AND 57TH STREETS
SCULPTOR: HENRY MOORE (1967)

Opposite:
"Nuclear Energy"
sculpture by
Henry Moore
(Philip A. Turner)

292

Between Regenstein Library and Ellis Avenue, halfway down the block, is a great bronze sculpture—12 feet high, weighing 3 tons, which stands on a base of black polished granite. Entitled Nuclear Energy, this extremely simple but impressive work of art by the distinguished British sculptor Henry Moore commemorates man's achievement in completing the first atomic chain reaction—as explained in one of the 4 plaques mounted on a slab of marble. Under a Stagg Field bleacher near this same spot, on December 2, 1942, Enrico Fermi and 41 other distinguished scientists accomplished the great breakthrough that introduced the Atomic Age. Speaking of the sculpture, Moore has explained that it relates both to the mushroom cloud of a nuclear explosion and to the shape of a human skull, with reminiscences of church architecture in the lower part. Walk all around it, to appreciate all its facets.

Continue north to 56th Street, then turn left.

LABORATORY FOR ASTROPHYSICS AND SPACE RESEARCH
933 E. 56TH STREET
ARCHITECTS: SKIDMORE, OWINGS AND MERRILL (1964)

This 2-story cast concrete structure with recessed walls of glass windows is a part of the University's Institute for Nuclear Studies and carries out research in the space sciences.

HIGH-ENERGY PHYSICS BUILDING
935 E. 56TH STREET
ARCHITECTS: HAUSNER AND MACSAI (1967)

The 3-story and penthouse building is actually a reinforced concrete research laboratory for the physical sciences. The simple, sturdy design serves the purpose well.

Return to Ellis Avenue. Cross 57th Street. The buildings on the east side of the street are part of the main University Quadrangle. They are a mix of original structures, like Snell Hall, and some more recent construction such as the Chemistry Building. This WALK will take you through the University Quadrangle, but first it is essential that you see some of the buildings outside the Quadrangle. Also you will see a brand new quadrangle.

SNELL HALL
5709 S. ELLIS AVENUE
ARCHITECT: HENRY IVES COBB (1893)

294

Snell Hall, an all-female dormitory, connects to Hitchcock Hall, an all-male dormitory. The connection is only on the exterior! The hall has an Indiana limestone facade styled in the English Gothic period. It is an integral part of the early Quadrangle and today stands with all its newer neighbors as a part of an excellent tradition of developing and growing with the spirit of the times.

SEARLE CHEMISTRY BUILDING
5715 S. ELLIS AVENUE
ARCHITECTS: SMITH, SMITH, HAINES, LUNDBERG
AND WAEHLER, OF NEW YORK (1967)

This 5-story structure is mainly a series of scientific laboratories and offices. It is sheathed in Indiana limestone to harmonize with its neighbors. However, the Gothic design has been simplified and creates no visual "cacophony" whatever.

Cross the street and walk west through the gate.

KERSTEN PHYSICS TEACHING CENTER
5720 S. ELLIS AVENUE
ARCHITECTS: HOLABIRD AND ROOT (1985)

With the completion of this building, the Science Quadrangle becomes the ninth of the university's quadrangles. It is instructive to compare this to the original Cobb-designed quadrangle seen later in the WALK. The corner site demanded a formal limestone facade to complement the surrounding buildings. The side of the building facing the quadrangle is less formal. The building is organized around a central circulation spine that forms a pedestrian bridge at the second level and links the Research Institute across the street. This spine supports all vertical circulation and provides space for displays and meeting areas for students and faculty. If you look up into the Post-modern gabled entrance you will see steel bristles attached to the upper supports. This is a unique anti-pigeon device.

Walk further into the quad to see a stunning white building.

JOHN CRERAR LIBRARY
5730 S. ELLIS AVENUE
ARCHITECTS: THE STUBBINS ASSOCIATES
OF CAMBRIDGE, MASSACHUSETTS;
LOEBL, SCHLOSSMAN AND HACKL (1984)

The John Crerar Library is a 4-story regional science library. Situated at the hub of the physical and medical science block for easy access to both areas, it was planned as the fulcrum of a new quadrangle—the first to be built in two decades. The limestone facade is in keeping with the character and tradition of the existing campus buildings. The focal point of the project is a 3-story skylighted atrium space containing a large, suspended, aluminum and crystal sculpture entitled *Crystara* by artist John David Mooney.

To account for the anticipated water table, the library's lower level and pedestrian connections are located 7 feet below grade while the main floor is raised 7 feet above grade. The main floor features the primary entrance, circulation, reference, meeting areas, administrative offices, and the John Crerar Room. The 2nd level contains collections in biological and medical sciences. The 3rd level has collections in the general physical sciences.

The inspiration for the impressive, free-standing arch is the Gothic arch on the old Abbott Building. You can see this only by climbing the library's stairs and looking to your left. The tall building to the right of the old Abbott Building is the Cummings Life Science Building which we will see later.

Behind you is the Henry Hinds Laboratory. To get a better view, walk back through the gate and cross to the east side of Ellis Avenue.

HENRY HINDS LABORATORY
East 58th Street and Ellis Avenue
Architects: I. W. Colburn and Associates;
J. Lee Jones (associate architect) (1969)

The University's Geophysical Sciences Building was the first in the science center that now occupies the entire block. Much of the design was determined by the demands of present-day research and teaching in the geophysical sciences. It seems at first to have no relation to the neo-Gothic buildings of the original Quadrangle directly across from it, but its design includes many concessions to the earlier style. The brick walls (for instance), which carry the load, are covered with a thin layer of Indiana limestone, the material used in the older buildings; the brick is allowed to show only here and there; the numerous towers, though of highly individual form, attempt to bring the entire building into greater harmony with the Gothic-towered structures of the old campus. Note the metal bay windows that are not only colorful, but highly practical.

296

Henry Hinds Laboratory
(Philip A. Turner)

Cross back to the west side of the street. If it is a weekday enter the lobby to see Ruth Duckworth's wonderful ceramic environment entitled *Earth, Water, Sky* (1968-1969). Continue south past the red brick store. Turn right and walk about ½ block.

CUMMINGS LIFE SCIENCE CENTER
950 E. 58TH STREET
ARCHITECTS: I. W. COLBURN AND ASSOCIATES;
SCHMIDT, GARDEN AND ERICKSON;
HAROLD H. HELLMAN, UNIVERSITY ARCHITECT (1973)

The stunning high-rise research center is designed with vertical brick piers in relief against a background of the limestone facade. The varying pattern of the bases of the piers is delightful. The narrow windows clearly indicate the necessarily confined interior research laboratories.

297

Colburn has treated the facade with different materials and height than the Geophysical Sciences Building just around the corner. Nevertheless, there is a strong similarity in style and both buildings appear to be part of a great medieval fortress through which one enters across a symbolic moat. Both rely on their contemporary flying buttresses for their vertical lines; both buildings achieve a rightful place on a campus that includes many outstanding architectural contributions.

The structure is 10 stories high with two penthouses and is the tallest building on campus. The construction is reinforced concrete. There are forty narrow towers located at the perimeter of the building; they contain exhaust ducts from laboratories. The towers are dark red face brick, and the main structure is clad in Indiana limestone.

Walk back east, but stop at the plaza to your right. This is the Surgery-Brain Research Pavilion, seen in WALK 21. The giant disc is by Arnaldo Pomodoro, whose work we saw earlier. Even though it is 14 feet in diameter and weighs tons it can be easily rotated! Try it.

Cross back to the east side of the street.

COBB HALL
5811 ELLIS AVENUE
ARCHITECTS: HENRY IVES COBB (1892);
FOR REMODELING: BURNHAM AND HAMMOND (1967)

This structure, at the central west edge of the Quadrangle, is one of the original members. It is 4 stories with an Indiana limestone exterior that includes bay windows. The undergraduate classrooms and facilities include an auditorium, biology laboratory, and art gallery.

There is a marble bust by Lorado Taft on the south wall of the main entrance. It is of Silas B. Cobb, for whom the building is named.

Walk east on the footpath on the north side of Cobb Hall.

UNIVERSITY OF CHICAGO QUADRANGLE
57TH AND 59TH STREETS, BETWEEN ELLIS
AND UNIVERSITY AVENUES
ARCHITECTS: HENRY IVES COBB;
SHEPLEY, RUTAN AND COOLIDGE;
CHARLES KLAUDER; AND OTHERS (1890 TO THE PRESENT)

This is the original campus of the University of Chicago, called

298

"the Quadrangle." Occupying 4 blocks, the Quadrangle as a whole follows the original plan prepared by Henry Ives Cobb in 1890—a large central quadrangle flanked by 3 small quadrangles to the south and 3 more to the north, all surrounded by buildings of Indiana limestone in the late English Gothic style. Cobb himself designed all the buildings that were constructed before 1900, and later architects used the neo-Gothic style exclusively through the 1940s. This mass of Gothic structures comprises the architectural heritage to which subsequent architects generally deferred.

The University Administration Building sits on the main north-south axis at the western perimeter of the Quadrangle. A 6-story structure with a highly modified Gothic exterior, it contains the mamor administrative offices and the University of Chicago Press. As you step into the Quadrangle, you are struck by the planned arrangements of structures, walks, roads, landscaping—into a large, intricate, but orderly web of convenience for students and faculty. Buildings are laid out on the various axes and sub-axes, and many do not meet the eye at first glance. It is a joyful experience to wander onto a small Gothic chapel that is partly hidden behind a large academic building and surrounded by trees. Yet each building has been designed or renovated to form a complex of similar disciplines, conveniently located for students.

If you are standing in the center of the Quadrangle, the buildings to the southeast are the business school.

JULIUS ROSENWALD HALL
1101 E. 58TH STREET
ARCHITECTS: HOLABIRD AND ROCHE (1915);
FOR RENOVATION: SAMUEL A. LICHTMANN (1972)

This Indiana limestone, English Gothic structure is a part of the complex of business school buildings. There is a completely modernized group of classrooms, offices, and library to replace the former geography disciplines.

Rosenwald, along with several other of the original Gothic structures in the Quadrangle, has been successfully renovated inside while retaining the original qualities of the exteriors. The University is to be commended for this.

The student newspaper, the Maroon, quoted Eero Saarinen, ("Campus Planning: The Unique World of the University" Architectural Record, November 1960), during the time when he was consulting architect to the University of Chicago:

Wandering in the University of Chicago today, one is amazed at the beauty achieved by spaces surrounded by buildings all in one discipline and made out of a uniform material; where each building is being considerate of the next, and each building—through its common material—is aging in the same way. It is significant that on a small court on the University of Chicago campus (referring to the one used by Summer Nights, which is the University's festival of performing arts, presenting everything from classic ensemble to full-scale opera, call 962-3348 for information) built between 1894 and 1930, three different architects—Henry I. Cobb; Shepley, Rutan, and Coolidge; and Charles Klauder—built the four different sides of the court. All are in the Gothic style, and the court gives us today a beautiful, harmonious visual picture.

The cohesiveness of the old quadrangles does not rest entirely on the use of the Gothic style. Some of the buildings defy this tradition, conforming only in the material used. In large part the harmonious effect is due to the architects all envisioning their buildings as contributions to a larger unity.

Directly to the east of Rosenwald Hall is The Walker Museum.

THE WALKER MUSEUM
ARCHITECT: HENRY IVES COBB (1893);
FOR ADAPTIVE REUSE: NAGLE HARTRAY AND
ASSOCIATES (1980)

Designed by Cobb as a geological museum, it is now in adaptive reuse as a part of the business school. Go in and see how the firm of Nagle Hartray and Associates totally changed the inside in 1980 to make it serve its new function.

Continue east to University Avenue. The building on your right is Albert Pick Hall.

ALBERT PICK HALL FOR INTERNATIONAL STUDIES
5828 S. UNIVERSITY AVENUE
ARCHITECTS: RALPH RAPSON AND ASSOCIATES;
BURNHAM AND HAMMOND (1971)

Albert Pick Hall is at the extreme eastern edge of the Quadrangle. As you approach it, your eye catches the remarkable combination of planes and surfaces—all in gray limestone to match the color of its neighbors. It is like emerging from the 12th to the 20th century in one short WALK. The Gothic spiral is there,

300

not only in the limestone, but the great flying buttresses—some of which are corbeled, and others supported on columns. The entire effect of the great verticality that reaches for the sky is indeed a strong architectural statement.

The University Avenue entrance has an interesting use of glass and metal for a portion of the facade. Their horizontal lines seem to balance the aforementioned verticality. The Adlai Stevenson Institute of International Affairs, formerly housed in the Robie House, moved here in 1976.

There is a strong metal sculptural work near the entrance. The sculptor is Virginio Ferrari and the title is *Dialogo*. The work rests on a 14-foot square limestone base from which the four separate forms rise toward the center.

Walk across the street. On the southeast corner of 58th Street and University Avenue is the internationally famous Oriental Institute.

ORIENTAL INSTITUTE
1155 E. 58TH STREET
ARCHITECTS: MAYER, MURRAY AND PHILLIP (1931)

The Oriental Institute contains one of the world's major collections of art, religious, and daily life objects from the Ancient Near East: Egypt, Palestine, Syria, Anatolia, Mesopotamia, and Iran. The timeline covered is from approximately 5000 B.C. to about 100 A.D. Open Tuesdays to Saturdays 10 a.m. to 4 p.m.; Sundays noon to 4 p.m.; closed Mondays. Admission is free.

Across the street is the Chicago Theological Seminary.

CHICAGO THEOLOGICAL SEMINARY
5757 S. UNIVERSITY AVENUE
ARCHITECT: HERBERT H. RIDDLE (1926)

This striking red brick structure with stone trim is an unique combination of English Georgian and Gothic design. The 162-foot tower can be seen from the Quadrangle or from the Quadrangle Club 1 block away.

A driveway bisects the building on the ground floor. In the west wing are two chapels (one seating 200), a library, and the classrooms. The stained glass windows of the larger chapel were executed by the Willett Stained Glass Studios of Philadelphia. The residential floors are located in the east wing.

Walk east on 58th Street.

301

Robie House
(Olga Stefanos)

WOODWARD COURT
5825 S. WOODLAWN AVENUE
ARCHITECT: EERO SAARINEN (1958)

This residence hall for women students is interesting architecture, although it is not up to the very high standards of design established by Saarinen in the Laird Bell Law Quadrangle. (See WALK 21.)

At the northeast corner of Woodlawn Avenue and 58th Street is Frank Lloyd Wright's famous Robie House.

⊚ ROBIE HOUSE
5757 S. WOODLAWN AVENUE
ARCHITECT: FRANK LLOYD WRIGHT (1909);
FOR RESTORATION: FRANK LLOYD WRIGHT OFFICE,
WESLEY PETER, IN CHARGE (1964);
SKIDMORE, OWINGS AND MERRILL (1967);
CONSULTING ARCHITECT FOR RESTORATION:
JOHN VINCI (1983)

This house was designated a National Historic Landmark in 1963. It was renovated in 1964—the funds coming from public

302

subscriptions—after the house was donated to the University by William Zeckendorf. Built as a private home, this is probably the best-known example of Wright's Prairie House.

The Citation by Chicago's 1957 Architectural Landmarks Commission reads:

In recognition of the creation of the Prairie House—a home organized around a great hearth where interior space, under wide sweeping roofs, opens to the outdoors. The bold interplay of horizontal planes about the chimney mass, and the structurally expressive piers and windows, established a new form of domestic design.

The Citation on a second plaque, presented by the 1968 Commission, which includes preservation of historical as well as architectural landmarks, reads:

Robie House combines all the elements of Wright's mature style. It is his boldest example of a Prairie House design and one of the most significant buildings in the history of architecture.

In 1967 the Robie House was restored and refurnished in its original style. It now houses the Alumni Association offices. Subsequent restoration of the south balcony was done in 1983 under the direction of John Vinci. There are free tours Monday through Saturday at noon. Call 753-2175 for information.

Now turn east on 58th Street, and stop at Dorchester Avenue to see a surprisingly unconventional group of recently constructed buildings—homes for Chicago Theological Seminary faculty.

CHICAGO THEOLOGICAL SEMINARY FACULTY QUADRANGLE
Northwest corner of East 58th Street
and Dorchester Avenue
Architects: Loebl, Schlossman, Bennett and Dart,
Edward D. Dart, partner in charge (1963)

No attempt was made here to harmonize the architecture of these houses with that of the older buildings around them. On the contrary, they defy previously accepted patterns with refreshing individuality. Instead of following the lines of the street, for instance, as the endless rows of houses in Chicago—and most other cities—do, their sides face the street on a diagonal, as if deliberately set askew. The roofs, instead of being flat or gabled, slope steeply from one side to the other with wide overhang. All eight houses, harmonizing well with each other, are clustered around a central green that is elevated so that it can slope down to the sidewalk.

A plaque on the house at the corner reports an award for excellence in architecture.

This is the end of WALK 20. To return to the Loop, walk north to 57th Street and then east 3 blocks to the elevated station of the Illinois Central suburban line that brought you to Hyde Park.

21

1. Sonia Shankman Orthogenic School
   1365 E. 60th St.

2. Public Administration Center
   1313 E. 60th St.

3. New Graduate Residence Hall
   1307 E. 60th St.

4. Laird Bell Law Quadrangle
   1111 E. 60th St.

5. School of Social Service Administration Building
   969 E. 60th St.

6. Social Services Center
   950 E. 61st St.

7. Midway Studios
   6016 S. Ingleside Ave.

8. Fountain of Time

9. The University of Chicago Medical Center

10. William Rainey Harper Memorial Library
    1116 E. 59th St.

11. Social Science Research Building
    1126 E. 59th St.

12. The University President's House
    5855 S. University Ave.

13. Rockefeller Memorial Chapel
    1156–80 E. 59th St.

14. Ida Noyes Hall
    1212 E. 59th St.

15. Henry Holmes Belfield Hall
    5815 S. Kimbark Ave.

16. University High School
    5834 S. Kenwood Ave.

17. Emmons Blaine Hall
    1362 E. 59th St.

18. Bernard E. Sunny Gymnasium
    5731 S. Kenwood Ave.

19. International House
    1414 E. 59th St.

20. Museum of Science and Industry
    E. 57th St. at South Lake Shore Dr.

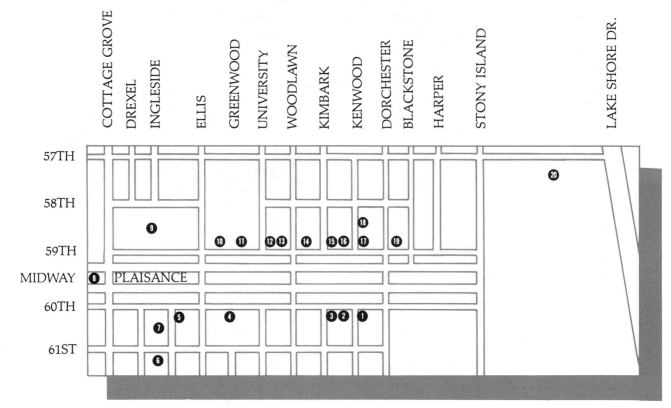

WALK • 21

MIDWAY PLAISANCE: ITS SOUTH AND NORTH SIDES

WALKING TIME: 1½ hours. HOW TO GET THERE: Take an Illinois Central [I. C.] suburban train at its Randolph Street and Michigan Avenue underground station, and get off at 59th Street. [All express trains and many of those marked "Special" stop at 59th. Check before boarding the train.] Or, if you go by car, take the South Lake Shore Outer Drive south to 47th Street, turn west under the I. C. railroad's viaduct, and then south on Lake Park Avenue [1400 E]. Continue on Lake Park to 59th Street, where this WALK begins.

Midway Plaisance stretches from Jackson Park on the east to Washington Park on the west, between 59th and 60th streets. Before coming down from the I.C. elevated platform, look west for an overall view of the Midway Plaisance, a block wide and some dozen blocks long, all green lawns, trees, and sidewalks, with two one-way drives and two local drives for east-west traffic.

This great green mall was first constructed as part of Frederick Law Olmstead's original South Park Plan of the 1860s. Later, in 1893, it served as the amusement and ethnographic section of the World's Columbian Exposition.

Other reminders of that famous world's fair are the enormous gilded statue of the Republic, by Daniel Chester French, now placed farther on in Jackson Park, where it is passed daily by hundreds of commuters on their way to and from the Loop, and the Museum of Science and Industry, which is the last stop on this WALK. (Though it stands 2 blocks north of the Midway, it seems an appropriate ending for a Midway WALK.)

Called merely "The Midway" by neighborhood residents, this parkway is especially popular with University of Chicago students, who use its long stretch of sunken lawns for sunning and studying in summer and for exercise in winter, when it is flooded for ice skating.

● This WALK is within the Hyde Park-Kenwood Historic District, roughly bounded by 47th and 59th streets and Cottage Grove and Lake Park avenues

Overleaf:
University of
Chicago Law Library
(Philip A. Turner)

Statuary marks each end of the Midway. On the east stands a sturdy mail-clad warrior on horseback, a tribute from Chicago's Czechoslovakians to their first president, Masaryk. The figure is supposedly one of the Blanik knights, who—according to legend—slept in a mountainous cave in Czechoslovakia until the time should come to arise and rescue their country. On the west is Lorado Taft's Fountain of Time, which will be included in this WALK. On the north side of the Midway near Ellis Avenue is a statue of the Swedish botanist, Linne.

This WALK starts on the south side of the Midway just west of the Illinois Central Railroad.

You are now on the South Campus of the University of Chicago. A considerable portion of this campus was developed through Chicago's urban renewal program, enabling the University to expand and achieve greater service to the community and its students and faculty.

SONIA SHANKMAN ORTHOGENIC SCHOOL
1365 E. 60TH STREET
ARCHITECTS FOR RENOVATION AND ADDITION:
I. W. COLBURN AND ASSOCIATES (1966)

This rather strange combination of a renovated church and a 3-story residential wing houses this famous school for emotionally disturbed children, founded by the equally famous Dr. Bruno Bettleheim. The school is part of the University. The ceramic untitled sculpture under the arcade is by Jordi Bonet (1965-6). The university has an extensive collection of modern art pieces on display all through the campus.

Walk west.

PUBLIC ADMINISTRATION CENTER
1313 E. 60TH STREET
ARCHITECTS: ZANTIZINGER, BORIE AND MEDARY (1937)

The Gothic design of Indiana limestone and brick houses the offices of twenty-three city, state, national, and international organizations interested in government and public administration. The structure is 4 stories tall and contains an extensive library that serves the in-house organizations as well as University of Chicago scholars. The donor for the construction was the Spelman Fund of New York. The main floor lounge contains portraits of Louis Brownlow and Charles Merriam, two of the center's founders.

Continue west.

308

NEW GRADUATE RESIDENCE HALL

1307 E. 60TH STREET
ARCHITECT: EDWARD D. STONE (1963)

This building was originally the Center for Continuing Education, the University's conference and hotel center, made possible by funds from the W. K. Kellogg Foundation. It is now a dormitory. Especially noteworthy are the patterns in the concrete, which are continued onto the underside of the cantilevered roof.

Continue west. You will pass the Industrial Relations Center at 1225 E. 60th Street, also affiliated with the university, and come to the University of Chicago Law School.

LAIRD BELL LAW QUADRANGLE

1111 E. 60TH STREET
ARCHITECTS: EERO SAARINEN (1960);
FOR ADDITION: COOPER-LECKY (1985-7)

This elegant low quadrangle is far and away the most successful building on the campus of the university. It blends well with its neighbors.

At the east end of the building is a completely closed auditorium, which contrasts markedly with the enormous library west of it, for the library uses all-glass walls set at angles to each other. Inside the building, the auditorium is connected by wide corridors with lecture rooms and lounges that extend to the west. Actually, there are 2 auditoriums—one set over the other. One is used as a court room for demonstration and the other for lectures. The stunning sculpture in the pool outside, called *Construction in Space in Third and Fourth Dimensions*, is the work of Antoine Pevsner, who created it specifically for the Law School.

At this writing, an addition extending the back of the building was under construction. A major reconstruction was also underway. All windows were being replaced with a thicker glass to make the building more energy efficient.

Continue west.

SCHOOL OF SOCIAL SERVICE ADMINISTRATION BUILDING

969 E. 60TH STREET
ARCHITECT: LUDWIG MIES VAN DER ROHE (1965)

The Social Service Administration Building of the university, the last building to be noted on the south side of the Midway, is a

Mies van der Rohe creation. Black steel and glass and an open plan give the structure an imposing appearance. It seems not at all out of place or off tempo and fits well with the other buildings on 60th Street. The policy of inviting distinguished 20th century architects to design new buildings has been most rewarding to the campuses of Harvard, Yale, and the University of Chicago.

Walk south on Ingleside Avenue to the northeast corner of 61st Street.

SOCIAL SERVICES CENTER
950 E. 61ST STREET
ARCHITECTS: HAUSNER AND MACSAI (1971)

The University of Chicago has assumed an active role in serving the adjacent community through this Social Services Center. Students are trained and nearby children and mothers are helped. Through child care training, the mothers are made to feel confident and better able to meet their responsibilities.

The structure is plain, and presents a facade of efficiency and strength. The exterior material is Indiana limestone.

The cost of construction was shared by the U.S. Department of Housing and Urban Development and the U.S. Department of Health, Education and Welfare's Children's Bureau.

Backtrack north on Ingleside Avenue.

◉ MIDWAY STUDIOS
6016 S. INGLESIDE AVENUE
ARCHITECTS: OTIS F. JOHNSON (1929);
FOR RENOVATION: EDWARD DART (1965);
FOR ADDITION: LOEBL, SCHLOSSMAN,
BENNETT AND DART (1972)

The university donated this building and land to Lorado Taft—this is where he successfully executed many sculptural commissions throughout his career. Today it is the art center for the university and contains major studio workshops. Painting is taught in Taft's stone-cutting studio; sculpture is taught in the former plaster casting workshop. Painting is also taught in a former studio and lithography in still another. One former studio now serves as a student center and Taft's private studio is used by students for independent work. All in all, it represents a fine tribute to a great sculptor of the late 19th and early 20th centuries.

Return to 60th Street and walk west. Here you can see a later addition and, in front of it, what appears to be a concrete auto-

310

mobile. Actuallly it is a 1957 Cadillac Sedan imbedded in 16 tons of concrete by artist Wolf Vostell in 1970, titled *Concrete Traffic*. Continue west to Cottage Grove Avenue. At the east entrance to Washington Park is one of the most monumental fountains in Chicago.

FOUNTAIN OF TIME
WEST END OF MIDWAY PLAISANCE,
AT ENTRANCE TO WASHINGTON PARK
SCULPTOR: LORADO TAFT (1922)

After an interval of neglect, Lorado Taft's haunting sculpture called *The Fountain of Time* has fortunately been restored. A hooded, "craglike" figure of Time (to use Taft's own adjective in describing his mental image), with his back to the Midway, gazes across a pool at a long procession of human beings as they move through life. The Chicago sculptor said that his inspiration came from these lines in a poem by Austin Dobson:

Time goes, you say? Ah no!
Alas, time stays; we go.

Both the immobility of Time and the onward sweep of human life are well expressed in this unusual sculpture.

Be sure to walk around it in a clockwise direction, to view it from every angle. On what seems to be the back is another procession of people, including a figure of the sculptor himself and his Italian assistant. A triangular marker on the ground points to them.

Now return east, but this time go to the north side of the Midway where the first complex of buildings will be the University Medical Center.

THE UNIVERSITY OF CHICAGO MEDICAL CENTER is located on the Midway between South Cottage Grove Avenue, South Ellis Avenue, and East 58th Street and covers about 25 acres at the southwest corner of the campus. It consists of interconnected hospitals and clinics with a total bed capacity of 722. The hospitals provide clinical teaching and research facilities for the Pritzker School of Medicine, the prototype of the medical school in the total academic setting.

The continued practice of adding so many buildings and wings of buildings all interconnected has resulted in a great limestone, metal, and glass monolith. There is no evidence of an original plan. The result is an appearance of constant improvisation—which it undoubtedly is.

Some of the newer buildings can be seen by walking a short distance north on Maryland Avenue. The multitude of buildings in the University of Chicago Medical Center makes it difficult to identify each one without a map of the area. A map of the University campus, available for the asking from the Office of the Registrar (call 962-7877), shows the location of all the facilities on the campus. Tours are available Monday through Friday at 10 a.m., leaving from the Admissions Office in Harper Memorial Library, and Saturday at 10 a.m., leaving from Ida Noyes Hall. Call 962-8650 for information.

FRANKLIN McLEAN MEMORIAL RESEARCH INSTITUTE
950 E. 59TH STREET
ARCHITECTS: SCHMIDT, GARDEN AND ERIKSON (1953)

PHILIP D. ARMOUR CLINICAL RESEARCH BUILDING
950 E. 59TH STREET
ARCHITECTS: SCHMIDT, GARDEN AND ERIKSON (1963)

ALBERT MERRITT BILLINGS HOSPITAL
950 E. 59TH STREET
ARCHITECTS: COOLIDGE AND HODGDON (1927)

BOB ROBERTS MEMORIAL HOSPITAL
950 E. 59TH STREET
ARCHITECTS: COOLIDGE AND HODGDON (1930)

NATHAN GOLDBLATT MEMORIAL HOSPITAL
950 E. 59TH STREET
ARCHITECTS: SCHMIDT, GARDEN AND ERIKSON (1950)

GOLDBLATT OUTPATIENT PAVILION
950 E. 59TH STREET
ARCHITECTS: SCHMIDT, GARDEN AND ERIKSON (1961)

NANCY ADELE McELWEE MEMORIAL HOSPITAL
950 E. 59TH STREET
ARCHITECTS: COOLIDGE AND HODGDON (1931)

GERTRUDE DUNN HICKS MEMORIAL HOSPITAL
950 E. 59TH STREET
ARCHITECTS: COOLIDGE AND HODGDON (1931)

CLARISSA C. PECK PAVILION
950 E. 59TH STREET
ARCHITECTS: SCHMIDT, GARDEN AND ERIKSON (1961)

Bernard Mitchell
Hospital
(Jim Wright
courtesy University
of Chicago)

CHARLES GILMAN SMITH HOSPITAL
950 E. 59th Street
Architects: Schmidt, Garden and Erikson (1953)

SURGERY-BRAIN RESEARCH PAVILION
950 E. 59th Street
Architects: Schmidt, Garden and Erikson (1977)

SILVAIN AND ARMA WYLER CHILDREN'S HOSPITAL
950 E. 59th Street
Architects: Schmidt, Garden and Erikson (1966)

MAGNETIC RESONANCE FACILITY
950 E. 59th Street
Architects: Perkins & Will (1986)

ARTHUR RUBLOFF INTENSIVE CARE WING
950 E. 59th Street
Architects: Perkins & Will (1983)

BERNARD MITCHELL HOSPITAL
950 E. 59th Street
Architects: Perkins & Will (1983)

A. J. CARLSON ANIMAL RESEARCH FACILITY
5820 Ellis Avenue
Architects: Schmidt, Garden and Erikson (1968)

CHICAGO LYING-IN HOSPITAL
5841 Maryland Avenue
Architects: Schmidt, Garden and Erikson (1931)

Continue east on 59th Street.

WILLIAM RAINEY HARPER MEMORIAL LIBRARY
1116 E. 59th Street
Architects: Shepley, Rutan and Coolidge (1912);
for renovation: Metz, Train, Olson
and Youngren (1972)

This impressive English Gothic structure was for many years the main library of the University of Chicago. Since the completion of the Graduate Regenstein Library, Harper now serves the undergraduate student body. As can be seen, it is part of the original Quadrangle group. It has 3 stories and a high, handsome, commanding tower. The main reading room is reminiscent of a 12th-century collegium with its high wooden trusses and equally high Gothic windows. Tours are available Monday through Friday at 10 a.m., leaving from the Admissions Office here, and Saturday at 10 a.m., leaving from Ida Noyes Hall. Call 962-8650 for information.

SOCIAL SCIENCE RESEARCH BUILDING
1126 E. 59th Street
Architects: Shepley, Rutan and Coolidge (1912)

This solid greystone Gothic structure serves as part of a great 12th-century facade along the north side of the Midway.
Continue east.

THE UNIVERSITY PRESIDENT'S HOUSE
5855 S. University Avenue
Architects: Henry Ives Cobb (1895);
for renovation: Arthur Myhrum (1969)

This fairly large, 3-story limestone and Roman brick, English Tudor Gothic house is set at the corner of University Avenue and the Midway Plaisance. Directly to the east is the mammoth Gothic Rockefeller Chapel. Strangely, the house is not overpowered by the chapel, principally because of the equally strong open, green spaces that separate the two.

The house has been remodeled several times. The original entrance was on the Midway and is now on University Avenue.

314

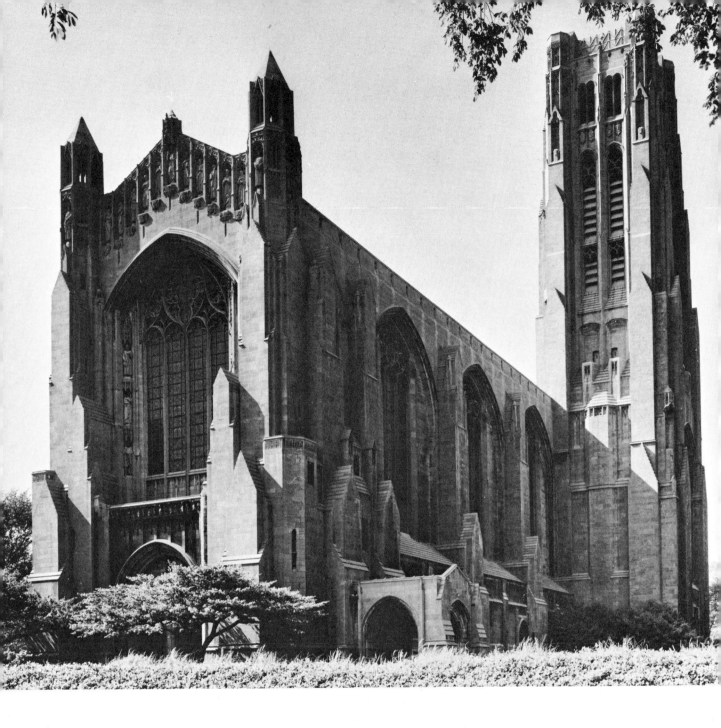

The delightful garden to the east is a part of the grounds that is used for receptions when weather permits. One must confess that although the house appears gloomy from the exterior, the garden and the Midway Plaisance Park upon which it faces more than compensates for any of its shortcomings.

Next, walk east to Rockefeller Chapel.

Rockefeller
Memorial Chapel
(Philip A. Turner)

ROCKEFELLER MEMORIAL CHAPEL
1156-80 E. 59TH STREET
ARCHITECTS: BERTRAM G. GOODHUE
AND ASSOCIATES (1928)

At East 59th Street and South Woodlawn Avenue stands Rockefeller Memorial Chapel, one of the most imposing buildings of the university's campus, donated by and named in honor of the founder of the University of Chicago. This is an excellent example of the late Gothic style by a prominent architect interested in the Gothic revival. The Carillon Tower bells (72 of them) are noteworthy for the excellence of their tones and the quality of their sound. They were given, a few years after the chapel was completed, by the same donor in memory of his mother, Laura Spelman Rockefeller.

The chapel is the scene of many university functions, such as concerts, pageantry, graduation ceremonies, and other convocations.

The colorful banners hanging inside Rockefeller Chapel come from a collection of 44 liturgical banners created by Norman Laliberte for the Vatican Pavilion at the 1964-5 World's Fair held in New York. The banners are known officially as the Mary MacDonald Ludgin Collection.

As you stand outside Rockefeller Chapel on the corner of East 59th Street and Woodlawn Avenue, look north for a glimpse of 2 other places of worship—the beautifully executed red brick tower of the University of Chicaogo Theological Seminary's chapel 1 block north and 1 block east, at East 58th Street and University Avenue and the exquisite spire of the First Unitarian Church—1 block farther north, at East 57th Street and Woodlawn Avenue.

Continue east on the north side of the Midway, passing other University of Chicago buildings—Ida Noyes Hall, the laboratory school of the university, and International House—before turning north to 57th Street.

IDA NOYES HALL
1212 E. 59TH STREET
ARCHITECTS: SHEPLEY, RUTAN
AND COOLIDGE (1916);
FOR RENOVATION:
VICKREY/OVERSAT/AWSUMB (1983-6)

This student activities center has meeting rooms, student lounges, a cinema, and a recreational pool. Tours of the campus are available Saturday at 10 a.m., leaving from Ida Noyes Hall. Call 962-8650 for information.

The Laboratory Schools Complex structures are linked with each other by passageways or walks.

EMMONS BLAINE HALL
1362 E. 59TH STREET
ARCHITECT: JAMES GAMBLE ROGERS (1903)

This building has the admissions office and is part of the teacher training program of the University. The Lab Schools serve grades kindergarten to 12th. Besides Blaine Hall they consist of:

HENRY HOLMES BELFIELD HALL
5815 S. KIMBARK AVENUE
ARCHITECT: JAMES GAMBLE ROGERS (1904)

Blaine and Belfield Halls are French Gothic in Indiana limestone.

UNIVERSITY HIGH SCHOOL
5834 S. KENWOOD AVENUE
ARCHITECTS: PERKINS & WILL (1960)

The exterior of this building is modern in every sense of the word and fits in well with its Gothic neighbors. The exterior of limestone, aluminum and tinted glass is pleasant and inviting. Besides classrooms, the building contains a library, cafeteria, and student lounge.

BERNARD E. SUNNY GYMNASIUM
5731 S. KENWOOD AVENUE
ARCHITECTS: ARMSTRONG, FURST
AND TILTON (1930)

This Gothic structure of Indiana limestone contains a 2-story gymnasium and swimming pool. There are also exercise rooms, locker rooms and offices. The nearby athletic field is more than ample for the various athletic events and daily exercise routines.

Walk east on 59th Street.

INTERNATIONAL HOUSE
1414 E. 59TH STREET
ARCHITECTS: HOLABIRD AND ROOT (1932)

The stately modified Gothic structure, built of limestone, is one of 4 such centers founded by John D. Rockefeller, Jr. The other 3 centers are located in New York City; Berkeley, California; and Paris, France. Although these different houses share common origins and goals, each is a separate institution with no formal or legal ties to each other.

Although International House of Chicago was established in 1932 as a department of the University of Chicago, it is financially self-supporting and has its own Board of Governors which establishes general policy for the House and is responsible for its overall operation, subject to final review by the University's Board of Trustees.

International House serves as a social and cultural center for approximately one thousand foreign students, staff, and visitors associated with the University each year. The building has the capacity for approximately 500 residents. The director of International House also serves as adviser to foreign visitors for the University of Chicago.

Now return to Dorchester Avenue and walk north to East 57th Street. On the way note the stunning apartment building on your right followed by the elegant old Cloisters Apartments—both of which house many faculty families. At East 57th Street turn east to Jackson Park and the Museum of Science and Industry.

MUSEUM OF SCIENCE AND INDUSTRY
EAST 57TH STREET AT SOUTH LAKE SHORE DRIVE
ARCHITECTS: D. H. BURNHAM AND COMPANY,
CHARLES B. ATWOOD, DESIGNER (1891-2);
FOR RESTORATION: GRAHAM, ANDERSON, PROBST,
AND WHITE FOR THE EXTERIOR;
SHAW, NAESS, AND MURPHY FOR
THE INTERIOR (1929-40);
FOR THE ADDITION:
HAMMEL, GREEN, AND ABRAHAMSON (1986)

Before climbing the stairs at 57th Street and Lake Park (where you can get an Illinois Central suburban train back to the Loop as frequently as at 59th Street) walk 1 block east into Jackson Park for a good view of the Museum of Science and Industry. A visit inside, as with the museums around Burnham Park (see WALK 17), rates a separate trip. You could spend days here without seeing all the exhibits.

318

Just a view of this enormous building is an experience. Erected as the Palace of Fine Arts for the 1893 Columbian Exposition, it follows an elaborate Greek revival style—precisely duplicating various parts of temples on the Acropolis at Athens. Ionic columns, doorways, and the giant-sized carytids (13 feet tall, weighing about 6 tons each) are copied from the Erectheum; the carving on the metope panels and frieze is reproduced from the Parthenon. Materials used, however, were not those of the Acropolis temples. For the original "temporary" building heavy brick walls were merely covered with plaster, and the Ionic columns were constructed of wood lattice frame, then covered with a plaster composition called staff.

Though widely admired as the showpiece of the Columbian Exposition, this building and others in the neoclassical style brought forth the bitter statement from the Chicago architect Louis Sullivan so often quoted: "The damage wrought by the World's Fair will last for half a century from its date." Whatever its influence on architecture, however, the "Palace of Fine Arts" has become a decidedly modern museum with chief emphasis on technology, a popular place visited by millions of people each year.

The transformation was by no means simple or painless. The Palace of Fine Arts building was abandoned in 1920, when the Field Museum, which had been using space here, moved to its own building nearer the Loop. Not until several years later was this building rescued from neglect. The extraordinary amount of

Museum of Science
and Industry
(Robert J. Frett
courtesy
Illinois Bell)

319

money needed to restore both exterior and interior as a permanent building and to establish it as an industrial museum came largely from Julius Rosenwald, though his initial contribution of $3 million was apparently inspired by a bond issue of $5 million for this purpose—a bond issue passed by the voters of the South Park District. (Rosenwald's later contributions brought his total gift up to about $7.5 million dollars.)

For this particular WALK, however, just look at the building and ponder on the incongruity between the beautiful, Greek-temple exterior and the 20th century science and technology it houses!

The exhibits in the museum are varied. Some are permanent, such as the simulated coal mine, a small-scale model of a fantasy-land castle—with lights that light and willow tree that weeps, and the U505 submarine; some are seasonal, such as the Christmas trees of all nations; some are on loan or visiting exhibits.

In 1986 the Henry Crown Space Center was added. It was designed by Hammel, Green and Abrahamson of Minneapolis, Minnesota. The 36,000 square foot building contains 12,000 square feet of space exhibits, including actual space craft, satellites, and space probes. The addition also houses the Omnimax Theater, a 76-foot diameter dome screen surrounding a 334-seat auditorium. The presentations are planned to change two or three times a year.

The museum is open Monday through Friday, 9:30 a.m. to 4 p.m.; Saturday and Sunday, 9:30 a.m. to 5:30 p.m. Summer hours: 9 a.m. to 5:30 every day. Omnimax Theater shows: from 10 a.m., hourly; most evenings. Call 684-1414 for information. Admission to the museum is free; Omnimax Theater: adults, $4; children and senior citizens, $2.50.

22

1. Administration Building and Clock Tower

2. Florence Hotel

3. Pullman Stables

4. Greenstone Church

5. Market Hall

6. Pullman Housing

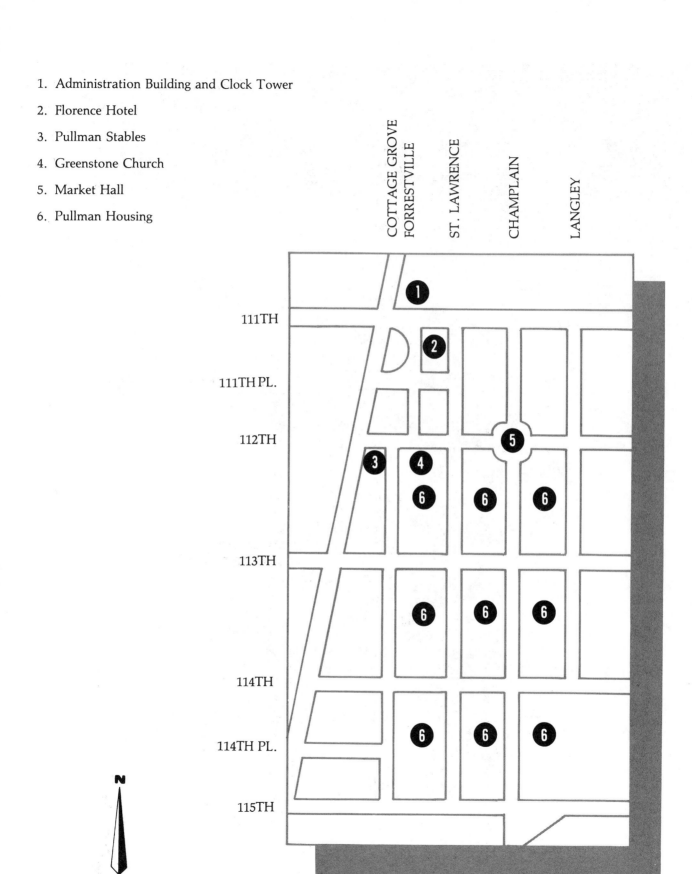

WALK • 22

WALKING TIME: 1 hour. HOW TO GET THERE: Take an Illinois Central [I. C.] suburban train at East Randolph Street and North Michigan Avenue [underground station] to Pullman. [Inquire about which train you should take.] Time—about 30 minutes. If you drive, take the Dan Ryan Expressway [Route 94] to 111th Street, Pullman Exit. Drive west to the second stop light.

The community of Pullman, near Lake Calumet on metro Chicago's Far South Side, was built as a model industrial town by George M. Pullman, an early Chicago industrialist. The town and all its buildings, one of the first developments in this part of the Chicago area, were designed by architect Solon S. Beman and landscape engineer Nathan F. Barrett. In the late 1870s Pullman selected this site for his Pullman Palace Car Company, which manufactured his recently devised Pullman railroad cars. (The first sleeping car was built in 1858, and the Pullman Palace Car Company was formed in 1867.)

For his model company town Pullman bought a huge tract of land bordering the western shore of Lake Calumet, which covered 4,500 acres of what was then undeveloped prairie in the Village of Hyde Park (not yet a part of the City of Chicago). Most of this land was owned by the Pullman Land Association with only the factory belonging to the Pullman Palace Car Company.

Pullman built the town on land bordered by 104th Street on the north, 116th Street on the south, by the Pullman Railroad on the east, and by the Illinois Central Railroad on the west. The town, which would be served by the Illinois Central Railroad, was designed with most of the community facilities near the IC depot at 111th Street—a hotel, a church, a school and an arcade building with stores, offices, library, theater, and bank—everything owned, of course, by the Pullman company. Work began on the Pullman plants and the first of the 1,750 housing units in 1880. Early the next year the first residents began moving into the row houses and the cheaper apartment buildings planned for lower-income workers. The factories of the car company were located

● This entire WALK is within the Pullman Historic District. Note that all the buildings were designed by the same architect, Solon S. Beman

Overleaf:
Pullman Square
(Philip A. Turner)

323

Pullman Works
(Philip A. Turner)

north of 111th Street. Other related enterprises, such as the Union Foundry and the Spanish Curled Hair Company (later Sherwin Williams Paint Company) were located between 104th and 106th streets and 115th and 116th streets respectively.

A walk through Pullman today gives you the sense of visiting a small town of the past, with the houses, hotel, and village square much the same as they looked a hundred years ago—an excellent showcase of town planning principles of the late 19th century. In this "model town" project Pullman was doubtless motivated partly by philanthropy as understood in his day and partly by enlightened self-interest. He believed that his employees would be happier if they could live near their work, in houses or apartments more attractive than the usual workers' homes, surrounded by all the facilities needed for daily living.

But Pullman's model town failed to bring happiness to his workers. Unrest hit the community—in those days made up mostly of workers of Scandinavian, Dutch, British and Irish descent—because they couldn't own their own homes and they felt that rents were too high. (Contrary to other sources, there was never a "company-owned" store. The company leased stores, but did not operate them.) By 1889, when petitions were filed for the annexation of Hyde Park to Chicago, feeling was so high among the Pullman workers that they voted for annexation over Mr. Pullman's opposition. Still the community remained very much an independent town within the city and for a while it prospered. As orders and production increased in the Pullman plants, more workers settled there, until the population by 1892 included more than 20 nationalities.

Real trouble lay ahead, however. The decline of the company town began with the depression of 1893-94, following the great boom Chicago had experienced with the Columbian Exposition of 1893. Unemployment rose and wages dropped, but rents remained pretty much the same. Mr. Pullman's refusal to restore his employee's wages to their previous figures and his prompt dismissal of several members of a committee that had called on him to discuss the matter precipitated a company-wide strike.

Since some of the workers belonged to the American Railway Union headed by Eugene V. Debs, the strike quickly became a nationwide issue, with an organization called the General Managers Association coming to the support of Pullman. After considerable violence and destruction of property (none of it in Pullman), as well as the workers' refusal to run the trains,

326

Pullman Square
(Olga Stefanos)

President Cleveland sent federal troops to take over and run the trains—so that the mail could go through. Although at first the president's action caused greater violence, it ultimately broke the strike. Eugene Debs was thrown in jail and his union weakened to the point of ruin. And Pullman's bitter, defeated workers returned to their jobs on his terms, not theirs. The only victory they won was a decision by the Illinois Supreme Court not long afterward that the Pullman Company's charter did not give it the right to own and manage a town. After Pullman's death, the successor management made no appeal, and so ended Mr. Pullman's Utopian dream of a perfect village for his workers!

Yet the buildings remain. After 1907, with a change from wood to steel cars, a greater number of Polish, Italian, and Greek immigrants came to Pullman, and older residents began to move out. From 1920 to 1940 the Pullman area remained fairly stable, merely becoming an older community. In 1957, the original plant of the Pullman Company moved its facilities further east. Since then, a number of industrial plants have developed on the original factory site.

327

Pullman Clock Tower
(Olga Stefanos)

ADMINISTRATION BUILDING and CLOCK TOWER
CORNER OF EAST 111TH STREET AND
SOUTH COTTAGE GROVE AVENUE

The Administration Building complex, constructed in 1880 was originally about 700 feet in length. The red face brick structure was made up of three parts: a center section, and two flanking wings. The center section contained three floors of corporate offices of the Pullman Palace Car Company.

In 1907, a large addition was attached to the southern wing. This addition, approximately 60 feet in height, begins south of the

328

center section and continues south parallel to the old wing, the facade of which was covered with the installation of the new structure. Its architectural treatment is only vaguely sympathetic to the original appearance, and because of differing design characteristics (especially with respect to height and property setbacks), the symmetrical qualities of the original complex have disappeared completely.

Cross the street.

FLORENCE HOTEL
Corner of East 111th Street and
South Cottage Grove Avenue

Named after George Pullman's favorite daughter, this elaborate 4-story building with many gables and turrets, was (and is) one of the first buildings to greet the visitor to the town when stepping the Illinois Central train at the 111th Street Station. During the early history of the town, many persons roomed here while either studying the various aspects of the community or visiting on George Pullman's personal invitation.

Although slight changes have been made to the facade, and a large annex added to the northeast corner of the building after 1910, the hotel's fine overall appearance and pleasing qualities are readily associated with the district.

Walk south on Forestville Avenue, though the park, and turn west on 112th Street.

PULLMAN STABLES
Corner of East 112th Street and
South Cottage Grove Avenue

According to a town rule, all residents (except the manager of the plant, who had his own stable behind his house) and visitors had to keep their horses here, apparently to prevent unnecessary clean-up tasks as well as to provide a profitable service. The volunteer fire company was also housed in this building for a number of years, and was known for its good service.

Around the turn of the century, a popular Sunday afternoon activity was to rent a carriage team, tour the countryside, and enjoy a family picnic. The company provided for this service at the stables, and individuals could rent a horse and buggy for $3 a day.

A service station and auto repair shop now occupy the building, but interesting reminders of the past are still apparent, including

329

two carved horses' heads located above the 112th Street entrance to the garage.

Walk east on 112th Street to St. Lawrence Avenue.

GREENSTONE CHURCH (PULLMAN UNITED METHODIST)
CORNER OF EAST 112TH STREET AND
SOUTH ST. LAWRENCE AVENUE

The Greenstone Church is perhaps the most charming building in the entire district. Its name derived from the green color of its Pennsylvania serpentine-stone facade. The massiveness of the masonry coupled with the large spire and arches suggests the Gothic Revival (of Richard Upjohn, to whom Beman apprenticed) and the Romanesque (of architect H. H. Richardson).

Since the Presbyterians had rented the church in 1885, the Catholics and Swedish Lutherans asked Pullman's permission to build their own structures. He resisted their pleas for a while, but finally leased property to them so they could build. Swedish Elim Lutheran Church (1888), and Holy Rosary Roman Catholic Church (1890), both designed by Beman, were constructed on vacant land some blocks west of the town to satisfy the needs of these congregations.

Today, the Greenstone Church is in excellent condition. Both the interior and exterior have undergone extensive restoration, under the direction of architect Charles E. Gregersen, and it remains much the same as it did when George Pullman attended services there.

Walk east.

MARKET HALL
AT THE INTERSECTION OF EAST 112TH STREET
AND SOUTH CHAMPLAIN AVENUE

By deliberate design, the building was placed in the middle of the intersection to break up the sometimes monotonous regularity of the streets' grid system. The top floor was removed in the 1930s and the remainder gutted by fire in 1972. It still awaits restoration.

Now take a walk down Champlain Avenue, toward 115th street, then west, and walk back north along St. Lawrence Avenue.

PULLMAN HOUSING

The housing in Pullman is of predominantly brick construction. Much of the brick was produced in brickyards to the south of the town. There were only two freestanding houses (for managers of the Allen Paper Wheel Works). All the others were arranged in rows of 2 to 28. Although there are roughly a dozen basic housing types, variation of roof lines, general configuration, and detail produced a much greater variety in the appearance of the housing.

While the homes of Pullman's elite were generally located on the parks and boulevards, those of the poorest residents were relegated to the back streets. Between these extremes, a deliberate attempt was made to mix the quality and size of the housing. It was not uncommon to find the home of a skilled worker, or even foreman, next to a boarding house.

Unlike other housing of the era, an effort was made to provide cross-ventilation and direct sunlight into all major rooms of the homes. One of the more advanced ideas in the design of Pullman's housing was the use of separate storm and sanitary sewers, which remain unique in Chicago.

Pullman Row House
(Olga Stefanos)

331

WALK • 23

FRANK LLOYD WRIGHT IN OAK PARK
AND RIVER FOREST

WALKING TIME: 2½ hours. HOW TO GET THERE: Take a Lake Street CTA elevated train headed for Oak Park at any of the Loop L stations, and get off at Oak Park Avenue. Walk 1 block north to Lake Street and then 2 blocks west to Kenilworth Avenue, where this WALK starts. If you drive, take the Eisenhower Expressway, turn off at Harlem Avenue, go north about 1 mile to Lake Street, then 4 blocks east to Kenilworth Avenue.

23

We are indebted to the Oak Park Public Library and W. R. Hasbrouck for developing this WALK in earlier editions. Oak Park is a community with high architectural awareness and much restoration work has been accomplished in the past decade and a half. We are indebted to the Frank Lloyd Wright Home and Studio Foundation, and especially to Donna Sack, for assistance in updating and revising the information in this WALK.

The Oak Park Center (a committee of the Frank Lloyd Wright Home and Studio Foundation) coordinates many architectural tours in Oak Park and operates the Oak Park Visitors Center at 158 Forest Avenue. Before beginning your WALK through Oak Park, you may want to stop at the Visitors Center where they sell a wide assortment of maps and guides. They also sell a map that includes pictures of all the buildings referred to; it would be an especially appropriate souvenir of your WALK. If you wish to have a guided tour of Unity Temple, The Frank Lloyd Wright Home and Studio, or a recorded walking tour of the area, tickets are available here. The cost for all three tours is $7. They also conduct special warm-weather tours. Call 848-1978 for more information.

In 1973, The Frank Lloyd Wright and Prairie School of Architecture Historic District was accepted for inclusion in the National Register of Historic Places. Two of the buildings in the district have been named National Historic Monuments: Unity Temple (1974) and The Frank Lloyd Wright Home and Studio (1976).

Opposite: Unity Temple
and interior view
(Philip A. Turner)

1. Unity Temple and Parish House
   875 Lake St.

2. Horse Show Fountain
   Lake St. at Oak Park Ave.

3. Francisco Terrace Apartments
   Lake St. and Euclid Ave.

4. George Furbeck House
   223 N. Euclid Ave.

5. Charles E. Roberts House and Stable
   321 and 317 N. Euclid Ave.

6. Rollin Furbeck House
   515 Fair Oaks Ave.

7. William G. Fricke House
   540 Fair Oaks Ave.

8. H. C. Goodrich House
   534 N. East Ave.

9. Edwin H. Cheney House
   520 N. East Ave.

10. W. E. Martin House
    636 N. East Ave.

11. Harry S. Adams House
    710 Augusta Blvd.

12. O. B. Balch House
    611 N. Kenilworth Ave.

13. H. P. Young House
    334 N. Kenilworth Ave.

14. Frank Lloyd Wright Home
    428 Forest Ave.

15. R. P. Parker House
    1019 Chicago Ave.

16. Thomas H. Gale House
    1027 Chicago Ave.

17. Walter Gale House
    1031 Chicago Ave.

18. Francis Wooley House and Stable
    1030 Superior St.

AUVERGNE
EDGEWOOD
THATCHER
KEYSTONE
FORREST
PARK
FRANKLIN
ASHLAND
LATHROP
JACKSON
MONROE
WILLIAM

19. Dr. W. H. Copeland House
400 Forest Ave.

20. Nathan G. Moore House and Stable
333 Forest Ave.

21. Arthur Heurtley House
318 Forest Ave.

22. E. R. Hills House
313 Forest Ave.

23. Mrs. Thomas H. Gale House
6 Elizabeth Court

24. P. A. Beachy House
238 Forest Ave.

25. Frank Thomas House
210 Forest Ave.

26. River Forest Tennis Club
615 Lathrop Ave.

27. J. Kibben Ingalls House
562 Keystone Ave.

28. Chauncey L. Williams House
530 Edgewood Pl.

29. Isabel Roberts House
603 Edgewood Pl.

30. William H. Winslow House
and Stable
515 Auvergne Pl.

31. E. Arthur Davenport House
559 Ashland Ave.

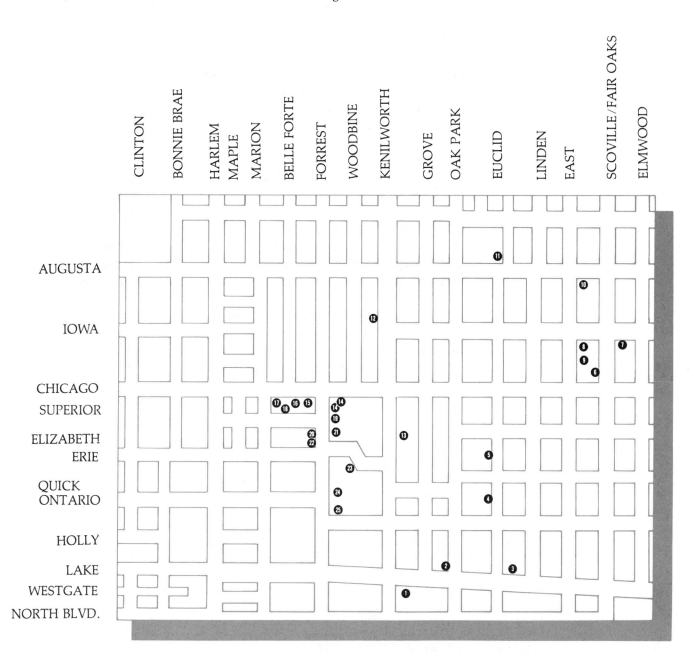

Frank Lloyd Wright was one of three distinguished architects who turned their backs on the accepted style of classic design and created new forms for people of the late 19th and early 20th centuries. The two others, who preceded him and doubtless influenced him in his earlier years, were Henry Hobson Richardson and Louis H. Sullivan. Each was a man of great talent and originality.

Of the three, Wright gave the most attention to domestic architecture, and over the years he developed a new style of home, now known worldwide as the "Prairie House." The Robie House (1909) on the University of Chicago campus (see WALK 20) is probably the most familiar example.

The Chicago area is incredibly fortunate in having a practically complete record of Wright's progress in his early years—25 structures that he built in Oak Park and 6 additional buildings in neighboring River Forest. The buildings listed for this WALK cover a period of only about 20 years in Wright's life.

You will be surprised at the early designs, especially those before 1900; steep gables and dormer windows have little resemblance to the style now associated with Wright's name. But the impact of the type of house he had developed by the end of that period continues to be felt today in house designs all over the world. Low roof lines, wide eaves, horizontal planes, and casement windows—all are characteristics of the Prairie House. The Prairie style was Wright's first expression of organic architecture; in it he incorporated site, material, plan, decoration, and finish into a unified whole to meet a specific functional requirement.

If you could choose a chronological order—which is obviously impractical!—instead of the geographical order that must be followed, you would more easily observe the record of changes in Wright's style. Unless otherwise indicated, the buildings listed here are not open to the public.

◉ **UNITY TEMPLE and PARISH HOUSE**
875 Lake Street
Architect: Frank Lloyd Wright (1908);
for the restoration: Unity Temple Congregation and the
Unity Temple Restoration Foundation (1973, 1979-80)

The Unity Temple, a Unitarian Universalist church, is Wright's only public building in Oak Park. The Temple is an esteemed international landmark. Wright was faced with three problems when designing this church: budget, urban location, and two uses. Abandoning traditional religious forms and symbols, Wright's solutions were both innovative and revolutionary—the cubic form without a steeple, the use of poured concrete, and the bi-nuclear plan.

A common entrance unites and separates the Temple and Unity House. Drawing the eye upward, the light streaming in from the skylight and windows is the major religious element in the Temple. With the pulpit placed front and center, Wright located seats on 3 sides, so that the minister and the congregation would be close to each other. (Years later Wright used a similar floor plan for the Greek Orthodox church he designed in Milwaukee.)

Unity House was designed to meet the secular and social needs of the congregation. As in his domestic architecture, Wright made the fireplace the focal point of the room, the heart of this church "home."

Through the combined efforts of the congregation and the Unity Temple Restoration Foundation (independent of the church), Unity Temple has undergone massive restoration. On the exterior, the 18-level roof has been restored and in 1973 the exterior was resurfaced. The foyer was fully restored in 1979, including return to the original color scheme and restoration of the entryway doors. In 1980 Unity House was returned to its original color scheme, as was Unity Temple itself. The lighting fixtures have been also been restored.

Frederick Koeper, (*Illinois Architecture*. Chicago: The University of Chicago Press, 1968, p. 204) referring to Wright's design of the Unity Temple, has paid special tribute to him in these words: "Like the music of Bach, the architecture of Wright develops magnificent variations on simple themes."

Unity Temple may be visited on Monday through Friday between 2 p.m. and 4 p.m. and on Saturday and Sunday at 2 p.m. The entrance fee is $4.

Walk east on Lake Street to the corner of Oak Park Avenue.

HORSE SHOW FOUNTAIN
LAKE STREET AT OAK PARK AVENUE

This fountain was designed by sculptor Richard Bock in 1909. It was reconstructed and relocated to this site in 1969. Wright suggested portions of the design concept.

Walk east and cross Euclid Avenue.

FRANCISCO TERRACE APARTMENTS
Lake Street and Euclid Avenue
Architect: Frank Lloyd Wright (1895);
for the reproduction: Harry Weese
and Associates (1978)

This building represents a last ditch preservation effort. When Wright's internationally-known building was razed, pieces were salvaged and reused here. For more information see *A Guide to Chicago's Historic Suburbs On Wheels and On Foot* (Swallow/Ohio University Press, 1981).

Walk north on Euclid Avenue 1½ blocks.

GEORGE FURBECK HOUSE
223 N. Euclid Avenue
Architect: Frank Lloyd Wright (1897)

The dormer and porch additions have destroyed the original proportions of this brick home with wood trim.

Continue north to the next block.

CHARLES E. ROBERTS HOUSE AND STABLE
321 and 317 N. Euclid Avenue
Architects: Burnham and Root (1883);
for the remodeling and addition:
Frank Lloyd Wright (1896)

This home, designed by Burnham and Root, was built in 1883. In 1896 Wright was architect for the interior remodeling. He designed the stable around the same time. The stable has been moved to its present site and converted into a home.

Continue north to Chicago Avenue. Turn east to Fair Oaks Avenue, then turn north again.

ROLLIN FURBECK HOUSE
515 Fair Oaks Avenue
Architect: Frank Lloyd Wright (1897)

This house is historically important because it marks the beginning of Wright's three-year period of design experimentation.

Continue north to the corner.

WILLIAM G. FRICKE HOUSE
540 Fair Oaks Avenue
Architect: Frank Lloyd Wright (1901-02, remodeled 1907)

This house has a stucco exterior with wood trim. The garage was added when the house was remodeled in 1907.

Walk west on Iowa Street, then turn south on East Avenue.

H. C. GOODRICH HOUSE
534 N. EAST AVENUE
ARCHITECT: FRANK LLOYD WRIGHT (1896)

This house has a clapboard exterior and a high roof. It was probably designed in 1895.

Continue to walk south.

EDWIN H. CHENEY HOUSE
520 N. EAST AVENUE
ARCHITECT: FRANK LLOYD WRIGHT (1903-04)

This 1-story brick house was originally set within gardens enclosed by brick walls. It has no basement or attic. There are striking resemblances to the Robie House, which Wright built in Chicago (see WALK 20).

Backtrack north on East Avenue, past Iowa Street.

W. E. MARTIN HOUSE
636 N. EAST AVENUE
ARCHITECT: FRANK LLOYD WRIGHT (1903)

This house has a stucco exterior with wood trim. At one time there were extensive formal gardens on the south side.

Continue north to the corner. Turn west on Augusta Boulevard to Euclid Avenue.

HARRY S. ADAMS HOUSE
710 AUGUSTA BOULEVARD
ARCHITECT: FRANK LLOYD WRIGHT (1913-14)

This is the last of Wright's Oak Park homes. It has a brick and stucco exterior.

Continue west on Augusta Boulevard to Kenilworth Avenue. Turn south 1 block.

O. B. BALCH HOUSE
611 N. KENILWORTH AVENUE
ARCHITECT: FRANK LLOYD WRIGHT (1911)

This was one of Wright's first commissions after returning from his trip to Europe. It has a stucco exterior with wood trim.

Frank Lloyd Wright Home
(courtesy Frank
Lloyd Wright Home
& Studio Foundation)

Walk east on Iowa Street 1 block. Turn south on Grove Avenue 1 block. Turn west on Chicago Avenue 1 block. Turn south on Kenilworth Avenue.

H. P. YOUNG HOUSE
334 N. KENILWORTH AVENUE
ARCHITECT FOR THE REMODELING:
FRANK LLOYD WRIGHT (1895)

This is an 1895 remodeling; it retains the old farmhouse (around which Wright built the newer home) as the kitchen area.
Backtrack north to the corner. Turn west 1 block. This is the most important stop on the WALK.

◉ FRANK LLOYD WRIGHT HOME
428 FOREST AVENUE
ARCHITECT: FRANK LLOYD WRIGHT
(1889, REMODELED 1895, ALTERED 1911);

340

FOR THE RESTORATION: THE FRANK LLOYD WRIGHT
HOME AND STUDIO FOUNDATION (1975-86)

Playroom of the
Frank Lloyd Wright Home
(courtesy Frank
Lloyd Wright Home
& Studio Foundation)

◉ FRANK LLOYD WRIGHT STUDIO
951 CHICAGO AVENUE
ARCHITECT: FRANK LLOYD WRIGHT
(1898, ALTERED 1911);
FOR THE RESTORATION: THE FRANK LLOYD WRIGHT
HOME AND STUDIO FOUNDATION (1975-86)

The Frank Lloyd Wright Home and Studio is a co-stewardship property of The Frank Lloyd Wright Home and Studio Foundation and the National Trust for Historic Preservation. Restored by the Frank Lloyd Wright Home and Studio Foundation to the last year Wright lived and worked in Oak Park, 1909, the building is significant both architecturally and historically. It was here that Wright designed the now-famous buildings of his Oak Park years.

The residence began as a small Shingle style house. Wright experimented with so many design concepts in this building that it can be viewed as a working laboratory of his stylistic growth. His growing family precipitated the first major alteration, the addition

341

of the playroom to the east and the enlarging of the south facade which allowed for a larger dining room.

Attached to his home, the studio, built in 1898, integrated Wright's work and family life. Radically different from buildings of its time, the exterior is an expression of the interior and includes many features that anticipated the Prairie style. In the eleven years that Wright worked in the studio, he produced one quarter of his total life output.

The house and studio of Frank Lloyd Wright may be visited weekdays at 1 p.m. and 3 p.m. and Saturday and Sunday from 1 p.m. to 4 p.m. on the half hour. The entrance fee is $4. Call 848-1978 for information.

Continue west on Chicago Avenue to see three examples of Wright's early work.

R. P. PARKER HOUSE
1019 CHICAGO AVENUE
ARCHITECT: FRANK LLOYD WRIGHT (1892)

This is known as one of the "bootleg" homes because Wright began supplementing his income by moonlighting, against the terms of his contract with Sullivan. This home is designed in the Queen Anne style.

THOMAS H. GALE HOUSE
1027 CHICAGO AVENUE
ARCHITECT: FRANK LLOYD WRIGHT (1892)

This is another of the "bootleg" homes.

WALTER GALE HOUSE
1031 CHICAGO AVENUE
ARCHITECT: FRANK LLOYD WRIGHT (1893)

This clapboard-sided house was completed shortly after Wright had left the employ of Adler and Sullivan.

Continue west and turn south at the corner, then turn east on Superior Street.

FRANCIS WOOLEY HOUSE AND STABLE
1030 SUPERIOR STREET
ARCHITECT: FRANK LLOYD WRIGHT (1893)

Originally surfaced with narrow clapboards, this house has been resurfaced with imitation brick siding.

Continue east to the east side of Forest Avenue.

DR. W. H. COPELAND HOUSE
400 FOREST AVENUE
ARCHITECT: FRANK LLOYD WRIGHT (1909)

The remodeling of this house in 1909 was not entirely according to Wright's plans.

Cross to the west side of Forest Avenue.

NATHAN G. MOORE HOUSE AND STABLE
333 FOREST AVENUE
ARCHITECT: FRANK LLOYD WRIGHT (1895);
REMODELED AND RECONSTRUCTED (1923)

This is one of few houses Wright designed in an historical style—English Tudor. Composed of many materials and stylistic features, it was reconstructed by Wright in 1923 after a fire had destroyed the upper floor.

On the other side of the street is 318 Forest Avenue.

ARTHUR HEURTLEY HOUSE
318 FOREST AVENUE
ARCHITECT: FRANK LLOYD WRIGHT (1902);
REMODELED AND RECONSTRUCTED (1923)

This house, built of Roman brick, is one of the finest examples of Wright's Prairie style. The main living area was on the second floor and the children's playroom and laundry facilities were on the ground floor. It has been remodeled into two apartments.

On the other side of the street is 313 Forest Avenue.

E. R. HILLS HOUSE
313 FOREST AVENUE
ARCHITECT FOR THE REMODELING:
FRANK LLOYD WRIGHT (1902);
REBUILT (1976-7)

This house was a reconstruction of an existing house by Wright. The transitional style utilizes stucco with wood trim. The second story burned in 1975 and the house was reconstructed, using the original plans.

Walk east on Elizabeth Court.

MRS. THOMAS H. GALE HOUSE
6 ELIZABETH COURT
ARCHITECT: FRANK LLOYD WRIGHT (1909)

343

The combination of the flat roofs and cantilevered balconies is not typical of the Prairie style. This small home became extremely influential with European architects in the 1920s.

Backtrack west to Forest Avenue and turn south.

P. A. BEACHY HOUSE
238 FOREST AVENUE
ARCHITECT FOR THE REMODELING:
FRANK LLOYD WRIGHT (1906)

Incorporating an earlier house, the combination of brick, stucco, wood, and cement is atypical of Wright.

Continue to walk south.

FRANK THOMAS HOUSE
210 FOREST AVENUE
ARCHITECT: FRANK LLOYD WRIGHT (1901); RESTORED (1975)

Built of stucco on wood frame, this was the first Prairie style house in Oak Park. It has features typical of Wright's early years —leaded glass windows, arched entrance, and Sullivanesque beaded moldings. It was restored in 1975.

If you are tired and wish to end the WALK here, continue south on Forest Avenue to Lake Street and turn south 1 block. You will have returned to Unity Temple.

There are, however, 6 more Wright buildings to be seen. They are a few blocks away in River Forest. To continue the WALK, after 210 Forest Avenue, walk west on Ontario Street. Cross Harlem Avenue and continue west on Quick Street. When it ends at Lathrop Avenue, turn north.

RIVER FOREST TENNIS CLUB
615 LATHROP AVENUE
ARCHITECTS: FRANK LLOYD WRIGHT;
CHARLES E. WHITE, JR. AND VERNON S. WATSON,
ASSOCIATE ARCHITECTS (1906);
FOR RELOCATION AND ENLARGING: VERNON S. WATSON (1920)

The exterior is of stained wood and battened sheathing. Charles E. White, Jr., and Vernon S. Watson were associate architects. Originally located on another site, it was moved here and enlarged under the supervision of Vernon S. Watson in 1920. It has been extensively altered.

Continue north to the corner and turn west on Oak Street to Keystone Avenue. Turn south to 562 Keystone Avenue.

Williams House
(Philip A. Turner)

J. KIBBEN INGALLS HOUSE
562 KEYSTONE AVENUE
ARCHITECT: FRANK LLOYD WRIGHT (1909); REMODELED (1926, 1981)

This house has a cruciform plan with cantilevered balconies. It has been remodeled twice, first in 1926 and again in 1981.

Continue south to the corner. Turn west on Lake Street to Edgewood Place, and walk north.

CHAUNCEY L. WILLIAMS HOUSE
530 EDGEWOOD PLACE
ARCHITECT: FRANK LLOYD WRIGHT (1895)

This house has Roman brick below the window sills and stucco above.

Continue north.

ISABEL ROBERTS HOUSE
603 Edgewood Place
Architect: Frank Lloyd Wright (1908, 1955)

This house, built in the form of a cross, is especially distinguished by a 2-story living room. Wright remodeled the house in 1955.

Backtrack south to the corner, then turn west on Lake Street 1 block. Turn north on Auvergne Place.

WILLIAM H. WINSLOW HOUSE AND STABLE
515 Auvergne Place
Architect: Frank Lloyd Wright (1893)

The exterior is Roman brick and stone, with a terra-cotta frieze above. This house was Wright's first independent commission after he left the firm of Adler and Sullivan. The wide eaves, low roof lines, centrally located chimney, and plain surfaces on the lower portion are characteristics that are incorporated in Wright's later houses. The roof was recently replaced.

Backtrack to the corner and walk east on Lake Street, 7 blocks, to Ashland Avenue. Turn north.

E. ARTHUR DAVENPORT HOUSE
559 Ashland Avenue
Architect: Frank Lloyd Wright (1901)

The building materials here are horizontal stained wood board and battened sheathing. This is the last of the homes to be viewed in River Forest.

Return to Lake Street. Walk east, crossing Harlem Avenue, to the Oak Park Mall. Continue through the mall until you are back at Lake Street, which concludes the walk.

This WALK has taken you from Oak Park's Unity Temple to River Forest's Tennis Club. Throughout you have seen many examples of Wright's chief contribution to American architecture —buildings planned as individual homes, from some of his earliest to those of a later period in which he was working out various forms of the Prairie House.

346

24

1. Piper's Alley
   1608 N. Wells St.

2. 1636 N. Wells St.

3. 1616 N. LaSalle St.

4. Kennelly Square
   1751 N. Wells St.

5. Hemingway House
   1825 N. Lincoln Plaza

6. Crilly Ct.

7. 225 W. Eugenie Ave.

8. 235 W. Eugenie Ave.

9. 1700 N. North Park Ave.

10. 1701-1713 N. North Park Ave.

11. 1711-1719 N. North Park Ave.

12. 1718 N. North Park Ave.

13. 316 W. Menomonee St.

14. 334 W. Menomonee St.

15. 1839-40 N. Orleans St.

16. 1835 N. Orleans St.

17. 1817 N. Orleans St.

18. 1801 N. Orleans St.

19. 235 W. Menomonee St.

20. 1802 N. Lincoln Park West

21. 1814 N. Lincoln Park West

22. 1816 N. Lincoln Park West

23. 1826-34 N. Lincoln Park West

24. 1836 N. Lincoln Park West

25. 1838 N. Lincoln Park West

26. 1834-1838 N. Lincoln Ave.

27. 1832 N. Lincoln Ave.

28. 1830 N. Lincoln Ave.

29. 1915-23 N. Lincoln Park West

30. Lincoln Park Tower
    1960 N. Lincoln Park West

31. Lincoln Park Terrace
    2020 N. Lincoln Park West

32. Ogden Mall

33. Midwest Buddhist Temple
    3435 W. Menomonee St.

34. St. Michael's Church
    1633 N. Cleveland Ave.

CLEVELAND HUDSON LINCOLN SEDGWICK ORLEANS NORTH PARK CLARK LINCOLN PARK WEST WELLS LASALLE

ARMITAGE

WISCONSIN

MENOMONEE

WILLOW

ST. PAUL

EUGENIE

CONCORD

NORTH

WALK • 24

OLD TOWN TRIANGLE

WALKING TIME: 1½ hours. HOW TO GET THERE: Take a northbound CTA bus No. 22, or a No. 36 bus on State Street. Get off at North Avenue and walk 2 blocks west to Wells Street.

This WALK starts at North Avenue and Wells Street, at Piper's Alley—an indoor shopping-entertainment mall created from the original alley of the Piper Bakery of 1875.

◉ The Old Town Triangle Historic District is roughly bounded by North Avenue, Lincoln Park, and the extension on Ogden Avenue north to Armitage Avenue

PIPER'S ALLEY
1608 N. WELLS STREET
ARCHITECTS: STANLEY TIGERMAN AND ASSOCIATES (1976)

The conversion includes a collection of shops, restaurants, and theaters. Second City, a nationally known theater, is part of the Piper's Alley complex at 1618 N. Wells Street. Second City's exterior ornament is from the facade of Adler and Sullivan's Garrick Theatre—rescued when that theater was demolished.

Walk north on Wells Street to Eugenie Avenue.

1636 N. WELLS STREET
ARCHITECTS: SCHIFF AND FRIEDES (1972)

The LaSalle Street tower has an adjacent shopping and community center.

Walk east on Eugenie Avenue. The land on the north side of the street was cleared for a project still not built.

1616 N. LaSALLE STREET
ARCHITECTS: DUBIN, DUBIN, BLACK AND MOUTOUSSAMY (1972)

This building was built in 1972.

Walk back to Wells Street. Turn north to Kennelly Square, another large complex.

Overleaf:
Old Town Apartments
(Bill Engdahl, Hedrich-Blessing courtesy Harry Weese & Associates)

KENNELLY SQUARE
1751 N. Wells Street
Architects: Ezra Gordon and Jack Levin (1973)

This is another unique development. It is named Kennelly Square for former Chicago Mayor Martin H. Kennelly and the Werner-Kennelly warehouse at 1750 N. Clark Street, which has been remodeled and is part of this complex. The east building is called The Warehouse.

The development includes a 25-story high-rise apartment building on North Wells Street; a 10-story apartment building on North Clark Street; a 54,000-square-foot commercial space, swimming pool, restaurant, and community facilities. The shopping gallery is skylighted and is accessible by a bridge over an open sunken arcade where the restaurant is located.

Next, walk 1 block north on Wells Street to Lincoln Avenue to see another interesting high-rise apartment building, Hemingway House.

HEMINGWAY HOUSE
1825 N. Lincoln Plaza
Architects: Solomon, Cordwell, Buenz and Associates (1971)

The Lincoln Park community has become world renowned for the efforts of its citizens in restoring the charm of this late 19th century area. Interspersed among the restored old houses are new developments in a variety of forms. Hemingway House is one such new development: on a uniquely shaped site overlooking Lincoln Park, it includes a vacated diagonal street and a traffic island. The challenge was to provide space for an apartment tower, attractive shops, and parking without interfering with the charm of the neighborhood.

Hemingway House contains 260 apartments and 20,000 square feet of shops and offices. All parking is below grade. The tower on the north end of the site minimizes sun shading of adjacent yards and structures. The height of the 2-story commercial structure was scaled to correspond to the predominant height of the cornice line of existing structures on Lincoln Avenue, thus preserving the vertical scale of the entire block.

Now walk south, back to Eugenie Avenue. Walk west to Crilly Court, a famous bit of Chicago.

CRILLY COURT

BOUNDED BY ST. PAUL STREET ON THE NORTH,
WELLS STREET ON THE EAST, NORTH PARK AVENUE
ON THE WEST, AND EUGENIE AVENUE ON THE SOUTH.
DEVELOPER: DANIEL F. CRILLY (1885-1893)

Stephen F. Gale, Chicago's first stationer and first Fire Chief, owned 40 acres of country farm and meadowland just north of the city limits. He subdivided it in 1845. Five or six years after it was subdivided, Chicago annexed the land in 1850 and 1851. Then Charles Canda, a Frenchman, bought the inside lots at the heart of it all. Those lots were from Wells to Sedgwick, and from Eugenie to St. Paul.

Where Crilly Court is now, Canda owned a home and a barn with a large number of fruit trees. After he died in 1854, his widow Adele took the west half, and Florimond, his brother, took the east. (St. Paul Street was Florimond Street until 1936.) Colonel Florimond Canda, who had fought at the battle of Waterloo under Napoleon Bonaparte, was awarded a medal by Napoleon III and the Empress Eugenie, before coming to settle in Chicago in 1843. It was Florimond Canda who sold the property to developer Daniel F. Crilly in 1884.

Daniel Crilly created a street through the middle of the block, from St. Paul to Eugenie, which he named Crilly Court. He built the 4-story buildings on the east side of North Park Avenue. He purchased the building material from the building that stood where the present Germania Club stands today. He also moved a 3-story brick building from that site to the southeast corner of St. Paul and North Park where it stands today.

The building that fronts on Wells Street is characteristic of a building type in Chicago. In the Chicago Landmark Commission Guidelines, *Twelve Typical Building Types*, this building is used as a model, with a caption "Store Fronts with Apartments Above." The structure is particularly handsome as an example because of the bay window and the iron columns. It truly livens up the street.

At the end of World War II, this section of the city was overcrowded and rapidly deteriorating. The owner of several large walk-up apartment buildings decided to deconvert and rehabilitate his buildings, two of which were back to back, separated by an alley. By replacing old wooden porches with steel balconies and stairs, and transforming the yards into gardens and delightful play areas, he changed the entire character of the

351

Crilly Court
(Olga Stefanos)

buildings. The city, taking cognizance of his fine work, named the short connecting street to the west Crilly Court after its innovator.

Crilly Court established the procedure for much fine conservation and rehabilitation work that characterizes the Old Town Triangle. Many painters, sculptors, musicians, poets, authors, and architects have now made this area their home.

Over the years much remodeling has taken place. The houses have been extensively redone. The Crilly estate over the years leased units to well-known Chicagoans. Eugene Field, poet and journalist, was one, and Cyrus DeVry, Lincoln Park Zoo Director, was another. George K. Spoor occupied an apartment there for many years. An early movie producer, Spoor was known for his Keystone Cops and movies with Ben Turpin and Francis X. Bushman, who gave our Zoo gorilla his name. In order to preserve the films, it was necessary for Spoor to keep them in his icebox.

Commercial artist Haddon Sundbloom lived for many years in an apartment above the Wells Street stores. He was the creator of the kindly man on the Quaker Oats box as well as Aunt Jemima. For over 35 years his Coca-Cola Santa was an annual Christmas feature all over the world.

There are so many late 19th-century townhouses and walk-up apartment buildings here you may think that when you've seen one you've seen them all. Not so; each is a pleasant surprise, sometimes found tucked in between taller buildings or set back far from the street. The rich texture of the fine brickwork and stone ornament make an architectural "find" of many of the buildings.

352

Continue west on Eugenie to the west side of Crilly Court, where townhouses cover the entire side of this short thoroughfare. Crilly Court itself is a private road with characteristics that suggest a quiet side street in the west end of London about the time of Sherlock Holmes!

225 W. EUGENIE AVENUE
ARCHITECT: UNKNOWN (1874)

Walk across the street for a better view of this recently remodeled 3-story frame house, with a new stucco wall and patio that make for privacy, and a charming entrance and facade. It is a well-preserved example of a wood frame cottage. The windows are crowned with keystone pediments and surrounded by rope moldings. It has a denticulated bracketed cornice under the eaves. There is a habitable rear building, which may have survived the Chicago Fire.

Continue west.

235 W. EUGENIE AVENUE
ARCHITECTS: HARRY WEESE AND ASSOCIATES (1958)

This is a delightful contemporary structure of seven maisonettes. These comprise fourteen dwelling units of 2 stories each, the architect having placed two "layers" of 2-story townhouses in a row of seven.

Walk to the northwest corner of Eugenie and North Park avenues.

OLD TOWN APARTMENTS
1700 N. NORTH PARK AVENUE
ARCHITECTS: HARRY WEESE AND ASSOCIATES (1960-61)

The Old Town Apartments were designed to blend into the surrounding community through the use of similar building height and characteristics reminiscent of older buildings. The apartments in the complex have high ceilings, Franklin stoves, and hardwood floors. The conventional construction technique used masonry bearing walls and party walls. The exterior is of Chicago common brick, painted standing seam sheet metal, and painted millwork. Parking is at grade, partially under the building.

Cross to the east side of North Park Avenue.

1701-1705 N. NORTH PARK AVENUE
Architect: Unknown (1893)

1707-1709 N. NORTH PARK AVENUE
Architect: Unknown (1893)

1711-1713 N. NORTH PARK AVENUE
Architect: Unknown (1893)

Built by Daniel Crilly in 1893, these courtyard apartments are early examples of a Chicago building type that became popular in the 1920s. They have slender denticulated crowning cornices. They are part of the Crilly complex.
Walk north.

1717-1719 N. NORTH PARK AVENUE
Architect: Unknown (pre-1888)

Although the architect and date are unknown, the building was moved to the site in 1888. The building is without bays, but the relatively plain facade contrasts with a magnificent, richly carved, bracketed front porch, which is its only decoration.
On the west side of the street again, you will see a charming old church building, tucked away behind trees, with a patterned brick walk.

1718 N. NORTH PARK AVENUE
Architect: Unknown (1880s);
for the adaptive reuse: Ast and Dagdelen (1982-6)

This was originally St. Jacob's Lutheran Church and later the Church of the Three Crosses. More recently it became the home of the Old Town Players, a repertory theater group—oldest of many small theater groups in the city. The interior was most successfully remodeled into a delightful arena for classical as well as modern drama.

After testing several schemes for this particular site, it was decided that the church be subdivided to allow for the conversion into 3 town houses, each oriented east and west. The design respects the existing fabric of the community. The front of the building, which has exposure on Orleans Street, is restored to its original condition with the exception of three understated doorways that provide entry to the individual townhomes. The east exposure, once the entry to the Old Town Players and set back a half a block from North Parkway, is punctuated with protruding bay windows where originally there was a blank brick wall. A landscaped berm along North Parkway shields the parking area from the street and sidewalk and provides partial privacy to the courtyard.

At this point of the WALK, stroll along St. Paul Street, to view the charming townhouses, trees, shrubbery, and vines there. Then return to North Park Avenue. Continue north past Willow Street to Menomonee Street. At this point you may want to walk west a few blocks on Willow Street to see City Commons, a new 62-unit townhouse development between Willow, Orchard and Vine streets designed by Pappageorge Haymes in 1986. Unit entrances are off a communal interior drive/courtyard. Utilizing a variety of masonry, the design draws on the vernacular of Chicago's rowhouse architecture for its streetscape image.

If you have taken this detour, walk back east to North Park Avenue and walk north to Menomonee Street. Cross the street, then turn west.

316 and 334 W. MENOMONEE STREET

Here you see a successful rehabilitation of an old apartment building at 316 W. Menomonee Street; and next door another example of successful rehabilitation, set behind a lovely garden.

At Orleans Street, walk north.

1838-40 N. ORLEANS STREET
ARCHITECT: UNKNOWN (1886)

Originally the C. F. W. Schmidt residence, built in 1886, this very handsome double-fronted apartment building has wonderful terra-cotta liberally placed on the facade and stained glass at the top of every window.

1835 N. ORLEANS STREET
ARCHITECT: UNKNOWN (1879)

Note too, across the street, the charming old vine-covered townhouse and patio have been well maintained.

Now walk back south on Orleans Street.

1817 N. ORLEANS STREET
ARCHITECT: UNKNOWN (1883)

Note this rehabilitated, 3-story, red brick house. Originally the Bertha Ehman house, it was built in 1883. The front stoop has been removed, but the lively line of the arched windows at the 3rd story gives this building distinction and a Moorish flavor.

Continue south.

1801 N. ORLEANS STREET

The Orleans apartment building is a rather poor facsimile of a New Orleans facade.

Continue walking south on Orleans to Menomonee Street.

235 W. MENOMONEE STREET
ARCHITECT: UNKNOWN (PRE-1930)

Farther east on Menomonee stands a daring rehabilitation of an apartment building: the 3rd story has been removed in order to give the 2nd-floor living room a ceiling 2 stories high. Excellent!

At this point you may want to see the Midwest Buddhist Temple and St. Michael's Church, a Roman Catholic church— instead of at the end of the WALK. If so, turn to p. 356 for the addresses and descriptions. You can pick up WALK 24 again at this point.

Walk east again on Menomonee Street and turn north on Lincoln Park West.

1802 N. LINCOLN PARK WEST
ARCHITECT: UNKNOWN (1874)

Originally the Henry Meyer house, this is a rare example of an extant farm house. It has keystones in carved wood arches, a light decorative element, added to gentrify the house. The brick wall and fine old trees make a delightful pattern.

Farther north in the same block you come to two red brick, high-ceilinged houses.

1814 N. LINCOLN PARK WEST
ARCHITECT: UNKNOWN (1878, 1886)

Originally the Samuel Anderson (Mr. Anderson was a merchant) apartment building, this was built in two stages; the rear third of the building in 1878, and the front two-thirds of the building in 1886. The facade of this 4-story walk-up is appointed with the plastic artistry of terra-cotta. These include the lunette at the top of the bay, and the window spandrels. The house is in fine condition—surely the result of tender loving care.

356

1816 N. LINCOLN PARK WEST
ARCHITECT: UNKNOWN (1890)

Although little information is available about this building, it is in fine condition and has also received tender loving care.
Continue north.

1826-1834 N. LINCOLN PARK WEST
ARCHITECTS: ADLER AND SULLIVAN (1884, 1885)

Originally the Ann Halsted townhouses, this row of 2-story, red brick townhouses is set back from the building line. The three southern units were built in 1884, and the northern two, the following year. These are among the few surviving examples of Louis Sullivan's early architectural design and planning. They have a special charm, due partly to the terra-cotta ornamentation. Close observation will show that the terra-cotta ornaments on the two halves are not quite the same. The corbel brackets on the northern two have a more vegetative origin and are less geometric than the three to the south. Notice the south part where the debt to Sullivan's early mentor, Philadelphia architect Frank Furness, is more pronounced.
Continue north.

1836 N. LINCOLN PARK WEST
ARCHITECT: UNKNOWN (1884)

This and the following house were known as the two Wacker houses. Charles Wacker—first chairman of the Chicago Plan Commission—for whom Wacker Drive was named (see WALK 8 and WALK 9) lived next door and his mother-in-law lived in this house. It has small eave brackets, intricate turned columns, and wood fretwork on the entrance canopy in a floral motif with delicate metal filigree on the canopy roof. The large front bay window has incised, fluted exterior casings in the classic manner on a base with capitals. They extend on the ground floor in a way sympathetically emulated by the sloping fascia of the entrance canopy.

1838 N. LINCOLN PARK WEST
ARCHITECT: UNKNOWN (1874)

The showpiece in this group is this brick-and-frame Swiss-type house, which has unusually heavy wood ornament above the first floor. Frederick Wacker's unusual house has a fairy tale quality.

With all the characteristics of a Swiss chalet, combined with an Italianate feeling, there is a wide overhanging veranda, supported by curved brackets, open-work hoods above the windows, and carved wooden spindle railings flanking the broad stairway. This was the home of Charles Wacker (see above). In a garden at the rear are two more brick houses, coach houses, built by Charles Wacker at the turn of the century. The 2-story frame house with a garden to the north is another example of how a well-maintained house can be kept livable and delightful.

Make a short detour—turn to your right at Lincoln Avenue and walk southeast.

1834, 1836, and 1838 N. LINCOLN AVENUE
Architect: Unknown (1876)

These rowhouses with triangular projecting bays were built in 1876. They have unified stone fronts, with decorative elements above the windows, and a fully-bracketed cornice and a broad frieze.

1832 N. LINCOLN AVENUE
Architect: Unknown (1880)

This and the next building were known as the Thekla Koch residence. This three-family residence is a fine example of the Second Empire style. The Mansard roof has the original fishscale slate. The large-paned glass was technologically progressive for its time.

1830 N. LINCOLN AVENUE
Architect: Unknown (1878)

A generation after this building was constructed, it was embellished in the then-popular Italianate style, seen in the brackets under the eaves, the dentils, and the projecting Chicago bay. A walk in the alley to the rear is most rewarding, for the houses all have delightful rear patios. At the time of the Old Town Art Fair, usually held the second week in June each year, some of these patios are opened to the public.

Now return to Lincoln Park West, and continue north.

1915-1923 N. LINCOLN PARK WEST
Architect: Unknown (1880)

Still farther north are fascinating rehabilitated townhouses built by Adolph Olsen in 1880. Even with the insignificant buildings near the center, this group of townhouses maintains the street facade. An interesting feature is the way in which the cornice outlines the 2-story dormer windows and the triangular pediments. It has the original slate imbrications on the mansard roof.

LINCOLN PARK TOWER
1960 N. LINCOLN PARK WEST
ARCHITECTS: DUBIN, DUBIN, BLACK AND MOUTOUSSAMY (1967)

This apartment building has a first-rate design. It is well sited with respect to Lincoln Park and Ogden Mall.

Continue north across Armitage Avenue.

LINCOLN PARK TERRACE
2020 N. LINCOLN PARK WEST
ARCHITECTS: DUBIN, DUBIN, BLACK AND MOUTOUSSAMY (1972)

The circular balconies give this high-rise reinforced concrete apartment building an individual appearance that does not in any way echo the Lincoln Park Tower, designed by the same architects. The low structure on the Armitage side of the building is a ground-level and below-ground parking facility.

At this point you are close to the northern end of the former Ogden Avenue—now the Mall in this area.

OGDEN MALL

The Ogden Mall is an important phase of the Department of Urban Renewal's exciting plans for rehabilitating the Old Town and Lincoln Park Conservation areas (see WALK 26). Ogden Avenue, a diagonal thoroughfare which formerly ended at Clark Street on the northeast, has been closed to vehicular traffic southwest to North Avenue and converted into a pedestrian mall. The Mall is a major axis of a green belt connecting Lincoln Park to the residential areas to the west. It has become the symbol of a renewed community.

Follow the alignment of the Mall, continuing in a southwesterly direction to Wisconsin Street. First, pass two small apartment buildings with shops at grade level. The urban renewal plans called for a combination of residential, commercial, and institutional development along the Mall.

The patient persistence of Lewis W. Hill, former Commissioner of Urban Renewal and Development and Planning, is largely responsible for the apparent success in implementing the plan.

Walk south on Orleans, past Wisconsin, then turn west on Menomonee Street.

MIDWEST BUDDHIST TEMPLE
435 W. Menomonee Street
Architect: Hideaki Arao (1972)

From a distance of 2 or 3 blocks, the Midwest Buddhist Temple—also known as the Temple of Enlightenment—appears to be set on a high plateau. As one gets closer, it is apparent that although it is on flat ground, the illusion persists until one is almost next to it. The reason for this is the unusual method the architect used in setting the chapel up high above the main portion of the structure.

The chapel has a shingled, modified gable roof which at a distance gives the appearance of a pagoda. The base of the temple is made up of a concrete wall that is striated by a rough, bushhammered technique. The first floor wall continues up above the first floor ceiling line to become the parapet wall for a deck that surrounds the chapel.

The rectangular floor plan places a large social room directly beneath the chapel. The social room is set a few feet below grade, with an open corridor at grade level on the two long sides. The corridor gives access to classrooms and offices.

The chapel can be reached from the social room as well as from outside. The main entrance consists of an impressive concrete stairway leading to heavy iron gates with the bushhammered concrete wall on either side. One first reaches the deck before entering the chapel. The deck is actually the roof over the corridors. It provides the means to hold ceremonial processions as well as a place to accommodate large crowds waiting to enter the chapel. The exterior walls of the chapel are stucco finished with windows of translucent glass.

Upon entering the chapel, which has white walls and ceiling and heavy timber trusses, one is aware of its simple character. There is an altar at the south end consisting of a gold-leaf sanctuary and shrine that contains a small gold, standing Buddha. The altar holds 2 large brass candelabras and vases with lovely floral arrangements.

360

The exterior remains the boldest part of the temple. It has the strength and vitality of the ancient Japanese shrines along with the simple straight lines of contemporary architecture. The nearby parsonage was built after the temple was completed, and the lovely Japanese garden was also added later. The temple has its own parking area.

Walk West to Cleveland Avenue, then walk south.

Midwest Buddhist Temple (Chicago Department of Urban Renewal)

ST. MICHAEL'S CHURCH
1633 N. Cleveland Avenue
Architect: August Wallbaum (1866-9, 1872-3)

St. Michael's, a complex of buildings extending south to North Avenue, includes the enormous church at Eugenie Street, and a convent, rectory, elementary school, gymnasium, high school, and community center. The brick and stone church was originally built in 1866-9 and partially destroyed by The Great Fire of 1871. It was restored in 1872-3 and expanded over the intervening years to its present size.

361

The semi-Gothic-Romanesque-German Baroque character of the exterior and interior of the church comes as a pleasant surprise, if one is not an absolute architectural purist. The interior has an enormously high ceiling with Gothic-type vaulting supported by slender columns with semi-classic capitals.

The great monumental altar is carved wood with many sculptured figures capped by a figure of St. Michael with a great sword and great jeweled crown overhead, over which stands a jeweled cross. There are murals on either side of the altar. All in all, it is a fascinating Baroque setting.

Originally, St. Michael's was a large German-speaking Roman Catholic parish. Today, one mass on Sunday is given in Spanish; the other is in English. This reflects the changing character of the neighborhood.

The urban renewal program has made St. Michael's a part of the Ogden Mall, with a large pedestrian masonry court, or square, at the entrance facade.

Walk north on Cleveland Avenue to Eugenie, then east 3½ blocks to Crilly Court. Walk east on Eugenie Avenue to Clark Street to board a southbound CTA No.22 or 36 bus to return to the Loop.

25

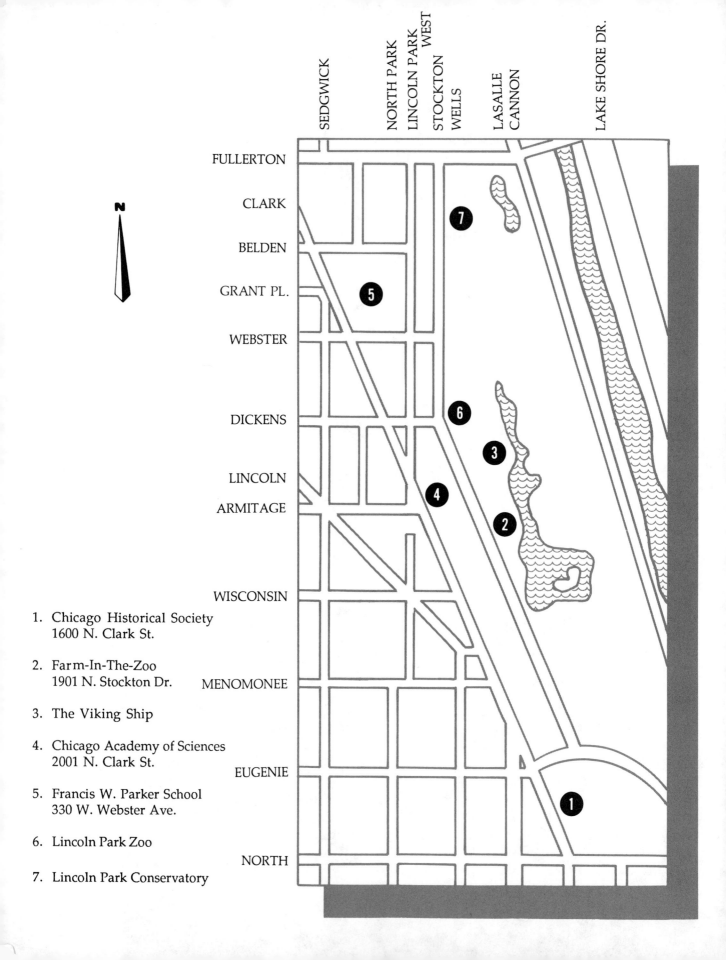

N

FULLERTON

CLARK

BELDEN

GRANT PL.

WEBSTER

DICKENS

LINCOLN

ARMITAGE

WISCONSIN

MENOMONEE

EUGENIE

NORTH

SEDGWICK

NORTH PARK

LINCOLN PARK WEST

STOCKTON

WELLS

LASALLE

CANNON

LAKE SHORE DR.

1. Chicago Historical Society
   1600 N. Clark St.

2. Farm-In-The-Zoo
   1901 N. Stockton Dr.

3. The Viking Ship

4. Chicago Academy of Sciences
   2001 N. Clark St.

5. Francis W. Parker School
   330 W. Webster Ave.

6. Lincoln Park Zoo

7. Lincoln Park Conservatory

WALK • 25

LINCOLN PARK: MUSEUMS, ZOOS, CONSERVATORY

WALKING TIME: 1½-2 hours [more if you want to enter the museums]. HOW TO GET THERE: Take a northbound CTA bus No. 36 [Broadway] on State Street or No. 22 [Clark] on Dearborn Street [1 block west of State Street], and get off at North Avenue [1600 N] and Clark Street.

Lincoln Park was named for President Abraham Lincoln. It is Chicago's largest park, covering some 1,000 acres of land just off the lake all the way from West North Avenue (1600 N) to West Hollywood Avenue (5700 N). This WALK, however, will take you only through the southern part of the area, no farther than Diversey Avenue (2800 N). In this section you are in the old Lincoln Park, as it was before the various northern extensions—on land redeemed from the lake—were added. And here you will find most of the park's special attractions.

At the southernmost border, where Dearborn Street ends at Lincoln Park, a rugged bronze figure of Abraham Lincoln stands to greet you—ignoring the bench, designed by Stanford White, behind him. This Lincoln statue, by Augustus St. Gaudens, is only one of nearly thirty large, miscellaneous statues in Lincoln Park—of such disparate personages as Garibaldi, Hans Christian Andersen, Beethoven, Shakespeare, John Peter Altgeld, and Emanuel Swedenborg. Perhaps the most unexpected in this locale are the large nude figure of Goethe and the conventional equestrian statue of Ulysses S. Grant, though he appears not at all in Grant Park—where St. Gauden's seated Lincoln is a main attraction!

Only a few steps away from the Lincoln statue is—appropriately—the Chicago Historical Society, especially famous for its Lincoln and Civil War materials.

Overleaf: Statue of Alexander Hamilton (Allen Carr)

365

CHICAGO HISTORICAL SOCIETY
WEST NORTH AVENUE AND NORTH CLARK STREET
ARCHITECTS: GRAHAM, ANDERSON, PROBST
AND WHITE (1925);
FOR NEW WING: ALFRED SHAW AND ASSOCIATES (1972);
FOR THE ADDITION: HOLABIRD AND ROOT (1986-8)

The Chicago Historical Society has occupied its building—a 2-story brick structure with a well-proportioned Georgian facade—since 1925, but the Society was organized a hundred and thirty years ago, in 1856.

An imposing gray limestone west wing was completed in 1972. This wing makes it possible for the society to exhibit many important items that heretofore had to be stored in the basement.

In referring to the building addition, Andrew McNally III, president of the society, told the trustees:

The planned addition to our building will provide space for our collections, space for new exhibits, space for handling school children, and space for us to conduct lively and exciting programs.

To anyone interested in this country's history, a visit to the museum is already a "lively and exciting" experience. The past comes vividly to life through dramatic displays, period rooms, costumes of famous Americans, and a collection of early autos and horsedrawn vehicles, as well as through the exhibits of manuscripts, paintings, prints, and maps. Seasonal contributions by the museum are an old-fashioned Christmas tree and an old-fashioned Fourth-of-July celebration with a reading of the Declaration of Independence, speeches, a band, and fireworks. Old Hollywood films are sometimes shown Sunday afternoons.

At this writing, new construction is about to begin. A new west entrance and an additional 28,000 square feet of space will be added, mostly for storage. A new restaurant will be in the glass and steel rounded projection at the south end, along with a bookstore. The design includes large display windows at street level within a sheltering sidewalk arcade.

The museum is open daily 9:30 a.m. to 4:30 P.M.; Sundays and holidays noon to 5 p.m. Admission: adults $1.50; children 6-17 and senior citizens 50 cents; Mondays free. For information, call 642-4600.

Just north of the Chicago Historical Society, with its records of the City by the Lake and of the people who made the records, is the tomb of one of those historic people—Ira Couch. Ironically, the rather small Couch Mausoleum is often overlooked, though its presence is proof that the Couch family won a lawsuit against the city to keep it here when the city cemetery was discontinued and the graves moved to private cemeteries. Ira Couch, originally a tailor, in 1836 became one of Chicago's pioneer hotel owners—the proprietor of the Tremont House, then located at the northwest corner of Lake and Dearborn streets. The only other reminder of the park's earlier function is a boulder farther north, placed by the Sons and Daughters of the American Revolution over the grave of David Kennison, the last participant in the Boston Tea Party to die—in 1852, when he was 115 years old!

Lincoln Park Zoo is a favorite haunt of thousands of Chicago's young at heart. It is actually 3 zoos—the Farm-in-the-Zoo, the Children's Zoo, and the over-one-century-old main zoo of the traditional kind. A short distance north of the Chicago Historical Society building, on Stockton Drive, is the zoo's miniature farm. The main zoo area, including the Children's Zoo, is farther north.

FARM-IN-THE-ZOO
1901 N. STOCKTON DRIVE
ARCHITECT: CHICAGO PARK DISTRICT (1964);
FOR THE RENOVATIONS AND ADDITION: JOHN MACSAI
AND ASSOCIATES (1986-7)

Spread out along the west side of Lincoln Park's South Pond, the Farm-in-the-Zoo is just a short walk from the Lincoln statue, through the underpass to the north. Originated as a way of familiarizing city children with the farm animals they never see, it has proved equally fascinating to children coming in from the country. You will find here not only the smaller farm animals—chickens, ducks, geese, pigs, sheep—but horses and cows as well. In the dairy barn are cows for milking and in another are beef cattle. In still another barn, horses are on display. The milking parlor in the dairy barn with all its modern equipment may not seem natural to a generation old enough to remember watching the "hired hand" squirt the milk from the cow into a big open pail (now considered unsanitary), occasionally aiming a stream into the mouth of a waiting cat beside him. But the present generation, of course, finds the farm machinery—milking machines and tractors and all the rest— more natural and more interesting.

In the main barn are many exhibits and demonstrations. There you can see samples of what is actually produced on a farm and

learn how many ways they are used. You can also watch the process of manufacturing a number of things that are made from farm products or especially needed on the farm—fertilizer, leather, or soap, for instance. Renovations and the addition of a teaching center to the barn were underway at this writing.

The Farm-in-the-Zoo is open daily 9:45 a.m. to 5 p.m. Free.

Across the road from the Farm-in-the-Zoo is the David Kennison Boulder (already referred to), which marks the grave of the last survivor of the Boston Tea Party group, who died in Chicago in 1852, when he was 115 years old.

THE VIKING SHIP

Just northwest of the South Pond is a carry-over from the 1893 World's Columbian Exposition. This is the very boat—a copy of a 10th century Viking ship—that was built by Norway at that time and sailed across the Atlantic with a crew of 12 men. They brought official greetings from their country to the citizens of Chicago.

Another museum in Lincoln Park is the Chicago Academy of Sciences, a small natural history museum, which stands just 1 block north of the David Kennison Boulder.

CHICAGO ACADEMY OF SCIENCES
2001 N. Clark Street
Architects: Patton and Fisher (1893);
for auditorium: Skidmore, Owings and Merrill (1953);
for gallery: Environ, Inc. (1984);
for exterior rehabilitation: Environ, Inc. (1986)

Founded in 1857, only one year after the founding of the Chicago Historical Society, this is the city's oldest museum—in fact the oldest scientific museum in the west. It housed Chicago's first planetarium. Here too Chicago's past is brought vividly to life—a past, however, long antedating anything you may have seen in the Chicago Historical Society's exhibits. For here you may walk through a section that reproduces Chicago of 350 million years ago—when it was a coal forest! And a series called "Chicago Environs" presents dioramas showing animals and plants that flourished here when the area was still open prairie, swamps, forest, and beaches. They have changing exhibits and special education programs.

Officially the Matthew Laflin Memorial, this building is a real tribute to one of Chicago's early businessmen. Matthew Laflin

Opposite top:
Lincoln Park
Farm in the Zoo
(Philip A. Turner)

Opposite bottom:
Chicago Academy
of Sciences
(Olga Stefanos)

369

came to Chicago in the 1830s, having sold out his business in the east to a man by the name of du Pont! He started one of the first stockyards in Chicago, near enough the hotel he had built to synchronize the two businesses. Another of his business ventures in Chicago was a bus line—which he later sold to somebody by the name of Parmelee! This restless innovator shared an ambition with many other early Chicago leaders—to rest at last in the city's cemetery with an imposing monument above him. Like many others he was distressed when the graves and monuments there were moved and Lincoln Park substituted. But though he couldn't be buried where he had hoped to be, he could have an impressive monument in the park. That monument is the Chicago Academy of Sciences building, for which he provided $75,000—the Chicago Park District adding $25,000 from its own budget. The interior has undergone remodeling, but the Romanesque exterior still stands as a worthy memorial indeed for one of Chicago's earliest successful businessmen.

The building has recently undergone some restoration work, including exterior cleaning, replacement of damaged stonework, and replacement of the stairs in an effort to return the structure to its previous grandeur.

The Academy is open 10 a.m. to 5 p.m. every day but Christmas. Adults: $1; children and senior citizens: 50 cents. Free on Monday. Call 871-2668 for information on exhibits and lectures.

Before continuing in the park, cross Lincoln Park West at Webster Avenue to see the Francis W. Parker School.

FRANCIS W. PARKER SCHOOL
330 W. WEBSTER AVENUE
ARCHITECTS: HOLABIRD AND ROOT (1962, 1986)

This U-shaped, 3-story, hard-burned red brick structure replaced an ancient 4-story half-timber Tudor Gothic building constructed in the early 1900s. Note the sculptured figures of children at the main entrance facing Clark Street. They were produced by sculptor Abbott Pattison, an alumnus.

An outstanding independent private school (pre-kindergarten through 12th grade) this was one of the first progressive schools in the country, following the creative teaching concepts of John Dewey and Francis Parker. This is the school that brought a cow to graze in the front yard, so that city children could have some touch of experience with the country. (This was in the days before

370

the Farm-in-the-Zoo at Lincoln Park across the street.) Visitors sometimes question the wisdom of the overall architectural plan—placing the building on the Clark Street side of the property and leaving the side facing the park, which is some of the most valuable land in Chicago, for a play field. The school's board of trustees, however, who are as progressive as its policies, agreed to allow the green belt from the park to continue to Clark Street as its contribution to the community.

In a delightful courtyard facing south you will see a reflection pool, flower garden, and stainless steel sculpture by John Kearny. This charming setting is often the background for school functions, such as plays, receptions, and other ceremonies. The brick wall separating the courtyard from the play field contains some original terra-cotta plaques from the razed Garrick Theatre Build designed by Adler and Sullivan—first known as the Schiller Building, which stood at 64 W. Randolph Street until its demolition in 1961. (The Second City theater group also used stones from this building. See WALKS 15 and 24.)

In 1986 a third floor was added to the east wing, to match the west wing; a connecting corridor was added at that level between the wings; and the art studios were expanded on the lower level to the east. The science rooms were updated and the library enlarged. The little school was expanded to the west with a brick to match the main school, and the kindergarten rooms enlarged; all windows were replaced with double glazed insulated glass.

LINCOLN PARK ZOO
BETWEEN STOCKTON
AND CANNON DRIVES AT 2200 N

Lincoln Park Zoo is Lincoln Park's biggest exhibit. Founded in 1868, it occupies 35 acres of the park's total acreage and is maintained by the Chicago Park District. In fact America's oldest zoo, Lincoln Park Zoo has had to modernize while keeping its 19th Century flavor. Traditionally a zoo simply tried to maintain the largest possible variety of animals, usually displayed in small, easy-to-clean cages. Beginning in the 1960s this philosophy began to change. It is now believed that a more natural setting benefits the animals and gives the visitor a more positive and instructive experience.

The Lincoln Park Zoo and the Children's Zoo were consolidated in an ambitious expansion and remodeling program the first phase of which was completed in 1971. Harry Weese and Associates

were the chief planners and architects. They worked with the staff of the Chicago Park District and Board of Commissioners. Robert Black, chief engineer for the district, was in charge of construction. The Lincoln Park Zoological Society, a private non-profit organization, has been active in the zoo's expansion. A second major phase is underway at this writing.

Great ingenuity is necessary because Lincoln Park Zoo, being in the heart of the city, has a limited site. Natural habitats are being created by the remodeling of interiors and exteriors of the old buildings, yet their wonderful character is being retained. The newest construction consists of unique, multi-functional structures that burrow into the ground and are covered with a blanket of landscaping. This reduces their visual impact on the park, and creates a terrain of winding paths and gentle hills.

The zoo is said to have more than 1,800 different kinds of animals, birds, and reptiles, representing a good cross-section of animal life. The grounds are open daily 8 a.m. to 5 p.m.; buildings open daily 9 a.m. to 5 p.m. Free.

THE CHILDREN'S ZOO
ARCHITECT: CHICAGO PARK DISTRICT (1959);
FOR THE RENOVATIONS AND ADDITION:
HAMMOND BEEBY AND BABKA (1986)

The Children's Zoo, located at the north end of the South Pond, is open the year around. Some of the baby animals that were born at the zoo during the previous winter and spring are exhibited outdoors during the summer months. At this writing, major renovations to the building, including the addition of a learning center, are underway. The Children's Zoo is open daily 10 a.m. to 5 p.m. Free.

KROC ANIMAL HOSPITAL
ARCHITECT: CHICAGO PARK DISTRICT,
MAURICE THOMINET CHIEF ARCHITECT (1976)

SEA LION POOL
ARCHITECT: CHICAGO PARK DISTRICT (1969)

REPTILE HOUSE
ARCHITECT: EDWIN CLARK (1922)

This was originally Chicago's only aquarium, remodeled into the present reptile house in 1936.

PRIMATE HOUSE
(FORMERLY SMALL ANIMAL HOUSE)
ARCHITECT: EDWIN CLARK (1927);
FOR THE RENOVATIONS: JOHN MACSAI AND
ASSOCIATES (1984)

SMALL MAMMAL HOUSE
ARCHITECT: UNKNOWN (1889)

GREAT APE HOUSE
ARCHITECTS: BRENNER, DANFORTH AND ROCKWELL,
DANIEL BRENNER CONSULTING ARCHITECT (1976)

ANTELOPE and ZEBRA HABITAT
ARCHITECTS: WELTON BECKET ASSOCIATES (1982)

LARGE MAMMAL HABITAT
ARCHITECTS: SKIDMORE, OWINGS AND MERRILL,
MYRON GOLDSMITH CHIEF ARCHITECT (1982)

FLAMINGO DOME and WATERFOWL LAGOON
ARCHITECT: CHICAGO PARK DISTRICT (1978)

LION HOUSE
ARCHITECTS: DWIGHT PERKINS (1912);
FOR THE REMODELING: HAMMOND, BEEBY AND BABKA (1986-7)

Be sure not to miss the brick and tile Lion House, winner of a Gold Medal from the American Association of Architects. Note the delightful dancing lions above the entrance arch.

CROWN-FIELD CENTER
ARCHITECT: BRENNER, DANFORTH AND ROCKWELL (1979)

Of the recent projects, the Crown-Field Center is an amazing multipurpose building. Mixed into one, dug-in, unobtrusive building are the zoo's offices, a gift shop, an auditorium, two classrooms, and an indoor apartment for a large family of lemurs! As if this weren't enough, the upper level of the building is ringed with an outdoor walkway and contains a small mammals exhibit in the center.

PENGUIN and SEABIRD HOUSE
ARCHITECTS: DANFORTH ROCKWELL CAROW (1981)

BIRD HOUSE
ARCHITECTS: JARVIS HUNT (1900);
FOR BIRD OF PREY HABITAT: SKIDMORE, OWINGS AND MERRILL (1983);
FOR THE RENOVATIONS: SCHMIDT, GARDEN AND ERICKSON (1986-7)

ZOO ROOKERY
ARCHITECTS: ALFRED CALDWELL (1936);
FOR THE RENOVATION: CHICAGO PARK DISTRICT, IRA M. BERKE (1968)

The Zoo Rookery is at the extreme north of the Lincoln Park Zoo. Here land and water birds make their home in a large attractive rock garden, and are free to come and go as they like.

On the northwest corner of the Lincoln Park Zoo is the Lincoln Park Conservatory, which covers 3 acres of land.

LINCOLN PARK CONSERVATORY
WEST FULLERTON PARKWAY AND STOCKTON DRIVE
ARCHITECTS: J. L. SILSBEE (1892, 1902);
ADDITION (1904);
FOR THE MAIN ENTRY MODIFICATION:
CHICAGO PARK DISTRICT (1950);
FOR REBUILDING OF PROPAGATING HOUSES:
CHICAGO PARK DISTRICT (1985-6)

The greenhouse, constructed of copper glazing bars with clear glass side windows and translucent wire-glass for the roof, protects a seemingly infinite collection of plants. The show houses, some of which date back to 1892, display a large collection of potted palms, a fernery, and a bit of real tropics where tropical fruit trees are propagated. (The Conservatory has 18 propagating houses, which sometimes may be seen by a visitor.)

Four annual exhibits have become traditional: a show of azaleas in February and March; of lilies and spring plants in April; chrysanthemums, of course, in November; and poinsettias and Star of Bethlehem in December and January.

This is considered one of the finest conservatories in the country. Incidentally, most of the flowers that appear in Chicago's numerous parks are started in the greenhouses connected with this conservatory. Don't overlook the park's outdoor gardens near the conservatory—Grandmother's Garden, water-lily ponds, fountains, and formal gardens.

Open daily 9 a.m. to 5 p.m. During their 4 major annual shows: 10 a.m. to 6 p.m. (9 a.m. to 9 p.m. Friday). Free.

Lincoln Park's Casting Pond lies along Stockton Drive north of Fullerton Parkway. The casting pond can be used by anyone interested in developing that particular fisherman's skill. And just beyond the casting pond and the ball-playing areas stands a golden statue of Alexander Hamilton, erected in 1952, designed by the architect Samuel Marx. (See also WALK 29.)

This is the northernmost point in your WALK. If you go over to the statue and up onto the plaza on which it is mounted, you will have a rewarding view. The Elks Memorial stands to the west (see WALK 29). To the north, the direction that Hamilton himself is facing, and slightly east, is a bronze figure of John Peter Altgeld, the governor of Illinois who lost his political career but gained eternal fame for his courage when he freed the men he was convinced were unjustly charged with the bombing during the Haymarket Riot in Chicago. To the east you will see the Diversey Yacht Club, and to the south (if you are willing to turn your back on the great gentleman!) a panoramic view of Chicago's always impressive skyline.

26

1. 1443-45 N. Hudson St.

2. Pickwick Village
   515-29 W. Dickens Ave.

3. 540 W. Dickens Ave.

4. Dickens Square
   550-54 W. Dickens Ave.

5. Walpole Point
   2140 N. Lincoln Ave.

6. 2100 N. Hudson Ave.

7. Policeman Bellinger's Cottage
   2121 N. Hudson Ave.

8. 2134-38 N. Hudson Ave.

9. 2111-21 N. Cleveland Ave.

10. 2114-16 N. Cleveland Ave.

11. 2125 N. Cleveland Ave.

12. 2124 N. Cleveland Ave.

13. 2129-31 N. Cleveland Ave.

14. 2137-41 N. Cleveland Ave.

15. Grant Hospital
    550 W. Webster

16. Contemporary Art Workshop
    542 W. Grant Pl.

17. 455 W. Grant Pl.

18. 2215 N. Cleveland Ave.

19. 2234-36 N. Cleveland Ave.

20. 515 W. Belden Ave.

21. 534 W. Belden Ave.

22. 538-544 W. Belden Ave.

23. 2310 N. Cleveland Ave.

24. 2314 N. Cleveland Ave.

25. 2325 N. Cleveland Ave.

26. 2328 N. Cleveland Ave.

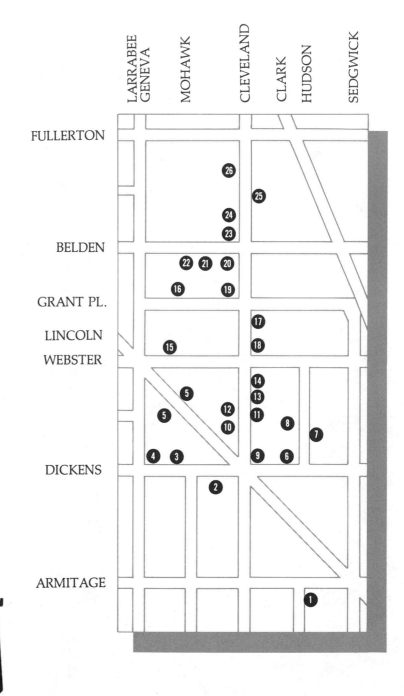

WALK • 26

LINCOLN PARK CONSERVATION AREA

WALKING TIME: 1½ hours. HOW TO GET THERE: Take a northbound CTA bus No. 10 [Lincoln-Larrabee] on Wells Street [4 blocks west of State]. Get off at Dickens Avenue [2100 N] and walk west on the south side of the street.

You are now in the heart of the Lincoln Park Conservation area, where many improvements have been made and are still taking place. The city through urban renewal and the citizens through active participation in planning and cooperation with the city have produced an outstanding program for the rehabilitation of the entire 3-square-mile area (Dickens Street to Fullerton Parkway, Larrabee Street-Geneva Terrace to Clark Street). The little sign "LPCA" that you see on windows or doors stands for Lincoln Park Conservation Association and—being interpreted—means: "We believe in the future of our area and are willing to work and fight for it if necessary." Call 477-5100 for information.

Note first the new brick parkways and recently planted trees, especially if you recall this area as it used to be— muddy or dusty, where grass never grew.

The WALK will take you around a number of streets in the area where you can see interesting results of the conservation efforts. Selected because they are in close walking distance of each other, the streets offer outstanding examples of architectural rehabilitation. So many houses have been remodeled successfully here that comment cannot possibly be made on each. What is significant is that so much good remodeling has been done that a whole area has been upgraded to the point of enormous charm, grace, and vitality.

Walk west on Armitage Avenue from Clark Street and turn south on Hudson Street.

● Portions of the WALK are in the mid North Historic District roughly bounded by Armitage, Fullerton and Lincoln avenues and Clark Street

1943-45 N. HUDSON STREET
ARCHITECTS: NAGEL AND HARTRAY (1969)

This group of 50 townhouses was built on a small site surrounded by 3- and 4-story turn-of-the-century townhouses and walk-

Overleaf:
Pickwick Village
(Philip A. Turner)

379

ups. The project demonstrates that a high density low-rise solution in scale with the neighborhood is possible even in a site zoned, and sold originally, for a high-rise project.

Walk north on Hudson Street to Dickens Avenue.

PICKWICK VILLAGE
515-29 W. Dickens Avenue
Architect: Stanley Tigerman (1965)

The complex of eight 3-story townhouses is built on an open court with shrubbery and a piece of abstract sculpture. Each house has a rear patio screened off from neighbors and passersby. An off-street parking area is provided. This is a well-planned housing group, which blends with its older neighbors but still has the advantage of new facilities.

Cross to the north side of Dickens Street and walk west.

540 W. DICKENS AVENUE
Architect for the remodeling: Arthur Carrarra (1959)

The exterior of this house (painted white) has been remodeled, with its entrance placed at grade instead of at the former 2nd-floor location. The architectural style of the 1870s has been retained outside, while the interior has been made contemporary with new lighting, new fixtures, and a new central fireplace. Charming gardens can be viewed from the street over the old iron picket fence.

Continue west. On the north side of the street, farther west, is an example of fine rehabilitation, not only of individual buildings but of a whole development.

DICKENS SQUARE
550-54 W. Dickens Avenue
Architect for restoration: Seymour Goldstein (1963)

Six old structures, which had been in deplorable condition for years, were successfully restored to the original appearance of their exteriors and rehabilitated inside. At 550, the center of the first 2 stories is effectively treated with glass from floor to ceiling. Gardens, patios, and open courts have been grouped around the buildings. The entire development is enclosed by a red brick wall with a series of arches, providing rhythm—as well as privacy—to this enclosure of 19th century gentility.

Continue on west to Larrabee Street. Along Larrabee Street from Armitage Avenue north to Webster Street and extending back southeast along Lincoln Avenue to Dickens Avenue is the huge Walpole Point complex.

WALPOLE POINT
2140 N. Lincoln Avenue
Architect: Seymour Goldstein (1973)

Here, in the heart of the Lincoln Park Conservation Area, a new kind of neighborhood has been redeveloped. On a rather "tight site," the architect has successfully managed to plan a series of play yards, gardens, green areas, tot lots, and patios in between structures and open parking areas. There are many inviting open terraces, sunken courtyards, and walks that together make Walpole Point a pleasing experience.

There are two types of dwelling units—townhouses and apartments. Eighty of the townhouses were intended initially for ownership by moderate-income families. The remaining 76 townhouses have been retained by the developer for renting. The 96 apartments are rental units also. The developer's long-range plans call for selling all the remaining townhouses to middle-income families. Combinations of the red brick, peaked, cantilevered roofs with angled double windows and arched openings give the effect of variety and distinctive character.

Now you are back at Lincoln Avenue and Cleveland. Continue east 1 block to Hudson Avenue and turn north.

2100 N. HUDSON AVENUE
Architects: Booth and Nagle (1968)

This is a quiet short block of charming, old, well-maintained houses owned by professional writers, painters, and sculptors. The contemporary character of this modern group of 6 townhouses is shown by the trim, clean lines.

Continue north.

POLICEMAN BELLINGER'S COTTAGE
2121 N. Hudson Avenue
Architect: W. W. Boyington (before 1871)

On the east side of the street, a plaque on the building states: "This is Policeman Bellinger's Cottage, saved by heroic effort from Chicago Fire of October 1871." It is clear that even heroic efforts could not save many houses, for the majority in this area were built after 1871.

Note how well maintained the houses are at 2115-17 N. Hudson Avenue and 2116-18 N. Hudson Avenue across the street. At 2127 and 2131 N. Hudson Avenue are examples of charming and successful rehabilitation.

Continue north.

2134-38 N. HUDSON AVENUE

On the west side of the street are some well-maintained, restored and remodeled townhouses, grouped around a well-landscaped courtyard.

Now return south 1 block to Dickens Avenue. Now walk east on Dickens to the northeast corner of Dickens and Cleveland avenues.

2111-21 N. CLEVELAND AVENUE

These townhouses have been successfully converted into apartment buildings. The below-grade patio at 2111-15, with marble floors and stone walls, adds charm to the exterior. The original entrance doors and roof cornices have been refinished. New glass panels at the below-grade apartment give the structure an air of modernity.

Walk north on Cleveland and look west.

2114 and 2116 N. CLEVELAND AVENUE

On the west side of the street, at 2114 and 2116, are two red brick townhouses constructed about 1880. Wooden bay, turret windows, and a mansard roof make this remodeled apartment very attractive.

Continue north.

2125 N. CLEVELAND AVENUE

On the east side again, you see excellent rehabilitation work in the facade—yellow brick at the 1st floor and stained pinewood at the 2nd floor, with a balcony and glass panel doors that reach from floor to ceiling.

2124 N. CLEVELAND AVENUE

Across the street is a red brick, mid-Victorian house built about 1880, with delightfully slender white Doric columns at the

382

entrance and balcony overhead, and a mansard roof with fascinating iron picket work at the roof peak. This building has been remodeled into apartments with no loss of the original charm.

2129-31 N. CLEVELAND AVENUE
ARCHITECT: RICHARD BARRINGER (1958)

These two townhouses are of red brick with bay windows and entrances at grade, instead of at the 2nd floor as they were before remodeling. The exterior facades retain most of the original dour appearance, but the interiors have been done over successfully.

2137-39-41 N. CLEVELAND AVENUE

Here is still another series of old townhouses successfully remodeled into apartments—three ivy-covered houses of brick and stone. Here too, new entrances at grade replace the former 2nd-floor entrances; yet the charm and general character of the old facades have been retained.

Walk north to Webster Avenue.

GRANT HOSPITAL
550 W. WEBSTER AVENUE
ARCHITECTS: HOLABIRD AND ROOT (1975);
SOLOMON, CORDWELL AND BUENZ (1982);
FOR NORTHWEST WING: JOHN JACOFFEE (1983)

Note the rebuilding process whereby the original mediocre structure has given way to a pleasant contemporary design that fits with its neighbors.

The exterior of the latest addition was designed to blend with the hospital's existing buildings by matching the adjacent building's heights, materials, and window placement. The addition, connected to the two existing structures, houses general offices, laboratories, multi-purpose meeting rooms, and an auditorium.

Walk around the hospital, on the Geneva side. Walk north. The Contemporary Art Workshop is located directly to the north of Grant Hospital.

CONTEMPORARY ART WORKSHOP
542 W. GRANT PLACE
ARCHITECTS: UNKNOWN (c. 1885, c. 1925)

2234-36 N. Cleveland
(Philip A. Turner)

Originally the Borden-Wheelen Dairy, the rear building was built shortly after the Chicago Fire. The front building dates from some 40 years later. This is now an artists' workshop where sculpture is also taught. John Kearney, a well-known Chicago sculptor, founded and heads the workshop. A tour can be arranged by calling 472-4004.

Walk east to the corner of Cleveland Avenue and Grant Place.

455 W. GRANT PLACE

At the corner of Cleveland Avenue and Grant Place is a newly constructed 3-story apartment building of hard-burned brick, built around an open court. The court entrances are below grade in a patio facing Grant Place. This is a well-planned complex that blends with the surrounding, older structures.

Walk south on Cleveland Avenue.

2215 N. CLEVELAND AVENUE
ARCHITECT: BRUCE GRAHAM (1969)

Here is a stunning example of a well-designed urban townhouse—2-story, monolithic concrete, including a walled-in garden that completely encloses the site. There are travertine marble walks and a black steel bar gate.

Walk north on Cleveland Avenue.

2234-36 N. CLEVELAND AVENUE

This is a 3-story frame duplex townhouse. The brick face on the grade level and wood siding at 2nd- and 3rd-floor levels are painted gray. Black and white trim around the windows and white Corinthian columns at the entrance complete this charming, very old structure, built around 1874.

Turn west on Belden Avenue to view a complex of townhouses.

515 W. BELDEN AVENUE

This complex of about 20 2-story townhouses is built around an open court. Although fairly well designed, the density is much too high and can only result in noise, traffic, and neighborhood congestion.

Continue west.

534 W. BELDEN AVENUE

On the other side of the street, farther west, are some red brick townhouses remodeled into apartments. From the white limestone and glass entrances to the new balcony at the former entrance, this is a most successful enterprise.

538-544 W. BELDEN AVENUE

A marvelous old sandstone apartment building. The remodeling includes metal grillwork on the balcony, black trim around doors and windows, and a black cornice on the ornate roof— for a most attractive effect.

Backtrack east to Cleveland Avenue and turn north.

2310 and 2314 N. CLEVELAND AVENUE

Here you see two well-restored Victorian brick houses with mansard roofs.

Continue north.

2325 N. CLEVELAND AVENUE

This is a 3-story house painted gray, set back from the street, with an iron picket fence. A square bay window and roof turret give this 1880 house a definite stamp of individuality.

2328 N. CLEVELAND AVENUE

A 3-story limestone-faced house that is embellished by Romanesque revival columns and ornaments. The addition of frame stairs and balustrade fit rather than detract from this well-restored old house.

Walk back to Belden Avenue and east on Belden to Clark Street. Note the delightful square at Belden with benches, landscaping, and the limestone sculpture attributed to Lorado Taft. At Clark note how Grant Place has been closed to through traffic. This is a good spot to rest.

At this point you can board a southbound No. 22 or 36 bus on Clark Street to return to the Loop.

27

1. Cenacle Retreat House
   513 W. Fullerton Ave.

2. St. Paul's Church and Parish House
   2335 N. Orchard

3. Children's Memorial Hospital
   2300 Children's Plaza

4. De Paul University—Lincoln Park Campus

5. Chalmers Pl.

6. Arthur J. Schmitt Academic Center
   2323 N. Seminary Ave.

7. Stuart Center
   2324 N. Seminary Ave.

8. Clifton Hall
   2312 N. Clifton Ave.

9. Church of St. Vincent DePaul
   1010 W. Webster Ave.

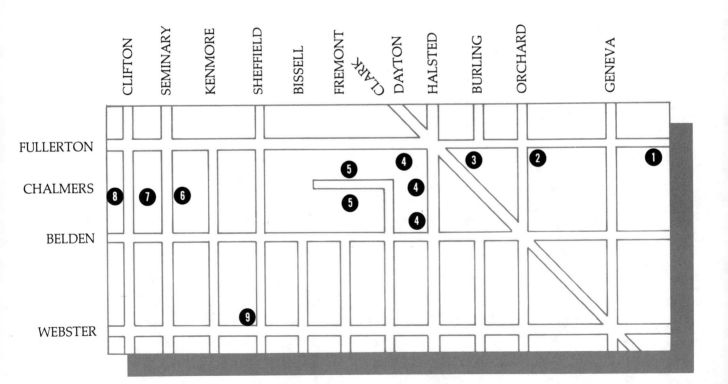

WALK • 27

DePAUL UNIVERSITY: LINCOLN PARK CAMPUS

WALKING TIME: About 1½ hours. HOW TO GET THERE: Take a northbound CTA bus No. 36 [Broadway] on State Street or a No. 22 [Clark Street] on Dearborn Street [1 block west of State]. Get off at Fullerton Avenue [2400 N]. Walk west to Cleveland Avenue [500 W], where this WALK starts.

This WALK will take you primarily on a tour of DePaul University's Lincoln Park Campus. En route you will encounter many well-kept old townhouses. A stroll through the area will quickly demonstrate the pride with which its people and institutions regard their community—a factor essential to success in almost any community conservation effort.

Before you reach the first of DePaul's academic structures, you will come to a number of other points of interest. In the first 2 blocks on Fullerton, going west from Clark Street (which are not the most exhilarating part of the WALK), you will pass the Cenacle Retreat House.

CENACLE RETREAT HOUSE
513 W. FULLERTON AVENUE
ARCHITECT: CHARLES POPE (1965-7)

This large convent building was constructed of hard-burned brick. This is an imposing, well-maintained addition to the community.

Continue west on Fullerton Avenue.

ST. PAUL'S CHURCH and PARISH HOUSE
2335 N. ORCHARD STREET
ARCHITECT: BENJAMIN FRANKLIN OLSON (1951, 1959)

The parish house was erected in 1951. After a large fire had destroyed the earlier church of St. Paul's, the new church was built in 1959. The design is modified Spanish Romanesque, with red brick and stone trim. The tall, well-proportioned spire, which is well-located, gives the church the proper, much-needed height.

Overleaf: Schmitt Center
DePaul University
(Philip A. Turner)

389

The buildings relate well to each other, for the site planning is good.

Continue west. At 700 W. Fullerton Avenue is the nationally known Children's Memorial Hospital.

CHILDREN'S MEMORIAL HOSPITAL
2300 CHILDREN'S PLAZA
ARCHITECTS: SCHMIDT, GARDEN AND ERICKSON (1961);
FOR THE ADDITION: PERKINS & WILL (1981-2)

This is one of the various hospitals served by Northwestern University's Medical School. (See WALK 12.) The design of the hospital building, which was developed at various stages by the same architects, is strong but not too severe.

Children's Memorial Hospital modernization program by Perkins & Will was done in two phases. First a high-rise elevator core and a triangular-shaped diagnostic/treatment wing were constructed. This consolidated the hospital's emergency, surgery, radiology, anesthesiology, laboratories, and pharmacy departments in expanded, modern space. In the second stage, four floors were added to the main hospital to consolidate in-patient services and existing buildings were renovated. Perkins & Will received the Merit Award of the Chicago Building Congress in 1982 "for blending of the latest technology with the tradition of a century of care

390

for the children on the historic landmark site of Children's Memorial Hospital."

Just west of the hospital are the buildings formerly occupied by McCormick Theological Seminary and now part of DePaul University's 25-acre Lincoln Park Campus. (DePaul also operates a downtown branch, at 25 E. Jackson Street.) Cross Halsted and continue west on Fullerton to the 1976 addition to DePaul University, an area stretching from Fullerton Avenue south to Belden Avenue and from Halsted Street west to Sheffield Avenue.

DePAUL UNIVERSITY—
LINCOLN PARK CAMPUS
2323 N. SEMINARY AVENUE

DePaul University
(Olga Stefanos)

Although the official address of this campus is 2323 N. Seminary Avenue, the Lincoln Park Campus of this fine university occupies much of the area bounded by Halsted Street (800 W) and Racine Avenue (1200 W), Fullerton Avenue (2400 N), and Webster Avenue (2300 N).

Enter at the first gate with an opening for pedestrians on Fullerton Avenue and take a little time to enjoy this beautiful campus. Note especially the Stone Building, a classroom building (1968) and the McGaw Memorial Library (1963)—both contemporary in design—and the James G. K. McClure Memorial Chapel (1963), a Georgian structure. All three buildings were designed by Holabird and Root. There is no jarring effect in the contrasting architectural styles because the site planning is first-rate and the space is adequate.

Turn west and stroll around Chalmers Place, a private square.

CHALMERS PLACE

In this pleasant green area, comparable to Louisburg Square in Boston, are privately owned 3-story, 19th century townhouses facing on the north and south sides of the Place. To the west is the University's limestone Commons building, in collegiate Gothic. It is now the Theatre School of DePaul University (which was formerly the Goodman Theatre School). West of the Commons is a second green space and square facing which are Francis V. Corcoran Hall and Francis X. McCabe Hall, student residences, and Theodore J. Wangler Hall, a gymnasium.

Now return to McClure Chapel and walk south to Belden Avenue, then west under the El tracks to DePaul's original Lincoln Park Campus. The first building of interest here is Alumni Hall, at

391

1011 W. Belden, a huge limestone building with granite base, which houses the University's athletic center.

Walk west several blocks. On Seminary Avenue turn north of Fullerton Avenue.

ARTHUR J. SCHMITT ACADEMIC CENTER
2323 N. SEMINARY AVENUE
ARCHITECTS: C. F. MURPHY ASSOCIATES (1967)

Just west of Alumni Hall is one of the outstanding structures on the campus, an imposing, 5-story concrete building with classrooms, faculty and administration offices, and seminar rooms. By raising the entrance level well above the street, the architects have given this structure an imposing approach and the effect of great height. The cantilevering of the upper level will remind you of the 222 N. Dearborn Building, also designed by C.F. Murphy Associates. (See WALK 4.)

Walk across the street.

STUART CENTER
2324 N. SEMINARY AVENUE
ARCHITECTS: C. F. MURPHY ASSOCIATES (1971)

Directly across the street from the impressive Arthur J. Schmitt Academic Center is the Stuart Center designed by the same architects in the same theme of great masses of concrete planes and surfaces. Although not nearly as overpowering a structure, it does manage to maintain its own individuality. This is probably due to the fact that only a portion is higher than 1 story and thus presents a strong horizontal mass extending from a 3-story windowless section which gives it the appearance of a modern Mayan Temple.

The interior holds a pleasant surprise because the reception hall, cafeteria, lounge, and snack room wrap around a large grass atrium. The 3-story section contains a religious services area, meeting rooms, and offices for advisers. Near the main entrance and cafeteria are art exhibits for free public viewing.

Walk through the building, heading west.

CLIFTON HALL
2312 CLIFTON AVENUE
ARCHITECTS: FREIDSTEIN AND FITCH (1970)

The University Center extends west from Seminary Avenue to Clifton Avenue and there on the opposite side is a pleasant and spacious-looking student residence hall. Again, concrete forms vertically and horizontally frame the large windows of the individual rooms. Although DePaul is primarily a commuter university, there is demand for housing by a substantial number of students. The quiet and warm lounge sets the tone for the entire structure—scholarly dedication.

Before returning east on Belden Avenue, if you are interested in seeing the church built by the Vincentian Fathers, who founded DePaul University, you might walk east to Sheffield Avenue and then turn south to Webster Avenue.

CHURCH OF ST. VINCENT DePAUL
1010 Webster Avenue
Architect: J. J. Egan (1895-97)

This very large edifice is constructed with gray limestone skin in a French Romanesque style. The nave has a high, barrel-vaulted ceiling supported by the ribs that are extended from the free-standing columns. At the transept, there are two large arches that are sprung from opposite corners to form an X in the ceiling.

The semi-circular apse contains a white marble sculptured altar with two small altars on either side. As you turn to leave, note the stained-glass windows, especially the great rose window, with its circles-within-circles pattern. The blues, reds, and vermilions are quite lovely when the sun is shining.

Now walk back to Belden Avenue and east to Lincoln Avenue. There are several fascinating restaurants, bars, and theaters in the vicinity.

28

1. Columbus Hospital
   2520 N. Lakeview Ave.

2. Francis J. Dewes House
   503 W. Wrightwood Ave.

3. 466 and 468 W. Deming Pl.

4. 470-480 W. Deming Pl.

5. St Clement's
   Roman Catholic Church
   642 W. Deming Pl.

6. 2461 N. Geneva Terrace

7. 525-531 W. Arlington Pl.

8. Lincoln Park Presbyterian Church
   600 W. Fullerton Pkwy.

9. 618 W. Fullerton Pkwy.

10. 638 W. Fullerton Pkwy.

11. 646 W. Fullerton Pkwy.

12. Church of Our Savior
    530 W. Fullerton Pkwy.

13. Park West Tower Apartments
    444 W. Fullerton Pkwy.

14. 345 Fullerton Apartments
    345 W. Fullerton Ave.

15. 2400 W. Lakeview Avenue Building

16. Wrigley Mansion
    2466 W. Lakeview Ave.

17. 426 W. Arlington Pl.

18. 429 W. Arlington Pl.

19. 438 W. Arlington Pl.

20. 418 W. Arlington Pl.

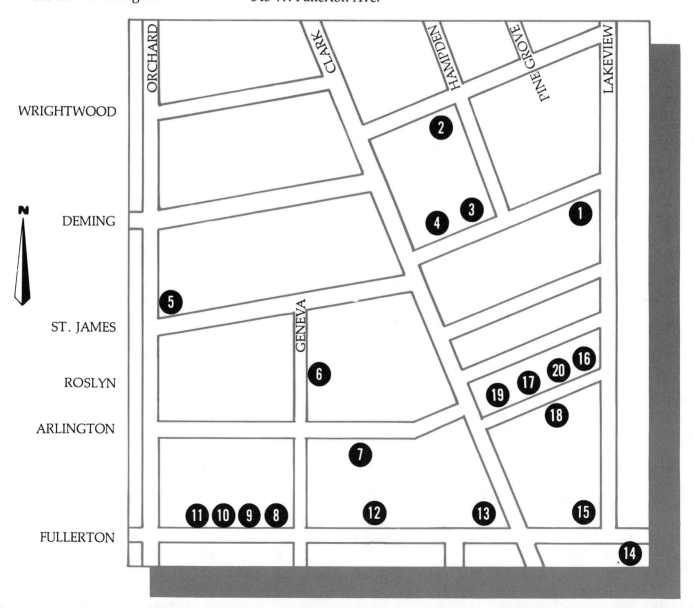

WALK • 28

DEMING PLACE AND NEARBY STREETS

WALKING TIME: 1 hour. HOW TO GET THERE: Take a north-bound CTA bus No. 151 [Sheridan] on State Street. Get off at Roslyn Place [2500 N] at the edge of Lincoln Park, and walk 2 blocks north to Deming Place [2534 N].

Deming Place at Lake View Avenue consists primarily of high-rise buildings. Later on in this WALK, you will enjoy the pleasant surprise of seeing charming residential 19th- and early 20th-century townhouses. You will also have the pleasure of following streets with houses set back of spacious lawns with great and handsome old trees. Some of the streets will curve and thus add to the element of surprise. Walking here is a delight.

The first stop is at the corner of Deming Place and Lake View Avenue.

⦿ Part of this WALK is in the Lakeview Historic District, roughly bounded by Wrightwood Street, Lake View Avenue, Sheridan Road, Belmont, Halsted and Wellington streets.

COLUMBUS HOSPITAL
2520 N. LAKEVIEW AVENUE
ARCHITECTS: DeSINA AND PELLEGRINO;
CONSULTING ARCHITECTS: ALBERT SCHUNKEWITZ
AND S. CHAN SIT (1973)

The 10-story north wing is formidable in comparison with the main hospital building. The precast stone panels against the tinted glass windows with their anodized aluminum trim give a strong emphasis to the vertical lines of both facades. The entrance and portico on the corner has additional strong vertical lines in the striated bronze columns.

The power plant and parking garage just to the west has equally strong vertical lines. This time it is in the striated and bushhammered reinforced concrete facade.

Columbus Hospital has expanded to the extent that it now covers almost the entire south side of Deming Place from Lake View Avenue to Clark. Architecturally, the hospital unfortunately

Overleaf: View of Fullerton Avenue (Philip A. Turner)

397

lacks unity and reflects the fact that each phase was a separate design function.

Directly across the street, at 400 West Deming Place, is the genteel Marlborough Apartments, making quite a contrast to the Columbus Hospital neighbor. The Indiana limestone facing on the two lower floors along with the brick work and bay windows of the twelve floors, makes this charming building a pleasant sight.

Now walk west on Deming Place to Hampden Court, then 1 block north to Wrightwood Avenue (2600 N).

◉ FRANCIS J. DEWES HOUSE
503 W. Wrightwood Avenue
Architects: Adolph Cudell
and Arthur Herez (1896)

There on the corner is the Francis J. Dewes House—a limestone structure in baroque style, with enormous male and female figures supporting the upper balcony of wrought iron, a departure from the exclusively female caryatids of ancient Greek sculpture! Heavy ornament surrounds the entrance and upper window. A mansard roof tops off the building.

Walk back south on Hampden Court to Deming Place passing a contemporary 6-story red brick building with Cor-Ten steel balustrades on the balconies. Cor-Ten steel was used on the Daley Center building and Chicago's Picasso sculpture (see WALK 4).

Next, walk west on Deming Place. Although many of the comments that follow may sound repetitious, you may be sure that the buildings referred to will not look repetitious, for all have a most welcome individuality.

466 and 468 W. DEMING PLACE

The twin townhouses with their ivy-covered red brick facades are a joy to behold—the huge bay windows with their black painted wood trim; the playful dormer windows and brickwork at the 3rd floor, crowned with a delightfully curved and graduated brick wall. It is a reminder of 19th century Boston or Philadelphia. (Chalmers Place on WALK 27 has some similar houses.)

470-480 W. DEMING PLACE

These are five townhouses with red brick facades and individual bay windows.

Opposite: Francis
J. Dewes House
(Allen Carr)

398

Window detail at
2436 Orchard Street
(Allen Carr)

Now walk west to Clark Street and note that you are at the southern end of a 2-mile strip of ethnic restaurants, art galleries, taverns, boutiques, and health food stores. This is a recent phenomenon and is the result of several former Old Town merchants moving here and attracting new merchants to what is known as New Town.

Cross Clark Street (which runs northwest-southeast in this part of the city) and continue west on Deming Place. Here the street starts to curve and the buildings are set back farther from the street. The lawns seem actually greener and the trees bigger and shadier! Continue west to Orchard Street.

ST. CLEMENT'S ROMAN CATHOLIC CHURCH
642 W. DEMING PLACE
ARCHITECT: GEORGE D. BARNETT (1917-18)

At the corner of Deming Place and Orchard Street stands St. Clement's Roman Catholic Church, just beyond St. Clement's Convent, at 622 W. Deming Place. French Romanesque, with limestone facade and a rose window over the entrance, this church has a pleasant surprise awaiting visitors who go inside. Above the spot where the apse and transept meet is a dome with mosaic tile figures that give the viewer a feeling of being in the 11th or 12th century.

Retrace your steps back east to Geneva Terrace, and turn south. Here, unexpectedly, are again some 19th-century townhouses with gardens and trees.

Opposite:
St. Clement's Church
(Allen Carr)

2461 N. GENEVA TERRACE

Note the small house at the rear of the garden—built in pre-Civil War style.

Continue south on Geneva Terrace. When you reach Arlington Place, walk east.

525-531 W. ARLINGTON PLACE

Note the pristine red-brick and stone facade with white wooden Ionic columns, all in good scale. This also reflects the style of the period before the Civil War.

Return to Geneva Terrace and continue south to Fullerton Avenue. At the corner of this block you come to a church.

LINCOLN PARK PRESBYTERIAN CHURCH
600 W. FULLERTON PARKWAY
ARCHITECT: CLINTON J. WARREN (1888)

The limestone structure is built in the Romanesque style. It is old but well maintained.

Continuing west on Fullerton Avenue is an entire block of 19th-century townhouses. Note in particular these examples.

618 W. FULLERTON PARKWAY

This 3-story house is completely covered with ivy.

638 W. FULLERTON PARKWAY

This is a typical 19th century house with a bay window.

646 W. FULLERTON PARKWAY

This is a pleasant 3-story brick house.

Turn and walk back east on Fullerton Avenue past Geneva Terrace and several more 19th century townhouses, set back 25 feet, with well-kept lawns and trees. Continue east.

CHURCH OF OUR SAVIOR
530 W. FULLERTON PARKWAY
ARCHITECT: CLINTON J. WARREN (1889)

The Episcopal church is a charming structure of the late 19th century, in English Romanesque design. The interior walls are of unglazed terra-cotta, an unusual early use of that material.

402

Continue to walk east. Situated at the corner of Fullerton Avenue and Clark Street, is a 20-story apartment building.

PARK WEST TOWER APARTMENTS
444 W. Fullerton Parkway
Architects: Dubin, Dubin, Black and Moutoussamy (1972)

The 200-apartment building has been expertly placed on the site so as to command excellent sight lines for most of the apartments.

Cross to the south side of the street and continue east.

345 FULLERTON APARTMENTS
345 W. Fullerton Avenue
Architects: Harry Weese and Associates (1973)

These striking concrete twin towers, located on a corner site overlooking Chicago's Lincoln Park, have a particularly powerful base and entrance. In order to minimize the effect of the new development on the park, and to maintain the tall, narrow scale of the other buildings along the street, a twin-tower design was chosen. The two 30-story towers are situated along the south and west lot lines, increasing the feeling of openness at the base and minimizing the effect of one tower upon the other. The towers share a common lobby of glass. While each facade is parallel to the street, the setback of one tower from the other allows equal views of Lake Michigan, the city, and the park.

At the northwest corner of Fullerton Parkway and Lake View Avenue is a building designed by Ludwig Mies van der Rohe.

2400 W. LAKE VIEW AVENUE BUILDING
Architect: Ludwig Mies van der Rohe (1963)

This building was planned by the famous architect, Ludwig Mies van der Rohe. The handsome structure is sheathed in aluminum, with columns exposed at the base and the vertical lines carried by mullions.

The luxurious character of the apartments is indicated by the exterior plate glass and the marble walls of the lobby, to say nothing of the swimming pool adjoining the lobby.

Walk north 1 block. At the corner of Lake View Avenue and Arlington Place is the Wrigley Mansion.

◉ WRIGLEY MANSION
2466 N. Lakeview Avenue
Architect: Richard E. Schmidt (1897)

The fine old building has been well maintained. The exterior has limestone base and brick facade, with brick and terra-cotta quoins at the four corners and abundant ornamentation at the 3rd-floor level. The rooms have high ceilings. At this writing, a new owner has indicated he will rehabilitate the house into one or two residences.

Walk a few steps west on Arlington Place to see another 19th century townhouse, also well preserved.

426 W. ARLINGTON PLACE

Observe the brick-and-limestone facade with arches over the wooden bay windows.

On the other side of the street is 429 Arlington Place.

429 W. ARLINGTON PLACE

This 3-story house has a limestone facade.

Back on the north side of the street is another 19th century house.

438 W. ARLINGTON PLACE

This is a 3-story Gothic revival in stone.

418 W. ARLINGTON PLACE

A little farther east, the last stop of this WALK, is a pleasant old brownstone. It also has been well maintained.

29

1. 2626 N. Lakeview Ave.

2. 2650 N. Lakeview Ave.

3. 2700 N. Lakeview Ave.

4. 2704-2710 N. Lakeview Ave.

5. Elks National Memorial Building
   2750 N. Lakeview Ave.

6. 330 and 340 W. Diversey Pkwy.

7. 2800 N. Lake Shore Drive West

8. St. Joseph Hospital
   2900 Lake Shore Drive West

9. Stone Medical Center
   2800 N. Sheridan Road

10. Brewster Apartments
    2800 N. Pine Grove Ave.

11. Britton I. Budd Apartments
    and Green Senior Center
    501 W. Surf St.

12. Commodore Apartments
    559 W. Surf St.

13. Greenbriar Apartments
    550 W. Surf St.

WALK • 29

LAKE VIEW, DIVERSEY, SURF

WALKING TIME: 1 hour. HOW TO GET THERE: Take a north-bound CTA bus No. 151 [Sheridan] on State Street or Michigan Avenue and get off at Wrightwood Avenue [2600 N].

2626 N. LAKE VIEW AVENUE
ARCHITECTS: LOEWENBERG AND LOEWENBERG (1970)

This 40-story apartment building and its handsome Y-shaped ◉ neighbor—also a 40-story apartment building—are excellent examples of two owners and their architects cooperating so that nearly every apartment in each building enjoys excellent sight lines.

Part of this WALK is in the Lakeview Historic District, roughly bounded by Wrightwood Street, Lake View Avenue, Sheridan Road, Belmont, Halsted and Wellington streets.

2650 N. LAKE VIEW AVENUE
ARCHITECTS: LOEBL, SCHLOSSMAN, BENNETT AND DART (1973)

The tinted glass and anodized aluminum window frames against the striated vertical lines of the concrete give the 40-story building a delicate and slim line. The bay windows are well placed and go toward creating a domestic appearance, in spite of the great height of the structure.

Now walk north on Lake View Avenue.

2700 N. LAKE VIEW AVENUE
ARCHITECT: DAVID ADLER (1920)

This handsome structure is the former Ryerson Family Mansion. (The Ryersons also owned homes on Astor Street. See WALK 15.) The house here on Lake View Avenue is said to be a replica of an 18th century London townhouse. It is now occupied by a community organization.

Continue north.

2704-2708-2710 N. LAKE VIEW AVENUE

North of the Ryerson Mansion are 3 townhouses, all in the same style and tied together with a common roof and party walls—a

Overleaf:
Elks Memorial
(Olga Stefanos)

characteristic seen in so many of our modern rows of townhouses. A stone base, dark red brick facade, wooden columns painted white, and slightly different ornamentation and details at each entrance give these houses an effect of special charm and grace. Note the delicate transom tracery over the doorways.

Next, on the same side of the street, is the monumental Elks National Memorial.

ELKS NATIONAL MEMORIAL BUILDING
2750 N. Lake View Avenue
Architects: Egerton Swartout (1926);
for the Magazine Building:
Holabird and Root (1967)

The building was originally constructed in memory of Elks who had died in World War I. The Memorial building consists of a great central rotunda—75 feet in diameter, 100 feet high—and 2 main wings. The base and columns support the huge dome, which is made up inside of pieces of marble from all over the world. The entrance is—of course—adorned by two bronze elks! The Magazine Building is a later addition, to provide a place for the many documents of the society. Indiana limestone is used throughout. The Elks Memorial main building is open to visitors daily from 10 a.m. to 5 p.m.

At the northeast corner of West Diversey Parkway and North Sheridan Road, diagonally across from the Elks Memorial, are two aluminum-sheathed tower apartment buildings, designed by Mies van der Rohe and developed by the late Herbert Greenwald.

330 and 340 WEST DIVERSEY PARKWAY
Architect: Ludwig Mies van der Rohe (1957)

The two towers are expertly sited so as to give each apartment a spectacular view. The columns are exposed at the ground level; mullions divide the windows and carry the vertical sweep upwards. The two structures have a sculptured, almost poetic quality.

Walk east on Diversey Parkway.

2800 N. LAKE SHORE DRIVE WEST
Architects: Solomon, Cordwell and Buenz (1970)

As you approach this imposing apartment structure, note the buff color of the reinforced concrete exterior. The rugged columns and spandrels spaced in a rhythmic pattern give the block-long exterior an interesting facade.

This building is a classic example of a Chicago residential high-rise. The concrete structure is simply and clearly expressed on the exterior, with bronze tinted glass infilled. The slight exterior bays express the internal unit layout and break down the facade into humanly scaled pieces. Occupying a choice piece of land with views of the park and lake in two directions, the complex includes full recreational facilities with a heated swimming pool, saunas, private plaza and roof decks, and hospitality rooms at the building's top.

If at this point you are feeling palpitations, go directly north behind the 2800 building and there you will find St. Joseph Hospital.

ST. JOSEPH HOSPITAL
2900 N. Lake Shore Drive West
Architects: Belli and Belli (1963)

This complex of buildings contains the main 3-winged, 12-story structure, parking decks, and nurses building. The hospital serves the entire north side with its modern facilities. The design, unfortunately, is eclectic and does not achieve what the designers set out to accomplish.

Before returning to Sheridan Road, you will be rewarded by looking south into Lincoln Park to see three important pieces of sculpture.

First is a standing figure in bronze of John Peter Altgeld, governor of Illinois during the Haymarket Square riot and bombing of 1893. His courage and liberalism in pardoning three of the men convicted of murder are described at the end of WALK 25.

Next is an allegorical bronze of Johann Wolfgang von Goethe—a male figure of heroic scale, dedicated in 1913 to this great poet and author by the German-speaking community of Chicago.

About 100 yards south of the Goethe statue is a sculptured memorial to Alexander Hamilton, the first Secretary of the Treasury of the United States. The figure of Hamilton, standing erect, though made of bronze is appropriately painted gold. It is mounted on a huge black granite structure, which makes a dramatic contrast. This monument was erected in 1952 from funds supplied in memory of Kate Sturgis Buckingham—the person who herself had left funds for the Buckingham Fountain in Grant Park in memory of her brother. (See WALK 1.) The memorial was designed by Samuel Marx.

Next is the building at the northwest corner of West Diversey Parkway and Sheridan Road.

STONE MEDICAL CENTER
2800 N. Sheridan Road
Architects: E. F. Quinn and
Roy T. Christiansen (1951);
for the renovation: Loebl,
Schlossman and Hackl (1983)

Stone Medical Center demonstrates the outcome of adaptive reuse in architecture. This 3-story light gray limestone former union headquarters now serves as a medical office building. With limited new building options, imaginative rehabilitation was the most practical choice. A new glass and metal frame entrance, interior atrium and signage graphics were created to establish a strong visual identity from both streets and from Lincoln Park. The interior was completely gutted for the construction of the atrium, physicians' suites, laboratory facilities, conference rooms, and a coffee shop which also serves the general public. The pair of Egon Weiner statues entitled *Brotherhood* have been repositioned, flanking each side of the entrance. Each group consists of four kneeling figures, representing the four races of mankind (often

Stone Medical Center
(Olga Stefanos)

410

identified as African, American Indian, Asian, and European), all of whom are kneeling as a symbol of man's dependence on a higher power and community unification.

Now, walk 1 block west on Diversey Parkway.

● BREWSTER APARTMENTS
2800 N. Pine Grove Avenue
Architects: R. H. Turnock (1893);
for remodeling: Mieki Hayano (1972)

The red polished marble appears at the entrance moldings and window columns of the first floor. By all means obtain permission to enter. Once inside, you will see the delightful open grillwork and cage of the elevator, the light court, skylight and metal grillwork of the stairways. It seems strange that the original architect, who once worked with William LeBaron Jenney, should have produced so remarkable a building only once in his lifetime.

The remodeling work and design have been handled with sensitivity and good taste. Indeed, the architect for the remodeling deserves the kudos of a grateful city. He has even added a fine touch of drama by constructing the metal ornament that is set in the parkway just in front of the main entrance.

The apartments have been tastefully remodeled and now have modern wiring and plumbing. Nevertheless, this 9-story structure with its high ceilings and bay windows—rugged, rough-faced with dark gray granite—seems out of place—something like a sleeping giant—right on Diversey Parkway with all its noise and movement.

Walk north on Pine Grove Avenue to Surf Street.

BRITTON I. BUDD APARTMENTS
AND GREEN SENIOR CENTER—
501 W. Surf Street

The Britton I. Budd Apartments and Green Senior Center, though no great architectural masterpiece, are worth noting because of their function. This remodeled structure, operated by the Chicago Housing Authority, is a mecca for many of the older citizens of the area.

Walk west along Surf Street to the corner of Broadway. Here, on opposite sides of the street, stand 2 huge apartment buildings, which were constructed near the turn of the century.

COMMODORE APARTMENTS
559 W. Surf Street
Architects: Edmond R. Krause (1897);
for the rehabilitation:
Nakawatase, Rutkowsky, Wyns and Yi (1985)

GREENBRIAR APARTMENTS
550 W. Surf Street
Architects: Edmond R. Krause (1904);
for the rehabilitation:
Architects International (1985)

These dignified brick structures have open courts, high ceilings, and smooth brick walls. The design of each facade is modified Georgian. Entrances are from Broadway as well as from the courtyards facing West Surf Street. When the sun is in the west, it shines through the lobbies into the courtyards. Louis Sullivan lived in the Greenbriar Apartments for eight years.

Both buildings are well maintained, affording tenants excellent living quarters. They have been recently rehabilitated, including the restoration of the lobbies, the replacement of all mechanical systems, and the restoration of the woodwork.

This WALK has shown you, among other things, quite a variety of apartment buildings—examples of modern architecture, from Mies van der Rohe's to the Chicago Housing Authority's and buildings dating back to the 1890s: the Brewster and Commodore.

You are at Surf Street and Broadway in the center of a strip of interesting boutiques, restaurants, taverns, and art galleries. It is called New Town. You crossed a portion of it in the previous WALK. Stroll a couple of blocks north and enjoy some of the fascinating sights and rhythm of this section of the city.

Whenever you wish to return to the Loop, you can take a No. 36 CTA bus on Broadway or return east to Sheridan Road where you will find the No. 151 bus going south.

30

1. 3801 N. Alta Vista Terrace

2. 3805 N. Alta Vista Terrace

3. 3802 N. Alta Vista Terrace

4. 3812 N. Alta Vista Terrace

5. 3814 N. Alta Vista Terrace

6. 3819 N. Alta Vista Terrace

7. 3814 N. Alta Vista Terrace

8. 3826 N. Alta Vista Terrace

9. 3830 N. Alta Vista Terrace

10. 3845 N. Alta Vista Terrace

11. Graceland Cemetery

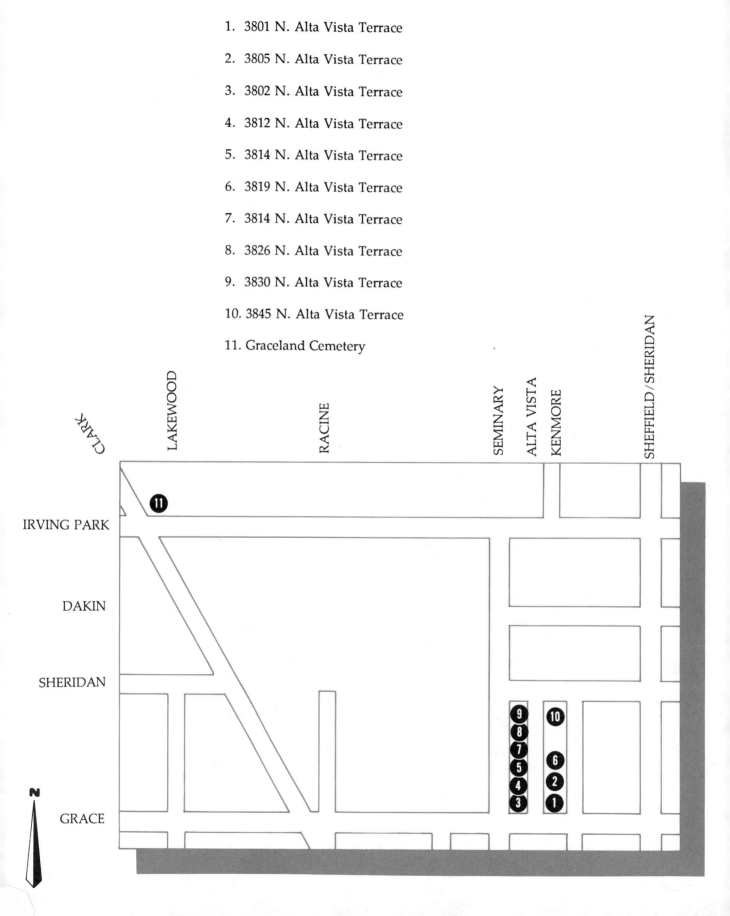

WALK • 30

ALTA VISTA TERRACE-GRACELAND CEMETERY

WALKING TIME: 1 hour or less. HOW TO GET THERE: Take a northbound CTA bus No. 22 [Clark Street] on Dearborn Street. Get off at Grace Street [3800 N]. Walk 2 blocks east, past the House of the Good Shepherd Convent, to Alta Vista Terrace [1054 W].

◉ **ALTA VISTA TERRACE**

EAST OF NORTH SEMINARY AVENUE BETWEEN
WEST BYRON AND WEST GRACE STREETS

This short block has townhouses on both sides of a narrow street, which might be in Boston or Philadelphia or London. It seems to belong to a past century; it is definitely not a street of today. The well-maintained old houses were constructed at one time by one builder, who gave each house an individuality in design—almost certainly J. C. Brompton, who worked for Samuel Everly Gross, the developer of the street.

Alta Vista Terrace was designated in 1972 as an Architectural Landmark District. This designation was made by the Chicago Historical and Architectural Landmarks Commission with the consent and approval of the Chicago City Council. This action will prevent encroachment or destruction of the district. The owners volunteered this action and enthusiastically participated in all the public hearings.

3801 N. ALTA VISTA TERRACE

In this house, on the east side of the street, limestone columns surround a wooden entrance in a pleasant eclectic design.

3805 N. ALTA VISTA TERRACE

An attempt at classic detail in the facade makes this another eclectic design. Note the stained-glass transom.

◉ Alta Vista Terrace Historic District is bounded by West Byron, West Grace, North Kenwood and North Seminary streets

Overleaf:
Alta Vista Terrace
(Allen Carr)

415

Above: Landmark marker
Alta Vista Terrace
(Olga Stefanos)

Right: View of
Alta Vista Terrace
(Olga Stefanos)

3802 N. ALTA VISTA TERRACE

On the other side of the street is a classic Georgian facade. The large wooden cornice at the roof line and over the entrance relate well with the bay window of the living room. Good scale.

3812 N. ALTA VISTA TERRACE

Here is another stained-glass transom over the entrance doorway.

3814 N. ALTA VISTA TERRACE

This house has a Greek revival facade, with Doric pilasters at the entrance and windows. A wooden cornice at the roof level gives the facade a sense of good scale.

3819 N. ALTA VISTA TERRACE

On the east side again is still another stained-glass transom—clearly one of this architect's favorite features. The house has Ionic wood columns at the entrance and 2nd-floor windows, and a bay window at the 1st-floor level.

3824 N. ALTA VISTA TERRACE

Back on the west side of the street, you see a limestone facade and bay window. A doorway in natural finish completes this interesting townhouse.

416

Some doorway
treatments at
Alta Vista
(Allen Carr)

3826 N. ALTA VISTA TERRACE

An English half-timber facade gives variety to the facades here at the northern end of the street.

3830 N. ALTA VISTA TERRACE

This house has an old brick facade of good scale and workmanship.

3845 N. ALTA VISTA TERRACE

On the east side again, the last house on this WALK has a wooden cornice and red brick trim.

On your return to West Grace Street, walk behind the houses on the west side of Alta Vista Terrace. You may catch a glimpse here and there of some attractive patios and gardens.

Now walk west along Grace Street to the stop light at Clark Street. Turn north to the next stop light. Cross Irving Park Road to the entrance of Graceland Cemetery.

GRACELAND CEMETERY
West Irving Park Avenue and
North Clark Street

After entering the gate, proceed in a northerly and easterly direction until you reach a small lake at the northeast corner of the cemetery. By walking around the lake you will see some of the most incredible monuments ever assembled. They are of every size, shape, and style, yet within certain areas, there is a flow of continuity. Where else but at a museum would one find an assemblage of such eclectic forms—the ancient pyramid, the obelisk, the classic columns, and Gothic turrets?

The names on the various tombstones and sculpture read like a Who's Who of early Chicago. Such names as Ryerson, Field, Armour, Pullman, Palmer, Wacker, Glessner, and Rockefeller-McCormick serve to remind us of the stability of that era. Along with mayors Harrison and Busse, the distinguished architects Louis Sullivan, Daniel Burnham, and Mies van der Rohe are included. For more detailed information see *A Guide to Chicago's Public Sculpture* (University of Chicago Press, 1983).

Monuments in Graceland Cemetery

Top left: Lorado Taft's "Death" on the Graves Family Plot

Below: Louis Sullivan's tombstone

(Sidney Kaplan, M. D.)

Getty Tomb designed
by Louis Sullivan
(Philip A. Turner)

◉ GETTY TOMB
ARCHITECT: LOUIS H. SULLIVAN (1890)

You will find the Getty Tomb in the northeast section of
Graceland Cemetery, on the northwest side of the lake. The lower
half of the structure is plain, unadorned stone. The ornamentation
of the upper half and of the bronze doors are exquisite, with two
designs well harmonized. The tomb was proclaimed an
Architectural Landmark:

In recognition of the design which here brings new beauty to an
age-old form: the tomb. Stone and bronze stand transformed in
rich yet delicate ornament, a requiem for the dead, and inspiration
to the living.

After leaving Graceland Cemetery, you will undoubtedly agree
that the Getty Tomb transcends in beauty all other monuments
there.

31

1. 806 W. Buena Ave.

2. 822 W. Buena Ave.

3. 4230 N. Hazel St.

4. 4234 N. Hazel St.

5. 4243 N. Hazel St.

6. 839 W. Hutchinson St.

7. 840 W. Hutchinson St.

8. 832 W. Hutchinson St.

9. 826 W. Hutchinson St.

10. 814 W. Hutchinson St.

11. 817 W. Hutchinson St.

12. 803 W. Hutchinson St.

13. 808 W. Hutchinson St.

14. 800 W. Hutchinson St.

15. 750 W. Hutchinson St.

16. 740 W. Hutchinson St.

17. 730 W. Hutchinson St.

18. 726 W. Hutchinson St.

19. 716 W. Hutchinson St.

20. 706 W. Hutchinson St.

21. 654 W. Hutchinson St.

22. 650 W. Hutchinson St.

23. 4230 N. Marine Dr.

24. 645 W. Hutchinson St.

25. 651 W. Hutchinson St.

26. 657 W. Hutchinson St.

27. 703 W. Hutchinson St.

28. 707 W. Hutchinson St.

29. 713 W. Hutchinson St.

30. 715 W. Hutchinson St.

31. 721 W. Hutchinson St.

32. 727 W. Hutchinson St.

33. 737 W. Hutchinson St.

34. 747 W. Hutchinson St.

35. 757 W. Hutchinson St.

36. Boardwalk
    4343 N. Clarendon Ave.

37. Pensacola Pl.
    4334 N. Hazel St.

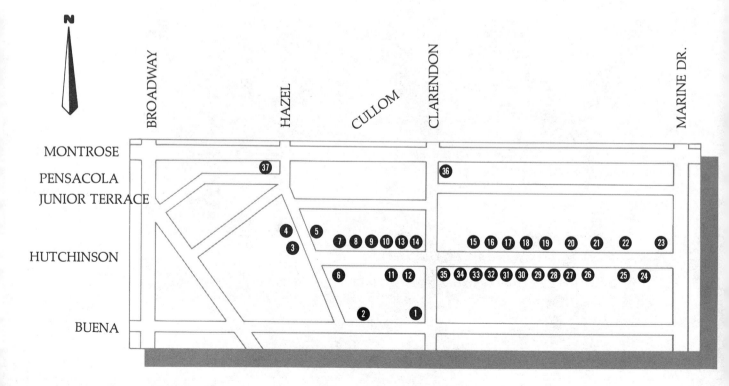

WALK • 31

HUTCHINSON STREET DISTRICT

WALKING TIME: 1 hour. HOW TO GET THERE: Take a north-bound CTA bus No. 145 on State Street. Get off at Buena Avenue [4200 N] and walk to the northwest corner to 806 W. Buena Avenue.

West Hutchinson Street is located in the community of Uptown, an area on the North Side which began as the Town of Lakeview in the mid-19th century and was incorporated into the city in 1889.

Most of the houses along West Hutchinson Street were built during the last decade of the 19th century and the first two decades of the 20th century. The unique character of the street derives from the large concentration of houses designed by architect George W. Maher and from the complementary Prairie House.

A variety of architectural styles prevailed during the years that West Hutchinson Street was being developed. Much of the 19th century residential architecture was characterized by revival of historical styles. The Queen Anne style is represented on Hutchinson Street as is the Romanesque style.

Altogether, the houses along Hutchinson Street represent a variety of architectural styles and present a capsule history of American residential architecture from the last decade of the 19th century through the first two decades of the 20th. It is important to know that George Maher was a contemporary of and also worked with Frank Lloyd Wright and George Grant Elmslie. All of them were as young as they were talented. They soon became leaders in the development of an indigenous American architecture—known as the Prairie school design and the Chicago school.

⊙ Portions of this WALK are in the Buena Park Historic District, roughly bounded by Graceland Cemetery, Maine Drive, Irving Park Road, and Montrose Avenue

806 W. BUENA AVENUE
ARCHITECTS: DOER BROTHERS (1917-18)

This Renaissance revival mansion was built for C. Zimmerman during the years 1917 and 1918. The main body of this 3-story

Overleaf:
840 West Hutchinson
(Charles Brooks)

423

residence is constructed of red common brick. The 2-story sun porches flanking the street facade are of limestone, as is the front portico. This large, formal portico, centered on the symmetrical facade, is supported on paired columns and frames the front entrance. The large rectangular windows of the 1st floor are topped by arched panels of limestone and decorated by simple roundels; wrought iron railings form mock balconies. The windows of the 2nd story are simply framed in brick, though cornice-like sills of limestone above the window frames are supported by brackets. An elaborate belt course, similar to the cornice in its design, marks the top of the 2nd floor. The treatment of the 3rd story is similar to that of the attic story of Renaissance palaces. At the 3rd story, decorative brickwork is a basic element of the design; headers of brick project from the surface, forming frames for the small windows and the panels between. The double hip roof is covered with green mission tile.

Walk west on Buena Avenue.

822 BUENA AVENUE
ARCHITECT: UNKNOWN (1907)

Claude Seymour built this house and lived here for about six years, and then moved into the larger house at 817 W. Hutchinson Street. This smaller, yet handsome 2-story home is constructed of warm orange brick. The two large round bays project from the street facade; rising a full 2 stories, they are topped by shallow conical roofs. The veranda, which extends the full length of the facade, reflects the bay shape only on the western end of the facade, where large windows open from the living room. Heavy brick piers support the roof of the veranda and also the low fence. Simple pilasters inconspicuously frame the corners of the facade. An interlace pattern of molding supports the glass in the front door and the top lights of the 2nd-story windows. The wood frieze under the eaves is decorated with garlands. The dormer windows, modified from the Palladian type, are surmounted by volutes which support a simple finial. The two modeled Queen Anne-style chimneys crown the simple roof line.

Now turn north on North Hazel Street and cross over to the west side of the street.

4230 N. HAZEL STREET

This is a striking brick and stucco house of contemporary design. Continue north.

4234 N. HAZEL STREET
ARCHITECT: RICHARD E. SCHMIDT (1904)

There has been some question as to which architect in Schmidt's office produced the design. Both William E. Drummond and Hugh M. G. Garden, young architects who were later to produce many fine Prairie school designs, were in Schmidt's employ. A similar design, labeled "L. Griffen House, Buena Park, Chicago," was published in the Chicago Architectural Club Catalog in 1902. More recently published materials have asserted Drummond's primary role in the design of the Wolff House, which was completed in 1904.

The Wolff House is a 2-story L-shaped residence constructed of brown brick. The broadly sloping, double hipped roof emphasizes the horizontality which is the trademark of Prairie school architecture. The top of the L faces the street. The 1-story wings project from the south and east facades, sheltering the main entrance and an enclosed porch. The emphasis on horizontality is apparent in the broad overhangs of the roof. The white limestone belt course, which forms the lower sills of the small 1st floor windows and the coping of the front porch, binds the design together. A white concrete mud sill which slopes sharply to the ground adds further horizontal emphasis.

Louis Wolff, a successful businessman, was a manufacturer of plumbing goods. He is listed in the Book of Chicagoans (1911) where it is noted that he was a member of the Chicago Automobile Club, the Chicago Athletic Club and the South Shore Country Club.

Continue north to 4243 N. Hazel Street—a combination studio, atrium and residence. The studio is the workplace of a fine arts painter.

4243 N. HAZEL STREET
ARCHITECT: UNKNOWN (1909);
FOR RENOVATION AND ADDITION: ANTHONY FRIGO (1975)

This house was constructed about 1909 and a new kitchen wing has been added at the rear. The art gallery was constructed for the use of the owners—the husband being a talented painter and the wife, a weaver of wall hangings.

Walk to the corner of Hutchinson Street.

839 West Hutchinson
(Charles Brooks)

839 W. HUTCHINSON STREET
ARCHITECT: GEORGE W. MAHER (1909)

Despite the rather awkward handling of certain elements in the design of this house, it is the work of George W. Maher. The house probably dates from 1909, when Maher was beginning to work with a new type of design, one that was inspired by English architects such as C. F. A. Voysey and the Viennese architect Joseph M. Olbrich. The 2-story facade of the house is long and covered by a steep hip roof which conceals a ballroom. The emphasis on horizontality, so basic to the Prairie school style, is evident in the long sill which joins the three small windows on the 2nd floor and the copper striations in the roof surface. In this design, Maher's concern for the role of the wall as enclosing surface is apparent. The cream-colored common brick is laid in a stretcher bond and the joints are not raked; thus, the flatness of the wall plane is emphasized. The windows are set deeply into the surface of the wall and are asymmetrically arranged, reflecting the arrangement of the interior spaces. Maher's motif-rhythm theory

426

of design called for the repeated use of the same decorative motif as a unifying element in the design. This theory is carried out by the repeated use of the low arch with short lateral flanges; the basic form is most apparent in the pediment over the main entrance. It is reflected many times: in the flower boxes to either side of the stair, in the coping on the chimney, and even in the catch basins of the downspouts.

840 W. HUTCHINSON STREET
ARCHITECT: GEORGE W. MAHER (1894)

When this house was built for John C. Scales in 1894, George Maher was still producing designs which displayed the influence of his ten-year stay in the office of Joseph Lyman Silsbee. This house is typical of the Queen Anne style in the irregularity of its massing and the variety of color and texture of the materials used.

A rubblestone base firmly anchors the 2-story house to the earth. The broad eaves of the veranda add horizontal emphasis while enclosing much of the south and east facades. Rubblestone walls extend above the 1st floor in the round elements of the design and in the chimneys. The 2nd story is decorated with elements suggesting medieval half-timber construction; dark brown molding is set off by the white stucco which covers the wall. The round bay on the south facade is topped by a conical roof surmounted by a large gable. Here Maher chose to work with medieval motifs: the bargeboard of the gable is cut in a trifoil shape. Behind this is a leaded glass window which is nearly flamboyant Gothic in style. Under the window is a terra-cotta cartouche.

The North Hazel Street facade is much more complex in its massing. The door, which is tucked under a deep overhang, is rounded at the top. Over this door is a tripartite Gothic-style window having wooden tracery at the top. On the west facade a 2-story rubblestone turret is surmounted by a faceted conical roof. There are few square corners in the plan of the Scales house; the design is held together by the heavy masonry base and by the repeated horizontals of the roof lines.

Walk east.

832 W. HUTCHINSON STREET
ARCHITECT: UNKNOWN (1921)

This 2-story brick house was built in 1921. The entrance is on the east side of the low ground story and the principal rooms of the house are on the 2nd story. The main features of the handsomely composed Hutchinson Street facade are the wide 2nd-story window and the gable directly above it. The window, occupying most of the width of the facade, is set into an opening with a pointed segmental arch; this arch echoes the configuration of the gable above. The Dutch-type gable is trimmed in stone and caps the Hutchinson Street facade. Projecting to the west is a small wing with a blank brick wall on the ground floor and an enclosed porch above.

Continue east.

826 W. HUTCHINSON STREET
ARCHITECT: GEORGE W. MAHER (1904)

W. H. Lake was a grain broker and senior partner in the firm of W. H. Lake and Company which was located in the Board of Trade Building. Lake, following the lead of his neighbor, John Scales, chose to commission George Maher as architect for his home, which was constructed in 1904.

In the Lake House, Maher developed his final version of the Farson House (1897) type. In this type of design Maher made his most significant contribution to the indigenous American architecture he worked so hard to develop. Unity is achieved by formal arrangement of elements within the design. The basic form of this house type is a massive rectangle with horizontal elements dominating the composition and drawing it together.

The 2-story rectangular facade of the Lake House is overshadowed by the deep overhang of the double hip roof, creating the most striking horizontal element in the design. The low rectangular dormer breaks the broad plane of the roof at its center. The three large windows are symmetrically arranged at the 2nd floor level; two panels containing simple art glass designs frame the central double hung window. The west windows, above the main entrance, are enhanced by a simple bowed limestone sill supported by a decoratively carved bracket. The main entrance below is framed by a simple wide band frame and two low, thick walls. A deep veranda extends from the center of the front facade to the east, adding another strong horizontal element to the composition.

Continue east.

814 W. HUTCHINSON STREET
ARCHITECT: UNKNOWN (1948)

This 2-story red brick house was built in 1948. Decorative elements in the design include limestone keystones over the windows, simple white shutters, and wrought iron.

Across the street is 817 W. Hutchinson Street.

817 W. Hutchinson
(Charles Brooks)

817 W. HUTCHINSON STREET
ARCHITECT: GEORGE W. MAHER (1913)

This house was constructed in 1913 for Claude Seymour. Drawings of the front facade were published in the Chicago Architectural Club Catalog for 1913. Seymour was a vice-president of Otto Young and Company, a jewelry company. Like many of his neighbors, Seymour was active in the Chicago Automobile Club and a member of many other fashionable clubs.

In his design for the Seymour House, Maher borrowed heavily from English country houses by C. F. A. Voysey and the firm of Parker and Unwin. The 2-story house is basically H-shaped, though a 1-story porch (not an addition) does break the symmetry of the facade. The many windows and their arrangement here are typical of Parker and Unwin's designs, but the geometric pattern

429

in the leaded glass is distinctly the work of Maher. This design and its variations are used consistently in all decorative elements to lend a measure of continuity; Maher called it his motif-rhythm theory. A motif similar to that used in the window glass is also found in the balustrades which enclose the front terrace. The large front door, containing a leaded glass window, is sheltered by a low arched canopy supported by four large, classically inspired brackets. The entrance to the property is a simple iron gate in a fence supported by large brick piers. Both the steps and the walkway leading to the house are of the same red brick as the structure itself.

Continue east.

826 West Hutchinson
(Charles Brooks)

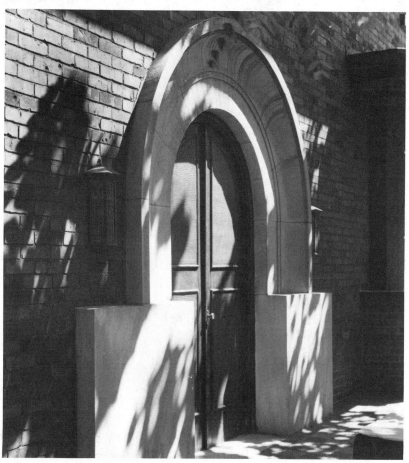

803 W. HUTCHINSON STREET
ARCHITECTS: SCHMIDT, GARDEN AND MARTIN (1910)

This 2-story house is a handsome, well-proportioned example of Richardsonian Romanesque design. The heavily rusticated limestone of the exterior walls emphasizes the massiveness of the structure. The simple forms are handled with great care; relationships between solid and void and the proportions used are evidence of the work of a good architect or an excellent contractor. The Clarendon Avenue facade contains two systems of complementary symmetry; under the double hip roof four windows are symmetrically arranged. The surrounding porch is divided by three broad arches, each springing from a thick pier; these piers are aligned with the window voids above. Entry to the house is by way of the porte-cochere on the Hutchinson Street facade or through the large door on the Clarendon Avenue side.

On the other side of the street is 808 W. Hutchinson Street.

808 W. HUTCHINSON STREET
ARCHITECT: W. F. PAGELS (1908)

This 2-story Prairie school style house is constructed of red brick, complemented by details of blond brick and carved limestone. The design of an arch flanked by rectangles (seen in the limestone details and the large 2nd-story window) may be due to the influence of George Maher. A wood frame porch, now removed, once sheltered the main entrance and balanced with the large window area on the eastern half of the street facade.

The next house east is the current residence of Governor James Thompson.

800 W. HUTCHINSON STREET
ARCHITECTS: HUEHL AND SCHMID (1906)

This house was constructed for A. E. Pyott. The large, 2½ story Prairie school style residence has a 1-story base of blond Roman brick. The 2nd story is of mock half-timber construction; here cream-colored stucco contrasts with brown wood. Limestone is used for the window sills and the capstones of the 1-story front porch on the Hutchinson Street facade.

Cross Clarendon Avenue and continue east on the north side of the street. The WALK will return on the other side.

750 W. HUTCHINSON STREET
ARCHITECT: GEORGE W. MAHER (1902)

The design of this house, especially the west facade, is a fine example of Maher's Farson House style. The west facade of this 2-story house is symmetrical. A low double hip roof is broken at the center by a classically styled dormer typically found in Maher's designs. The base of the roof is bordered by a shallow, classically inspired cornice. Below this cornice, a pattern of alternating arrows perforate the decorative molding which is supported by a row of dentils. The smooth surface of the cream-colored brick is broken by the main entry on the west facade. The entry is set in a large stone frame (reminiscent of Sullivan's Wainwright Tomb in St. Louis) projecting from the center of the 1st story. Above this, a small window is set behind a large frame which is supported by two colonettes. The capitals of the columns used throughout this design are very similar in style to those designed by Louis H. Sullivan. The facade is also broken by four large, simply treated windows.

The West Hutchinson Street facade is broken by a rounded 1-story sun porch, the roof of which projects to form a porte-cochere. The sun porch is very similar to those found in the designs of English country houses built at the end of the 19th century. The long wooden cornice is supported by the same unusually styled Sullivanesque colonettes. Today the owners of this house use the entrance off the porte-cochere as the front entry.

740 W. HUTCHINSON STREET

The main entrance of the house is set back from the street to provide privacy for the owners. Trim (such as the capstones surrounding the front porch and the window sills and lintels) is of limestone which contrasts with the deep red color of the brick walls.

730 W. HUTCHINSON STREET

Built during the last period of development on the street, the 2-story red brick house has details of Indiana limestone.

726 W. HUTCHINSON STREET
ARCHITECT: UNKNOWN (1898)

Though it has recently been remodeled, the 2½-story house retains its 1st-floor base of blond Roman brick. The front entrance and the 2nd story have been completely remodeled.

432

716 W. HUTCHINSON STREET
ARCHITECT: JOHN R. STONE (1901)

This classical revival style house stands in striking, yet instructive, contrast to the other homes along the street. The boldness with which the classical elements of the design have been executed in wood negates the basically simple brick volume of the house. The pedimented roof is supported by brackets and decorated with rows of dentils and egg-and-dart moldings. A simple tripartite window is surmounted by a richly modeled floral ornament. The pediment is supported by a colonnade of modified Ionic columns 2 stories in height. A matching white frame sun porch fills the 2nd story, breaking at its center to form a bay window; both are set in frames derived from the classically inspired Palladian style.

This house was the home of William F. Monroe. Mr. Monroe founded a well-known tobacco shop shortly before the turn of the century; though the ownership of the shop has changed, it still bears his name.

706 W. HUTCHINSON STREET
ARCHITECTS: HUEHL AND SCHMID (1905)

This 2½-story residence was built in the first decade of this century for Dr. John A. Robison. Constructed of cream-colored Roman brick complemented by limestone detail, the house is topped by a steeply pitched roof of red tile. Though the influence of the Prairie school of architecture is apparent in this design, many of the details are taken from classical architecture. The tripartite window in the attic dormer is divided by stout neoclassical columns. The windows are framed in limestone, which is also used in the belt course above the second story. The porch, which extends two-thirds of the length of the south and east facades, is supported by eight neo-Ionic columns.

654 W. HUTCHINSON STREET
ARCHITECT: UNKNOWN (1940)

During the last period of construction on the street, this 2-story red brick house was constructed. Note the 1-story projection to the east where the brick has been laid in a simple diaper, or diamond, pattern.

650 W. HUTCHINSON STREET
ARCHITECT: UNKNOWN (1937)

The design of this 2-story red brick house is enhanced by the use of limestone in the coping, belt course, and the 1st-floor window frames. Colonial details, such as the front door frame, also add interest to the design.

At the northwest corner is 4230 N. Marine Drive.

4230 N. MARINE DRIVE

The massing of this 2-story residence is simple and functional, and the diamond-shaped pattern in the brickwork of the West Hutchinson Street facade adds interest to the design.

Cross West Hutchinson to the south side of the street. The WALK now continues west on Hutchinson Street.

645 W. HUTCHINSON STREET
ARCHITECT: GEORGE KINGSLEY (1914)

This house is a fine, early example of the residential architecture of the 1920s and 1930s. The design of this 2-story structure is enriched by the careful use of high quality building materials. The rich color of the red brick facade is matched by the tile roof. The roof is framed with broad but simple gutters of copper, which have now acquired a green patina. Limestone is used for the window sills and in the plain entablature-like band under the eaves. The elaborate portico over the main entrance is suspended by chains anchored to the facade by limestone rosettes.

651 W. HUTCHINSON STREET
ARCHITECT: UNKNOWN (1914)

This 2½-story house has a 1st floor of red brick, while the 2nd story and the attic dormers are of wood frame construction, covered with gray stucco. The 1-story porch on the street facade has been filled in and a large picture window added.

657 W. HUTCHINSON STREET
ARCHITECT: UNKNOWN (1914)

This 2-story red brick house has recently been tuckpointed with bright white mortar. The entrance on the tree-shaded east facade provides privacy.

703 W. HUTCHINSON STREET
ARCHITECT: UNKNOWN (1940)

434

The limestone trim above the 1st-floor windows contrasts with the exterior walls of pink common brick in this 2-story house.

707 W. HUTCHINSON STREET
ARCHITECT: UNKNOWN (1912)

This 1-story bungalow has been remodeled; a 2-car garage now occupies the basement of the house, which has been faced in white permastone. Some elements of the original design remain; the main entry on the east facade is unchanged, yet the scale of the picture window is not the same as that of the original window.

713 W. HUTCHINSON STREET
ARCHITECT: GEORGE GARNSEY (1907)

This 2-story frame house was constructed during the 1st decade of this century. Narrow horizontal siding on the 1st floor contrasts with the shingle-covered 2nd floor. A Palladian window (a classically-inspired window divided into three parts) is set into the dormer, which is centered on the attic story of the street facade.

715 W. HUTCHINSON STREET
ARCHITECT: UNKNOWN (1911)

The sloping roof and broad eaves of the 1½-story house tend to diminish its size, making it appear to hug the ground. Actually this gray stucco house is quite large, for the gentle slope of the roof allows for a spacious attic story.

721 W. HUTCHINSON STREET
ARCHITECT: UNKNOWN (1951)

This 2-story red brick house was constructed during the last period of development on the street, during the late 1950s and early 1960s. Here the sandstone base and concrete panels at either side of the front entry add interest to the design.

727 W. HUTCHINSON STREET
ARCHITECTS: JENNEY AND MUNDIE (1897)

The randomly laid limestone base of this house lends it an air of informality; the character of the house emphasizes the suburban beginnings of Hutchinson Street. One of the first houses constructed on the street, it is 2 stories in height. A large polygonal porch, supported on neoclassical columns, frames the main entrance.

737 W. HUTCHINSON STREET
ARCHITECT: GEORGE KINGSLEY (1911)

This 2-story red brick residence is a very fine example of Prairie school domestic architecture. The design of the house is based on a balanced system of proportion. Though the 1-story enclosed porch on the Hutchinson Street facade does not extend the length of the house, axiality is maintained in the alignment of the four windows below the tripartite bay window of the 2nd floor. The recessed front entrance, containing a large double door flanked by two modified Corninthian columns, corresponds in the original design with the void of the 2nd-story sleeping porch, now enclosed. Indiana limestone has been used extensively as a unifying element in the design.

747 and 757 W. HUTCHINSON STREET
ARCHITECT: C. WHITNEY STEVENS (1909)

These houses, identical except for certain secondary elements of design, were constructed in 1909 for John H. and William H. Powell. These 2-story residences are constructed of common brown brick; the front facades are symmetrically arranged and dominated by a wide porch. The double pitch roofs are broken by rounded dormers on the front facades, but horizontality is stressed by the broad overhangs surmounting the roof and porch. The limestone belt courses, sills, and coping (of the front porch) reflect the white plaster which is used to highlight the overhangs. Decorative brickwork plays an important role in the overall design, breaking up massive elements (such as the piers that support the front porch) and accenting the horizontality of the second-floor facade.

Walk north on Clarendon Avenue. If time permits, walk 1 block north to Junior Terrace, a very short street, and note the first house at 805 W. Junior Terrace (of a Mediterranean design) along with 811 W. Junior Terrace (of the George Maher period). Both houses along with others in the block are superb examples of excellent maintenance. You will now see a pair of new high-rises. At the corner of Clarendon and Montrose avenues is Boardwalk.

BOARDWALK
4343 N. CLARENDON AVENUE
ARCHITECTS: STANLEY TIGERMAN AND ASSOCIATES (1974)

This 28-story apartment complex is of reinforced concrete glazed with solar bronze float glass. The base of the building contains commercial space, a swimming pool with bath house, tennis court, and a landscaped plaza deck.

Walk west on Montrose to Hazel Street.

PENSACOLA PLACE
4334 N. HAZEL STREET
ARCHITECTS: STANLEY TIGERMAN AND ASSOCIATES,
ASSOCIATE IN CHARGE: ROBERT FUGMAN (1978-81)

The Janus piece to Boardwalk, this middle-income housing and commercial complex struggles with its schizophrenic site. On one side are Lake Shore Drive and the wealthy; on the other rooming houses and tattoo parlors. Thus imbalanced, the complex denies resolution, the difference between the two facades becoming even more pronounced when they are juxtaposed.

Walk around to see the west side of the building as well. At this point, return east to Clarendon Avenue to reboard a bus to the Loop.

INDEX

Photographs in italic

439

441